ACTA ARCHAEOLOGICA

ACTA ARCHAEOLOGICA SUPPLEMENTA

ACTA ARCHAEOLOGICA

Editor

KLAVS RANDSBORG

VOL. 78:2

OXFORD

WILEY · BLACKWELL
2007

Published by ACTA ARCHAEOLOGICA & Centre of World Archaeology (CWA), Director Klavs Randsborg
Archaeological division, SAXO-Institutet, University of Copenhagen, Njalsgade 80, DK-2300 Copenhagen,
Denmark
Phone +45 35329478 Fax +45 35329495 randsb@hum.ku.dk
www.worldarchaeology.net

Editor Professor Klavs Randsborg

Type setting etc. by Architect Rimas Steponaitis, rimas@rimas.info
Printing & reproduction house P. J.Schmidt Grafisk, Vojens
Publishing house Wiley - Blackwell
Orders: Wiley - Blackwell Publishing, 9600 Garsington Road, Oxford OX4 2DQ, UK
customerservices@oxon.blackwellpublishing.com

ISBN 978-1-4051-8421-2
ISSN 0065-101X

ACTA ARCHAEOLOGICA

SUPPLEMENTA

Editor
KLAVS RANDSBORG

VOL. IX

OXFORD

WILEY - BLACKWELL
2007

ACTA ARCHAEOLOGICA Vol. 78:2, 2007
ACTA ARCHAEOLOGICA SUPPLEMENTA IX
CENTRE OF WORLD ARCHAEOLOGY (CWA) - PUBLICATIONS 5

STONE AGE STUDIES

IN POST-GLACIAL EUROPE

Edited by
KLAVS RANDSBORG

OXFORD

WILEY - BLACKWELL
2007

CONTENTS

Acta Archaeologica vol. 78:2, 2007, pp 1-78

Copyright 2007
ACTA ARCHAEOLOGICA
ISSN 0065-001X

EZERO - KALE

FROM THE COPPER AGE TO THE BRONZE AGE IN THE SOUTHERN BALKANS

Inga Merkyte

CONTENTS

INTRODUCTION

I. BEGINNINGS

This paper is a sequel to the monographic publication of the Late Copper Age settlement site of Lîga at Telish, municipality of Cherven Bryag, in northern Bulgaria (Merkyte 2005)[1]. In the Early Bronze Age, the ruins of this settlement were re-used as a cemetery site with burials in Copper Age tradition, interestingly.

The prelude for the research in the area was the perennial excavations at a neighbouring settlement site, Redutite [2], which held evidence on four horizons, attributed to the Early and Late Copper Age, as well as to a period between the end of the Copper Age and the Bronze Age. This so-called Transitional Period is poorly understood due to very few finds compared to the rich Copper Age. Seemingly, the Copper Age settlements in Bulgaria, including many tell-sites, were abandoned and new localities sought out, typically in new environments; this implies utilization of diversified resources by reduced groups interlinked by wider social networks and small-scale exchanges. In the Early Bronze Age (EBA) social conflict was on the rise, resulting in the construction of veritable fortified sites, as at Kale, not far from Lîga.

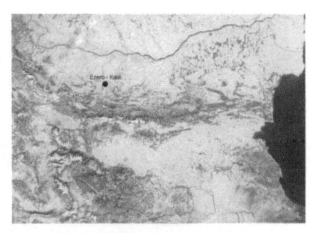

Fig. 1. Geographical position of Ezero-Kale (near Telish) in northern Bulgaria.

Indeed, the Copper Age settlement of Ezero, in fact, the two-partite site of Sadovec-Ezero and Sadovec-Kale, or just Kale (Kale being the high fortified part), was also investigated during the years of the Lîga campaign 2000-2002. Ezero is positioned in a gully by a small river or stream and has a long Copper Age sequence with some traces of the Transitional Period, but the twin-site also has archaeological material from other periods and may in fact have been linked by a "drawbridge" of 7(+) metres. The locality was much disturbed by plunderers, the more readily accessible Kale by bulldozing, and Ezero by very deep wide trenches - almost archaeological in nature, with vertical sides - which rather easily could be cleaned and studied in detail by the Lîga team. The Ezero tell may have been mistaken for a Thracian (or Roman) monument holding items of costly metals.

The present site should not be confused with the Ezero Tell located in the central part of Bulgaria close to Nova Zagora, which is the eponymic site and benchmark for the Early Bronze Age development (Georgiev et al. 1979). The Ezero-Kale site at Sadovec has been known at least since 1935 when Welkov made a short note on it (Welkov 1935). Later it was included in a catalogue on the cultural monuments in the district of Pleven (Mitova-Džonova 1979, 61). But the need for a proper archaeological investigation grew acute in 2002 as a scientific response to the immense looting activities mentioned above, which

---

1 The campaign of 2000-2002 was devised as a research programme focusing on the cultural development of the Telish region at the end of the 5th millennium and the beginning of the 4th millennium. The excavation team comprised of Bulgarian and Danish scholars and students led by Professor Klavs Randsborg, University of Copenhagen and the Bulgarian archaeologist V.V. Gergov, then at the History Museum in Pleven, who has spent a life-time on research in the region. The results, centred on the Lîga excavations, were summed up in the quoted work (Merkyte 2005).

On the present occasion I would much like to express my gratitude to the members of the excavation teams and, not least, to the research group studying the data in great detail and preparing the material for publication. Especially, I would like to acknowledge the valuable contributions made by Søren Albek, Petar Zidarov, Maya Dimitrova Valentinova, Julij Stoyanov, Milen Kostov Kamarev, Emil Vankov, Nikolay Krustanov, Radka Zlateva-Uzunova, and Kristoffer Enggaard. Izolda Maciukaite has effectively turned however precise excavation drawings of pottery into small artistic master pieces.

2 In earlier publications the name of this site - Redutite - was used interchangeably with Telish, as it is located on the eastern fringes of Telish village. For instance, "Telish IV culture" (Gergov 1994a) is based on the materials discovered in the 4th settlement at Redutite. But after discovery of Lîga site also situated at the NE fringes of Telish such synonymous use of toponyms is no longer applicable.

Fig. 2. Caves at the entrance to the Belilka gorge.

started in the autumn of 2001[3]. The rescue work was aimed mainly to document and to some extent to re-excavate and fully document the trenches opened by the looters, who here - no doubt due to some archaeological field experience - dug almost like professionals, with control over the movement of soil and even clean vertical profiles or sections.

II. LOCATIONS
Ezero is located 5 km west of Sadovec, in the Dolni Dabnik municipality in NW Bulgaria (Fig. 1). It rises as a distinct hummock in a steeply sloped gorge

3 Nowadays, unfortunately, such fate hits nearly every archaeological site in Bulgaria, since local communities are insensible to the damage and the laws and the police too ineffective to prevent looting. Archaeological excavations have to be carried out with armed guards, since there is a constant threat that looters, technically often well-equipped, will destroy an excavation before the archaeologists finish their investigation. Members of the Liga team were even shot at when attempting to stop the bull-dozing of an archaeological site (the looters are in particular going for items of noble metals, coins etc., which have a value on the international arts market). Some looters obviously have experience from archaeological digs. The eponymic site of Krivodol, only partially excavated, is today a dense mesh of 4-5 m deep ditches.

Sadly, the lot where the Liga site is located has recently been purchased by looters with the intention to have unrestricted access to the remaining burials. This acquisition has been halted for the time being by a lawsuit initiated by V. Gergov.

formed by the river Belilka. At Sadovec, Belilka flows into Vit, an important tributary of the lower Danube, which in turn is running just 25 km north of the site. The area can be considered as the footsteps of the Balkan range in the south, with fertile plains occasionally interspaced by dramatic limestone peaks and plateaus. Karst topography has developed along the rivers Belilka and Vit, holding at least 20 significant caves and a number of rock shelters suitable for prehistoric occupation (Fig. 2). Pockets in the narrow gorges functioned as traps for game hunting. The area is rich in flint sources; the most extensive one is located just north of Sadovec, below Golemanovo Kale - a Late Antiquity[4] stronghold also containing prehistoric remains including distinctive materials of the Late Copper Age and Early Bronze Age (Todorova Simeonova 1968; Todorova 1992; Uentze 1992) (Fig. 3).

Access to Ezero is by natural means only possible through the narrow gorge and by crossing the waters of the meandering river several times (Fig. 4). Communist period regulations of the water course involved construction of a concrete channel running north of the river, dramatically cutting rocky slopes

4 In Bulgarian historical and archaeological terms this period covers the 4th-6th centuries AD.

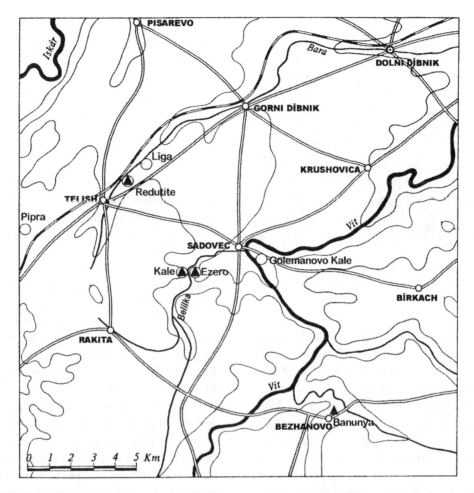

Fig. 3. Map of investigated sites around Sadovec. ● (circles) mark Late Copper Age settlements, ▲ (triangles) mark sites dated to the Transitional Period. The base map (Valev 1992) shows the situation prior to the creation of the dams of the 1960s.

but used only occasionally for irrigation purposes. In some places the river has created small washouts in the steep limestone walls where waters are almost still, attracting schools of fish. The closest low point allowing entrance to the gorge is at a cave known as Sedlarkata, 300 m west of Ezero. The cave is the most impressive one in the area, with several entrances and two galleries with a total length of 1071 m. Almost certainly, it must have been enjoyed also in prehistory, but modern transformation of the cave into storing rooms for feta-like cheese, even if no longer in use, has eliminated any traces of its uses in the past.

Due to the difficult access the beautifully situated Ezero site has remained extremely well-preserved until recently. Traces of occupation are found on a saddle-like hillock encapsulated between steep ranges

of hills. In the gorge, the hillock is surrounded by the river bend on three sides; in the past it was likely completely enclosed by the water, since washed out walls of the hillock indicate that at least seasonally it was an island (Fig. 5). Perhaps this explains the peculiar name attributed to the site, Ezero meaning "lake" in Slavic languages. Needless to say, that the site is invisible in the general landscape, as its top is lower than the upper edges of the narrow gorge (Fig. 6). The top of the hillock is an area of ca. 65x40 m, but traces of occupation were only found on the southern part, or ca. 2/3rd of the hillock. The northern uninhabited part is approximately 14 m above the river and higher than the southern one by some 6 m. Due to the natural shape of the site, aeolithic sand - forming the occupation layers - only accumulated on the southern

Fig. 4. The site of Ezero, located in the gorge of Belilka, can only be reached by crossing the river several times.

part. Thus, the northern part remains as blunt rock, uncovered by soil and vegetation. There are no detectable traces of human activity, which could have made an impact on its appearance.

At its highest and most northern point the Ezero hillock is approximately 173 m above sea level. The range of surrounding hills is rising over the site by 7 m on the northern side and by more than 15 m on the southern one. The Kale site is just opposite Ezero towards the north, on the very edge of the gorge (Fig. 5). An open semi-circular rampart is enclosing Kale ("fortress" in Turkish language, now a loanword in Bulgarian) from the northern plains of the plateau and thus marking it distinctively, although archaeological remains are also found outside the rampart (Fig. 7). Indeed, the locality, especially Ezero, rather looks like a refuge than an ordinary settlement.

III. "WIGGLES" IN THE CHRONOLOGICAL TERMINOLOGY

Writing about issues related to the 5th-4th millennium BC in Bulgaria is inevitable to state a "personal" perception of the terminology of temporal phases and even cultures. After nearly three decades of scientific debate there is still no consensus about how to view the period covering nearly the whole of the 4th millennium BC. The Copper Age (sometimes also called the Chalcolithic or the Eneolithic in Balkan archaeology)

terminated in a stepwise fashion during the period 4200-3800 BC (Fig. 8). The earliest dates relate to the eastern part of the country, the latest ones to sites in western Bulgaria (Todorova 1986; 2003; Georgieva 1992; Görsdorf & Bojadžiev 1996). Archaeologically "stable ground" only re-appears with the advent of the Early Bronze age (EBA) proper as attested at Ezero, Djadovo, Karanovo and other tell sites in the Thracian plain.

The beginning of the EBA is fixed by a number of radiocarbon dates (Bojadžiev 1992; 1994). The earliest horizon at Ezero, the XIIIth, is dated within the range 3350-2900 BC (calibration with OxCal v. 4.0.5). Unfortunately, exactly this period, from ca 3300 till almost 3000 BC - cf. the atmospheric curve IntCal04 (Reimer et al 2004) - still has unresolved plateau problems. These explain the broad margins of the calibrated dates. The beginning of the EBA Ezero A culture is also defined by connections with Aegean sites, first and foremost the dates available for Kumtepe B and Troy I, which are being dated to 3150 BC (Panayotov 1995)[5].

The period between the end of the Copper Age and the beginning of the Early Bronze Age has been coined the Transitional Period (Todorova 1979a). Since the term "transitional" does not have clear socio-cultural implications, attempts were made to extend the terminal phase of the Copper Age and to introduce a new phase with, basically, an EBA socio-cultural content. New terms such as "Final Copper Age" (or "Post-Copper Age") (dated to 4200-3700 BC) and "Proto-Bronze Age" (dated to 3700-3200 BC) entered Bulgarian archaeological literature in the early 1980s (Todorova 1981; see Vajsov 2002a Fig. 177 for comparison of chronological divisions). A more radical stance has been advocated first and foremost by L. Nikolova, who chose to ignore the chronological gap and subdivide the period from c. 4050-3600 BC into several phases respectively termed Final Copper Age IA (c. 4050-3950 BC), IB-C (c. 3950-3870/3840 BC), and II (c. 3870/3840-3700/3600 BC) (Nikolova 1999). The period following after 3600 BC was regarded as EBA proper (ibid.). A third group of archaeologists,

---

5 A recent study has demonstrated, for the first time, an unexpectedly longer occupation of Kumtepe B, ranging between 3370-2910 BC (Kromer et al. 2003).

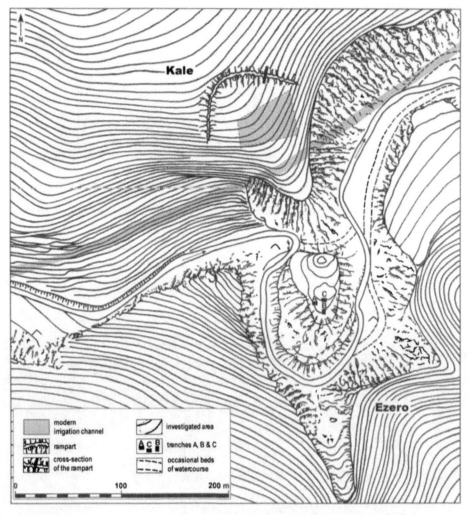

Fig. 5. Topographical map of the Kale-Ezero sites, with indications of the investigated areas.

with a preconceived critical but inconclusive stance, tends to operate with terms like "the so-called Transitional Period", cautiously avoiding any active participation in the debate.

What remains valid is, that up to this day much of the debate is "wandering in darkness" and that an understanding of the processes shaping the SE Balkans in the 4th millennium BC is only at its beginning, as often, largely due to accumulation of more archaeological data and better dating techniques. With the current knowledge it is even possible to argue that the Transitional Period in economic orientation, cultural contents, population numbers, technology, and likely ideology is closer to the Neolithic than to the "Metal ages". In other words, that it is "sub-Chalco-

lithic". The issue is further elaborated below. Until substantial evidence becomes available the present author will tend to use the "traditional" denomination of the cultural phases: The periods dominated by KSB (KGK VI) cultural traits will be regarded as Late Copper Age. KSB stands for the Copper Age "Krivodol-Sălcuţa-Bubanj Culture" in NW Bulgaria and adjacent regions in former Yugoslavia and Romania, while KGK signifies the central and eastern Bulgarian and adjacent Romanian Kodžadermen-Gumelniţa-Karanovo VI Culture. All "transitional" manifestations (the cultures or rather social groupings of Galatin, Telish IV, Sălcuţa IV, Jagodin, Pevec, etc.) will be treated as belonging to the Transitional Period.

Fig. 6. The sites of Kale (foreground, high location) and Ezero (middle ground to the right, lower location) as seen from NW.

Fig. 7. Ezero and Kale sites as seen from SE; note the wall at Kale.

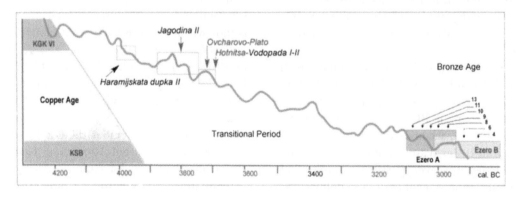

Fig. 8. Chronological scheme showing the duration of the Transitional Period with plotted intervals of the C14-dated sites attributed to the Transitional Period and plotted dates of the Early Bronze Age site of Ezero at Nova Zagora (not Ezero at Telish). After Vajsov 2002a, with modifications.

SETTLEMENTS

IV. THE EZERO SETTLEMENT

The looters at Ezero carried out their undertaking rather "professionally". They dug three trenches; two of these until bedrock level. The main trench was dug in the centre of the site, through 2.35-2.55 m of cultural deposits. It was orientated E-W and measured 2.70x1.85 m. In the archaeological report it was denominated "Trench C" (Trench C is also the central trench) (Fig. 5). The second trench, "Trench A", was located on the western slope of the site: its completely vertical profile established some 4 m into the settlement mound with a width of 2.90 m. The cultural levels were 2.65-3.05 m thick (the variation is due to the uneven surface of the bedrock). The third trench, "Trench B", was made by the looters at the southern slope. The southern slopes are less steep, reaching only ca. 55 degrees. Therefore, exposure of the full sequence of layers in Trench B would have demanded more effort from the looters than the work in Trench A. In Trench B bedrock was not reached, and the exposed layers only comprise 2.20 m in thickness.

A small trial extension was made by the archaeologists at the foot of Trench B. It contained finds dated to the Early Copper Age, seemingly in situ. The upper layers of the extension contained materials dated to the two earliest phases of the Late Copper Age. In some places the looters had also dug short tunnels, following burned and better-preserved debris. Data from all three trenches have been combined by the author to produce a general image of the overall development of the site. Indeed, the site proves to hold a unique potential for understanding the Copper Age in NW Bulgaria. It is a multilayered-settlement and can in fact be regarded as the first discovered tell settlement in the area. Traditionally, the area subscribed to KSB cultural practices, with less attachment to a particular settlement site than the "classical tell-culture" - KGK VI. It should be noted, that it is not unusual to encounter multi-layered sites in the KSB area, for instance Krivodol, which was settled at least five times during the Late Copper Age (Mikov 1948; Nikolov 1984). And yet, this did not result in the creation of a new landmark - a tell - since Krivodol occupied a promontory location on top of a hill and thus did not rise from a plain.

Tells are usually found in plains; over time they grow into significant mounds altering the fluxing line of the landscape. Their physical appearance is shaped by recurrent construction and deconstruction of coherent structures made of clay and wood. For many scholars tells have been the symbol of permanence and sedentism/stability, although recent studies have modified such views (Bailey 1999).

It has become a tradition in Southern Europe to render the multi-layered sites in terms of horizons or building horizons, which are then equated to "settlements" (in the meaning of habitation areas). Both notions are understood implicitly and rest completely on individual perceptions of each scholar. Most would agree that a building horizon is a set of physical events, which have transformed the appearance of a site. Such events can vary in duration and intensity and would include many different actions such as construction of structures, repair works, re-arrangement, destruction and decomposition. The later two however are falling into a grey zone. The logic of causality dictates that they should be seen as the final stage of an earlier development, but at the same time they are being significantly modified by the subsequent users of the site, thus entering into the process of construction of the new inhabitants. Other grey zones include the case where a site is not being re-occupied for habitation but used for other often unidentifiable purposes. Therefore, it would be more correct to read the history of a site in terms of events with varying degrees of interrelatedness rather than using the static notion of horizon. However, for the sake of communication, the term "horizon" (used along with "occupation" and "settlement") will be applied here; it refers to all periods of time when a site was in use leaving detectable traces of use.

V. HISTORY OF THE EZERO SETTLEMENT

The interpretation of the development of the Ezero site was based on a thorough cleaning of the profile walls created by the looters, whereby drawing and recording of layers was made possible, as well as extraction of finds from the layers (Fig. 9). The greatest challenge was to compare and correlate the layers of the three trenches. The most informative and fullest sequence of events was established in Trench A, at the western slope (Fig. 10, Pl. 1). However, if it had been investigated alone the results would not have been completely reliable. The general sloping of the bedrock is from the high north towards the south. Hence the deposits at the western slope were affected by the natural shape of the ground, pushing the soil both down the slope towards the west and in the general direction, towards the south. Such complications of interpretation of cultural deposits are well-known in archaeology. One of the notorious cases relates to Krivodol itself, where V. Mikov, the first researcher of the site, identified eight or nine building horizons while excavating the western slopes of the site (Mikov 1948). Later investigations have corrected the number to five.

At Ezero, the central trench, Trench C, became the yardstick of correlations (Fig. 11, Pl. 2). But even this rendered complications. As might be expected, the central part of the site had undergone the most dramatic modifications over time. Both digging of pits and levelling of terrain over time had created a number of disturbances, so that an analysis of this trench alone would also have provided a blurred picture. The southern trench, Trench B, which was not excavated to bedrock has only been affected by the southern landslide and became an important supplement towards the understanding of the use of space at Ezero. The correlation of the layers was based on visual and physical properties but also on chemical analyses allowing determination of the amount of calcium, humus and phosphate in the respective layers.

Settlement Horizons 1-8
The site and settlement history of Ezero is highly complex. We may recon up to eight distinct phases, for the sake of systematics termed settlement horizons, even if the last ones are ephemeral. The main occupation takes the form of several subsequent phases.

1. Early Copper Age
2. Late Copper Age
3. Late Copper Age
4. Late Copper Age

Fig. 9. Recording of profile information in Trench C at Ezero.

5. Late Copper Age
6. Transitional Period
7. Early Bronze Age
8. Late Antiquity Period

The occupants of the *1st settlement horizon* arrived at the site during the time of the Early Copper Age[6]. Soil was accumulated on an uneven rocky surface. Trying to create a more plain terrain the settlers exposed the bedrock at certain places, which served as foundations. In Trench A, a wattle and daub dwelling was erected above a layer of wooden planks, which rested on the rock surface and effectively sealed the occurring depressions and pits. The wooden planks were covered with a 1-1.5 cm thick layer of light coloured clay, which acted as a floor. This settlement burned down, an event which left distinct layers of ashes and severely burned daub in Trench A, but not in the centrally located Trench C. In Trench B, the level of this event was not reached. Among the destruction debris were rather large pieces of daub with imprints of wood, 2-3 cm and 7-8 cm in diameter. The daub was richly tempered with straw. The surface of the walls was well smoothed. The destruction debris also contained large fragments of thick-walled pottery, both dark black and light brown in colour (Pl. 6: 1-5). The

---

6 In the field diaries the sets of layers comprising horizons were numbered from top to bottom, thus the 1st horizon here (the oldest) was termed the 6th in the field notes.

Fig. 10. Trench A, located at the western slopes of the Ezero site.

shards were tempered predominantly with sand. The main part of the fragments had polished surfaces and was decorated with excised and incised geometric motives. The decoration is organised in zones seemingly covering the whole surface of a vessel. One shard with an incised decoration was also incrusted with yellow pigment (Pl. 6:3). The discovered material is showing a low degree of fragmentation; it is representing the remains of 4-5 vessels. Two of these have a dark grey black surface. Some shards were reddened due to the intensive heat during the conflagration. One big container represented by six shards demonstrates an interesting combination of clay and lime plastering in the interior (Pl. 6:4). To make the adhesion easier, the internal surface was densely scratched. Lime plas-

tering is known to be suppressive of germs (Merkyte 2005, with references).

The closest parallels to this pottery are found in a material excavated at the Brenica site in the Vratsa area (Nikolov 1978; Todorova 1986). Although only loosely defined, Brenica has become a type-site defining the earliest phase, Phase I, of the three-phased Gradeshnitsa culture of the Early Copper Age in the western part of Bulgaria. Based on that, the layers comprising the 1st settlement horizon are dated to the beginning of the Copper Age.

The remains of the *2nd settlement horizon* were attested directly on top of the thick and rather uniform layers of burned debris belonging to the first settlement. A hiatus layer, which must have accumulated

Fig. 11. Trench C, located at the centre of the Ezero site.

after the abandonment of the Early Copper Age settlement, must have been removed in a course of levelling the terrain and redistributing of the soil. In Trench A, a distinct and powerful layer of charcoal, likely stemming from house floor planks, separated the remains of the two settlements. In some places this layer was reaching 10-15 cm in thickness. In support of this interpretation it was noted that the layer below the assumed floor level was compacted and firm despite the fact that the main component was pieces of burned daub. Traces of an oven, being around 1.10 m in diameter, were also recorded. Unfortunately, the oven was nearly completely destroyed by a tunnel excavation on the part of the looters.

The number of finds, mainly shards, amounted to only a handful, but they undeniably belong to the

Fig. 12. Trench B, located at the southern slopes of the Ezero site.

Late Copper Age (Pl. 6:6), falling well into line with the much greater ceramic collection from the subsequent occupation (Pl. 6:6-14 & Pl. 7); C14-dating confirms this finding (see below). The 2nd settlement horizon, as indicated by the layer of charcoal, also burned down, leaving a rather thick layer of burned daub, breaking in large flakes in Trench A.

The area covered by Trench C was also used for built structures during the occupation period of the second settlement, hence the layers attributed to the second settlement contained high concentration of flakes of burned daub and charcoal. In Trench B, the layers of the second settlement were not reached.

The *3rd settlement horizon* was established on top of the layers accumulated after the destruction of the second settlement. These layers had a greatly varying thickness clearly reflecting the efforts of creating plain surfaces before the erection of dwellings in this settlement horizon. Indeed, despite the complicated terrain and the forces of landslide the settlers succeeded in creating plain house floor levels, as recorded in both Trench A and Trench B.

There is evidence to suggest that the third settlement horizon existed over a considerable time span. In Trench A, multiple remains of a house floor were discovered, which appeared in the form of compacted layers of clay, grey greenish in colour. The floor was originally plastered with a thin layer of lime (Pl. 4: 1). Three subsequent restorations involved addition of a new layer of clay and plastering with either clay or lime: the first time it received a new clay plastering, the second time a lime plastering and finally a clay plastering. The last floor level is remarkably compact and firm. It is covered with a rather uniform layer of red burned clay (reaching up to 15 cm in thickness) containing pieces of charcoal. The origin of this layer is somewhat uncertain, since the remains belonging to this settlement found in the other two trenches did not show any traces of conflagration. Perhaps fire was used in isolated cases in order to remove decaying structures.

The most interesting vestiges attributed to the 3rd settlement horizon were uncovered in Trench B. Floor levels could not be clearly distinguished, except as separate patches of grey greenish compacted clay, but on top of these patches, at the eastern periphery of the trench, an integral group of domestic features was found. The group consisted of a clay bin and an oven (Fig. 13). The bin, or stationary pithos, was made of unbaked whitish clay, with walls 6.5-9 cm thick splaying upwardly from a flat base. The clay was tempered with straw. The bin is circular in shape, 58x60 cm in internal diameter and 76 cm in external diameter. The preserved maximum height is 31 cm (Fig. 14). The contents of the bin were water sieved, but no cereals or other plant remains were recovered (seeds and any other organic material are only rarely preserved in contexts not affected by fire). Next to the bin, in fact to the south of it, separated by merely 1-2 cm were the oven remains. The oven was discovered in the eastern wall of the trench, partially destroyed by the looters. The oven underwent several changes during its time of use (Pl. 4:2). Likely the changes were caused by natural landslide rather than due to a long duration of use. The oven was built directly on the floor, and the same whitish clay with organic temper was used for its construction. The first oven was 1.20 m in external diameter. The second dome was constructed just above the first one, on a layer of shards and minor stones. Its external dimensions were 1.40 m. The third dome is separated from the second one by some 10 cm of burned clay. This last oven was expanded till 1.75 m in eternal diameter and almost melted in with the bin.

Although it can be argued that the recurring restorations of the structures were necessitated by the unstable terrain, the high amount of pottery attributed to the 3rd settlement horizon indicates a long and intense occupation of the site in this particular period of the Late Copper Age. In fact, it would not be wrong to state that half of the collected pottery at Ezero stems from this particular occupation, which also produced the highest amount of animal bones, although on the whole the number of recovered animal bones was peculiarly low (likely reflecting off-site disposal). A few fish vertebral discs (reaching 2 cm in diameter) and numerous shells of the Unionidae, as well as of the Helicidae and Enidae, families were also collected from the layers of the 3rd settlement horizon, especially in Trench B.

The settlement mound of Ezero has the common shape of a cone, narrowing significantly towards the top as determined by the natural laws in action. According to calculation the maximum area available for habitation during the period of the 1st to 3rd

Fig. 13. Remains of a Late Copper Age oven and adjacent storage bin in Trench B, attributed to the 3rd settlement horizon at Ezero.

Fig. 14. Storage bin of unbaked clay in Trench B, attributed to the
3rd settlement horizon at Ezero.

settlement horizons was 50 m in N-S direction and 22 m in E-W direction. During the later settlements the area of habitation diminished by 10% per each occupation. Attempts to hinder landslide were pronounced during the 4th settlement horizon, when the slopes were stabilised by limestones. The layers formed as result of the abandonment of the 3rd settlement horizon present a complex sequence of events implying a significant distance in time between this and the subsequent occupation.

The areas covered by Trenches B and C were not used for construction of dwellings during the time of the *4th settlement horizon.* The remains of a collapsed unburned daub wall (with a preserved thickness of 22 cm) in Trench C, situated on top of the layers created during the occupation of the 4th settlement horizon indicates that this area was left un-built. The only interesting feature in Trench B related to the 4th settlement horizon was the imprint of a post with a flat base; the hole dug for the pole was 60+ cm deep and 30 cm in diameter. Its function cannot be explained easily, since it was not connected with any apparent structure. The most evocative remains related to the 4th settlement were observed in Trench A. Above a rather compact layer created after a lengthy abandonment of the 3rd settlement was a distinct 5-10 cm thick grey black layer containing charcoal. This layer had a regular plain appearance, suggesting that it was based on a levelled surface. Just above it was a number of shards laying on their flat faces, indicating that the layer was in fact the remains of a wooden plank floor. On top of it were thick layers containing burned daub and ashy clusters/lenses. This settlement is also dated to the Late Copper Age.

The following *5th settlement horizon* has the most complicated depositional history of all. Reconstruction of the events which left their imprint in the layers attributed to this occupation of the site is not straightforward, even though the pottery involved is still of Late Copper Age date.

Fig. 15. The rampart at Kale as seen from S-SW. (The rampart is running from the right foreground towards the left, then right in the distance.)

In Trench A, a shallow trench measuring 1.80 m in length/width? was observed. It was about 0.30 m deep and covered with lime stones - obviously an attempt to stabilize the terrain, perhaps as a foundation for a built structure. The layers above the line of stones contained many fragments of pottery of Late Copper Age date, which were mostly distributed in a heterogeneous grey soil of undetermined nature (soft, containing tiny fragments of burned daub and charcoal but also unburned clay and ancient organic matter observed as voids). As inclusions in this layer there are also sections of distinct layers of burned daub, ashy material and layers rich in charcoal. Obviously these layers represent some kind of destruction, likely of the upper part of a dwelling containing the highest amount of wooden or other ignitable structural elements. The sequence of layers and their fragmentary nature gives the impression that human involvement was far greater than the natural processes of destruction and decomposition. Perhaps the edges of the site had at certain point in time become an area for deposition of structural debris, burned remains of structures being pushed out on the slope for gaining an additional number of square meters.

Trench B provided information, different in nature from the above, concerning the 5th settlement horizon. On top of the debris related to the 4th settlement horizon occupation was an added layer of clay rich

soil reaching 10 cm in thickness after the older layers had been levelled. The clayey layer is interpreted as a floor layer. Above it is a uniform and homogeneous layer created after burning of organic matter, likely wooden planks. Directly on top of this again is a distinct compact layer of reddish burned daub reaching 40 cm in thickness plus a layer containing burned daub and charcoal. Evidently, this sequence represents the conflagrated remains of a built structure. Moreover, there is also a regular circular spot of calcinated matter measuring 18 cm in diameter in between the burned fragments of daub; this is interpreted as a wooden pole as seen in section.

The most significant event taking place in the area of Trench C during the period of the 5th settlement horizon was the excavation of a large and deep rounded pit measuring 1.20-2.00 m in width/length and being 2.00 m deep. The purpose of this pit is unclear. There are five layers of fill in the pit, basically containing the same kind of material as the surrounding layers. In any case, an interpretation as pit for deposition of waste, or for sourcing of materials, can be wholly excluded.

The last clearly discernible occupation at Ezero left traces of varying intensity in the three investigated trenches. Based on the discovered materials, it is dated to the above-mentioned Transitional Period, which thus represents the *6th settlement horizon* - or rather site

Fig. 16. The Ezero site (middle ground, right) with adjacent plateau (left) leading towards the Kale site (upper left), as seen from W; the dashed line marks the outline of the rocky surface covered by dense vegetation. The plateau and Ezero may in prehistory have been linked by a short wooden or tow bridge.

Fig. 17. Working situation at Kale (as seen from N towards Ezero). Note the soil heaps created by the looter's bulldozer.

use - of Ezero. In Trenches A and C this occupation is mainly attested by pits intrusive in relation to the layers of the previous Late Copper Age occupation. During the Transitional Period, apart from the pits, a separate light grey clayey and humuous layer was established across the entire surface of the site. It likely represents the occupational surface of the period. The only evidence to more extensive alterations of the site can be studied in Trench B. After the termination of the 5th settlement horizon, well-sorted, homogeneous soil was added to the southern part of the site. This layer created a compact and exceptionally levelled surface. A number of limestones and shards was distributed in it, but there were no actual traces of permanent structures even though the layer was 40 cm in thickness. The number of pottery finds attributed to this phase is very limited. It is therefore likely that the project of establishing a new settlement at Ezero was abandoned at a very early stage. Instead one focused on the above-lying Kale site (fortified in the Early Bronze Age around 3200-3000 BC).

A particular episode of site should be highlighted. Sometimes around 3300 BC (Ua-24359: 4375+/-45 BP) a female body was entered into the layers attributed to the Transitional Period. The body was found at the very edge of the site, in Trench B, less than a meter below the present day surface. A full description of this interesting find is presented below.

A few pits and a mixed layer below the top soil and above the layers attributed to the 6th settlement horizon of the site may be of even later date - perhaps the Early Bronze Age - which is otherwise only represented by a handful of unstratified pottery shards. We may, tentatively, term this occupation the *7th settlement horizon* at Ezero, even though the finds and structures may only reflect a few casual visits to the site.

A thick layer of topsoil, at some points reaching 1+ m, also suggests the use of the site in later periods. For instance, a layer of limestones close to the surface recorded in Trench B is not a natural phenomenon. They are too fragmented to be used as house foundation, but sufficient to stabilize the slopes - a persistent activity at the site since the Copper Age. Based on a few surface finds of wheel-made pottery it is tempting to connect this layer - the *8th settlement horizon* of Ezero, as we may term it following the above terminology - with the Late Antiquity Period, which has also left ephemeral traces at Kale in the form of a few shards. Again, these, in number limited and scattered finds may only represent a few casual visits to the site.

VI. THE ARCHAEOLOGICAL REMAINS AT KALE

As a feature in the landscape, the Kale site is readily recognizable due to its powerful semi-circular enclosure effectively demarcating it on the northern side and enclosing an area of ca. 100 (N-S) x 90 (E-W) m (Fig. 15). On the southern site the steep slopes of the plateau determine the edges of the site. Today, these slopes are severely eroded, a process intensified by

the creation of the above-mentioned water channel of concrete running parallel to the stream, made in order to create a more efficient irrigation system for the area, even though no longer in use. The physical distance between the Kale site and the Ezero site is approximately 20 m today. In the past, this distance would have been 7 m at most, making it natural to expect a hanging bridge or the like uniting Ezero with Kale and the wider world beyond the gorge (Fig. 16). While co-existence of the two sites cannot be proved - it is only expected - the settlers of Ezero must have constructed such a bridge irrespectively of whether Kale was occupied or not. Energy expenditure would simply have been too high for the settlers of Ezero if they had had to satisfy themselves with moving only along the long passage in the gorge created by the river. Also, a hanging bridge could easily be severed in case of an emergency.

At Kale, cultural debris are also found outside the enclosure, but their full extent has not been investigated. The looters bulldozed the southern part of the enclosed area, in some places reaching a depth of 0.50-0.60 m (Fig. 17). This depth was likely motivated by surveying with metal detectors. Upon inspection by the archaeologists, a few spots still contained small piles of amorphous fragments of copper or bronze. The area was covered with abundant small finds, mainly belonging to the Late Copper Age or the Transitional Period. There were also finds dated to the Early Bronze Age and a small number of sporadic items attributed to the Late Antiquity period, among these wheel-made pottery shards (Pl. 13:18-21), a glass bead, a spindle whorl, and likely a few tiny iron rods. The archaeological rescue work involved shovelling of the surface in the central exposed area and recording of features, which might have escaped the looters. Immediately below the loose soil, remains of a Late Copper Age settlement were discovered (Fig. 18). The most complete feature comprised part of a floor with a massive saddle quern measuring 34x25 cm. Nearby, ca. 1 m away, was a plano-convex grinder measuring 25x12.5 cm. Saddle querns are considered stationary installations, almost exclusively found inside dwellings. Edges of the quern were covered with a thick layer of red ochre; a distinct centrally placed circular depression indicated that the quern also held a secondary function: it had been used for pound-

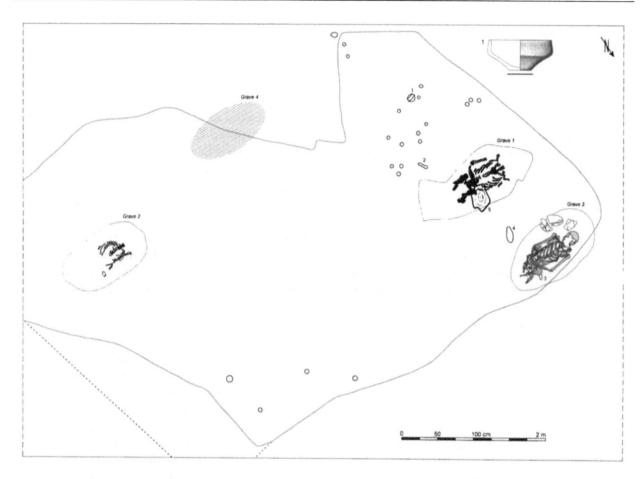

Fig. 18. Plan of the investigated Medieval graves at Kale, as well as house remains of the Late Copper Age. The dashed line marks the reconstructed width of the house; circles mark postholes.

Fig. 19. Milling stones at Kale. Note the saddle quern with a circular depression belonging to its secondary period of use (as a pounding surface).

ing lumps of ochre (Fig. 19). Such finds are occasionally accounted also at other Late Copper Age sites, for instance Okol Glava (Gaul 1948), revealing the multi-functionality of grinding installations usually in-

discerned in field reports. Several pottery concentrations were found in association with the quern allowing a dating of it to the Late Copper Age. The said floor remains, although incompletely preserved, show that the house was orientated N-S; it can be estimated that it was 6.5-7 m wide (Fig. 18). The investigated remains of the Copper Age settlement did not show any traces of conflagration, but the heaps of soil left by the looters, located towards the East-NE contained considerable amounts of burned daub; the date of this incendiary destruction episode is unclear.

On the mentioned floor level, skeletal remains of four individuals were also discovered. The bones were generally well preserved, but the greater part of the skeletons were disturbed or moved away during the bulldozing (Fig. 18, 20). The graves appeared to be rather densely clustered, all orientated E-W, with the

Fig. 20. Working situation at Kale, note Medieval Grave 3 and the milling stones of Fig. 19.

Fig. 21. Southern part of the cross-section of the rampart at Kale. The measurement stick marks the outer face of the stone wall.

head towards west. The graves appeared 0.5-0.6 m below the present day level. All were pit burials without coffins or grave goods. Grave 1 contained remains of a grown-up female (according to the angle of sciatic notch), the scull and legs were not present, but the position of the remaining bones indicates that the dead was laid on the back in outstretched position with the hands collected on the stomach. Grave 2 only contained bones of the chest: thoracic vertebrae, scapula and ribs. Several phalanges discovered in the grave reveal that the buried individual was 14-20 years old (depending on the sex, which was not determined); the epiphyses of the phalanges were just fused (Mays 1998). The dead person was placed on the back. Grave 3 contained the best-preserved skeletal remains (Fig. 20). All the principle bones, except a main part of the legs, were present. The dead was laid on its back in

an outstretch position. The hands were collected in the pelvic area. Sexual traits typical for males were observed both on the scull and the pelvic bones. The height could be estimated to around 1.70+ m, based on the length of humeri (humerus dexter 34.7cm/ humerus sinister 33.8 cm). Based on dental wear, the age at death was estimated to be 35-45 years.

The distance between the outer edges of the pelvic bones in Graves 1 and 3 is 1.17 m. Grave 4 was recognised in the form of a part of a scull and an amorphous concentration of fragmented bones. It was located to the south of Graves 1 and 2, ca. 2 m from Grave 1 (Fig. 18). The size of the bones indicates that they belonged to a juvenile. A number of human bones were also found scattered on the surface, mainly in the SE area of the site.

Since the graves did not contain any grave goods,

Fig. 22. Close-up of the highest point of the stone wall of the rampart at Kale.

their dating is open for speculations. The E-W orientation and the position of the bodies, with the hands gathered in the pelvis area, along with the fact of the lack of grave gifts, imply that these burials subscribe to the Christian tradition. The lack of coffin puts them into Medieval period. Such "un-datable" burials are frequently found during archaeological excavations. For instance, seven such burials were discovered at the Redutite site (Gergov, pers. comm.; Neikov 2001), but they are barely mentioned in archaeological reports.

The looters had not destroyed the entire site, some parts were seemingly left intact. Mapping of the surface finds indicated that different parts were occupied during different periods. During the Copper Age and the Transitional Period the area close to the edges was occupied. It stretched until the central part of the enclosure (which did not exist at that time). The Early Bronze Age finds were clustering higher up, from about the central part of the enclosed area till the enclosure. Shards of Early Bronze Age date were also found outside the enclosure, but

this amount is too insignificant to suspect a noteworthy occupation. Incidentally, the same preferences in area of occupation was also observed at Liga and other sites: the Copper Age settlers are attached by the edges of the plateaus while the Bronze Age communities tend to select higher and more commanding altitudes, even at the same location. At Kale, the scattering of Early Bronze Age finds may also indicate an abandonment of the Ezero site and a concentration on the former.

The Enclosure

Apart from the above features, the archaeological team used the opportunity to investigate the enclosure wall itself. A depression or even complete interruption of the outline could be sighted in the Western side of the wall; still, it was uncertain whether this was the place of an original gate (and a more rewarding place to investigate) or merely a later modification made by the shepherds moving along the edges of the gorge. Instead, a place in the NE part where the wall

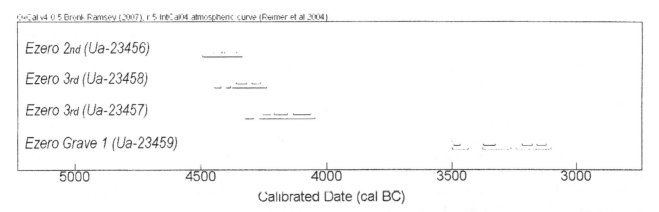

Fig. 23. Calibrated C14 dates of samples from Ezero.

was preserved to its highest, ca. 1.50 m, was chosen for excavation.

The initial expectation was that the structure would be dated to 4th-6th AD. Therefore, it was quite a surprise that not a single potshard in the excavated section could be attributed to this period. Instead, the find assemblage was exclusively of Early Bronze Age pottery made in the Orlea-Sadovec tradition (Pl. 13:1-17). Two shards could be attributed to the Late Copper Age - not unnaturally on a Late Copper Age settlement site. EBA pottery was evenly distributed in all layers of the excavated structure, although the total amount did not exceed some 30 shards.

The discovered remains show at least two phases of wall (Pl. 5). The first phase includes the creation of a kind of "emplecton": Two parallel rows of stones, ca. 1.40 m apart, were laid in a circular manner enclosing a part of the plateau from the unprotected eastern, northern and western sides. The rows of stone were placed upon a foundation made of stones on top of each other in three layers. The area between the two rows of stones was filled with layers of common soil and light yellow grey clay - all in thin multiply separated layers. The stones are noteworthy small and fashioned in two ways (Fig 21 & 22). The dominant group is a flat, brick-shaped blocks measuring 30x10 to 55x15 cm. Another group is made of rounded or angular stones, which do not have an elongated shape, they are measuring 15x10 to 30x30 cm. There are no traces of any particular binding material between the stones, as can be seen in the structures from Late Antiquity at Sadovec-Golemanovo Kale and at Pipra.

However, the rows of stones were reinforced from the exterior with the same kind of material, light clay and common soil. Each stone row originally reached a thickness of about 1 m. The exterior reinforcements would have added 0.80 m in thickness. The presently preserved height of the stone structure (in the wall) is 1 m. It should be noted that virgin soil was not reached over the whole section of the excavation trench. It is clear that the stone wall was never expected to stand alone. From the moment of creation it was stabilised with added soil, basically comprising of light yellow grey clay.

It has not been established whether a wooden palisade was erected on top of the wall, although this is highly likely. The total width of the rampart would originally have been around 5 m, while the "emplecton" part is around 3.5 m wide. A second phase included a further stabilisation of the wall, which at that moment has already started to disintegrate. A new layer of soil was applied to cover the earlier wall, thus sealing it completely.

It remains a puzzle what was the source of the soil used for the rampart. Usually, the soil for a rampart is procured by excavating a moat at its foot. The excavation trench extended for more than 7 m from the outer faces of the stone wall, both in the northern external direction and in the southern internal direction. No traces or even indications of moats were discovered. Perhaps the excavation trench was not long enough, but bearing in mind that the main material holding the stone structure together was light clay, this was likely collected from a more distant place, specially selected for the purpose. For the second covering, common surface soil was used, not differing significantly from the topsoil of the site. Indeed, the common find of EBA shards supports such an assumption (the two Late Copper Age shards also stemmed from this particular layer).

Early Bronze Age and even earlier fortifications are not an uncommon phenomenon in the territory of Bulgaria. Usually, they have moats and soil ramparts, occasionally with palisades. The use of stone seems to be an early Bronze Age innovation, albeit stone-walled houses are well known from Copper Age sites like Durankulak and Galatin (Todorva 2002; Georgieva 1988).

Stone walls (occasionally with moats/ditches) made for enclosing purposes have been attested from the earliest EBA layers at the tells of Mihalich, Ezero, Djadovo, Kazanlak, Sveti Kirilovo, and possibly others (Mikov 1948; Georgiev et al. 1979, 130 with references; Leshtakov 2005). The best-documented stone installations are at the Ezero tell, close to Nova Zagora. Stone walls encircling a site have been found in several EBA-horizons, including the oldest one, Ezero XIII (Georgiev et al. 1979). It is interesting to note that here stones were brought to the site from lime stone quarries lying 7-8 km away from the site (Georgiev et al. 1979, 121), thus demonstrating the planned and organised nature of such undertakings. By contrast, momentous creativity is probably behind for instance the stone walls at the Late Copper Age site of Galatin (discussed in Merkyte 2005 with references). The oldest stone wall at Ezero XIII included two parallel rows of stone blocks set 1.50 m apart (Georgiev et al. 1979, 121). The space between the rows was filled with smaller stones. The same method was used for erection of a wall during the later Xth horizon. Here two parallel rows of stones were laid at a distance of 1.50-2 m, the space between them filled with smaller stones and clay (Georgiev et al. 1979, 123). A similar wall, measuring 1.60 in width and with a preserved height of 1.20 m, was discovered at Mihalich, municipality of Svilengrad, (Mikov 1948), as confirmed by recent excavations (Leshtakov 2005)[7].

The section across the wall also gave opportunity to study the deposited layers. The wall, as also the whole surface of the enclosed area, was covered with a rather thick layer of top soil almost 0.5 m thick - at the wall at least - of sandy loam: dark brown to brown black in colour and with a considerable amount of charcoal, indicating periodical surface burning. Below this layer was a lighter calcareous sandy loam layer loaded with lime pebbles and occasional pottery shards, likely the top layer at the time of the construction of the wall. This layer, also reaching around 0.50 m in thickness, was only observed at the foot of the wall and not in the central part where the salvage actions were concentrated. Below it was a more homogenous clayey layer medium brown in colour, which contained no archaeological finds, and was thus interpreted as virgin soil (Pl. 5).

VII. C14 DATES OF THE EZERO SETTLEMENT

Four samples collected during the rescue excavations at Ezero have been AMS dated by the Uppsala Laboratory of Ion Physics, Sweden (Fig. 23). The earliest sample, of charcoal, Ua-23456, was collected from the northern wall of the Trench A and relates to the second occupation of the site, of Late Copper Age date. The produced result is 5560+/-50 BP ($\delta^{13}C$ value is –24.6). The calibrated age at 95.4% probability is 4492-4334 BC.

Two charcoal samples were used to date the third occupation (also Late Copper Age), both were collected from Trench A. One of these derived from the eastern wall, Ua-24357, and was dated to 5340+/-45 BP ($\delta^{13}C$ value is –25.2). Another, Ua-24358, was collected from the southern wall and resulted in 5470+/-45 BP date ($\delta^{13}C$ value is –26.0). Both dates at the standard 95.4% probability were calibrated to a combined period spanning 4324-4237 BC.

Finally, part of a well-preserved humerus from a female skeleton (of the Transitional Period/Early Bronze Age) was dated to 4575+/-45 BP (Ua-24359, $\delta^{13}C$ value is –20.9). In calendar years this corresponds to 3499-3103 BC (95.4% probability). Unfortunately one of the serious plateaus in the calibration curves exists exactly around 4500 BP.

---

7 Although, according to M. Stefanova, who has carried out control excavations at Mihalich after V. Mikov's investigations in the 1940s, the discovered stone rows were likely remains of "a big stone building" (Stefanova 2000).

FINDS

VIII. COPPER AGE POTTERY AT EZERO

Despite the fact that the main body of pottery from Ezero-Kale stems from mixed surface collections, it presents an interesting case of development from the Late Copper Age till the Early Bronze Age. More importantly, survival of certain Copper Age traits in the Early Bronze Age material attests to a gradual, almost organic transition in pottery production. The Transitional Period lives up to its nomination being a period of absorbing of new ideas and influences and reshaping the long-lived traditions of the Copper Age. The Ezero site produced materials predominantly of the Late Copper Age, while from Kale also derives a rather rich collection of pottery attributed to the Transitional Period and the Early Bronze Age.

The earliest Copper Age pottery was found in the lowest layers at Ezero. As has been mentioned, it was richly decorated in geometric, predominantly rectilinear, excised or incised motives, which cover the whole exterior surface. This kind of decoration determines that the pottery has to be relatively thick-walled; the surfaces were burnished, often lustrous (Pl. 6:1-5). Both light and dark surfaced pottery was produced. Although there are no C14 dates for this horizon, based on parallels, it should be dated to the first quarter of fifth millennium, the so-called Brenica phase of the Early Copper Age in NW Bulgaria (Nikolov 1978).

The subsequent occupation of the Ezero site produced four temporally different sets of pottery collections, which, however, share a number of common traits, allowing an attributing of Settlement horizons 2, 3, 4 & 5 to the latest phase of the Copper Age. It is a common trait that dark-coloured pottery dominates (dark brown, grey black, or grey brown), but lighter nuances like light brown were not unusual. A number of shards also had intense red burnished surfaces, typically on the inside. The darker surfaces seem to represent a technological choice. Sometimes the undecorated interior has a lighter colour than the decorated exterior, demonstrating that pottery colours were controlled by the aesthetic canons of the time. In fact, the material also demonstrates a very precise control

of colouring when sometimes only a chosen part was darkened while other parts of the surface were left lighter. Most probably this has been achieved with quenching (for description of the method, see Carlton 2002). Bowls are significantly over-represented in the uncovered material, a bias likely stemming from an easier identification of bowl fragments. Therefore, any typological considerations are put aside, attempting only to produce immediate overall trends. Several combinations of tempering constituents have been recorded, but there is a very clear dominance of only four types of fabrics: (a) only well levigated clay used without any added substances; (b) sand or/and sorted coarse grains of rock; (c) (b) in combination with organic matter; and (d) (b) in combination with chamotte.

It is common for the mentioned sets of pottery that the walls are usually well burnished, often lustrous. The use of slip has only been observed in the case of coarse, thick-walled pottery. The interiors are also often burnished, although even in the case of bowls the exteriors were more often surface treated. It is also notable that vessels with handles or lugs or any other handle-like applications, like knobs, are a rarity, especially when compared with materials from neighbouring Lîga or Redutite. The trademark of the KSB culture - vertical handles - virtually vanished from the Late Copper Age Ezero collection. (Vertical handles reappear among the shardage of the Transitional Period.)

The amount of pottery associated with the 2nd settlement horizon is limited (Pl. 6:6) and generally conform to the traditions reflected in the pottery of the 3rd settlement horizon, which produced the richest collection (Pl. 6:7-14 & Pl. 7). Typical for the 3rd settlement horizon is well smoothed and burnished surfaces decorated with graphite. During this phase the pottery can be decorated both in positive and negative ways. Decoration with graphite paint rendered in a negative way - that is, when unpainted areas comprise the overall design - is thought to be a characteristic of the Gumelniţa tradition and considered as non-existent on KSB sites (Todorova 1995:89). Interestingly, negative graphite decoration was in use in western

Bulgaria during the Early Copper Age but then disappeared, in fact at the same time as it was adopted by the communities in Thrace and north-eastern Bulgaria (Chokhadzhiev 2000), perhaps indicating a transfer of at least women to the latter regions.

The significant number of such shards indicats that it was not an exotic feature at Ezero (Pl. 6:10-11). Shards with complicated graphite painted designs rendered by using the negative technique were also discovered at Kale. Two of these shards, likely from the same vessel, were also decorated with red ochre paint on top of the graphite decoration. Ochre decoration was also attempted rendered as a negative decoration. Interestingly, red painted decoration appears at Ezero during the time of the 3rd settlement horizon (Pl. 7:8, 10). In rare cases the same vessels painted red could also be painted in light yellow or whitish colours (Pl. 7:8, 10). One of the dark-walled vessels was complexly covered with whitish paint as a background for red painted circles and rectangles (Pl. 7:8).

It is difficult to say how great a part of the pottery received red painted decoration, but it was as nearly as common as graphite painting. A saddle quern from Kale with abundant traces of ochre (Fig. 19) indicates that the demands for red paints were high. Based on that, it is tempting to associate the Late Copper Age settlement at Kale with the 3rd settlement horizon of Ezero. It should, however, be noted that red painted pottery was also rather common during the subsequent 4th settlement horizon. And one red painted shard was even recorded in the layers of Trench B attributed to the 5th settlement horizon. There are also other traits allowing a connecting of the Kale Late Copper Age settlement with the 4th settlement horizon of Ezero. Hemispherical bowls of varying proportions decorated with horizontal flutes covering the whole body were one of the most replicated elements in the Kale material (Pl. 11). Such bowls, according to present knowledge, only occurred during the period of Ezero's 4th settlement. Therefore, it is also plausible to assume contemporaneity between the Kale settlement and the 4th settlement horizon of Ezero. The material of the 5th settlement horizon of Ezero is only remotely related to the materials found at Kale.

Besides painted decoration occurring both internally and externally, the pottery of the 3rd settlement horizon of Ezero is often decorated with oblique flutes placed on rims and lips, externally as well as internally (Pl. 7:5). Rim shaping is often achieved by faceting of the inverted part above the shoulder. In this way, bowls achieve an angular, wavy outlook, rather close to fluting. Impressed decoration, for instance made with edges of shells at right angles (Pl. 6:13) or by punctuates are also occurring, but only sporadically. Graphite decoration includes different designs using groups of three clustered lines, either organised in spirals, rectilinear designs, meanders or enframing other elements such as triangles and rhombs with ovals inside. Rare in the region is the so-called "wolf's teeth" decoration - hanging graphite triangles (Pl 7:9), which is very common in Thrace in the Karanovo VI period (Todorova et al. 2003, Table 11). Rustication with barbotine is present but seems to be significantly reduced compared with other Late Copper Age sites in the area.

The shapes of the vessels can only be discerned from a very fragmented material, so a full repertoire of pottery cannot be recreated. However, all the main shapes of bowls characteristic for the Late (or Latest) Copper Age are represented. These include bowls with straight inverted rims, with thickened rims, thickened and rounded rims, and straight thickened rims with sharply pointed lips. The last type is very pronounced compared with the Lîga material (but not unusual in Latest KSB sites, including Sǎlcuţa (Berciu 1961: Fig. 85 (6,11) & 101 (9,10)), and Redutite, the 4th settlement, which belongs to the Transitional Period (Yordanova 2001[8]). Another type related to the first one is a bowl with a sharply marked shoulders and a flared outverted rim (Pl. 7:8-9). The lip can be either sharply pointed or rounded. Such bowls are also present in the area of KGK VI, but are considered as atypical (Todorova et al. 2003:251). Among the investigated material regular hemispherical bowls are rather frequent (Pl. 7:11); they grow even further in popularity after the 3rd settlement horizon at Ezero, and became one of the arch-types during the Transitional Period. Another feature of the Transitional Period – the S-profiled vessels – seemingly started to emerge during the samme settlement phase (Pl. 6:14).

8 The author is deeply grateful to Asia Yordanova, MA, for permission to study her unpublished thesis on the pottery from Redutite, the 4th settlement (attributed to the Transitional Period).

Looking at the category of pottery with restricted orifice/curvature, the most dominant specimens are big biconical jars with thickened rims (Pl. 6: 8-9). Over the period of the subsequent two settlements they develop in two directions. One type is characterised by a globular body and inverted rim, the other preserves the biconical outline terminated with straight cylindrical neck/rim. In terms of relief attributes there are two main groups - small conical handles vertically perforated and located around the place of the turning point and small, conical knobs applied on walls with an even curvature, be it straight-walled bowls or spherical jars.

Actually, these observations are raising questions about the cultural affinities of the site. Except for the red painted decoration of pottery[9], basically limited to Northern and Western Bulgaria, the main attributes of the ceramic material are more emblematic for the Late KGK VI sites found in Thrace (negative graphite paint, high complexity of painted designs, lack of handles, etc.). Certainly, this is not the only case of "shifting" across traditional borders of cultural complexes. The extensive sequence recorded in the Devetaki cave at Lovech have also raised questions about cultural affinity, in particular the pottery from Horizons V and VI, which is dominated by KGK VI traits with very close parallels to the Ovcharovo XI-XIII occupation (Mikov & Dzhambazov 1960; Atanasov 2002[10]). At the same time, the Yunatsite Late Copper Age layers unexpectedly yielded pottery fashioned in the KSB tradition, despite its geographical location at the western corner of the Thracian Plains, the core area of the KGK culture (Katinčarov et al. 1995).

This settlement also sees pottery with specialised functions, such as pots with spouts below the rim, some rather big with an orifice reaching 25 cm in diameter (Pl. 6:7), and pots (always the same type - restricted spherical pots) with a centrally located hole in the base, a special type of funnel. It has been argued elsewhere that such pot-funnels, together with big bowls, are part of an installation used for produc-

tion of cheese (cf. Hvass 1985). Several such vessels have been recorded at Lîga (Merkyte 2005, Fig. V.14). These two cases are eloquent traits of the period, which sees a gradually growing differentiation among pottery types, expanding the repertoire of functionally determined separate vessel types.

Pottery discovered in the 4th settlement horizon follows the tradition of the previous occupation (Pl. 8). Among the recovered shards the number of graphite painted ones has decreased, other types of decoration (incised lines, grooves, impressions with fingernails and fingertips, impressions made with edges of shells, multiple rows of small circular or lens-like pits) being dominant. The material is too limited to determine whether this distribution of decoration types is a general trend or merely a reflection of localised technological traditions on the site. A general trend is however suspected in the growing popularity of fluting. On two-partite bowls it would be used in an oblique fashion on the upper part above the turning point (Pl. 8:5). In the cases of sharply marked turning points oblique fluting (performed as a distinct row of short oblique flutes) is placed in the area of the turning point to smooth the sharp angle (Pl. 8:6). But most often fluting is seen on regular hemispherical bowls, where it is applied horizontally over the entire surface. Finger trailing and cordons with finger imprints are also common elements (Pl. 8:12 & 7). Cordons with finger imprints are used to separate the rim from the body. In bowls they are placed on the turning point in the same way, as a row comprised of oblique fluting. The shard collection of the 4th settlement horizon also produced a greater amount of handles and bosses, although handles are still rare. Dominant are vertical ear handles with a sharp upper edge (Pl. 8:14), vertically perforated tab handles (Pl. 8:5), and vertically perforated triangular tab handles (Pl 8:13).

The pottery collection of the 5th settlement horizon subscribes to the general trends of the previous settlements (Pl. 9). Graphite paint is likely declining but not unusual. The motives are no longer bound to restricted repertoires of elements, but demonstrate a full range of various combinations. The "traditional" spiral decoration is found side by side with strict rectilinear motives where groups of lines are organised in straight angles. Graphite decoration can be com-

---

9 Red painted decoration has recently also been acknowledged on KGK VI sites attributed to the latest phase of the cultural complex (Georgieva 2005), cf. below.

10 The author is deeply grateful to Cvetelin Atanasov, MA, for permission to read his unpublished thesis on the pottery from Devetaki Cave.

bined with fluting and/or impressed decoration such as round or oval pits/punctuates (Pl. 9:21).

Along with the usual bowl types there are also types with a more angular outline. The turning point can be stressed with a massive angular cordon or step, or the lip can be cut and the rim shortened so that it appears to be flat and angular (T-sectioned) (Pl. 9:18). Faceting of the rims is also performed.

IX. LATE COPPER AGE POTTERY AT KALE

The pottery from the Kale site mainly comes as unstratified material, only a minor part was discovered in situ. Despite that, there are no indications of more than one episode of occupation during the Latest Copper Age. It was mentioned above that a definite relation between the Late Copper Age occupation at Kale and the occupations at Ezero cannot be unambiguously established. In theory, it is possible that none of the Ezero settlements were contemporary with the Late Copper Age occupation at Kale, even though this is unlikely.

The pottery of Kale can be considered as more representative than the shards extracted from the trench walls of Ezero, since the former were collected from disturbed contexts across nearly the entire surface. The Copper Age pottery is easily distinguished among the shards from later periods due to its paste and surface treatment (Pl. 11). The surfaces are usually burnished or well-smoothed, dark brown or grey blackish colours dominate, but some lighter shades also occur. There are several examples of use of negative graphite decoration, in rare cases in combination with red ochre. Sometimes the decoration is carried out with red ochre alone. As also the case at Ezero, especially in layers not affected by fire, not all decoration patterns can be reconstructed due to calcareous crust firmly adhering to the surfaces. Certain elements emerge as persistent groups, though. These are graphite painted equilateral triangles, either open or closed at the base, in varying sizes and most commonly filled with lines (Pl. 11:1-2, 14-15). Such triangles reappear in the Early Bronze Age pottery performed in shallow grooves. Interestingly, one of the hemispherical bowls was equipped with a row of holes just below the lip, an element also characteristic of EBA pottery (Pl. 11:15).

Among the discovered fragments of pottery there were three different "askoi" (two of the fragments were discovered during excavation of the walled enclosure). These vessels are well-burnished, grey black in colour, tempered in different combinations of constituents (both sand, chamotte, and organic matter) as typical for Late Copper Age pottery. One example stands out by being of egg-shell quality, with a wall-thickness only reaching 3 mm. Horizontal fluting covering the entire body of vessel is also a characteristic feature of the Kale pottery assemblage. Among such vessels, bowls with hemispherical curvature dominate. A hitherto unseen shape with fluted body is a globular vessel with closed orifice and equipped with four tab handles (Pl. 11:10). The handles are perforated vertically on both sides of the protruding central part, which reminds of earlier zoomorphic handles. The shape of such handles was evidently functionally determined, enabling suspension (and hanging?) of the vessel. One such vessel was also decorated with curvilinear graphite lines, which likely reveal the way and the direction of stringing (Pl. 11:10). Notably, this vessel contained crushed shells in its paste (cf. below).

As in the Ezero material, flutes can also be arranged obliquely, as "rows" marking the place of the turning point. The most popular type of the KSB pottery repertoire - biconical cups - may appear as cups with a cylindrical, straight neck. Other peculiar shapes include vessels with a hemispherical body and everted rounded rims, creating a smooth S-profile (a few examples of a somewhat more inexpressive S-profile were already found in Ezero's 3rd settlement horizon (Pl. 6:14). Also bowls fashioned with thickened, often internally rounded rims appear. All these peculiar features can be recognised as seminal for the pottery of the Transitional Period (Georgieva 1993).

X. POTTERY OF THE TRANSITIONAL PERIOD

Pottery of the Transitional Period was discovered as single fragments at Ezero, representing the 6th settlement horizon at the site (interestingly, they were largely uncovered in Trench B) (Pl. 10:1-10); but primarily such pottery was collected at Kale. As can be expected, vessels with S-profile dominate. Dominant too are vessels with ear handles emerging at the lip or just below it. The lip is everted and the side or the top of it can be marked with nail or stick imprints (Pl. 10:7), thus creating a rather cranellated appearance. Handles are mostly rounded, but occasionally they may be sharp-angled (Pl. 10:8). A distinct group consists of broad strap handles, which often are shell-tempered. Some small vertical rounded handles terminating at the level of the vessel lip do resemble handles of the so-called "milk-jug"/"Milchtopf" type, known particularly in the Černavoda I culture (along with other Central European groups), but, unfortunately, the wall fragments attached to the handles are too small to confirm this (Pl. 12:16).

Bosses disappear in the Transitional Period, but a version of an oblong horizontal tab-handle with two-partite points may have replaced them. The notorious handles of the "Scheibenhenkel" type, which have gained status as the prime attribute defining pottery of the Transitional Period, were also discovered (Pl. 12:10-12). Three examples stem from Kale. A type genetically related to these is found at Ezero: instead of the discoid lower terminal, the handle is terminated with an arrow-like thickening at its base (Pl. 10:3). One of the "Scheiben" handles is decorated with short impressions along its edges perpendicular to the central axis - greatly resembling Early Bronze Age (EBA) handles found at Yunatsite, Horizons XVII-XIV (Katinčarov & Matsanova 1993, Fig. 7) (Pl. 12:11). Another "Scheiben" handle has also demonstrated links with EBA pottery traditions, namely through a composite decoration with a band of shallow grooves (characteristic of EBA pottery) (Pl. 12:12). Along with specimens with a flared upper part there is also a distinct group of vessels with closed, conical, straight, and long necks, usually decorated with a continuous incised decoration and incrusted with whitish or yellow paste (Pl. 12:8-9). Analogous examples are known from the Romanian site of Cheile Turzii (Roman 1971, Fig. 39:1).

The repertoire of bowl shapes, especially the dramatic ones with a pronounced turning point, decreased in the Transitional Period. The emblematic ones are hemispherical bowls and bowls with thickened lip. In terms of decoration there is a distinctive group of vessels - both bowls and jars - that are entirely covered with brushing. Such decoration (or

Fig. 24. Ceramic shard with characteristic striations and white incrustation, Transitional Period, Kale.

rather type of rustication) was already known on Late Copper Age sites, for instance Lîga (Merkyte 2005, Pl. 6:20). Whereas Late Copper Age brushing seems to be finer and more organised, the striations thinner, later brushing is cruder, and more intense, and the striations are deeper (Fig. 24). In some cases it also incrusted with whitish paste. Graphite and other paints are no longer applied. A complete novelty in pottery production is the use of crushed shells as tempering constituent. This can be used alone or together with sand. In some cases shells are so abundant that they comprise more than 25% of the total body volume. Shell tempering is not reserved to certain types of pottery, and it can be both present and absent within the same typological group (cf. Pl. 12:8 & 9). In this sense, shell tempering appears rather like a "fashion" (copying foreign elements which are considered superior or exotic) rather than a technologically sustained implementation. According to the described traits and following the ordering suggested by P. Georgieva (1993), the materials can be attributed to the Galatin culture.

XI. EARLY BRONZE AGE POTTERY
The pottery attributed to the Early Bronze age (EBA) stems from surface collecting at Kale and, mainly, the trench made across the semi-circular rampart. Only a few EBA fragments were found at Ezero, unassoci-

ated with any particular feature (Pl. 10:10). In terms of general appearance, paste, and surface treatment the EBA pottery is continuing the same traditions of production, which were observed in the material attributed to the Transitional Period. A few EBA fragments even contained crushed shell as tempering material[11]. But essentially the vessels are made of clay tempered with sand in different concentrations and different granular sizes.

The EBA pottery subscribes to the trends, which define the Orlea-Sadovec Cultural Group, a southern variant of the Magura-Coţofeni Culture (Aleksandrov 1992) (Pl. 13). The pottery shares a number of common traits with the Bulgarian EBA Ezero A Culture but primarily it is directly influenced by Romanian Coţofeni traditions. These influences should not be seen as transformations of foreign elements melted into local traditions, but are rather direct borrowings without significant modifications. It is characteristic for the Orlea-Sadovec group to accentuate the lip of a vessel. The lips are often prolonged and marked with impressions of different shapes, usually creating a cranelated curvature of the lip. One of the typical fingerprints of this tradition is a row of pits or holes placed horizontally just below the lip. Another part of the EBA pottery from Kale is decorated with shallow grooves and punctuates which together create a mosaic of complicated geometric motives. In single cases there is also decoration with low applied cordons of impressions of finger or stick. Such elements, including grooving (sometimes termed pseudo-fluting), are characteristic for the Coţofeni tradition. Not surprisingly, the closest parallels to the Ezero-Kale pottery are found in the Sadovec Golemanovo Kale materials (Todorova 1992, Fig. 14), some fragments can even be considered as identical[12].

The genesis of the Orlea-Sadovec group is not completely understood (Aleksandrov 1992). However, it is most likely that the group is a direct derivative of local pottery production traditions of the previous periods (presence of conical bowls with thickened lips, hemispherical bowls, handles raised above the

rim, bowls with everted rim, etc.). What is clear in the Kale material is that the Orlea-Sadovec production tradition is reserved for kinds of "domestic" pottery. Vessels of such a character include usually big jars with unrestricted orifices and simple body curvature, hence likely related to storage functions. Pottery with shallow grooves - the Coţofeni tradition - can be considered as fine ware, the decoration being applied on jars and jugs with spherical bodies and dramatic curvature, and often with highly placed ear handles. A secure attribution of fragments of bases to a particular period can be a difficult task. In a few cases it could be established that the EBA pottery had pronounce, footed bases (Pl. 13:6-7). The EBA pottery is generally thin walled. The surfaces are smoothed, although often fallen off. In rare cases surfaces can be burnished. Notably, the EBA pottery also bears traces of higher firing temperatures than earlier.

XII. POTTERY OF THE LATE ANTIQUITY PERIOD

During the initial fieldwork, the pervasive opinion as to the presence of the rampart at Kale was that it belonged to the Late Antiquity (Early Byzantine) period (4th-6th century AD). It was viewed in the same light as the neighbouring strongholds at Sadovec-Golemanovo Kale and Pipra. Therefore, before even starting the cross-section excavation of the rampart, systematic attempts were made to collect all the materials attributable to this period in order to explain the presence of the wall structure. Surprisingly, only a dozen pottery shards (together with a fragment of a spindle-whorl, a glass bead, and a few iron rods), which are attributable to the Late Antiquity period, were discovered at Kale (Pl. 13:18-21). Ezero only yielded a handful of such shards. All shards are wheel-made of levigated clay, in two cases with fine sand as a tempering constituent. They are light grey or medium grey in colour. The shapes conform to the types known form Sadovec-Golemanovo Kale (Uentze 1992).

XIII. THE CHIPPED STONE ASSEMBLAGE

The flint material collected from Ezero (30) and Kale (106) lacks stratigraphical as well as contextual sensi-

---

11 Shell-tempered pottery is rather common in other Early Bronze Age sites discovered in NW Bulgaria and attributed to the Coţofeni Culture (Panayotov & Aleksandrov 1988).

12 (cf. Todorova 1992, Fig. 14 and Pl. 13: 17 here)

tivity for any truly serious analysis (Pl. 14:9-16). How-ever, overall trends can be observed, especially when the collections from both sites are compared, a comparison only concerned with a coarse scale tool function based on morphological attributes. The Ezero collection is predominantly of tools made on blades such as blades with retouched or utilised lateral edges and end scrapers. This is in accordance with other Late Copper Age sites, for instance Lîga (Albek 2005). Other tools in this limited collection include a sickle element with gloss, a combined double burin with retouched lateral edge, a truncated blade, the middle part of a blade with denticulate edge outline, and end scrapers on flakes. A few tools have hafting notches. As on other contemporary sites blades with parallel edges dominate. Only a few amorphous flakes have no traces of use. The blanks were produced by direct soft or indirect percussion. In terms of raw material, the local grey Sadovec flint is dominating. The Sadovec flint source is one of the main sources of primary flint in the area. Here are two layers of flint nodules, formed in different periods at the end of the Cretaceous (Valev 1992). One is rather light grey in colour, opaque and coarse-grained, and spotted with whitish inclusions. The other type is more glossy and darker with a fine grain structure. The first type has been preferred during the Copper Age. The Ezero material also includes a few examples of "foreign" flint, which manifests itself due to an even microcrystalline structure and a wax-yellow colour. Undoubtedly, these items entered the material as ready-made products.

A higher diversity within the flint assemblage is observed at Kale. The overall statistics are quiet similar to other prehistoric sites: Among 106 collected flints there were 5 exploited cores and 59 flakes and blades with retouch or traces of utilisation. The grey spotted Sadovec flint together with its finer variety make up 32% of all collected pieces. A new type of raw material dominates, a brown grey opaque flint spotted with whitish inclusions. In a way this resembles Sadovec flint but only in a patinated state. Closer investigation reveals that the colouring is geologically determined; the spots are also bigger and more diffuse than in Sadovec flint. The brown grey flint makes up 42% of the total collected material. It was also present among the artefacts collected at Ezero, but only as

few pieces. The remaining 36% of the artefacts are distributed among seven other types of raw material, including whitish Pipra flint (21%). The grey brown flint is likely local as well (found within a radius of 10 km), while its domination in the Kale material is temporally determined.

This group of flint artefacts form a coherent assemblage, which is produced according to different principles than the tools observed in the Late Copper Age material, namely by being made on large flakes, not blades[13]. The dimensions (length x width) of the flakes used for tool production are, for instance, 7.5x5.2, 6.0x4.4, 5.5x3.7, 6.1x4.0, etc. (Pl. 14:9-11); they are crudely produced with direct hard percussion. The retouch is also crude covering only some parts of the edge. The un-retouched areas bear traces of utilization typical for cutting edges. Some flakes are combined tools with emblematic scraper retouch on the distal end and traces of utilization along the lateral edges. A more conventional group of end-scrapers seems to be related to this group of artefacts (Pl. 14:14). They are typified by heavy steep retouch. Two steeply retouched blades discovered at Ezero probably also represent this and same temporal horizon.

The macrolithic features of the discussed set of artefacts points to a distinct flint industry not rooted in the Copper Age. Analyses of flint inventories collected on sites dated to the Transitional Period, such as Hotnitsa-Vodopada and Redutite IV have demonstrated a continuation of Copper Age lithic traditions (Gergov et al. 1986; Sirakov & Tsonev 1995; Sirakov 1996). On the other hand, the publications related to Bulgarian Early Bronze Age sites, such as Ezero (Georgiev et al. 1979) do not contain any parallels to the macrolithic tools of Kale.

In recent years, there has been a growing awareness in Northern and Central Europe that Early Bronze Age flint industries - usually overshadowed by metal tools - survive in rather crude, conventionally unrestricted shapes generally defined as "macrolithic forms" (Kopacz & Valde-Nowak 1987; Eriksen in prep.). Perhaps the same processes took place in the Balkans at an earlier period, with the onset of the

---

13 Blades - versus flakes - are defined as being detached pieces at least twice as long as wide and having parallel longitudinal scars on the dorsal face (Crabtree 1972:24).

Bronze Age metallurgy. It should be noted that in general there is a similarity with the material published from Hotnitsa-Vodopada settlement at Veliko Tarnovo (heavily retouched flake tools which also show a clear tendency towards macrolithic features). The material from Telish-Redutite IV, also of the Transitional Period, includes just two flint artefacts (only about 30 such items were collected from the whole site) (Gergov et al. 1986), which of course is insufficient for any diachronic (or other) analysis. A lithic industry based on flakes as the primary blanks for tool production is also attested at Troia I-VII (Gatsov 1998), but it is still unclear when this technology started, nor are the further chronological and geographical properties of the macrolithic industry known.

Unambiguous domination of flakes in relation to blades has been noticed as typical for the late phases of the Vinča complex (Radovanović 1996). According to I. Radovanović, such development is contrasting with the chipped stone industries attested in the area of the KSB and, for instance, the Tiszapolgár Culture to the North (ibid. 1996), where blades dominate. It is therefore open for debate whether Vinča lithic traditions actually penetrated north-western Bulgaria to the east, or whether the reliance on flake-industries based on local resources and - especially - "macrolithic forms" was dictated by localised circumstances, such as being in a "pioneer position" in a new environment, or by novel technological preferences.

It is also worth mentioning the find of three pointed flint artefacts from Kale (Fig. 25). Two of these are regular triangular bifacial points, while the third is an exceptional one. Both the triangular points are incomplete. The smaller specimen (preserved height of 2.3 cm), with a slightly concave base, has no tip, while the bigger specimen (preserved height of 3.9 cm) is lacking tip as well as base. Such points find their closes stylistic parallels in the material from Hotnitsa-Vodopada, attributed to the Transitional Period (Sirakov & Tsonev 1995), but are also known from earlier periods, in fact Late Copper Age sites attributed to both the KGK and the KSB cultural traditions (ibid.). One similar bifacial point was indeed found in the Lîga 2 context (Merkyte 2005, Plate 23:16). However, their augmented numbers during the Transitional Period, even in such a "peaceful" region as NW Bulgaria cannot be left unnoticed and likely indicate an increase

Fig. 25. Flint points, Kale.

of on-site clashes. The third pointed flint artefact from Kale (preserved length of 3.2 cm) is made on a thin truncated blade without any scars, so that the surface has not been modified by pressure flaking otherwise typical for bifacial points. The edges, which are slightly convex, are bilaterally retouched. The tip is again missing, but well-fashioned notches on both sides indicate the way this artefact was hafted and used - as an arrow-head. Similar notched points have been reported from a settlement at Durankulak (Todorova 1986, Figs. 54 & 78:3).

Finally, some tools found at Kale, clearly of a Late Copper Age date, by contrast demonstrate a canonised approach towards the production of tools. Nearly identical pieces (pear-shaped scrapers and end-scrapers with hafting notches) were found in the Lîga material (Merkyte 2005, Plate 22:1,2).

XIV. BONE AND ANTLER ARTEFACTS

The collection of bone and antler artefacts from Ezero and Kale amounts to 20 pieces. They are extremely well preserved due to the high content of calcium in the ground. Nearly all traces of breakage are recent, caused by looter' activities. Except for one case, their stratigraphic provenience could not be established. The one exception is a pointed tool with triangular section made on a long bone splinter discovered in Trench A, in the 2nd settlement horizon (Pl. 14:4).

10 pieces of worked bone were collected during re-excavation in Trench B at Ezero. These comprise complete items or tools (3) (Pl. 14: 2, 3), fragmented tools (4) (Pl. 14:6) and debitage shavings - all fragments of worked antlers (3). Such concentration of shavings and other items allows, perhaps, the speculation that these were contemporary and related to

Fig. 26. Antler socket (hoe), Kale.

Fig. 27. Edge fragments of small copper axe heads discovered at Kale. The fragments show that copper axes were in fact used for work.

the same area of production. Among the complete items was a non-utilitarian piece - a prismatic figurine made of pig metatarsus, normally regarded as a female representation (cf. Zidarov 2005:126f.). Another such figurine was collected at Kale. The latter was flattened to a nearly regular prismatic shape, completely grounding away the articulations of the distal epiphysis. Noteworthy finds from Trench B are a pointed tool with a convex section having been utilised as an awl (Pl. 14:3) and a bevel-shaped tool utilized as a chisel (Pl. 14:2). Also the top part of an antler tine shaped at opposite sides and with bevel was used as a chisel (Pl. 14:6).

The most remarkable find was made in Trench A. This was a flat anthropomorphic figurine carved in a rather stylised way, its femininity transparent from curved body lines and incised lines marking the pelvic triangle (cf. Gergov 2004). Around the pelvic triangle and in the area of the knees - typical of the period -

were rows of dots. The facial features were reduced to the presence of eyes; the legs were separated with an incised line. Unfinished attempt to drill a new hole in the area of the hands replacing the original ones, which grew open due to break of terminals, confirms its active use as pendant.

Somewhat enigmatic is a pointed bone artefact resembling a hook found at Ezero (Pl. 14: 7). Deep oblique striations visible on both surfaces together with an incomplete perforation of the ear suggest that the item is not complete. Its overall shape would be reasonably suitable for a function as harpoon point, but at the same time it has close affinity with a group of copper (and bone) items discovered in Redutite II: bone versions have been discovered at a number Late Copper Age sites, for instance Sâlcuţa (Berciu 1961, Fig. 66:3), and are interpreted as implements for knitting of nets or the like (Gergov 1987, Fig. 6).

The bone artefacts found at Kale also contained exceptional finds, including the just mentioned prismatic figurine. A pointed artefact, elegantly made on a long bone splinter (Pl. 14:8) and 13.4 cm long, is not completely understood functionally (the completely polished surface may imply that it was used as an ornament (a pin of some kind) rather than as an awl). A bone pin with a rounded head and a flattened distal end for keeping the hair in place or secure clothing may be of a later period than the Copper Age (Pl. 14:5), a likely parallel being found in the EBA layers of the Devetaki cave (Mikov & Dzhambazov 1960, Fig. 87:c). The Kale material has also yielded part of an antler socket with circular perforation for mounting (Fig. 26) and an antler tine with rounded distal point and polished end. Both items are traditionally considered as common agricultural tools used for working the ground (hoes). Both types of artefacts have a broad temporal range and are found at both Copper Age and Bronze Age sites (Mikov & Dzhambazov 1960; Georgiev et al. 1979).

On both Ezero and Kale the bone/antler material is dominated by awls (Trench B - 2 awls, Trench A - 1 awl, Kale - 2 awls), and chisels (Trench B - 1; Kale - 2, antler & bone, respectively). This underlines the importance of the production of skin clothing and of finer wood-working.

XV. OTHER FINDS

The ground stone tool collection included only two hammer stones and an adze, all found at Kale. A small mace-head of the post-Copper Age date was found at Ezero (Plate 10:11).

The most fascinating discovery, however, is two tiny fragments of the edges of copper axes from Kale. One fragment derives from the corner of a nearly straight edge (Fig. 27:1), the other from a middle part of a rounded edge (Fig. 27:2). Both fragments are important testimonies that copper axes were not merely prestige items, but functioned in the quotidian domestic inventory.

It is also quite probable that during this period - the final phases of the Copper Age - copper axes were entering a general system of exchange based on affirmation of social associations and ideology (cf. below). Therefore, the find of a miniature clay model of a double axe (L=4.3 cm), made of light un-tempered clay, in Trench B (precise position unknown) (Pl. 10:12) is regarded as a symptomatic element in the repertoire and sequence of "clay messages", reflecting upon central concerns of Copper Age communities.

A symbolically even highly loaded clay specimen has been found at the site of "Starozagorski mineralni bani" in Stara Zagora (Georgieva 2005, Fig. 4:1). This depicts a particular version of a double axe, which is merged with zoomorphic sceptres (L=6.2). The latter are generally regarded as heralds of the turbulent times of the Transitional Period. The sceptres are shaped as zoomorphic heads, with eyes and ears, yet they are not identical: one is likely to be a male, the other a female representation. The antipodal character (and the unity - cf. the juxtaposition) inherent in the structure of a double-axe is here employed to stress duality in nature.

It is interesting to note that production of miniature clay axes was rather common during the EBA. At Ezero Tell at Nova Zagora, 24 such axes have been recovered distributed through Horizons XIII-IV (Georgiev et al. 1979, Fig. 204; see also Stefanova 2000, Fig. 6:3). All but one of the Ezero axes were imitating battle-axes and, generally, could be matched with particular stone and metal counterparts (Georgiev et al. 1979, Table 299). Strangely, all the specimens were broken. The Kale specimen appears to be more abstract in shape than the other mentioned pieces, but

nevertheless, the possibility of tracing this tradition to the end of the Copper Age has important implications for the understanding of the genesis of EBA.

A cross-shaped clay object discovered at Kale is also worth mentioning; this is possibly a spindle whorl, measuring 4.8x5.0 cm, with a thickness of the central part of 1.6 cm. Two of the adjacent terminals are shaped as abstract zoomorphic heads (dog?) looking in opposite direction, the remaining two terminals are likely to be perceived as legs (Pl. 10:13). Cross-shaped clay items are rather wide-spread both in the KGK and KSB areas at the end of the Copper Age (Matsanova 1994, with references). They are usually interpreted as idols. A collection of 66 such items discovered at Yunatsite Tell, attributed to the last Copper Age settlement, was interpreted as representation of birds, likely eagle (ibid.). Notably, the absence of a uniform and canonised shape may indicate that the artefact had a practical function rather than being determined by ritual significance alone.

Apart from this, the collection of artefacts also yielded two miniature vessels, both representing the classical biconical cups of the Late Copper Age. Such cups - nearly identical miniature vessels have been discovered at neighbouring sites such as Sadovec-Golemanovo Kale (Todorova 1992, Fig. 11:3, 4) and Lïga (Merkyte 2005, Pl. 16:1). Both vessels were discovered in Trench A of Ezero and are attributed to the final phases of the occupation of the site. One specimen, measuring 3 cm in height and with burnished exterior, was discovered in layers belonging to the 5th settlement (Pl. 10:14), the other was found in the topsoil; both were tempered with medium coarse sand.

Among other idiosyncratic finds are three fragments of anthropomorphic figurines. Half of a lower female body (leg - minus foot - and abdomen), inexpressively shaped and broken lengthwise in the middle, was found at Ezero in Trench A. The discovered fragment is measuring 6 cm, the complete figurine being estimated to be around 9-10 cm in height. The item is made of clay tempered with chamotte and sand, and light grey brown in colour. The cut surface is very even, implying that it could have been a controlled and intentional breakage. Such fragments of figurines are "typical" Late Copper Age finds.

Two other fragments of figurines - both stemming from the surface collection of Kale - held some surprises. One is a right foot, grey black in colour, measuring 4.2 cm in width (the full length could not be measured), and thus belonging to a group of figurines reaching some 30 cm in height. Such figurines have also been recognised in the Liga material; in fact, there is a striking similarity between this massive, abstractly fashioned foot and the examples discovered at Lîga (Merkyte 2005, Pl. 18:12). But contrary to its equivalents, the Kale foot held a moderate amount of finely crushed shells along with an even higher amount of quartz grains in its paste. Another fragment - a pair of legs with toed feet, abstractly modelled - was also shell-tempered (along with moderate amount of sand). The leg fragment, measuring 2.1 cm in width and 2.5 cm in length was light reddish brown in colour and followed in terms of colour preferences Late Copper

Age traditions. The presence of crushed shells in the temper has also been determined in a clay spindle whorl found at Kale; an amount of fine sand was added to the paste. This spindle whorl is circular in shape and double convex in section, 4.7 cm in diameter, the height being 2.6 cm; the diameter of the central hole is 0.7 cm. The item is dark brown in colour. Lastly, it should be mentioned that among the materials discovered in Trench A at Ezero was also a fragment representing the corner of a clay model of a flat table. The surfaces were well-burnished, lustrous, medium brown with grey black patches. It was decorated with graphite paint on both surfaces, graphite lines organised in herring-like fashion centred on lines leading from the point of the corner towards the centre the table. The date is undoubtedly Copper Age.

GRAVES

XVI. HUMAN SKELETAL REMAINS AT EZERO

Human skeletal remains were already discovered during the very first visit to Ezero, when the immense damage that the looters have caused by their illicit activities were recognized. A human scull was unmistakably visible in the middle of a profile wall of a trench at the southern slopes of the site, later labelled Trench B (cf. above). The location of the scull dictated modifications of the usual excavation methods (excavating in horizontal layers), in so far that a terrace at the level of the scull was created for detection and studying further human bones likely belonging to the scull. No actual signs of a burial pit could be seen or felt, with the exception of the eastern edge of the area which bordered on a rather compact layer. The size of the area occupied by human bones implied that the body was positioned into a pit, not just covered with soil. The size of this area is 0.65 m in E-W direction, and 0,45 in N-S direction. Even though the bones were discovered very close to the slopes, all principal bones were recorded, which also speaks in favour of intentional deposition of the body, which was not affected by scavenging, as sometimes is the case with finds of human skeletal remains displaying an awkward position of the bones (for instance, the human remains discovered in the final layers of the Late Copper Age at Yunatsite Tell, close to Pazardzhik (Matsanova 2000)).

Still, the position of the discovered bones was indeed odd (Fig. 28 & 29). The scull was discovered 0.37 m below the present-day surface created by a modern ditch-like trench. The pelvis bones were lying significantly higher than the scull (0.19 m separated the uppermost part of the scull and the lowest edge of the right hip bone), 0.34 m below the present-day surface (Fig. 30 & 31). The long bones - in fact the distal end of the left tibia and the proximal end of the right femur - were the highest points of the skeleton. The scull was placed on the anterior side of this, the top orientated towards the south, perpendicular to the spine. The vertebral column was still firmly attached to the scull, so that the neck was wrung prior to the deposition of the body. A limestone slab measuring 19x7.5 cm was placed immediately on the scull. Such a position of bones implies that the dead was literally plunged into a small pit not more than a meter below the surface (Fig. 32).

The dead was laid prone, in a crouched position, resting on the upper part of the body and the knees, while the rump and the feet were sticking up, latter abutting against the wall of the pit (Fig. 32). The body was generally orientated E-W, with the head towards the west. The vertebral column gave a compass measure of 295° N (NW). The high contents of lime in the soil had resulted in superb conditions of find: all bones, as indicated, preserved and collected. Nevertheless, some bones, like those of feet and palm, were missing; others were fragmented due to the disturbances caused by looters. The bones had even gained a lime coating hindering recognition of traces of injuries and even prohibiting exact measuring. The skeletal remains were investigated by Y. Yordanov of the Bulgarian Academy of Science[14].

The bones were determined to belong to a female aged c40 (maturus) (Life expectancy during EBA was around 26 year for women, and 29.3 years for men (Yordanov & Dimitrova 1989)). The bones are too fragmented to estimate the height. The long bones have medium to strong relief, indicating a well-developed musculature. The scull was well-preserved and inspired a facial reconstruction, unfortunately not completed. According to the personal observations of Prof. Yordanov, this female had a highly protruding maxilla and a low expressed forehead; she was hardly considered a beauty in her days (pers. comm.).

Part of the humerus was submitted for dating to Laboratory of Ion Physics in Uppsala, Sweden. It was dated to 4575+/-45 BP (Ua-24359, $\delta^{13}C$ value is –20.9). In calendar years, this corresponds to 3499-3103 BC (95.4% probability, OxCal v. 4.0.5) with a statistical overweight on the period 3380-3103 BC) (Fig. 23). Unfortunately, one of the serious plateaus in

---

14 The author is very grateful to Prof. Y. Yordanov, Institute of Experimental Morphology and Anthropology, Sofia for undertaking the biological investigation of the recovered human bone material from Ezero, as well as from the Liga graves.

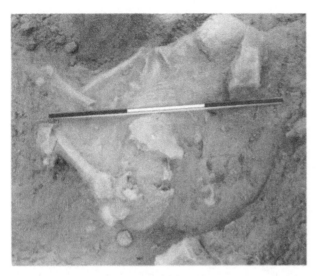

Fig. 28. Human skeletal remains discovered at Ezero, as seen from above. The measurement stick equals 60 cm.

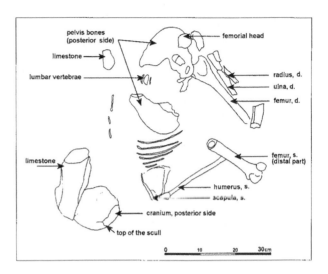

Fig. 29. Drawing of the human skeletal remains at Ezero, as seen from above.

the calibration curves exists exactly around 4500 BP. So perhaps, this deposition can be related to the EBA occupation at Kale, even suggesting a date for the Orlea-Sadovec cultural subgroup. No grave goods were discovered. A few shards and some casual flint blades were collected during excavation of the skeleton as belonging to the layers of the 5th settlement horizon at Ezero, into which this female was inserted. The violent nature of the deposition (literally throwing and plunging the body into a small, hastily excavated shallow pit, not even bothering to turn the body upside up, the stone placed (or thrown, as the last blow) on the head), the lack of grave goods, etc. would imply an act of criminal activity rather than a normal burial or even sacrifice. One can only wonder who and why anyone wished to mortify such an aged woman of about 40 years, with the average Early Bronze Age life-expectancy being about 28 years(Yordanov & Dimitrova 1989).

XVII. DATES OF THE LÎGA GRAVES

Since the publication of the Lîga excavations (Merkyte 2005), additional bone samples from the graves of the site have been submitted for dating to the Uppsala laboratory of Ion Physics, Sweden. Unexpectedly, these samples have produced younger dates than anticipated. In the presentation of the Lîga graves, the

possibility that a group of six centrally located burials (Graves no. 2-7, including a double interment), which were secondarily inserted into the layers of the settlement, might be of another date than the isolated burial found at the southern slopes of the site, and already C-14 dated prior to the publication (Merkyte 2005:153).

Three bone samples from the grave at the southern slopes were submitted; two produced credible dates placing it at the very end of the Copper Age (around 4000 BC, for details see Merkyte 2005, Figs. II.12, II.13 & III.5). Although this grave, termed Grave 1, had a southern orientation, and the remaining a northern orientation, the short distance between these graves and especially the nature of the grave goods made it plausible to assume a Late Copper Age date for all the then undated six burials. This anticipation was strengthened by the fact that the burials and the Late Copper Age dwellings preceding them had the same northern orientation.

Although the observations related to the graves and the cultural landscapes of the period presented in the original publication remain valid, it is in place to make needed corrections as to their chronological position. Actually, the new dates are even more intriguing. Unfortunately, the wiggles in C-14 curves allow for broad margins of the calibrated dates. The methods of C-14 dating are far from being impeccable,

Fig. 30. The human skeletal remains discovered at Ezero, as seen from the side.

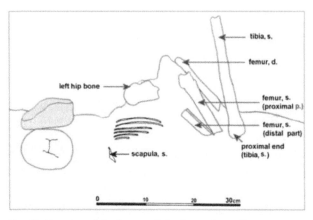

Fig. 31. Drawing of the human skeletal remains at Ezero, as seen from the side.

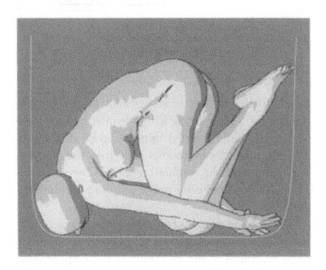

Fig. 32. Suggested reconstruction of the burial at Ezero.

hence, for instance, the surprising uncalibrated difference of 100 years between samples taken from two the individuals - a male adult and an infant - of double Grave 7. The sample related to the child appeared to be the younger one, likely because the amount of preserved collagen was lower. It should also be mentioned that one mistake has been embroiled in the original publication. The age of the child buried in the double-burial Grave 7a-b is 5 years, not 1½ (Merkyte 2005: 147). Actually, the reconstruction of the necklace associated with this child was been based on a five-year old model and therefore - as visual representation - remains accurate (ibid. Fig. XI.15).

Four samples (fragments of long bones), belonging to four individuals from three different graves from

Lîga have been submitted. The dating has produced the following results:

Grave 7a (adult, male, 25-30 years) – 4310+/-45 BP (Ua-24360, δ^{13}C value is –21.9)

Grave 7b (infant I, 5 years) – 4210 +/- 45 BP (Ua-24361, δ^{13}C value is –20.6)

Grave 5 (infant II, 8-9 years) – 4390 +/-40 BP (Ua-32696, δ^{13}C value is –20.2)

Grave 6 (juvenile, male, 18-19 years) – 4375 +/-40 BP (Ua-32697, δ^{13}C value is –20.9)

The calibrated ranges clearly place this compact group of burials within the Early Bronze Age, in spite of the character of the grave goods. The dates obtained from Graves nos. 5 and 6 are remarkably close, suggesting a temporal position of the burials within the period 3100-2900 BC (at 90+ % probability, δ^2), which can conceivably be narrowed to the period 3030-2920 BC (at 58+ % probability, δ^1). The human remains from Grave 7a-b have produced somewhat younger dates, ranging between 3040 and 2660 BC (at 92+ % probability, δ^2). The date for the bones belonging to the adult in the grave is rather close to the range suggested for Graves nos. 5 & 6. At 92.9% (δ^2) probability the calibrated results range between 3040-2870 BC. Since the double interment Grave 7a-b is located in between Graves nos. 5 and 6, and all the graves (i.e., Graves nos. 2-7) are fully excavated and appear to be organised in both longitudinal and latitudinal rows (a full description is presented in Merkyte 2005), their contemporaneity cannot be doubted.

Thus, it is plausible to suggest that the deposition of the dead of Graves nos. 2-7 took place sometime between 3030 and 2920 BC. It is not clear whether this burial site can be associated with the Early Bronze Age settlement at Līga (with Orlea-Sadovec materials), located higher up than the Copper Age settlements. Actually, the Copper Age strata were disturbed by at least one pit (of 1.50x1.20x1.15 m) containing fragmented EBA pottery and animal bones, generally interpreted as related to domestic refuse. This pit was less than two meters north of Grave no. 4 (Merkyte 2005, Pl. 1). Therefore, such combination of domestic and ritual spheres seems unlikely.

The new dates for the Līga burials strengthen the previous anticipation that the golden pendant recovered in loose soil close to Grave 1 (Merkyte 2005, 108, Fig. VI.17) was indeed related to this particular burial, since this is the only burial of Late Copper date (ca. 4000 BC, see Merkyte 2005, Fig. II.2) discovered up till now at Līga. Copper Age burials are indeed the expected context for the deposition of gold items in this part of Prehistory (Chapman 2002, Table 5.1).

XVIII. BURIAL CUSTOMS

The number of known earlier EBA burial sites in Bulgaria is still very modest. By contrast, proliferate knowledge has been accumulated on the Pit Grave Culture, which spread along the Danube and dotted the landscape with barrows, sometimes reaching impressive heights such as 8 meters. The two only available dates, from Placidol, NE Bulgaria, indicate that this development was slightly later than the Līga graves and can be placed in the period 2900-2600 BC (uncalibrated dates provided in Kitov et al. 1991.) The burial rites of the Pit Grave Culture also penetrated the Thracian plain (Panayotov 1989). At the same time, in north-western Bulgaria, there are sites where the dead are buried in flat burial sites, either as inhumations (Altimir), or, notably, in a cremated state (Galiche, Ostrov, Selanovtsi, and Krushovitsa) (ibid.). Some barrows (Tarnava) may contain both inhumed and cremated remains (Nikolov 1976).

In the Thracian plain, where the earlier tells were reoccupied with the arrival of the Bronze Age, there are also isolated finds of so-called intramural burials. Thus, five burials have been found in the Ezero tell at Stara Zagora, attributed to different horizons of the EBA (Georgiev et al. 1979). The earliest was found

in Horizon XIII, i.e. the beginning of the EBA. The dead was laid on its the back with crouched legs and the head orientated towards south-south west. The only grave good recognised by the excavators was a necklace of five dentalium beads and an oblong marble pendant with a perforated hole.

The only formal flat burial site in the Thracian plain has been discovered near the Bereket Tell, also at Stara Zagora (Kalchev 1996). 78 burials were found (among them four of the Karanovo VI date, but no further information); all the dead were laid in hocker position, predominantly on the left side, with the head orientated towards the south. Pieces of ochre were deposited at the sculls or below the skeletons. Generally, red ochre is one of the few recurring elements in all the burials dated to the EBA. Links with the Copper Age can be observed in two graves containing bucranion.

Indeed, what is characteristic of all the listed EBA burial types and sites is the lack of a unified conception of burial rites so persistently demonstrated on Copper Age grave sites. Indeed, disintegration and individual reformulation of the ritual regulations concerning burials can even be witnessed in one and the same burial mound, containing, for instance, several burials where the dead have different orientations and different body arrangements.

In this light, the burials of Līga stand out as a strongly coherent group, untypical of the EBA. All the dead were orientated towards the north (with an insignificant deviation towards the east). A northern orientation occasionally appears among the burials of the EBA, but only in rare cases. The bodies were arranged in hocker position on the right side with their heads facing westwards. The only exception is the double Grave 7a-b, where the adult male was laid on the back with crouched legs while holding the child lying in hocker on the right side. Supine arrangements with crouched legs are typical for the Pit Grave Culture (Panayotov 1989; Kitov et al. 1991), but in the case of the Līga double grave it could have been dictated by the need to arrange two bodies together. The grave goods were sparse (also characteristic for the period), but the included items are also rather unusual in an EBA context, such as a bone plate (made as a wrist guard, but likely used as a breast plate by the child it was associated with), a cattle horn, animal bones, a flint scraper, one necklace made of 8 dentalium shells and a bone pendant, shaped as imitation of a red deer tooth, and a necklace made of dentalium and cardium shells. Noticeably, among the Lîga EBA graves, personal items dominated. As can be seen from the cited burial in the Ezero Tell at Stara Zagora, dentalium shells were also in use elsewhere in the EBA. A necklace made of shells (dentalium?) has also been discovered in a primary grave of a child at Tarnava (Barrow I, Grave no. 3) close to Vratsa in NW Bulgaria (Nikolova 1976). But these can be regarded as exceptions in the burial inventory of the EBA, where necklaces only occur in rare cases and then made of metal beads (silver, gold) and/or beads made of bone/teeth (Kitov et al. 1991). Contrary, all the mentioned artefacts found in the Lîga burials are well-known in Late Copper Age grave sites in both coastal and north-eastern Bulgaria, for instance Durankulak (Todorova 2002), and in settlement sites such as Drama (Lichardus et al. 2000).

It has been convincingly argued that the early agricultural communities place their dead in hocker position on the left side, orientated towards the East (Häusler 1998). The most remarkable exceptions are the graves of the Hamangia and the later Varna cultures (5250/5200-4250/4150 BC), spread at the western coast of the Black Sea; here the dead are orientated towards the North (Todorova 2002). A northern orientation is often observed among forager communities, which actually are seen as the initiators of the Hamangia-Varna burial tradition (ibid.). However, bipolar modality, seen for instance in the Varna and Durankulak burial sites, where the males are buried outstretched on the back and females in hocker position on the right side allow the speculation whether women were perceived as more "Neolithic" than men. The coastal burial sites also raise questions regarding the control mechanisms within these societies, which can hardly be regarded as closed at the social level and yet manage to impose a well-defined gender determined bi-polarity in stark contrast to the neighbouring inland sites in north-eastern Bulgaria, such as Golyamo Delčevo, Ovčarovo, Polyanitsa, Radingrad, and others, where the dead, almost without any exceptions, were buried flexed on the left side with the head orientated towards the east (Todorova & Vajsov 1993).

Gender biased bipolar modality is also attested in the Tiszapolgár-Bodrogkeresztúr culture, where - by contrast - males are laid on the right side, while females are laid on the left (Häusler 1998; Derevenski 2000). Heads are orientated westwards in the early phase, and eastwards in the later one (ibid.). Northern orientation is unusual beyond the coast of Bulgaria. Newcomers from the (pre-)Pit Grave Culture, whose earliest appearance in Bulgaria has been attested at Durankulak, laid their preference on an eastern orientation and a hocker position on the left side or on the back with bent legs (Vajsov 2002a).

It is therefore evident to suggest that the burial rites attested in Lîga are rooted in the Late Copper Age traditions of the Black Sea coast. This was already suggested in the original publication (Merkyte 2005) and remains valid even with the corrections made on the date of the graves. Perhaps north-western Bulgaria can even be seen as an enclave for displaced communities or individuals from the coast.

INTERPRETATIONS

XIX. THE END OF THE COPPER AGE

In recent years, north-western Bulgaria has become a focus of post-Copper Age studies (Fig. 33). Re-evaluation of excavated materials - for instance Krivodol (Ganetsovski in print a), Okhrid-Grado (Ganetsovski 1996), Bagachina (Ganetsovski in print b), Davetaki Cave (with recent excavations by Gergov & Valentinova (2005)), and systematic research at Telish-Redutite (Gergov 1992), Galatin (Todorova 1979b, Georgieva 1988), and Rebarkovo (Georgieva 1994) - have much contributed towards the growing body of material as well as the scientific awareness of problems, developing methods, and new suggestions. At the same time, the publication of the highly important burial site at Durankulak has demonstrated that an anticipated change in demographic and social context by the end of the Copper Age was indeed real (Todorova 2002) - a fact still only painfully accepted by most Bulgarian scholars, as well as others from neighbouring areas.

The last burials at Durankulak following Copper Age traditions were dated to 4200/4150 BC. Later, at 3700 BC a completely new type of burial was documented at the same site, in fact barrows of Early Ochre Grave Complex (Vajsov 2002a). The termination and abandonment of the tell settlements in north-eastern Bulgaria at the end of the Copper Age (around 4200 BC), often with conflagration of the entire settlement - as was the case in Ovcharovo, Golyamo Delchevo, Polyanitsa, Durankulak and others - have been perceived as an important signal of external disturbances of the socio-cultural equilibrium in the region (Todorova 1986). The closing stages of the tell settlements on the Thracian plain have not been uncomplicated either and all were abandoned for some 1000 years until the Early Bronze Age. In fact, only Drama Tell, municipality of Jambol (Lichardus et al. 2000) and possibly Kaleto Tell, municipality of Chirpan (Georgieva 1999) has yielded some materials which could be attributed to the Transitional Period.

Although such interpretation of events is not devoid of opponents, new research seems to support it. The lifespan of the Varna culture has been prolonged with materials from the Kozareva Mogila

Tell (pottery painted with graphite and, hitherto almost unknown in the region, red ochre) (Georgieva 2005). This tell site also terminated in fire. Further late evidence comes from a submerged settlement site at Sozopol, chronologically succeeding the materials from Kozareva Mogila (ibid.). The final phase of the KGK VI culture, represented at "Starozagorski Mineralni Bani", has also produced some materials, which link this area with the broader regional development. Here too is pottery painted with graphite and red ochre, either in combination or alone (ibid.). In the next period, roughly after 4000 BC and until 3200 BC, evidence on the cultural development in the area between the Black Sea and the Adriatic is reduced to just two or three dozens sites with a clustered distribution and diffused temporal attribution.

Different explanations have been sought to elucidate the reduction of cultural visibility in the fourth millennium BC. These ranged from ideas of depopulation (Raduncheva 1976) to migration (Todorova 1986), insufficient research (Nikolova 1999), faults in the C-14 calibration curves (Bojadžiev 1994), among other ideas. The term Transitional Period, coined by Todorova in 1979, raised scholarly nuisance both in Bulgaria and abroad. Nevertheless, nearly 30 years after the term came into scientific circulation, the general picture of a region nearly devoid of material manifestations has not been changed significantly. Recent investigations of pollen cores from the Bulgarian coast substantiate the existence of this lacuna-period as an objective fact. There are no anthropogenic indicators apart from single pollen grains of Plantago lanceolata (ribwort plantain) and Polygonum aviculare (common knotgrass) (Filipova-Marinova 2007), which most likely are indicators of (some) grazing.

The main purpose of the present article is publication of the excavation results concerning the double settlement of Ezero-Kale. With this as background, the author has used the opportunity to pinpoint some of the issues which are sometimes overlooked in the rather heated scientific debates between adherents and opponents in particular of invasion theories as regards the close of the Copper Age.

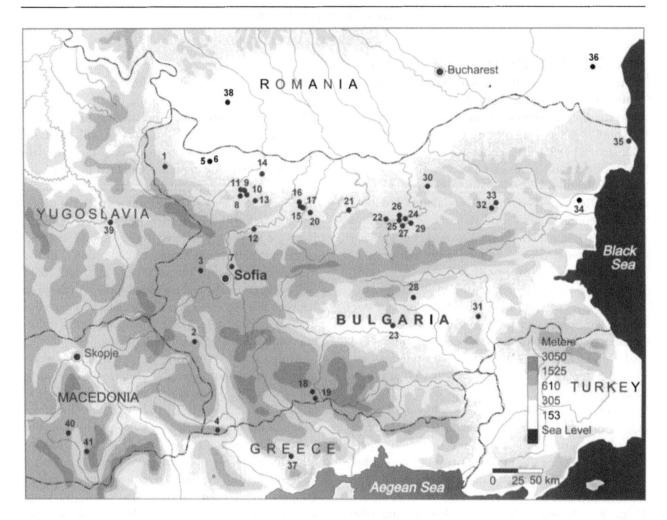

Fig. 33. Distribution map of known sites in Bulgaria attributed to the Transitional Period. Many sites are only represented by small collections of unstratified shards.

List of sites: 1 - Magura; 2 - Vaksevo; 3 - Peklyuk; 4 - Kolarovo; 5 - Bagachina; 6 - Bagachina-Staliyska Makhala; 7 - Okol Glava; 8 - Galatin; 9 - Lesura; 10 - Lesura-Golata Mogila; 11 - Lesura-Gradishteto; 12 - Rebarkovo; 13 - Okhoden-Kaleto; 14 - Lipnica-Tepeto; 15 - Telish-Redutite; 16 - Sadovec-Kale; 17 - Sadovec-Ezero; 18 - Jagodina Cave; 19 - Haramijska Cave; 20 - Bezhanovo-Banunya; 21 - Devetaki Cave; 22 - Emen Cave; 23 - Rupkite-Kale; 24 - Hotnica-Gorno Selishte; 25 - Hotnica-Paskova Bryast; 26 - Hotnica Vodopada; 27 - Shemshevo-Klise Bair; 28 - Ai Bunar; 29 - Kachica D; 30 - Koprivec; 31 - Drama; 32 - Ovcharovo Plato; 33 - Pevec; 34 - Ezerovo II; 35 - Durankulak.

Some of the key sites outside Bulgaria: 36 - Černavoda; 37 - Sitagroi; 38 - Sâlcuţa; 39 - Bubanj; 40 - Bakarno Gumno; 41 - Šuplevec.

XX. EXTERNAL IMPACT

The suggested external impacts involved in the long transition from the Copper Age to the Bronze Age in the Southern Balkans - via the extended Transitional Period - are several and diverse, in character as well as geographical space (Fig. 34). Their nature ranges from climatic change to human migration, over shifting cultural roles of individuals and groups to exchanges in various forms. The central question is to determine their mutual importance in development.

Climatic change

Climatic change has often been seen as a factor leading the region around the Black Sea into unrest and change. However, the classical idea of an overall peaking of benign weather, the so-called climatic optimum (Todorova 1986; 1989; 2002), may not be valid for Southeastern Europe. Recent climatic modelling suggests that Europe was influenced differently by the climate around 6000 BP (Cheddadi et al. 1996). A

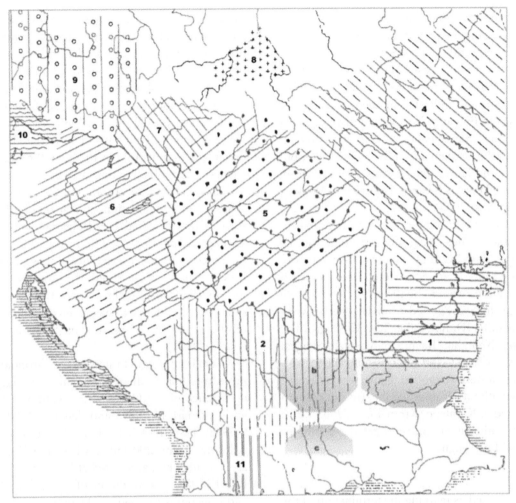

Fig. 34. Cultural groups at the beginning of the 4th millennium BC in the Balkans:

1 - Černavoda I; 2 - Sălcuța III-IV; 3 - Brătești; 4 - Cucuteni AB-B1/Tripolyje BII; 5 - Bodrogkeresztúr; 6 - Balanton Lasinja; 7 - Ludanice; 8 - Złotniki; 9 - Jordanów (Jordansmühl); 10 - Münchshöfen II; 11 - Šuplevec-Bakarno Gumno. After Kalicz 1992, Fig. 12, with modifications.

Social groupings on the territory of Bulgaria: a - Pevec; b - Galatin; c - Kolarovo-Jagodin.

thermal maximum has been identified in Scandinavia, Britain, and the Alps at a time when Southern Europe was experiencing cold winters, a decrease of Summer temperatures and overall wetter than present conditions (ibid.). Based on Greenland ice core analysis (sea-ice diatoms), the Holocene warming is seen as part of an integral process followed by an abrupt cooling phase from around 3800 till 3000 BC (Dahl-Jensen et al. 1998; Moros et al. 2006, Fig. 5). Depending on the globality of these indications, the most dramatic cultural changes should be expected during the latter period. In fact, this is the aftermath phase of the Copper Age.

Pollen core analyses in the swamp of Kardashinski located in a steppe zone of southwestern Ukraine (the flood plains of Dnepr) indicate that the July temperature around 4100 BC was colder than the present one by 2°C (the mean January temperature was higher, though), with the annual precipitation being 100 ml higher than today (Kremenetski 1995). These changes did not occur suddenly. The climatic optimum phase is recorded at Kardashinski as late as 3300-2800/2700 BP (ibid.). It is interesting to note that the first antropogenic indicators in the area only occur in the 6th century AD. The most dramatic change around 4000 BC is related to the Black Sea transgression and tectonic movements, which caused a dramatic rise of the sea level, exceeding the present day one by up to 5 m (Filipova-Marinova 2007). This certainly caused abandonment of a series of coastal sites (Todorova 1986; 1989; 2002). A general rise of the ground water table in the Balkans is also indicated by the appearance of pile dwellings in Bulgaria: Negovatsi, municipality of Pernik, Krainitsi, municipality of Dupnitsa (both in western Bulgaria), settlements at the Varna Lake, but especially around larger water basins such as Ohrid, Prespa and the Dipsilio-Kastoria Lakes in the Western Balkans (Mitrevski 2003).

While it is true that there is a certain global dimension to the various changes occurring during the 5th- 4th millennium BC, these do not appear synchronously at the same latitude, as would be expected if climatic alterations were to be the sole reason for the changes. The hiatus reported from Greece between the Late Neolithic (Dimini-Dikili Tash II-Sitagroi III) and the Final Neolithic (Rachmani-Mandalo-Sitagroi IV) cultures (ca. 4600-4100 BC)[15] is not echoed by a hiatus in the Western Anatolian plains, which first see cultural discontinuity in most of the 4th millennium BC, as attested at Kumtepe (Kromer et al. 2003). This implies that quite other, man-instigated reasons for change should be sought.

The Steppes

The dates accepted as marking the termination of the Copper Age in Bulgaria (Bojadžiev 1992; Görsdorf & Bojadžiev 1996) demonstrate that the period ended at the coast first and then, in a wavelike fashion, in the western part of the country. According to estimations, the process took 300-400 years, from roughly 4200 to roughly 3800 BC. Such an interpretation of the C14 dates leaves the impression of an epicentre of events, with the help of the logics of a domino effect placed in the north-eastern part of the country. While this can be considered true, at least to a certain extent, the influences and the mechanisms behind these influences, which were shaping the Balkans in the

fourth millennium BC, were far more complex than a unidirectional model would suggest. In fact, interaction with communities located at the northern fringes of the Black Sea (and beyond) and the penetration of these groups along the Danube have been seen as one of the more important causes of the decline of the Copper Age (Todorova 1986; Georgieva 1992). Despite numerous attempts to downplay the effects of this interaction, its role in inducing the said regional changes cannot be underestimated.

Thus, ignoring for a moment the classical discussion of the conflagration and abandonment of the then heavily fortified NE Bulgarian tells - already starting around 4500 BC (Todorova 1982) - and their reference to regional instability, a new player on the Lower Danube stage should be introduced. This is the so-called Early Ochre Grave Complex, which - rooted on the Steppes - has received much attention, most recently by J. Rassamakin (2004) and B. Govedarica (2004).

What is important to stress is the chronology of this novel tradition to the region. The seemingly earliest occurrence of the Ochre Grave Complex is recorded in Căinari, Moldova and dated to 4500-4330 BC (5580±50 BP, KIA 369) (Govedarica 2004). Căinari is located some 200 km north of the Danube estuary. Slightly later, as attested at Giurgiuleşti (4398±69 BC, Ki-7037), the tradition of ochre burials in pits and catacombs reached the Danube at its confluence with River Prut (Telegin 2002; Rassamakin 2004). By around 4200 BC the practice had crossed the Danube, as attested at Casimcea in Dobrogea, as well as at Reka Devnja and Kiulevča in Bulgaria (find inventories in Rassamakin 2004). The Casimecea burial is a seminal example of the formation of new elites. While certain burial inventories of the Ochre Grave Complex demonstrate an effort to mimic Balkan Copper Age elites (as for instance the Giurgiuleşti burials with their presence of three pointed sticks made of copper, bone plates, flint inserts, and sheet gold much in resemblance with the items found in Varna grave No. 43), there are clear signs of a novel symbolic language at Casimcea.

The Casimcea burial was discovered in 1938 during levelling work including removal of a big "tertre", a word with a double meaning: hillock and barrow. Also the burials at Giurgiuleşti (2 pit and 3 catacomb

---

15 This hiatus may to some degree be biased by a fragmental understanding of the causes leading to changes of settlement patterns, when, for instance, inland tells are being abandoned for the sake of coastal locations (Demoule & Perlès 1999). I am grateful to Lasse Sørensen, BA, University of Copenhagen who drew my attention to this circumstance.

Fig. 35. Limestone zoomorphic sceptre (length 17 cm) from the Casimcea burial, Romania; after Popescu 1941.

burials) are reported to have been discovered in natural hillocks, just like the two graves at Kiulevča (topmost part of a hillock). In any case, the location of these early graves of the Ochre Grave Complex seems to indicate that a shift towards barrow interment is to be expected, likely in response to increasing needs at legitimizing the presence of new social groups and their leaders.

The skeletal remains at Casimcea (undetermined) were associated with at least 15 bifacial spear-points (varying in length from 3.4 till 7.6 cm), 3 long flint blades (measuring 12.5 cm), likely for knives, and 5 polished flint axes (pointed-necked hollow-bladed - thus for finer wood-working), plus a massive flint scraper (Popescu 1941, Figs. 1-2). The grave inventory also comprised a highly important stone head, in fact an animalistic sceptre 17 cm long, which has become an icon of long and twofold discussions (Fig. 35).

The first group of questions concerning the Casimcea sceptre regards the implications of the geographical distribution of such sceptres, usually found as stray finds (cf. below). The second group centres on the meaning of the symbol as such, i.e., what it is represents, as well as the implications of the suggested representation. The author of the original publication saw in it both rhinoceros, hippo, and mastiff, while, as new sceptres were discovered, the group was mainly interpreted as representations of the heads of horses. Recently, there has been a tendency to discard the

stone heads as having any direct relation to horses in the symbolically otherwise highly charged artistic repertoire of Late Copper Age societies and even to abandon the idea of the items as being sceptres (Levine 2005).

While it is hard to take arguments such as "we cannot ask the Eneolithic people to describe them as "sceptres"" seriously (Levine 2005, 9), attention should be drawn to the unique characteristics of the Casimecea animal head, likely of a horse. It is the only such item made of soft rock - limestone, a material highly adjustable to modifications, thus allowing high degree of detail[16]. Therefore, it bears more details than the other sceptres made of hard rocks such as granite and porphyry. Incidentally, sceptres were likely also fashioned in organic materials, as for instance the bone sceptre from Krasnoe in Bulgaria (Georgieva 2005, Fig. 1:4). The regularly placed bands running across the nose of the Casimecea specimen, around the eyes, and also between the ears resemble straps of harnessing. This interpretation is by no means original; it has previously been set in the context of the earliest domestication of the horse (Anthony 1991). The debate has recently been

---

16 The present author agrees with P. Georgieva (2005) that two presumable limestone heads found at Redutite (near Līga, both in Telish village) are just curious stones fashioned by nature (see Gergov 1994b).

reheated by new dates for the famous domesticated Dereivka horses, which shifted down from the 4th millennium BC to the Scythian Iron Age (700-200 BC) (Anthony & Brown 2000). Seen in this light, the interpretation of the stone heads as representations of horses has been weakened. However, the type of harnessing represented on the stone head is not of the riding type, but the pulling one, inter alia used for camels and donkeys. The latter type does not include cheek pieces and bits, and is thus merely indicating taming but not yet domestication of the horse (including breeding in captivity).

What is also important to note is that the Casimcea sceptre bears traces of repeated hafting. The original hafting covered the whole butt end (as can be seen in difference of stone texture, comparing the facial part with the butt end), while the subsequent hafting was based on a groove and notch technique, created by a controlled blow ca. 1/3 from the butt end, made at the place of an earlier protuberance. In recent publications the sceptre has somehow lost its butt end (cf. Rassamakin 2004). Bearing in mind that such stone item hardly had the same use-wear pace as stone axes or even maces, it is feasible to suggest that it experienced a significant period of use and likely changed hands several times - accepting the idea that technology, i.e. the different hafting techniques, may reflect different social groups (Stark et al. 1995).

What then does the Casimcea sceptre represent on a functional level? Looking at ethnographic data, we are not left with many choices of interpretation of figurative stone objects made to be hafted. Good examples of the function and meaning of sceptres can be found in the non-literate states or kingdoms of West Africa. The sceptre is here a supreme symbol of power, often personifying the king himself as chief of one or several clans. Animals such as lions and leopards are often chosen to represent the royal authority. But there are also a number of cases where birds or plants, like pine apple, is the royal insignia. Such items were hardly chosen due to their good taste or usefulness, but rather because they encompassed a special symbolic meaning for the society.

Horse bones are sporadically reported from archaeological sites in the Balkans dated before the end of the 5th millennium; one has even been found in Redutite near Lîga (Spassov & Iliev 1998). But the areas which in particular supported wild populations of horses were further to the east, between the Danube and the Volga, exactly the area where the sceptres with horse heads are distributed. Here the horse was the largest hunt animal and a substantial source of meat, hide, and bone material. The communities in this huge region could even - by the well-established settled agriculturalists in the Carpathian-Balkan area - be perceived as horse-hunting people, thereby strengthening the farmer identity of the former. Horse sceptres would thus become emblematic, especially when participating in regional transactions.

In this context it is interesting to note that stone sceptres are known in two varieties, an abstract one and a more realistic (Fig. 36). The abstract ones are spread northeast of the Prut River, in the area where herds of wild horses were common, while the realistic sceptres are found south-south west of the Prut, where wild horses became extinct during the 5th millennium (Spassov & Iliev 2002).

Written sources of the 19th century on West Africa have recorded that sceptres did not necessarily stay with their owner. Rather, they would take a more active role, being presented (perhaps in authorized copy) as signs of authority when taxes had to be collected or borrowed by honoured travellers in order to ease their journey (e.g., Skertchly 1874, 147). While this may not have been the case in southeastern Europe at the end of the 5th millennium, the examples illustrate the extension of power such sceptres may present. In fact, the presence of sceptres and especially their even distribution reaching the Pelagonian Plains, for instance Šuplevec I (Kitanoski 1992, Miterevski 2003), suggest fundamental changes in the way relationships were now being constructed. Clay figurines, occurring in great numbers (and in different states of fragmentation) all over Southern Europe have rightly been seen as objects of personal enchainment of people (Chapman 2000), perhaps as material contracts. Such interpretation presupposes individual personal involvement, while the occurrence of sceptres indicates the creation of extended regional communication systems based on group identity and communal involvement.

Thus, the Casimcea grave most probably reflects fundamentally different systems of values and ideology from those of the Copper Age communities of

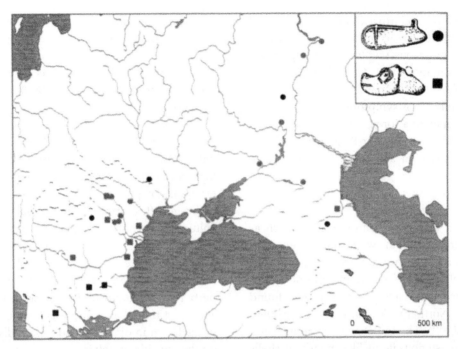

Fig. 36. Distribution map of stone sceptres: the realistic (square) and the abstract (dot) type; after Lichardus & Lichardus-Itten 1998, Fig. 5.

Varna and Durankulak on the Black Sea coast of Bulgaria, social groups which seldom included items interpreted as weapons in their burial repertoire. By contrast, Casimcea seems to represents the burial of a great hunter and likely that of a great warrior as well. In some societies, for instance West African Daho-mey, hunters used to hold a very prestigious status and were implicitly understood as great warriors, while the opposite is not the case. One of the Dahomean kings, Tegbessou, even married a renounced hunter and appointed him general of his troops. The Casim-cea individual carried with him to the afterlife no less than 15 skilfully made spears and was equipped with 3 very long knives, a very powerful scraper, and 5 well polished flint axes for wood-working and other duties (at least one of the axes has a rounded edge, a clear indication of active use). And just like the Da-homean kings, this hunter also took his most precious object, clearly indicating his high social position and particular network - the horse headed sceptre - with him into the grave and on to the afterlife.

The Ochre Grave Complex - later evolving into the Černavoda, Pit Grave, and Usatovo Cultures - cannot be given a joint label. In fact, the diversity reflected in the grave material across the North Pontic region

mirrors, on a grand scale, the diversity, which can be observed in any viable community, where personal position and achievements transform communal cus-toms. The intention behind the new elaboration was no doubt to demonstrate that the emerging elites of the Ochre Grave Complex were operating on a differ-ent ideational platform - allowing them to target ag-ricultural communities on the both sides of the lower Danube. At least two independent but simultaneous developments support this assumption: immense for-tification followed by complete abandonment of the Bulgarian tells (starting at 4500 BC and continuing till 4200/4150, a process also attested in Muntenia, i.e., the southeastern region of Romania), and rigor-ous fortification of the dramatically growing Cucuteni A-Tripolye B1 settlements (4500-4100 BC, according to the chronology of Manzura 2005).

Finally, it is important to pay attention to the burials found in the Medieval cemetery at Kiulevča (Graves 33 and 45) in the area of Shumen, inciden-tally the fertile region of the earliest Bulgarian capitals of Pliska and Preslav (Rassamakin 2004). Based on B. Govedarica's study (ibid. 2004) it is likely that these graves should be dated to the end of the 5th millen-nium BC and not the beginning of the 4th millennium

BC, as suggested by Todorova (ibid. 2002). One of the buried individuals was accompanied with a rather modest example of a stone sceptre measuring only 8 cm in length but equipped with 40 cm long bone handle. The date of the burials may be secondary in significance, but KiulevČa is symptomatic for the way it reflects the existence of a foreign inland community, which was capable of providing their dead with the necessary ritual attention according to Steppe fashions and traditions.

Exchange

It is obvious that tokens of communication such as sceptres are required both when interaction was based on social relations and on economic interests. The latter is likely the case of certain types of copper axes, for instance the heavy Jászladány type found from Greece to Northern Germany and even Denmark (Klassen 2000). The importance of copper and gold and other prestigious items like spondylus shells for broad scale networking has been acknowledged for a long time. But a wide range of other commodities, archaeologically less detectable, was certainly also in demand across cultural and social boundaries. It is known that certain kind of stones - flint and even graphite - not to mention tangible substances such as plants and fruits, also with limited distribution, could be in as great a demand as metals.

It is perhaps a surprise that a simple substance such as ochre also has a rather limited natural distribution. Ochre sources are located along the Danube, in the central and southern parts of Oltenia and Muntenia, at the Iron Gates, and in the northern part of Bulgaria (Brenica) (Gâţă & Mateescu 2003). Northern Serbia and Dobrogea may also hold deposits of ochre, although their location has not been established. A special kind of ochre containing opal has been identified at a number of archaeological sites along the Danube (including Gumelniţa and Sadievo at Nova Zagora) dated from the Neolithic till the La Tène Culture. The source of this particular type is in the western part of the Lower Danube, or around at the confluence of the Olt and the Danube, including Brenica (ibid.). Perhaps the limited accessibility of ochre explains why ochre-painted pottery is a characteristic only of the latest phases of the KSB (Krivodol-Sâlcuţa-Bubanj) Copper Age Culture in

NW Bulgaria, and only recently detected on pottery from Sozopol and Kozareva mogila dated to the latest phase of the KGK VI and Varna culture of the same age (Georgieva 2005): KGK as mentioned standing for the eastern Bulgarian Kodžadermen-Gumelniţa-Karanovo Culture.

Red ochre - abundantly used in burials of the Ochre Grave Complex - was likely one of the principal commodities circulating along the Danube. In this light, a burial at Csongrad-Kettöshalom, on the western banks of Tisza River in Hungary, ca. 50 km south of Szeged (the area of Tiszapolgár-Bodrogkeresztúr culture), may not be as peculiar as it has been perceived (Rassamakin 2004). It is a supine ochre burial, containing an obsidian blade 13.2 cm long, beads made of stone, gold and spondylus shells - thus a superb representative of the Ochre Grave Complex. The most remarkable find was a lump of ochre measuring 15 cm in diameter and reportedly held in a bag on the left side of pelvis.

The high value of ochre as a commodity can also be deduced from one of the EBA graves in Bereket in Bulgaria, where a male, along with a set of pottery vessels, was buried with a mortar used for crushing ochre (Kalchev 1996). Notably, only 10 out of 74 burials at Bereket had received some amount of ochre treatment. Interestingly, one of the EBA burials found in the Ezero Tell was sprinkled with crushed lime stone, perhaps as a replacement of ochre, the interpretation suggested by the authors of the publication (Georgiev et al. 1979), thus illustrating the limited availability of ochre.

Another interesting pattern emerges from the distribution of arsenic-copper items, mainly daggers. The provenience of this particular copper-alloy remains unclear, the opinions being divided between the North Pontic area, the Northern Caucasus (the Maikop zone), and - the most recent suggestion - the East Carpathian area, where daggers of Pusztaistvánháza (Bodrogkeresztúr) type have been dated to 4000 BC (Matuschik 1998). The Bulgarian specimens are dated to the period between ca. 4000-3600 BC. Seemingly, no such daggers can be associated with known copper ore deposit in Bulgaria (Vajsov 2002a, Fig. 197). The apparent concentration of arsenic copper items around the mouth of the Danube and the Dniester River, bordering on the Steppes, likely defines an area of particular use of this new technology and the routes of re-distribution (Vajsov 1993, Fig. 36).

In Bulgaria such daggers have been found in the cave of Haramijska Dupka (2 specimens), at Hotnitsa-Vodopada (4 specimens, along with a flat axe), Durankulak (3 (4) specimens), and at Galiche (1 stray dagger) (Vajsov 1993; Matuschik 1998), i.e., in all the parts of the country apart from the Thracian plain. The distribution pattern indicates that widespread exchange networks were still functioning despite re-allocation of the centres of production and settlement. However, stating that the presence of these daggers in Bulgaria demonstrates the spread of a particular "know-how" (Vajsov 2002a) is a slight exaggeration in the face of a rather limited amount of metal finds from the Early Bronze Age proper, and the Middle Bronze Age (MBA). Thus, Chernykh attributed only 144 items to these two main periods (ibid. 1978). In the same way that the presence of European smoking pipes and glass beads in African graves does not imply that the local populations possessed the knowledge of how to manufacture these items, there are no reasons to suggest that the metal daggers of this phase in Bulgaria were locally produced. Rather, they reflect an ability to interact and to enter the networks of exchange. Nevertheless, the occurrence of arsenic copper alloys in the Alpine production zone around 3800 BC may suggest that such production was based on transmitted knowledge from the east rather than independent innovation.

The so-called "Steppe population" was no doubt a heterogeneous entity made up of different social groups with diverse technological preferences rooted in the North Pontic zone, and only united by being in contrast to the settled and more advanced Copper Age communities of Southeastern Europe (cf. Barth 1969). This population underwent a twofold development, which schematically perhaps can be compared with that of the Vikings: first raiding, then trading. Mobile groups with a subsistence strategy mainly based on hunting or stock breeding would stage surprise flash attacks on the easily targeted agricultural settlements both to the south and the north of the Danube. The "Steppe peoples" were seemingly politically autonomous groups unconstrained by inter-lineage bonds or obligations set by established networking among, for instance, the Copper Age farmers of Bulgaria.

It is tempting to suggest that the massive devastations attested in the Late Copper Age tells of Ruse (Gaul 1948; Georgiev & Angelov 1952) and Yunatsite (Mazanova 2000 & personal observations), with dozens of skeletal remains - likely representing more than 2/3rd of the settlers - deposited in highly unnatural positions and covered with burned debris of the final Copper Age settlement, were in fact the result of such ongoing warring. Certainly, the balance of power changed along the course of the Lower Danube towards the end of the 5th millennium BC. The result was the establishment of novel groups - culturally with a stem from the Steppe - including highly advantageous middle-man positions along the major trade axis of the time. And just like the Vikings, perhaps, the material visibility of these groups, when away from their original area, was only detectable in the mortuary domain.

Presently, there are some 30 sites attributed to the Transitional Period in Bulgaria. While their relative and absolute chronological sequence remains unclear, the majority seems to be concentrating within the period 3900-3500 BC. Based on regional differences, the sites are even subdivided into various cultural groups. Thus, a Pevec group is distinguished in northeastern Bulgaria (with the sites of Pevec, Ovcharovo-Plato, Hotnitsa-Vodopada, and Koprivec), a Jagodina culture group was spread in the Rhodope Mountains (the caves of Jagodina and Haramijska Dupka), and a Galatin culture group is separated in the north western part of the country.

The material culture of these groups reflects different degrees of foreign influence. The Pevec Culture, which is regarded by some as a southern variant of the Černavoda I Culture (cf. Vajsov 1993), may be considered a complete break with earlier traditions, while the western "cultures" developed on own Late Copper Age foundations. The Hotnitsa-Vodopada site, dated to around 3700 BC and attributed to the Pevec culture group, has demonstrated hitherto unknown elements in the Bulgarian Late Copper context. The dwellings of the earliest horizon were pit structures with ovens constructed on the edge of the pit (Ilcheva Petrova 1995). Such pit-structures, 5-10 in total, were also discovered at Ovcharovo-Plato (Todorova 1998). The nearest area with such a building tradition is around the mouth of the Danube, which

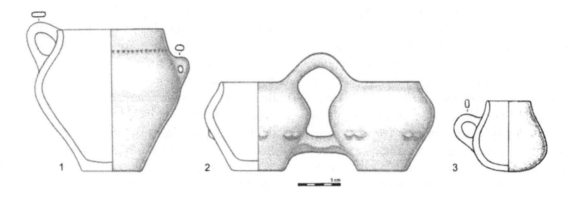

Fig. 37. Pottery of the Transitional Period discovered at Redutite, the 4th settlement; after Gergov 1992.

used to be settled by the Bolgrad-Aldeni II Group (also a variant of the Gumelniţa culture) at the end of the 5th millennium BC. This tradition also extends further east and north east.

Perhaps the occasional encounters of simple pit-dwellings in the Balkans during the span of the Bulgarian Transitional Period, such as those of Pilavo-Burilcevo on River Bregalnitca in Macedonia (Mitrevski 2003) and Panjevački Rit near Jagodina in the Great Morava Valley in former Yugoslavia (Tasić & Tasić 2003) can be explained by the presence of a migrant population with eastern roots. In any case, such technological manifestation - in marked contrast to the general trend of wattle and daub structures above the ground - should demarcate a distinct social group with discrete material biography. At Hotnitsa-Vodopada, such pit-dwelling structures were found spread over an area of 1775 m² (Ilcheva Petrova 1995), so this was not an insignificant temporary camp. Notably, when the oldest settlement was destroyed by flooding, a second one was established at the same locality but moved to a higher terrain, using a completely different building technique, namely wattle and daub. The second settlement occupied only 1025 m², and was abandoned after a conflagration. Both settlements are genetically related through a special type of oven - a pit oven 0.43-0.72 m in diameter and up to 0.66 m in depth - denominated "tandir" and likely used for bread baking. Contemporary examples can be found in the eastern steppe region (for instance around Don) (Ilcheva 1989). They signify a transformation in cui-

sine, which is an even stronger argument for the presence of foreign population.

A series of changes concerns the production of pottery in Bulgaria. The most apparent is the use of crushed shells as tempering material. Shell tempered pottery has been known in the North Pontic region since the earliest Neolithic. It has been an inherent feature in such culture groups as the Bug-Dniester Culture (based on stock breeding), the Sursko-Dnieper Culture (foragers), and the Mountain Crimean Culture (foragers) (Telegin 1987). Shell tempered pottery is also known from the Late Neolithic in Greek Macedonia (Urem-Kotsou et al. 2002). The use of shell tempering gradually decreased with time (Kotova 2003), and during the early stages of the Tripolyje culture it was mainly earmarked for production of kitchenware in the area between the Prut and the Dniester (Zbenovitch 1996). G. Schmidt has encountered shell-tempered pottery in the material from Cucuteni and termed it the "Cucuteni C" type, a term now generally applied for shell-tempered pottery (Schmidt 1932). In the area of the Sredny Stog/Skelya Culture this type of pottery, likely kitchenware, has been dated to Cucuteni A-Tripolyje B1 (Telegin 2002), leaving little doubt about the source of penetration of this particular technological tradition. The main part of this ware - likely for milking, as based on the shape analysis suggested by B. Hulthén for TRB pottery (ibid. 1998, Fig. 17) - resembles so-called funnel beakers of the North European Funnel Beaker Culture (TRB in Danish) and can perhaps explain the development of

S-profiles and rounded bottoms in the material dated to the Transitional Period in Bulgaria (e.g. Fig. 37).

Studies have demonstrated that shell-tempering improves the strength of vessels as well as their thermal shock resistance, suggesting that this kind of pottery was optimal for use as kitchenware, especially for cooking (Steponaitis 1984). The southern border of the distribution of the shell-tempered pottery is considered to be the Balkan Range (Georgieva 1993), and most of the northern Bulgarian sites have produced a share of this type of pottery. The 4th settlement at Redutite (Telish IV), attributed to the Transitional Period (Gergov 1992, 1994a), yielded shell-tempered pottery in an amount equivalent to 14.6% of the investigated pottery (Yordanova 2001). Crushed shells were found both in coarse wares and, to a lesser extent, in the fine wares (4.6% of the total amount of pottery) (ibid.).

A slightly different picture presents itself at the Hotnitsa-Vodopada settlement site (Ilcheva 2000). Here shell-tempered pottery accounts for 28% of the investigated material. The use of crushed shells is more frequently occurring within the group of fine wares (16% of the total). Such distribution is most likely temporally biased, but may also point to the source for the spread of this novel technological element - Hotnitsa-Vodopada holding a more easterly position than Redutite.

Investigation of the pottery from Sadovec-Ezero and Sadovec-Kale implies that shell tempering was not restricted to certain types of pottery. Likely, the earliest occurrence is recorded in the production of figurines, which in terms of artistic expression subscribe to Late Copper Age traditions. The amount of shell tempering could vary from very abundant to sparse. When comparing pottery of analogous shapes, some would contain crushed shells, others not. Also, shell tempering is not restricted to kitchenware but found in different vessel types, as well as in other clay items like figurines and spindle whorls. Shells are seldom found as the only added constituent in the paste; often shells are detected in combination with fine or coarse sand. All this indicates that shell tempering was used on an experimental platform; it was more of an issue of fashion than an element in a general relocation of the technological orientation. It seems that crushed shells as tempering material was replacing tempering with lime, a constituent often found in

Late Copper Age pottery of the KSB Culture. Seen in this way, it may represent a technological improvement, since preparation and integration of shells in to the paste is less complicated than that of limestone.

Foreign influences may also explain the appearance of certain novel pottery shapes and features, like rounded bases and vessels with everted rim and S-curvature, listed in the studies dealing with the Transitional Period (for instance Georgieva 1992; 1993; 2005). It is also important to mention the appearance of double vessels, such as those discovered in Redutite, the 4th settlement (Gergov 1992), and Vrachanka-Komarevo (Nikolov 1962) (Fig. 37). Composite vessels are naturally underrepresented in the excavated material, since they are rarely completely preserved and can be misinterpreted, as their shape echoes that of single vessels (biconical vessels with centrally located turning point). The Telish specimens exhibited in the Historical Museum of Pleven, show blackish soot clouds, which are typical for cooking wares. As such, they represent an innovation or alteration within the tradition of cuisine not attested during the time of the Late Copper Age. The origin of this element can be debated; connected pedestal bowls are known from Tripolyje sites, but such elaborate specimens are unlikely to have been used in food preparation. The only area, where multiple vessels with a domestic purpose can be recognised is within the Majkop Culture[17] (for instance, Rassamakin 2004).

Finally, a truly striking change, usually only swiftly mentioned, is the disappearance of anthropomorphic - mostly female - and zoomorphic figurines in the Transitional Period. Taken at face value, even the proponents of a smooth development would not deny that this reflects a radical transformation of the belief systems and of networking mediated with symbolic tokens. Therefore, quite rightly no doubt, I. Vajsov interprets the latest Durankulak kenotaphs containing figurines as an actual burial of figurines and all what they have represented in the overall ideological domain (Vajsov 2002b). The six figurines found at the above Hotnitsa-Vodopada settlement support the idea

---

17 Majkop Culture is dated to 3800/3700 – 3200 BC, albeit the existence of "pre-Majkop" phase makes it's beginning somewhat indistinct (Govedarica 2002).

Fig. 38. Handles of the Transitional Period with bowl-like depressions: 1 – Ordacsehi-Kécsi, SW Hungary (after Somogyi 2000:15); 2 – Redutite, the 4th settlement, NW Bulgaria (after Gergov 1992:5).

of ideological change since four of these were male, not female, representations (Ilcheva Petrova 1995).

Central Europe

The Danube has always played a role as a cultural border, as well as a route directing movement. Hence, in geographical terms, it is not surprising that much archaeological evidence is concentrated along the Danube and in its peripheral areas. It has been assumed and indeed proven that many of the changes shaping the cultural landscape of the Transitional Period in nowadays Bulgaria and the Balkans in general had an westerly direction, i.e., novel influences were arriving from the east.

Actually, one would rather have expected the cultural flows to follow the waters of the Danube, directing the movement of people and ideas from the west towards the east. In fact, certain elements developing in the Transitional Period must have originated in Central Europe. One of these traits - unlikely to represent an independent, parallel development - is vertical handles with a circular, bowl-like depression at the highest point (Fig. 38). Such handles have been discovered in Redutite, the 4th settlement (Gergov 1992), and at Hotnitsa Vodopada. The area of origin is considered to be within the contemporary Balaton-Lasinja Culture (for example, Kalicz 1992, Fig. 1:1), occupying most of southern Hungary.

Another supposed "Central European element" is vertical handles terminating with a disk-like application - the so-called "Scheibenhenkel" (Pl. 12:10-12). These handles have a rather wide distribution, from Pevkakia Magula in Greece to the former core area of the KSB complex which by then was transformed into a new phase of Sâlcuţa-Galatin culture, namely

north-western Bulgaria, southwestern Romania, and eastern Serbia. Vessels with disk-handles are found along the Danube until the Vajska necropolis (giving name to a contemporary culture of Vajska-Hunyadihalom (Vajska denominates the materials in Vojvodina, Hunyadihalom the ones in Hungary; the same cultural complex is known in Slovakia as Lažňany). Single fragments have been encountered in the valley of Drina, in Northern Hungary, and even in Poland at Krakow: a burial at Nowa Huta being the northernmost point of the distribution (Kaczanowska 1986).

The "Scheibenhenkel" also has an interesting and archaeologically useful restricted temporal distribution, allowing to correlate cultural manifestations over broader regions than previously. Bulgarian scholars tend to view the spread of these handles as a reflection of Central European influences (Georgieva 1992; Todorova 2003), while other scholars see the centre of evolvement within the core area of the Galatin-Sâlcuţa Culture (Brukner 1974; Jovanović 1998). The handles were originally recognised at Sâlcuţa in Romania, where they were found in great numbers and different varieties (Berciu 1961).

A statistical analysis of the materials from Redutite, the 4th settlement, shows that disk-handles made up 13.5% of all handles, dominated by the vertical variety placed either on the shoulders or at the highest point, thus exceeding the rim (Yordanova 2001). There is a great variability of pottery shapes, which can be associated with even greater variety of disk-handles in the area of north-western Bulgaria-south-western Romania (Berciu 1961; Roman 1971; Yordanova 2001; Ganetsovski in print b). The occurrence of disk-handles in the north-western, in fact the Central European areas of the overall distribution are restricted to medium-sized carinated bowls and small jars with cylindrical necks (Brukner 1974, Figs. 1, 2, 3, 4 & 5). Consequently, the area between Sâlcuţa and Telish should be considered the area of origin of disk-handles. The relationship with the Greek regions remains unclear, mostly due to the lack of evidence preceding the Rachmani Culture in Thessaly and Sitagroi IV in Northern Greece.

Disk handles represent a technological innovation. The handles are luted on to the vessel without the creation of a joint made up of perforation of the wall of the vessel and the hidden protrusion of the handle, as had been done previously. It is quite intriguing to try to understand the popularity of this single element, especially when it relates to shape rather than design. In this context it is worth mentioning that the only pottery shape, which "survives" the time span from the Copper Age till the Bronze Age is the "askos", a sack-like vessel with an orifice drawn to the side of the main axis of the vessel and equipped with a single handle, thus resembling a Greek vine bag - the askos. Perhaps, the popularity of certain containers is determined by their content, a content which was in demand and which could be associated with, for example, disk-handles as a kind of label. Ultimately, these labels became elements in the developing regional interaction, where exchange and trade, and feasting, ensured the circulation of goods, customs, and certain material items.

The ties with Central Europe can also be seen in the presence of baggy vessels with small vertical handles located at the level of the rim, the so-called milk jugs ("Milchtöpfe"). These vessels are more popular to the north of the Danube, though. Handles of "milk jug type" were also discovered at Kale, even though a reconstruction of the particular vessel shape was not possible. In addition, Redutite, the 4th settlement, held some vessels with a special kind of "red slip" - the entire vessel being covered with red ochre - a feature typical for Central European (Late) Lengyel and Bodrogkeresztúr pottery (Grancharov 1999, Fig. 40, 41).

In the Bulgarian scholarly discourse there is still a tendency to view the Transitional Period in a rather schematic way, stressing the change in subsistence strategy from settled forms to mobile stock breeding followed by a general decline of material culture, first and foremost manifested in the pottery production. Much of such modelling is based on accidental finds and randomly documented excavations.

Objectively, most of the settlements attributed to the Transitional Period are situated on top of Late Copper Age sites - thus demonstrating a certain continuity in topographical preferences, but not excluding that other locations were in use too. Early Bronze age (EBA) sites are often found at the same locality though shifted higher up in relation to earlier occupations, in fact, to a more commanding position with sufficient potential for expansion. Such topographical relations between the occupational phases of the Late Copper

Age/Transitional Period and the EBA have been observed at both Lîga and Kale. The areas which used to be occupied by the settlements of the earlier periods thus became backyards subsequently used for intensive activities by the settlers of the EBA settlements, causing transportation and erosion of earlier materials.

It should also be stressed that archaeological materials of the Transitional Period usually come from the topmost layers of settlement sites - layers which experienced negative erosion effects during the Sub-Atlantic Period, characterised by high precipitation levels. To these effects come the later destructive agricultural activities. This could indeed have biased the construction of the evaluation mesh of cultural manifestations related to the Transitional Period, which is also set in contrast to the colourful Copper Age.

But there are also examples contradicting the perception of short-lived sites characterizing the Transitional Period. Besides the already mentioned two occupation horizons at Hotnitsa-Vodopada, comprising almost 1 m of cultural layers (Ilcheva Petrova 1995), a new discovery at the village Bezhanovo shows an existence of 0.40-0.60 m thick cultural layers attributed to the Transitional Period (two settlement phases, both burned) and preserved by a later stone barrow (Valentinova 2006). The most recent excavations at the Devetaki Cave have demonstrated the existence of three subsequent occupations attributed to the Transitional Period (Galatin-Sâlcuţa IV Culture) (Gergov & Valentinova 2005). Ovens which have been associated with these occupations bear traces of multiple restorations, which took place 7 and even 11 times (ibid.). Bearing in mind that the pace of decomposition in a cave protected from rains and other climatic influences is much slower than on open-air sites, such evidence points towards an unexpectedly and enduring attachment to the site.

It was argued in the publication of the Late Copper Age materials from Lîga that the production of pottery is determined by social factors which are relatively time-resistant and that the rules of production are not affected by a changed production milieu (Merkyte 2005). The designs, with their active communicative content, readily understood by a social unit, were the last to be altered and replaced. Pottery - along with other items, which could be charged with symbolic meaning - was used to transmit (and

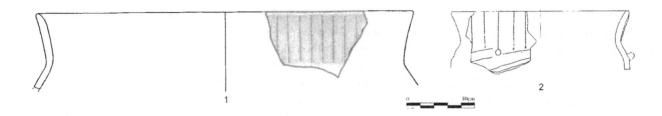

Fig. 39. Fragmented vessels of the Late Copper Age discovered at Kale (1), and at Sozopol (2), the submerged site (the latter after Draganov 1998).

thus preserve) cultural identity. The latter assumption is taken as a point of departure to elucidate two significant trends.

The first trend is increased interaction and mobility within the area of present day Bulgaria. Discoveries of finds of the red ochre painted pottery at Kozareva Mogila and at the submerged site at Sozopol show a hitherto unrecognised affinity with the western region, stretching from the Struma valley to north-western Bulgaria. An influx of graphite painted pottery in a negative manner - attested at Kale, Ezero, and the Devetaki cave (Atanasov 2002) - even speaks in favour of a movement of people. It is of course unknown whether the groups arrived from the KGK VI area south or north of the Danube, but in any case, the observation signifies an intensification of movement in western directions. A Late Copper Age burial discovered at Lepenski Vir (being under influence of the KSB - Krivodol-Sâlcuţa-Bubanj Ia Culture), but arranged according to KGK - Kodžadermen-Gumelniţa-Karanovo VI Culture traditions. (Letitsa 1972) certainly supports such an assumption.

Perhaps the dramatic increase in the number of settlement sites in Southwest Hungary and Northwest Croatia during the time of Balaton-Lasinja Culture (Kalicz 1992) coupled with the settlement expansion and higher accumulation of population in the Cucuteni A-Tripolyje B1 area (Manzura 2005) provide an explanation - at least in part - of the decline in population in Bulgaria after the Copper Age. It is estimated that a significant part of the estimated 72,000 inhabitants of Copper Age Bulgaria (Todorova 1986) drifted away or disappeared by other means, presumably leaving the whole of Thrace uninhabited (Vajsov

2002a; Todorova 2003), or, at least, rather sparsely populated during the Transitional Period[18].

In this light, it is highly interesting to discover two nearly identical containers with everted rims, resembling funnel beakers in shape, with identical decoration of the neck at Kale (Fig. 39:1) and at Sozopol (Fig. 39:2), separated by some 350 km. Both the use of red ochre and the production of vessels with everted rims are novel elements at the end of the 5th millennium BC. They signify an active and simultaneous absorption of cultural influences ongoing in the East Balkan region.

The second trend reflected in the pottery of the age is a fundamental alteration of the production, occurring simultaneously across the whole region from around 4000 BC. Regional differences are still being manifested, and ties with earlier periods can be traced, but completely novel shapes penetrate and define the pottery repertoire. The focus of the design is shifted from the area around or below the shoulders to the area of the neck/rim. The decoration is reduced to simple geometrical motives or altogether omitted. Clearly, the societies of the Transitional Period had undergone a process of cultural re-definition and evolvement of a new identity. It is therefore evident that the cultural milieu of neighbouring groups, shaping each other's identities (cf. Jones 1997), must have radically changed according to the dictum: We are created in ongoing relationships with others - if they change, we also change.

The explanation for this change is complex. Certain economic elements related to the production of

18 A number of metal stray finds in Thrace and other regions of Bulgaria dated to the 4th millennium BC (Todorova 1981; Vajsov 1993) certainly indicates that there was somebody to interact with.

pottery, like the provision of graphite and ochre, did not function anymore. Also, the social environment of high quality production was obviously gone. But basically the change seems to be an ideological one. The status of pottery had changed, with less stress on display and more on function, e.g. pouring of liquids and other contents.

The present evidence on site distribution gives the impression that certain areas were particularly favoured during the Transitional Period in Bulgaria. Such "enclaves" have been recorded around Veliko Tarnovo, with Hotnitsa-Vodopada as the best-investigated example, and in north-western Bulgaria, with a clear concentration around Sadovec and Galatin. New discoveries can also be predicted in the catchement area of the Struma/Strymnon River, with the Vaksevo-Studena Voda (Čochadžiev 2001) and Kolarovo sites (Pernicheva 2000), as well as in the Central Rhodopi Mountains (the caves of Jagodina and Haramijska). These enclaves were not isolated despite clear regional differences. The cultural traditions were all rooted in the previous period but also open for outside stimuli, effecting each region with a different emphasis. Some novelties may be traced back to a particular source, others, like the appearance of apsidal houses in Redutite, the 4th settlement (Gergov 1996), as of yet remain a mystery[19]. Certainly, reconstructing the Copper Age legacy during the long Transitional Period (leading to the Bronze Age) was not an uncomplicated process but nevertheless unavoidable due to the continuous "Europeadization" of the Continent.

Reflections on Method

Some scholars, for instance when caught by the surprise decline of the splendid Copper Age, concentrate on negative aspects when discussing the Transitional Period (for instance Todorova 1986; Georgieva 1992). It is not unnatural to view a cultural manifestation as relatively static during a particular period and its development thus uni-directional, but a danger of idealization is inherent in such a position, with changes seen as "decline", rather than a result of conscious selection and cultural strategies. Idealization is also manifested in conceptions of cultural transmissions. New difficulties arise when cultural groups expected to be in succession of each other in fact appear to be temporally associated, as is, for instance, the case with the Tiszapolgár and Bodrogkeresztúr Cultures of the Central European Copper Age (Johnson 1999).

Perhaps, one of the main strengths, indeed the very role of modern ethnoarchaeology is not to extend our knowledge on cultural materiality and how this functions, but rather to change the mind-set of a scholar, extending his or her understanding of gender roles, cultural motivation, parallel ways of decision-making, and so on, and to understand these dimensions not as buzz-words, but as existing variables shaping a living society. For instance, in the village of Banjeli close to Bassar in Northern Togo in Africa is possible to observe two different modes of claiming and establishing high status in the society. The chief of the village demonstrates his richness and power through subscribing to an ancient mode of organising his compound. He is rich and therefore allows himself to hire the only man still possessing the knowledge of ancient house construction to make a round house, i.e. a kitchen for each of his wives. The houses are elaborately painted, and every visitor will know that the king is indeed rich for there are eight painted kitchens (for competing wives). In the vicinity, one encounters another demonstration, namely a nouveau riche person, who chooses to manifest his resources by building a house of concrete blocks with tin roofing. In fact, a century ago the chief would probably have had tin roofing - as the only man in the area. In each case, a strive for the exquisite is noted. Also, the expectations of society upon their leaders may be changing from innovation to preserving the traditions of the past. Therefore, ideas of measuring the quality of pottery, for instance, in terms of painting and decoration - that is, in aesthetic appeal - have to be taken critically. As has been demonstrated at Lîga, two contemporary houses may contain completely different kinds of pottery. Just like the modern village of Banjeli in Togo held a traditional as well

---

19 In recent years there is evidence to suggest that apsidal houses can in fact be traced to Greece, as the most likely place of origin. An apsidal house of the Final Neolithic date has been reported in Rachmani (House Q) (Gallis 1996). An even earlier occurrence of apsidal houses dated to the Late Neolithic was recorded in the Makriyalos site situated close to the Thermaic Gulf in northern Pieria (Andreou et al. 1996). Thus, a Greek link is certainly not improbable.

as a modern compound, yet both built by rich men: Certainly, culture is never uni-dimensional.

Another disturbing position relates to cultural impact. When some archaeologists observe "foreign" artefacts in a grave - often of some standing - they often take for granted that the dead person (and his family or social group) had adopted, supposedly rather passively, a particular "symbolic code language" to become like the people from where the artefacts originated or after whom they were imitated (Manzura 2005). More likely, such is rather a question of mimicking a value system, just as the Africans of the 18th century AD did, when entering European glass beads and pipes into their own graves, no doubt without any illusion that they thereby would become European slave traders, including the mentality and ideology of such foreigners.

Again, culture is not a static factor, but constantly transformed by people in a conscious way, more often to provide status to its practitioners, rather than a new - thus dangerous - identity. The archaeological reference in this context is, for instance, to Steppe people with Danubian Copper Age artefacts in the graves (or vice versa)[20].

XXI. THE EARLY BRONZE AGE

The beginning of the Early Bronze Age - EBA (3200-2100/2000 BC) was marked by a wave of re-occupations of earlier tells. The Upper Thracian Plain, almost invisible in terms of cultural manifestations in the Transitional Period, now regained its former focal position. Some tells, like Karanovo, were occupied for a short episode only, others, like Ezero at Nova Zagora, with 13 settlement horizons (Georgiev et al. 1979), or Yunatsite with 17 settlement horizons (Katinčarov et al. 1995) demonstrate repeated use of space throughout most of the Bronze Age. The only formal flat necropolis found in Thrace was discovered next to the Bereket tell (Kalchev 1996). The burials attest to subscription to the traditional way of treating the dead: hocker positions on the left side but now also sprinkled with red ochre.

Steppe influences in this period (from the Pit-Grave Culture) had a new and more organised pro-

file, spreading mainly along the Danube but also penetrating into the eastern part of the country, leaving an unmistakable signature in the form of large burial mounds. This influence reached north-western Bulgaria a few centuries later at the time of the Coțofeni Culture (which includes a southern variant termed Orlea-Sadovec). At the threshold to the EBA, the western part of Bulgaria was also under some influence from the Černavoda III Culture, later replaced in the south-western part of the country by a local culture group termed Radomir with Central European ties (Alexandrov 1995). Despite this variety of influences the main orientation now shifted southwards, in the beginning towards the dynamic Troad area and later to the northern Greece mainland.

This development was characterized by a number of technological advances, such as "re-discovery" of metallurgy and a new uniformity of pottery types (cf. Chapter XI above), in addition to a novel organisation of settlement. Caves continue to be occupied or rather used during the EBA. Open air sites were established on prominent locations with the best possible, even commanding view. Stress on defensive measures was implemented either through enclosing walls, and/or ditches, or by constructing the houses along the edges of a site with joint outer walls. Such defensive features are seen at most of the sites. The transformation of the Kale site (cf. Chapter VI above) into a stronghold by erecting a stone wall is typical of the general development.

The transition from the Copper Age to the Bronze Age - via the very long so-called Transitional Period - thus landed Bulgaria in a periphery position vis-à-vis new dominant regions to the South, rather than linking up with Central Europe or the Steppes, as might have happened otherwise. The ultimate reason, of course, is the development of urban cultures in the Near Eastern Bronze Age since the mid-4th Millennium BC, and their expansive influence.

XXII. CONCLUSIONS

A series of highly detailed excavations and in-depth studies centred on the Telish region of north-western Bulgaria have revealed the intricacies of the important cultural transformations in Southern Balkans from the great Late Copper Age - via the bleak, but long, so-called Transitional Period - to the Early Bronze Age

---

20 Of course, such position does not exclude movement of people, nor mating between individuals from different social groups.

(EBA). In fact, these transformations, taking place around 4000 BC, represent a major cultural watershed in Europe, as well as in the Near East.

The Project

The excavations concentrated on the Late Copper Age riverside but agricultural settlement of Lîga - in the EBA used as a burial ground - and the twin-settlement of Ezero-Kale, of which Ezero sees several Copper Age and Transitional Period phases, and Kale was fortified by an enclosure wall in the EBA. The already published Lîga site (Merkyte 2005) submitted important chronological and cultural observations, including several most carefully excavated burned down houses in Phase 2. These structures had an indeed very rich inventory and provided crucial information on household structure and, not least, diversity of ceramic styles, in particular concerning the decoration. In fact, traditional Bulgarian Copper Age chronology would place the strictly contemporary houses up to 800 years apart, on the differences in pottery. The settling of Ezero - virtually hidden in a beautiful lush gully and encircled by a stream - starts in the Early Copper Age and ends in the Transitional Period, apart from occasional occupations or visits in the EBA (and even in Late Antiquity).

The Lîga studies tackled very many detailed problems of analysis and interpretation of structures and artefacts, but also the wider settlement of the Telish region, including a functional diversity of occupational sites towards the end of the Copper Age, no doubt an attempt at redefining the social economy of north-western Bulgaria in the face of the crisis of the virtual collapse of Copper Age society in the east of the country. At the same time, a wider acquisition of raw-materials is noted, for instance flint from far afield, and wider social networks, as exemplified by the diversity of pottery decoration styles.

The Ezero-Kale studies, presented here, concentrate on understanding the Transitional Period, in context. This period is much discussed in Bulgarian archaeology - sometimes seen as a prolonged Copper Age, sometimes as a prelude to the Early Bronze Age, and sometimes even denied. Clearly, it is both long and different in cultural content (however poor the archaeological data) from its temporal neighbours: Indeed, an archaeological phase in its own right, and

a very important one as such, despite the obvious decline in population and conventional "culture", when compared with the classical Copper Age known from the large tell settlements in southern Bulgaria, displaying marvels in ceramics and decoration, metal work in copper and gold, and the beginnings of a symbolic language, perhaps en route to writing.

The Transition

The Transitional Period, the long archaeological phase roughly between 4200/3800 and 3300/3200 BC (Fig. 40), is viewed differently depending on the geographical position of the observer. Some regions of the Southern Balkans did experience more dramatic changes than others. In the eastern and north-eastern parts of Bulgaria the transformations were so powerful that even today the scarcity of evidence must be accepted as evidence onto itself. Millennia old networks collapsed, and the area of Thrace - bound by strong agricultural traditions - did not manage to adapt but instead was left in a state of disintegration and demographic overspill.

The western regions were effected to a lesser extent, first and foremost due to the early strive of developing alternative subsistence strategies adjusted to temperate European conditions (for argumentation, see Merkyte 2005), but also due to its geographic distance from the source of massive unrest in the East. In the current scientific discourse there are growing efforts to downplay the role of Steppe communities in the termination of the Balkan Copper Age. Yet, an increasing number of dates and finds do suggest that even loosely organised groups from the Steppes were sufficient to create regional instability beyond the Danube. In a way, this situation probably echoed that of the Migration Period, when Central and Eastern Europe rather suddenly exchanged their advanced cultural profile with the dull manifestations of the "Early Slavic Culture", a phenomenon only duly understood thanks to Roman historians (Curta 2001; Barford 2001).

It has been argued that the western KSB cultural complex, contrary to the eastern KGK group, was more "open" to novelties and creative solutions in terms of securing an economic basis. This "openness" led to a transformation of the cultural outlook, which in fact, at the end of the Copper Age, was utterly loos-

Period	~BC cal.	Bulgaria — EAST	Bulgaria — WEST	Bulgaria — SADOVEC REGION	SW ROMANIA (OLTENIA, BANAT)	SERBIA	F.Y.R. MACEDONIA	HUNGARY (CENTRAL EUROPE)	GREECE E MACEDONIA – W THRACE	GREECE (THESSALY)	NE ROMANIA / UKRAINE-MOLDOVA	N EUROPE
Early Bronze Age	← 3300	Pit-Grave Černavoda III Ezero A-B	Magura-Coţofeni (Orlea-Sadovec)	Liga 3-4-Kale 3- Ezero 7-Glm.Kale II-	Coţofeni-Kostolac Baden	Coţofeni-Kostolac Baden Černavoda III	Sitagroi V	Baden IIb-IVa	Sitagroi V	Early Thessalian	Pit-Grave	Funnel Beaker (TRB)
Transitional Period	← 4000	Černavoda I Pevec	Sălcuţa IV Galatin II Jagodin	Ezero Grave / Redutite IV Ezero 6 – Kale 2	Herculane II-III Sălcuţa IV	Boleráz / Sălcuţa IV Bubanj-Hum Ib Vajska Hisar I / Bodrogkeresztúr A-B	Karamani II Šuplevec I-II- Bakarno Gumno II Crnobuki I-II	Boleráz (Baden Ia-IIa) / Hunyadihalom-Lažňany Balaton-Lasinja II-III / Bodrogkeresztúr A-B	Sitagroi IV / Mandalo, Thassos Mikro Vouni I	Petro-magoula / Rachmani	Horodiştea-Folteşti Usatovo / Cucuteni AB-B – Tripolye C	Ertebølle (Mesolithic)
Late Copper Age	← 4400	Kodžadermen-Gumelniţa-Karanovo VI-Varna	Krivodol I-V- Sălcuţa I-III- Bubanj Hum Ia	Ezero 5-Kale 1 (?) Ezero 4-Kale 1 (?) Redutite III Ezero 3 Redutite II Liga 2 Glm. Kale I Ezero 2 Liga 1	Sălcuţa I-III	Bubanj-Hum Ia Tiszapolgár Vinča D	Krivodol I-V- Sălcuţa I-III- Bubanj Hum Ia	Tiszapolgár / Lengyel	?	?	Cucuteni A2-A3 – Tripolye B1b-c	
Middle Copper Age	← 4600	Hamangia IV Polyanitsa Marica IV	Dyakovo		Vinča C	Vinča C	Vinča C Tm	Lengyel			Cucuteni A1-Tripolye B1a	
Early Copper Age	← 5000	Hamangia III Polyanitsa Marica I-III	Slatino Gradeshnica Brenica (6-3)	Redutite I / Ezero 1	Tisza	Vinča B2/C	Vinča B2/C Tm	Tisza-Herpály-Csőszhalom	Dikili Tash I-II Sitagroi II-III	Dimini	Pre-Cucuteni I-III Tripolye A1-A2	

Fig. 40. Comparative chronological table of Southeastern Europe, including the sequence of known sites in the Sadovec region, where ↑ marks the relative continuity of space use. Glm. Kale = Golemanovo Kale at Sadovec, cf. Fig. 3.

ing its distinctiveness. This is very well attested even in the highly limited Ezero material, yet containing a very broad repertoire of shapes and decoration motives, some of which are clearly rooted in outside traditions. The so-called Galatin-Sălcuţa culture emerging on this background can therefore hardly be expected to be uniform and homogenous. Increased interaction and securing of new alliances should be considered as responses to social pressures instigated by the transformation processes of the Copper Age communities. The Transitional Period therefore might also be called the period of communication.

Pottery remains the most readily appreciated medium for measuring these changes. The notorious "disk handles" not only allow a correlation of European cultural groupings, but also testify to the emergence of widely-raging subcultures, where "soft values" (ceremonial behaviour, including feasting, libation, and the like) were as important as material goods. The ritual/ideological focus thus shifted from the female to the male realm, an idea already advocated long time ago by M. Gimbutas (1982).

The study of the development of pottery in Bulgaria demonstrates a well-established boundary between the Final Copper Age and the Transitional Period. In general, the Copper Age ends with a horizon of painted pottery, where red ochre paints stand out among white-yellow colours and graphite decoration. In the succeeding period, the colours disappear. Such division was initially observed in the western part of the country (Čochadžiev pers. comm.), but recently also acknowledged elsewhere, including the coastal now submerged sites at Sozopol (Draganov 1998; Georgieva 2005).

The popularity of red paints applied on pottery, especially on this macro-regional scale, should not be perceived as accidental but related to the cultural changes elaborated above. Red, as well as other paints, was certainly favoured earlier, as for instance attested in the Liga 1 settlement material, but at the transition to the 4th millennium BC they gained a new weight. The use of red ochre expanded from the domestic into the mortuary domain among the "Steppe people". Likewise, the early use of crushed shells as tempering material in objects which can be considered intrinsic to the Copper Age cultures, such as clay figurines and spindle whorls - as has been attested at Kale - reveal that there was a clear cultural motivation behind the technological changes which were not forcibly implemented.

The Ezero Kale material has demonstrated both a number of foreign influences and internally-geared transformations, but also continuity, as revealed in the pottery shapes, which started to emerge at the end of the Copper Age and developed during the Transitional Period. A certain part of these shapes survived into the Early Bronze Age, at least in areas like NW Bulgaria, where there is sufficient data for a diachronic evaluation (compare for instance Georgieva 1993 on the Galatin-Sălcuţa culture with Panayotov & Aleksandrov 1988 on the EBA Coţofeni culture).

The Ezero-Kale site with its long cultural sequence, though only superficially explored, has thus made a valuable contribution towards the understanding of the complex processes reshaping Southeastern Europe at the end of the 5th and the beginning of the 4th millennium BC. It is also a symptomatic site, which witnessed the rise of the of grand "graphite painted pottery" cultures of the Copper Age, followed by a puzzle-like disintegration into small population and cultural islands with divergent orientations in the Transitional Period, and later - in the EBA - saw the beginning of the long processes of incorporation. Incorporation led to broad regional alliances, defined by focusing on the new centres of gravity in the South. It also led to (or was instigated by) social change, even competition and armed conflict, as exemplified by the heavy rampart at Kale.

BIBLIOGRAPHY

Albek, S. 2005. Flints. Merkyte, I. et al. 2005. *Liga. Copper Age Strategies in Bulgaria.* Acta Archaeologica 76:1. Acta Archaeologica Supplementa VI. Centre of World Archaeology (CWA) - Publications 2. 112-116.

Alexandrov, S. 1995. The early Bronze Age in western Bulgaria: periodisation and cultural definition. Bailey, D.W., I. Panayotov (eds.). *Prehistoric Bulgaria.* Madison, WI: Prehistory Press. 253-70.

Andreou, S., M. Fotiadis & F. Kotsakis. 1996. The Neolithic and Bronze Age of Northern Greece. *American Journal of Archaeology (AJA)* 100, No. 3. (Jul. 1996). 537-599.

Anthony, D.W. 1991. The domestication of the horse. Meadow, R. & H.-P. Uerpmann (eds.). *Equids in the ancient world* 2. Wiesbaden: Ludwig Reichert. 250-77.

Anthony, D. & D. Brown. 2000. Eneolithic horse exploitation in the Eurasian steppes: diet, ritual and riding. *Antiquity* 74:283. 75-86.

Atanasov 2002. Pers. Comm.

Bailey, D.W. 1999. What is a tell? Spatial, temporal and social parameters. Brück, J. and M. Goodman (eds.). *Making Places in the Prehistoric World.* London: UCL Press. 94-111.

Barford, P.M. 2001. *The Early Slavs.* New York: Cornell University Press.

Barth, F. 1969. Introduction. Barth, F. (ed.). *Ethnic Groups and Boundaries. The Social Organisation of Culture Difference.* London. 9-38.

Berciu, D. 1961. *Contribuţii la problemele neoliticului in Rominia in lumina noilor cercetări.* Bucureşti.

Bojadžiev, J. 1992. Probleme der Radiokohlenstoffdatierung der Kulturen des Spätäneolithikums und der Frühbronzezeit. *Studia Praehistorica* 11-12. Sofia. 389-406.

Bojadžiev 1994/Бояджиев, Я.1994. Абсолютна хронология и периодизация на българската праистория. Проблеми. *Годишник на Департамент Археология*, НБУ, т. 1. София. 249-254.

Brukner, B. 1974. Funde der Sălcuţa-Gruppe in der Vojvodina. *Istraživanija* 5. 27-31.

Chapman, J. 2000. *Fragmentation in Archaeology: People, Places and Broken Objects in the Prehistory of South Eastern Europe.* London & New York: Routledge.

Chapman, J. 2002. Domesticating the Exotic: The Context of Cucuteni-Tripolye Exchange with Steppe and Forest-steppe Communities. Boyle, K., C. Renfrew & M. Levine (eds.). *Ancient Interactions: East and West in* Eurasia. University of Cambridge. 75-92.

Cheddadi, R., G. Yu, J. Guiot, S.P. Harrison, I. Colin Prentice, 1996. The climate of Europe 6000 years ago. *Climate Dynamics* vol. 13, no. 1. Springer.

Chernykh 1978/Черных, Е. Н. 1978. *Горное дело и металургия в древнейшей Болгарии.* София.

Chokhadzhiev, S. 2000. Development of the Graphite Ornamentation in the Copper Age. Nikolova, L. (ed.). *Technology, Style and Society. Contributions to the Innovations between the Alps and the Black Sea in Prehistory.* B.A.R. International Series 854. 97-112.

Čochadžiev 2001/Чохаджиев, С. 2001: *Ваксево – праисторически селища.* Велико Търнаво.

Čochadžiev, S. pers. comm

Crabtree, D.E. 1972. *An Introduction to Flintworking.* Occasional Papers of the Idaho State Museum 28. Pocatello.

Curta, F. 2001. *The Making of the Slavs: History and Archaeology of the Lower Danube Region, c. 500-700.* Cambridge: University Press.

Dahl-Jensen, D., K. Mosegaard, N. Gundestrup, G.D. Clow, S.J. Johnsen & A.W. Hansen. 1998. Past Temperatures directly from the Greenland Ice Sheet. *Science* 282. 268-271.

Demoule, J.-P. & C. Perlès. 1993. The Greek Neolithic: A New Review. *Journal of World Prehistory* 7:4. 355-416.

Derevenski, J. S. 2000. Rings of Life: The Role of Early Metalwork in Mediating the Gendered Life Course. *World Archaeology* 31:3 (Human Lifecycles, Feb. 2000). 389-406.

Draganov, V. 1998. James Harvey Gaul and the Present State of Eneolithic Research in Northeastern Buklgaria and Thrace. Stefenovich, M., H. Todorova & H. Hauptmann (eds.). *In the Steps of Harvey Gaul.* Vol. 1. Sofia. 203-219.

Eriksen, B.V. in prep. Early Bronze Age Flintworking at Bjerre, Thy.

Filipova-Marinova, M. 2007. Archaeological and paleontological evidence of climate dynamics, sea-level change, and coastal migration in the Bulgarian sector of the Circum-pontic region. V. Yanko-Homback et al. (eds.). *The Black Sea Flood Question.* Berlin: Springer. 453-481.

Gallis, K. 1996. Habitation. Thessaly - The Northern Sporades. Papathanassopoulos, G.A. (ed.). *Neolithic Cultures in Greece.* Athens. 64-66.

Ganetsovski 1996/Ганецовски, Г., 1996. Праисторическото селище Охрид-Градо при с. Охрид, област Монтана. *Известия на музеите в севернозападна България*, том 24. Враца. 261-281.

Ganetsovski in print a/Ганецовски, Г. In print. Керамиката от праисторическото селище Криводол-Тепето.

Ganetsovski in print b/Ганецовски, Г. In print. Керамикта от късноенеолитното селище Багачина край Сталийска Махала, Монтанско.

Gatsov, I. 1998. Technical and typological analysis of the chipped stone assemblages from Troia. *Studia Troica* 8. Mainz am Rhein. 115-140.

Gaul, J.H. 1948. *The Neolithic period in Bulgaria.* Cambridge (Mass): Peabody Museum of Harvard University.

Georgiev & Angelov 1952/ Георгиев, Г., Ангелов, Н. 1952. Разкопки на селищната могила до Русе през 1948-1949. *Известия на Археологическия Институт* 18. София.119-195.

Georgiev et al. 1979/Георгиев, Г., Мерперт, Н., Катинчаров, Р., Димитров, Д. 1979: *Езеро. Раннобронзовото селище.* Българска Академия на Науките. София.

Georgieva 1987/Георгиева, П., 1987. Материали от преходния период между каменномедната и бронзовата епоха от Северна България. *Археология*, XXIX:1. 1-14.

Georgieva, P. 1988. Die prähistorische Siedlung in der Gegend Čukata beim Dorf Galatin bei Vraca. *Studia Praehistorica* 9. Sofia. 143-146.

Georgieva 1992/Георгиева, П. 1992. Этнокультурные измене-ния в преходном периоде от энеолита к бронзовой эпохе в Нижнедунайском районе. *Studia Praehistorica* 11-12. Sofia. 339-346.

Georgieva, P. 1993: Galatin culture. Georgieva, P. (ed.). *The Fourth Millennium B.C. Proceedings of the International Symposium Nessebur, 28-30 August 1992.* Sofia. 109-115.

Georgieva 1994/Георгиева, П., 1994. Прозчвания на селище от преходния период от енеолита към бронзовата епоха при с. Ребърково, Врачанско. *Археология* 1. 9-25.

Georgieva 1999/Георгиева, П. 1999. Селищна могила Калето

при с. Рупките, Чирпанско. *Годишник на Софийския Университет "Св. Климент Охридски"*, том 1. София. 7-50.

Georgieva 2005/Георгиева, П. 2005. За зоомопфните скиптри и последните етапи на късноенеолитните култури Варна, Коджадермен-Гумелница-Караново VI и Криводол-Сълкуца. *Studia Archaeologica Universitatis Serdicensis*. Supplementum IV. Stephanos Archaeologicos in honorem Professoris Ludmili Getov. София.144-166.

Gergov 1987/Гергов В. 1987: Медни находки от праисторическото селище в местността Редутите при Телиш, Плевенски окръг. *Археология* XXVIII: 4. София. 44-54.

Gergov 1992/Гергов В. 1992. Доисторическое поселение Телиш Редутите. *Studia Praehistorica* 11 12. Sofia. 347 358.

Gergov 1994a /Гергов В. 1994. Праисторическото селище Телиш – Редутите у проблема за прехода между енеолита и бронзовата епоха в България. *Годишник на Департамент Археология*, НБУ, т. 1. София. 303-306.

Gergov 1994б/Гергов, В. 1994. Каменни зооморфни скиптри от праисторическото селище Телиш-Редутите. *Марица-Изток, археологически проучвания*, том 2. София. 73-78.

Gergov, V. 1996. A dwelling of Telish IV. *Early Bronze Age Settlement Patterns in the Balkans (ca. 3500-2000 BC, calibrated dates)*, Part 2. Reports of Prehistoric Research Projects 1:2-4. Sofia: Agatho Publishers. 309-322.

Gergov 2004/Гергов, В. 2003. Спасителни археологически разкопки на праисторическо селище в м. Езерото при с. Садовец, Плевенско. *Археологически открития и разкопки през* 2003 г. АИМ-БАН. София. 39-40.

Gergov, V. pers. comm.

Gergov et al. 1986/Гергов В., И. Гацов, С. Сиракова, 1986. Кремъчни оръдия от праисторическото селище в местността Редутите при с. Телиш, Плевенски окръг. *Известия на музеите от Северозападна България* 10. 11-20.

Gergov & Valentinova 2005/Гергов, Б., Валентинова, М. 2005. Спасителни археологически разкопки в Деветашката пещера. *Археологически открития и разкопки през 2004*. АИМ-БАН, София.

Gimbutas, M. 1982. *The Goddesses and Gods of Old Europe: Myths and Cult Images*. Los Angeles: University of California Press.

Govedarica, B. 2002. Die Majkop-Kultur zwischen Europa und Asien: Zur Entstehung einer Hochkultur im Nordkaukasus währen des 4. Jts. v. Chr. Aslan, R., S. Blum, G. Kastl, F. Schweizer, D. Thumm (eds.). *Mauerschau: Festschrift für M. Korfmann*, bd. 2. Remshalden-Grunbach: Greiner. 781-800.

Govedarica, B. 2004. *Zepterträger – Herrscher der Steppen. Die frühen Ockergräber des älteren Äneolithikums im karpatenbalkanischen Gebiet und im Steppenraum Südost- und Osteuropas*. Mainz am Rhein: Philipp von Zabern.

Görsdorf, J. & J. Bojadžiev. 1996. Zur Absolute Chronologie der bulgarischen Urgeschichte. Berliner C-14 Datierungen von bulgarischen archäologischen Fundplätzen. *Eurasia Antiqua* 2. Mainz. 105-174.

Grancharov, M. (ed.). 1999. *Catalogue of Historical Museum of Pleven*. Pleven.

Häusler, A. 1998. Struktur und Evolution der Bestattungssitten zwischen Wolga und Karpatenbecken vom Äneolithikum bis zur frühen Bronzezeit. Ein diachron Vergleich. Hänsel, B. & J. Machnik (eds.). *Das Karpatenbecken und die Osteuropäische Steppe*. München-Raden. 135-162.

Hulthén, B. 1998. *The Alvastra pile dwelling pottery: an attempt to trace the* society *behind the sherds*. Stockholm: Historiska Museet; Lund: Keramiska Forskningslaboratoriet.

Hvass, S. 1985. Hodde. Et vestjysk landsbysamfund fra ældre jernalder. *Arkæologiske Studier* 7. København: Akademisk Forlag.

Ilcheva 1989/Илчева, В., 1989. Вкопани пещи-тандири от праисторическото селище Хотница-Водопада. *Археология* 3. 20-27.

Ilcheva Petrova 1995/Илчева Петрова, В. 1995. *Преходният период от каменно-медната към бронзовата епоха по материали от централна северна България*. Афтореферат. София.

Johnson, M. 1999. Chronology of Greece and S.E. Europe. Final Neolithic and Early Bronze Age. *Proceedings of the Prehistoric Society* 66. 319-336.

Jones, S. 1997. *The Archaeology of Ethnicity*. London & New York.

Jovanović, B. 1998. Sălcuţa IV, Krivodol and Bubanj. Stefanovich, M., H. Todorova & H. Hauptmann (eds.). *In the Steps of James Harvey Gaul*. Vol. 1. Sofia. 197-202.

Kaczanowska, M., 1986. Materiały typu „Scheibenhenkel" w Krakowie-Nowej Hucie, Hucie-Mogile (stan. 55). *Materiały Archeologiczne Nowej Huty* X. Kraków. 43-47.

Kalchev, P. 1996. Funeral rites of the Early Bronze Age flat necropolis near the Bereket tell, Stara Zagora. *Reports of Prehistoric Research Projects* 1:2-4. Sofia: Agatho Publishers. 215-225.

Katinčarov & Matsanova 1993/Катинчаров, Р., Мацанова, В. 1993. Разкопки на селищна могила при с. Юнаците, Пазарджишко. Николов, В., ed., *Праисторически находки и изследвания*. Сборник в памет на проф. Георги И. Георгиев. София. 155-173.

Katinčarov et al. 1995/Катинчаров, Р., Д., Мерперт, Н., Титов, В., Мацанова, В., Авилова, Л., 1995: *Селищна могила при с. Юнаците (Пазарджишко)*. т. 1. София: Агато и Диос.

Kalicz, N. 1992. Die Balaton-Lasinja-Kultur und ihre südlichen Beziehungen. *Studia Praehistorica* 11-12. Sofia. 313-333.

Kitanoski, B. 1992. Some Data on the Eneolithic Pelagonia. *Balcanica* (Belgrade) 23. Belgrade.

Klassen, L. 2000. *Frühes Kupfer im Norden. Untersuchungen zu Chronologie, Herkunft und Bedeutung der Kupferfunde der Nordgruppe der Trichterbecherkultur*. Jysk Arkæologisk Selskabs Skrifter 36. Aarhus.

Kopacz, J. & P. Valde-Nowak. 1987. From studies of flint industries of the Circum-Carpathian epi-corded ware cultural circle (C.E.C.C.). *Archaeologia Interregionalis. New in Stone Age Archaeology*. Wydawnictwa Universytetu Warszawskiego. 183-210.

Kotova, N.S. 2003. *Neolithization in Ukraine*. B.A.R. International Series 1109.

Kremenetski, C.V. 1995. Holocene vegetation and climate history of southwestern Ukraine. *Review of Palaeobotany and Palynology* 85. 289-301.

Kromer, B., M. Korfmann, & P. Jablonka. 2003. Heidelberg radiocarbon dates for Troia I to VIII and Kumtepe. Wagner, G., E. Pernicka & H.-P. Uerpmann (eds.). *Troia and the Troad*. Berlin: Springer. 43-54.

Letitsa 1972/Летица, 3. 1972: Гроб Салкуца културе са Лепенског Вира. *Starinar* XXI, 1970. Београд. 117-126.

Leshtakov 2005/Лещаков, К. 2005. Относителна хронология на пласта от бронзовата епоха в селищна могила Казанлък. *Studia Archaeologica Universitatis Serdicensis*. Supplementum IV. Stephanos Archaeologicos in honorem Professoris Ludmili Getov. София. 442-454.

Levine, M. 2005. Domestication and early history of the horse. Mills, D.S. & S.M. McDonnell (eds.). *The Domestic Horse: The Origins, Development and Management of its Behaviour*. Cambridge: University Press.

Lichardus, J. & Lichardus-Itten, M. 1998. Nordpontische Gruppen und ihre westlichen Nachbarn. Ein Beitrag zur Entstehung der frühen Kupferzeit Alteuropas. Hänsel, B. & J. Machnik (eds.). *Das Karpatenbecken und die Osteuropäische Steppe*. München-Raden. 99-122.

Lichardus, J., A. Fol, L. Getov, F. Bertemes, R. Echt, R. Katinčarov & I. Iliev. 2000. *Forschungen in der Mikroregion von Drama (Südostbulgarien). Zusammenfassung der Hauptergebnisse der bulgarisch-deutschen Grabungen in den Jahren 1983-1999*. Bonn: Habelt.

Manzura, I. 2005. Steps to the Steppe: Or, How the North Pontic Region was colonised. *Oxford Journal of Archaeology* 24: 4. 313-338.

Matsanova 1994/Мацанова, В. 1994. Кръгтати идоли от селищната могила при с. Юнаците, община Пазарджик. *Марица-Изток, археологически проучвания*, том 2. София. 53-61.

Matsanova 2000/Мацанова, В., 2000: Интрамурални «погребения» от късния халколит в селищната могила при Юнаците, Пазарджишко. Николов, В. ed. Карановски конференции за праисторията на Балканите, 1. *Тракия и съседните райони през неолита и халколита*. София: АИМ-БАН. 121-131.

Matuschik, I. 1998. Kupferfunde und Metallurgie-Belege. Zugleich ein Beitrag zur Geschichte der kupferzeitlichen Dolche Mittel-, Ost- und Südosteuropas. Mainberger, M. (ed.). *Das Moordorf von Reute*. Staufen: Teraqua CAP. http://unterwasserarchaeologie.de/publikation/1998/opu00001p.html

Mays, S., 1998. *The archaeology of human bones*. London & New York: Routledge.

Merkyte, I. et al. 2005. *Liga. Copper Age Strategies in Bulgaria*. Acta Archaeologica 76:1. Acta Archaeologica Supplementa VI. Centre of World Archaeology (CWA) - Publications 2.

Mikov 1948/Миков, В. 1948. Предисторическото селище до Криводол, Врачанско. *Разкопки и проучвания I*. София. 26-62.

Mikov & Dzhambazov 1960/Миков, В., Н. Джамбазов. 1960. *Деветашката пещера*. София.

Mitova-Džonova 1979/Митова-Джонова, Д. 1979. *Археологически паметници в Плевенски окръг*. София.

Mitrevski, D. 2003. Prehistory of the Republic of Macedonia-F.Y.R.O.M. Gramenos, D. (ed.). *Recent Research in the Prehistory of the Balkans*. Thessaloniki. 13-72.

Moros, M., K.G. Jensen & A. Kuijpers. 2006. Mid- to late-Holocene hydrological and climatic variability in Disco Bugt, central West Greenland. *The Holocene* 16: 3. 357-367.

Neikov 2001/Нейков, Н. 2001. *Преди 7000 години и след това - с. Телиш, Плевенско*. Плевен.

Nikolov 1962/Николов, Б. 1962. Праисторически селища във Врачанско. *Археология* 4. 65-711.

Nikolov 1976/Николов, Б. 1976. Могилни погребения от раннобронзовата епоха при Търнава и Кнежа, Врачански окръг. *Археология* 3. 38-51.

Nikolov B. 1978. Développement du Chalcolithique en Bulgarie de l'Ouest et du Nord-Ouest. *Studia Praehistorica* 1-2. Sofia.

Nikolov 1984/Николов, Б. 1984. *Криводол-древни култури*. София.

Nikolova, L. 1999. *The Balkans in Later Prehistory*. BAR International Series 793. BAR. Oxford.

Panayotov, I. 1995. The Bronze Age in Bulgaria: studies and problems. Bailey, D. W., I. Panayotov, I. (eds.). *Prehistoric Bulgaria*. Madison, WI: Prehistory Press. 243-52.

Panayotov & Aleksandrov 1988/Панайотов, И., Александров, С. 1988. За култура Магура-Коцофени в българските земи. *Археология* XXX:2. 1-15.

Pernicheva, L. 2000. The Final Copper Settlement of Kolarovo. Nikolova, L. (ed.). *Technology, Style and Society. Contributions to the Innovations between the Alps and the Black Sea in Prehistory*. B.A.R. International Series 854. 133-171.

Popescu, D. 1941. La tombe à ocre de Casimcea (Dobrogea). *Dacia - Revue d'archéologie et d'histoire ancienne* 7-8. Bucureşti. 85-91.

Radovanović 1996/Радовановић, И. 1996. Прелиминарна анализа кремене индустрије са локалитета Бодњк. *Гласник* 11. Београд. 41-54.

Raduncheva, A. 1976. *Prehistoric Art in Bulgaria from the Fifth to the Second Millenium B.C.* B.A.R. Suplementary Series 13. Oxford.

Rassamakin, J. 2004. *Die nordpontische Steppe in der Kupferzeit*. Teil I (Text) & II (Tafeln). Mainz: Philipp von Zabern.

Reimer P.J., M.G.L. Baillie, E. Bard, A. Bayliss, J.W. Beck, C. Bertrand, P.G. Blackwell, C.E. Buck, G. Burr, K.B. Cutler, P.E. Damon, R.L. Edwards, R.G. Fairbanks, M. Friedrich, T.P. Guilderson, K.A. Hughen, B. Kromer, F.G. McCormac, S. Manning, C. Bronk Ramsey, R.W. Reimer, S. Remmele, J.R. Southon, M. Stuiver, S. Talamo, F.W. Taylor, J. van der Plicht, C.E. Weyhenmeyer. 2004. *Radiocarbon* 46. 1029-1058.

Roman, P. 1971. Strukturänderungen des Endäneolithikums im Donau-Karpaten-Raum. *Dacia* XV. Bucureşti. 31-169.

Schmidt, H. 1932. *Cucuteni in der oberen Moldau, Rumänien, die befestigte Siedlung mit bemalter Keramik von der Steinkupferzeit bis in die vollentwickelte Bronzezeit*. Berlin, Leipzig.

Sirakov 1996/Сираков, Н. 1996. «Степната имвазия» на Балканите и преходът енеолит – бронзова епоха в светлината на каменни ансамбли от Севернат България. *Годишник на департамент археология*. т. II-III, Sofia.

Sirakov, N. & T. Tsonev. 1995. Chipped-stone assemblage of Hotnitsa-Vodopada (Eneolithic/Early Bronze Age transition in Northern Bulgaria) and the problem of earliest "steppe invasion" in Balkans. *Préhistoire Européenne* 7. 241-264.

Skertchly, J.A. 1974. *Dahomey as it is*. London: Chapman and Hall.

Somogyi, K. 2000. A Balaton-Lasinja-kultúra Leletanyaga Somogy Megyében (The Finds of the Balaton-Lasinja Culture in the Komitat Somogy). *Communicationes archaeologicae Hungariae*. Budapest. 5-48.

Spassov, N. & N. Iliev. 1998. The Late Pleistocene and Holocene Wild Horses of East Europe and the Polyphylethic Origin of the Domestic Horse. Stefanovich M., H. Todorova & H. Hauptmann (eds). *In the Steps of James Harvey Gaul*. Vol. 1. Sofia. 371-389.

Spassov N. & N. Iliev. 2002. The animal bones from the prehistoric necropolis near Durankulak (NE Bulgaria) and the latest record of

Equus hydruntinus Regalia. Todorova, H. (ed.). *Durankulak, Band II. Die prähistorischen Gräberfelder.* Teil 1. Deutsches archäologisches Institut. Sofia. 313-324.

Stark, M.T., J.J. Clark, M.D. Elson. 1995. Causes and Consequences of Migration in the 13th Century Tonto Basin. *Journal of Anthropological Archaeology* 14: 2. 212-246.

Stefanova, M. 2000. Control excavations at Mihalich in 1998-1999. (Preliminary communication.) Nikolova, L. (ed.). 2000. Analyzing the Bronze Age. *Reports of Prehistoric Research Projects* 4. Sofia: Agatho Publishers. 21-31.

Steponaitis, V. P. 1984. Technological studies of prehistoric pottery from Alabama: physical properties and vessel function. van der Leeuw, S.E. & A.C. Pritchard (eds.). *The Many Dimensions of Pottery.* Amsterdam: University of Amsterdam. 79-127.

Telegin, D.J. 1987. Neolithic Cultures of the Ukraine and Adjacent Areas and their Chronology. *Journal of World Prehistory* 1:3. Plenum Publishing Corporation. 307-331.

Telegin, D.Y. 2002. A Discussion on some of the Problems arising from the Study of Neolithic and Eneolithic Cultures in the Azov Black Sea Region. Boyle, K., C. Renfrew, M. Levine (eds.). *Ancient Interactions: east and west in Eurasia.* Cambridge: McDonald Institute. 25-48.

Todorova 1979a/Тодорова, X.1979. *Энеолит Болгарии.* София.

Todorova 1979b/Тодорова, X., 1979. Разкопки в м. «Джугера» край с. Рабърково, Врачански окръг. *Археологически открития и разкопки 24.* София. 26.

Todorova, H. 1981. Die kupferzeitlichen Äxte und Beile in Bulgarien. *Prähistorische Bronzefunde.* Abteilung IX. Band 14. München.

Todorova 1986/Тодорова, X. 1986. *Каменно-медната епоха в България.* София: Наука и Изкуство.

Todorova, H. 1989. Ein Korrelationsversuch zwischen Klimaänderungen und prähistorischen Angaben. *Praehistorica* XV-XIV. Internationales Symposium. Praha.

Todorova, H. 1992. Bericht über die Kontrollgrabung von 1979 auf Golemanovo Kale und Neuauswertung des prähistorischen Fundgutes. Uenze, S. (ed.). *Die spätantiken Befestigungen von Sadovec (Bulgarien). Ergebnisse der deutsch-bulgarisch-österreichischen Ausgrabungen 1934-1937.* Münchner Beiträge zur Vor- und Frühgeschichte 43. 2 Bd. München: Beck. 361-374.

Todorova, H. 1998. Der Balkano-Anatolische Kulturbereich vom Neolithicum bis zur Frühbronzezeit (Stand der Forschung). Stefanovich, M., H. Todorova & H. Hauptmann, H. (eds.). *In the Steps of James Harvey Gaul.* Vol. 1. Sofia. 27-54.

Todorova, H. 2002. *Durankulak, Band II. Die prähistorischen Gräberfelder.* Teil 1. Deutsches archäologisches Institut. Sofia

Todorova, H. 2003. Prehistory of Bulgaria. Gramenos, D. (ed.). *Recent Research in the Prehistory of the Balkans.* Thessaloniki. 257-328.

Todorova Simeonova, H. 1968: Die vorgeschichtlichen Funde von Sadovec (Nordbulgarien). *Jahrbuch des Römisch-Germanischen Zentralmuseums Mainz* 15. 15-63.

Todorova & Vajsov 1993/Тодорова, X., Ваисов, И. 1993. *Новокаменната епоха в България.* София.

Todorova, N., Leshtakov, P., Kuncheva-Russeva, T., 2003. Late Chalcolithic Pottery from Sudievo Tell, Nova Zagora District. Nikolova,

L. (ed.) *Early Symbolic Systems for Communication in Southeast Europe,* vol. 1. B.A.R. International Series 1139. 241-289.

Uenze, S. 1992. *Die spätantiken Befestigungen von Sadovec (Bulgarien). Ergebnisse der deutsch-bulgarisch-österreichischen Ausgrabungen 1934-1937.* Münchner Beiträge zur Vor- und Frühgeschichte, 43. 2 Bd. München: Beck.

Urem-Kotsou, D., K. Kotsakis & B. Stern. 2002. Defining function in Neolithic ceramics: the example of Makriyalos, Greece. *Documenta Praehistorica* XXIX. Neolithic Studies 9.

Valentinova 2006/Валентинова, M. 2006. Спасителни археологически разкопки на могила в м. Бануня, с. Бежаново, Ловешко. *Археологически открития и разкопки през 2005 г.* АИМ-БАН. София. 85-86.

Valev, P. 1992. Geologische und geographische Einführung. Uenze, S. (ed.). *Die spätantiken Befestigungen von Sadovec (Bulgarien). Ergebnisse der deutsch-bulgarisch-österreichischen Ausgrabungen 1934-1937.* Münchner Beiträge zur Vor- und Frühgeschichte, 43. 2 Bd. München: Beck. 23-33.

Vajsov, I. 1993. Die frühesten Metalldolche Südost- und Mitteleuropas. *Praehistorische Zeitschrift* 68:1. Berlin: Walter de Gruyter. 103-145.

Vajsov, I. 2002a. Das Grab 982 und die Protobonzezeit in Bulgarien. Todorova, H. (ed.). *Durankulak, Band II. Die prähistorischen Gräberfelder.* Teil 1. Deutsches archäologisches Institut. Sofia.159-176.

Vajsov, I. 2002b. Die Idole aus den Gräberfeldern von Durankulak. Todorova, H. (ed.). *Durankulak, Band II. Die prähistorischen Gräberfelder.* Teil 1. Deutsches archäologisches Institut. Sofia. 257-266.

Welkov, I. 1935. Eine Gotenfestung bei Sadowetz (Nordbulgarien). *Germania. Anzeiger der römisch-germanischen komission des deutsches Archäologischen Instituts* 19. 149-158.

Zbenovich, V.G. 1996. The Tripolye Culture: Centenary of Research. *Journal of World Prehistory* 10:2.

Zidarov, P. 2005. Bone Artefacts. Merkyte, I. et al. 2005. *Liga. Copper Age Strategies in Bulgaria.* Acta Archaeologica 76:1. Acta Archaeologica Supplementa VI. Centre of World Archaeology (CWA) - Publications 2. 124-131.

Yordanov & Dimitrova 1989/Йорданов, Й., Димитрова, Б., 1989. Антропологични данни за погребаните в могилните некрополи от Североизточна България (Ранна Бронзова епоха). *Разкопки и проучвания XXI.* София. 175-187.

Yordanov, Y. pers. comm.

Yordanova, A. pers. comm.

Author's address
Centre of World Archaeology,
Archaeology division SAXO Institute
University of Copenhagen
Njalsgade 80
DK-2300 Copenhagen,
DENMARK
toinga@yahoo.com
www.worldarchaeology.net

PLATES

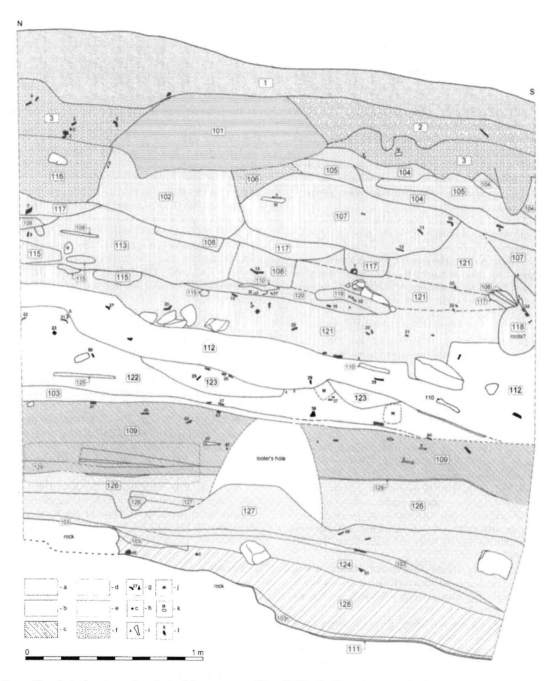

Plate 1. Ezero. Trench A, drawing and analysis of the eastern profile wall. (For the framed area - in broken line - above layer 126 to the left, see Plate 4.1.)

Schematic subdivision into settlement horizons:

a - 1st settlement

b - 2nd settlement

c - 3rd settlement

d - 4th settlement

e - 5th settlement

f - 6th settlement.

Finds:

g - ceramic shard

h - charcoal

i - animal bone

j - flint

k - piece of daub

l - shell.

Description of layers:

1 - top soil, sandy silt loam with high content of humus and small pieces of pottery and daub, firm, porous, brown to brown grey;

2 - heterogenous layer, high content of humus, containing pieces of burned daub and limestones stemming from layer 5, grey brown (interpreted as ancient top soil);

3 - sandy silt loam, sticky, rich in organic matter and grey pieces of daub, but also occasionally burned rounded pieces of daub. There are may particles of charcoal (2-4 mm) and some pottery shards, the layer is generally ill-sorted, colour varies from medium grey (in Trench C) to medium grey blackish (in Trenches A & B);

101 - intrusive layer, loose, but more firm than layer 102, grey black;

102 - silt mixed with small particles of burned clay, max. 3.5 cm, firm, well-sorted, loose, yellow grey;

103 - layer of charcoal and ashes, blackish;

103+ - as layer 103, but more intense layer of burned debris, blackish;

104 - layer containing bigger parts of burned daub, same colour as layer 102, yellow grey;

105 - loam silt, homogenous (even structure and colour), grey;

106 - intrusive (6st horizon), mixed layer of layers 102 and 107, grey with yellowish spots;

107 - compact, firm, grey;

108 - mixed layer, layers 115+113, grey but lighter than layer 115;

109 - silt loam with pieces of charcoal (up to 1 cm2), pieces of daub (up to 3 cm2), medium concentration, ill-sorted, very compact, sticky, grey, slightly lighter than layer 107 (formed after incendiary event);

110 - light kaolinic clay;

111 - clay, unburned, compacted, brown;

112 - as layer 109, with slightly bigger concentration of smaller burned pieces of daub (<0.5 cm²) and spots of white clay (up to 0.5 cm2), the same colour as layer 109.

113 - similar to layer 109 (silt loam), breaks in flakes, containing calcinated organic matter and charcoal (ca. 1-2 mm), light grey;

114 - silt loam, as layer 113, but more compact, with reddish tinge;

115 - ashes with charcoal, very dark grey;

116 - intrusive, as layer 113, but more mixed, and the amount of burned daub is bigger;

117 - burned daub, fragmented, the layer is firm but no compact pieces seen – destruction layer, daub tempered with abundant organic matter, yellow reddish;

118 - mixed layer (created by roots?), humuous, loose, two big fist-sized pieces of grey unburned daub;

119 - layer of severely burned daub, with remains of plastering on the top, reddish to grey reddish;

120 - mixed layer, layers 119+121;

121 - as layer 112, but with lesser amount of daub, soft, containing charcoal and organic matter (mainly seen as circular voids), grey, darker than layer 113;

122 - lime plaster, very loose, orange;

123 – layers 112+122, very porous, very mixed, fragile, some bigger concentrations of daub tempered with organic matter (0.5-1 cm2) grey to grey reddish;

124 - silt clay loam stamped floor level, firm, fragile, containing small particles of charcoal and some daub medium, grey to light grey brown;

125 - burned lime, white;

126 - like layer 124, but lower plasticity and contains bigger particles of daub (originating from layer 127) and charcoal, compact (more compact than layer 124), grey;

127 - layer containing very big pieces of burned daub (size varies between 1-20 cm2) with dark grey core (oven remains and other structural debris), reddish;

128 - like layer 127, but with higher amount of burned organic matter in between pieces of daub (the size of daub varies between 2 and 15 cm2), daub is more effected by fire than that in layer 127 (some pieces are vitrified), the amount of ashes and charcoal is also higher than in layer 127, reddish;

129 - remains of floor (see Plate 4 for close-up).

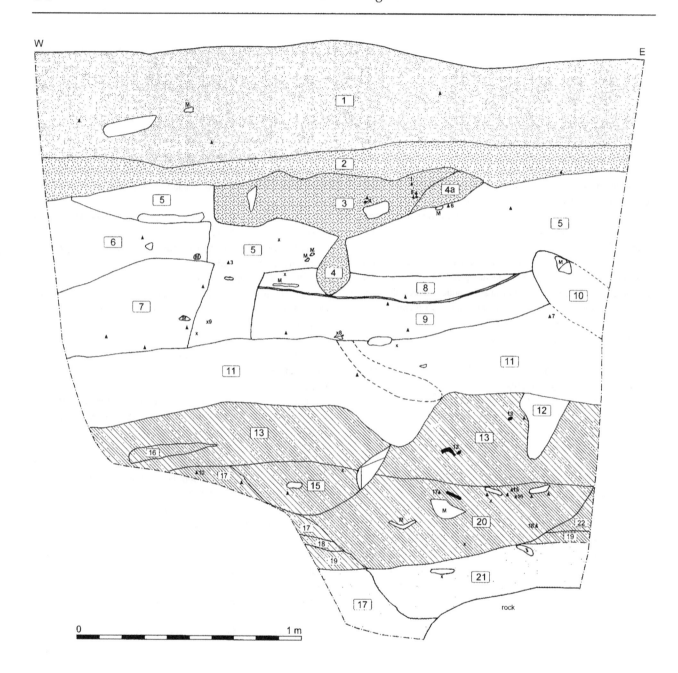

Plate 2. Ezero. Trench C, drawings and analyses of the northern (left) and eastern (right) profile walls. For general signature explanation,

see Plate 1.

Description of layers:

1 - top soil, sandy silt loam with high content of humus and small pieces of pottery and daub, firm, porous, brown to brown grey;

2 - heterogenous layer, high content of humus, containing pieces of burned daub and limestones, stemming from layer 5, grey brown (interpreted as ancient top soil);

3 - sandy silt loam, sticky, rich in organic matter and grey pieces of daub, but also occasionally burned rounded pieces of

daub. There are may particles of charcoal (2-4 mm) and some pottery shards, the layer is generally ill-sorted, more loose than layers 1, 2 & 5, colour varies from medium grey (in Trench C) to medium grey blackish (in Trenches A & B);

4 & 4a - secondary animal trench;

5 - sandy loam, calcareous, friable, humuous, some tiny particles of charcoal (2-4 mm), few pieces of burned daub, light grey in colour;

6 - sandy silt loam, calcareous, friable, porous, with some amount of humus, containing rounded pieces of grey unburned

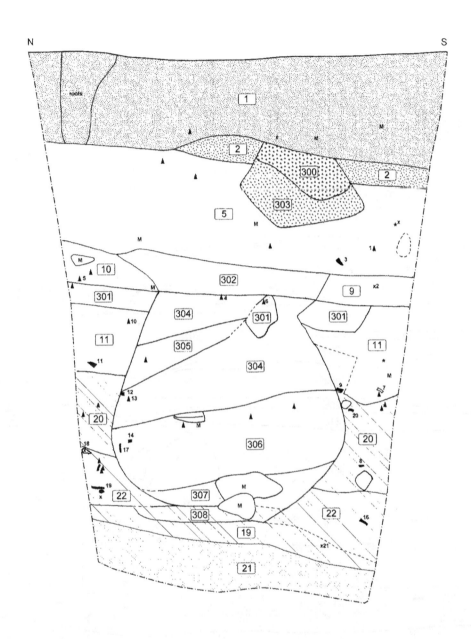

daub, many circular voids 2-4 mm after disappearance of organic matter, grey brown (less brown than layer 3);

7 - sandy loam. Friable, humuous, containing grey daub, organic matter, charcoal, coarse sand (1-2 mm), related to layers 8 and 9, but less compact, spotted with lighter coloured unburned daub, more homogeneous and more compact than layer 6, medium grey;

8 - sandy silt loam, lighter than layer 9, contents of charcoal higher than layer 5, firm, with visible flakes of unburned and burned daub, generally contains a great amount of organic matter;

9 - sand loam (similar to layer 7), calcareous, friable to firm, humuous, containing charcoal and organic matter, coarse sand (1-2 mm), medium grey.

10 - grey blackish layer;

11 - silt loam, calcareous, friable, very plastic, no humus, with few very coarse particles of sand ca. 4 mm, generally mixed layer with unburned and burned pieces of daub, many pottery shards, light grey reddish.

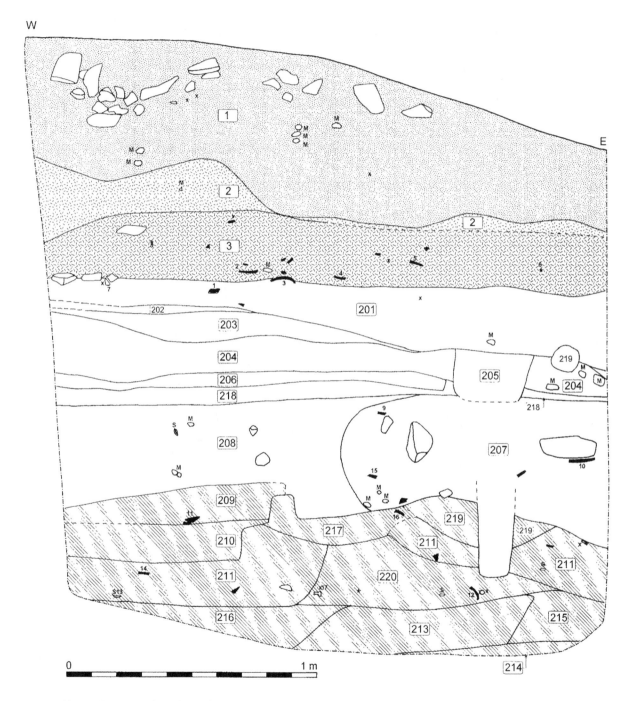

Plate 3. Ezero. Trench B, drawing and analysis of the northern profile wall. For general signature explanation, see Plate 1.

Description of layers:

1 - top soil, sandy silt loam with high content of humus and small pieces of pottery and daub, firm, porous, brown to brown grey;

2 - heterogenous layer, high content of humus, containing pieces of burned daub and limestones, stemming from layer 5, grey brown (interpreted as ancient top soil),

3 - sandy silt loam, sticky, rich in organic matter and grey pieces of daub, but also occasionally burned rounded pieces of daub. There are may particles of charcoal (2-4 mm) and some pottery shards, the layer is generally ill-sorted, porous, calcareous, medium grey blackish, when fresh – with greenish tinge;

201 - silty clay loam, more compact than layer 3, containing some charcoal, small shells and stones, light grey with greenish tinge;

202 - part of layer 201, layer of clay, grey white;

203 - grey blackish layer with blackish spots of extremely burned daub and charcoal, daub is originating from layer 204 (size 1-5 cm²), loose;

204 - layer of burned daub (destruction debris), reddish;

205 - layer containing pieces of burned daub, less compact than layer 201 and lighter than layer 207, light grey;

206 - fine, well-sorted layer of burned organic matter, blackish;

207 - layer containing slightly heat affected daub, grey whitish in colour (the same as grain bin), heterogenous, with small burned

pieces of daub (1-2 cm²) (originating from layer 209) more compact than layer 208, light grey;

208 - layer consisting of bigger particles of heat affected clay, very loose, less heterogenous than layer 207, containing many shells, grey to medium grey;

209 - layer of grey yellowish fragmented daub, destruction debris of 3rd settlement;

210 - as layer 209, but less compact, destruction debris of 3rd settlement;

211 - humuous layer, loose, friabe, containing fragments of burned and unburned daub, grey;

212 - mixture of layers 210 and 211;

213 - as layer 216, but more yellowish;

214 - layer of unburned clay – floor layer (related to layer 216), absorbing, retains water longer than the other layers, very plastic, well-sorted, medium sticky, brown to greenish;

215 - as layer 216, but very plastic, yellow grey;

216 - water-retaining layer, soft, many shells, few pieces of burned daub and charcoal, rather homogenous, with small fragments of limestone, brown to greenish;

217 - very loose layer with pieces of burned daub and charcoal, grey yellowish;

218 - as layer 208, but more firm with some charcoal, otherwise well-sorted, defines floor level, grey;

219 - well-defined layer rich in charcoal (remains of calcinated wooden pole?), grey black.

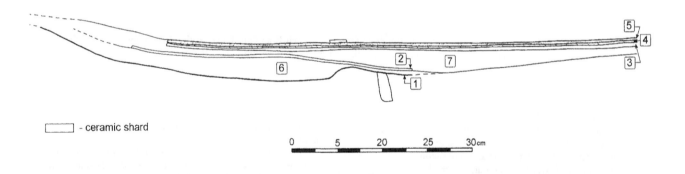

☐ - ceramic shard

0   5   20   25   30 cm

Plate 4.1. Ezero. Close-up drawing and analysis of the cross-section of floor levels discovered in Trench A, and attributed to the 3rd settlement (cf. the framed area, in broken line, above layer 126, to the left in Plate 1).

Description of layers:

1 - whitish lime plaster;

2 - brown reddish clay;

3 - reddish brown clay;

4 - brown yellow clay (a layer in between two layers of floor plastering);

5 - white lime layer with particles of charcoal and clay;

6 - greenish grey compacted clay layer;

7 - medium brown layer of clay containing particles of charcoal.

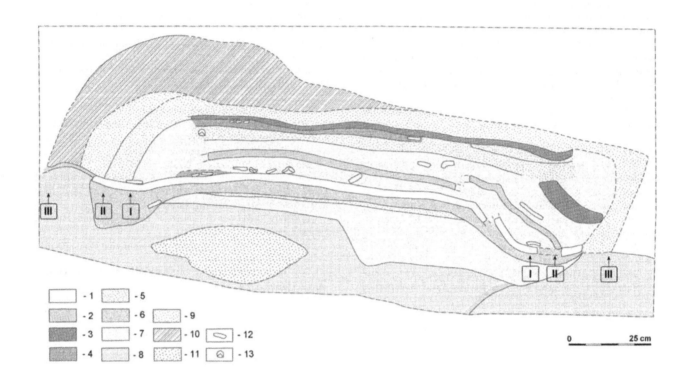

Plate 4:2. Ezero. Cross-section drawing and analysis of the oven found in Trench B and attributed to the 3rd settlement. I - outline of the original oven; II-III - marks the outline of subsequent restorations of the oven.

Description of layers (etc.):
1 - fragmented clay dome of the original oven;
2 - fragmented clay dome of the 1st restoration;
3 - fragmented clay dome of the 2nd restoration;
4 - blackish layer with calcinated organic matter;
5 - reddish layer of heat affected clay;
6 - red burned clay, very compact;
7 - as layer 6 but more friable;
8 - reddish brown clay;

9 - reddish clay attributed to the 1st restoration phase of the dome;
10 - reddish grey clay attributed to the 2nd restoration phase of the dome; heterogeneous layer comprised of heat affected clay particles and humus (looter's hole);
11 - ceramic shards;
12 - limestone.

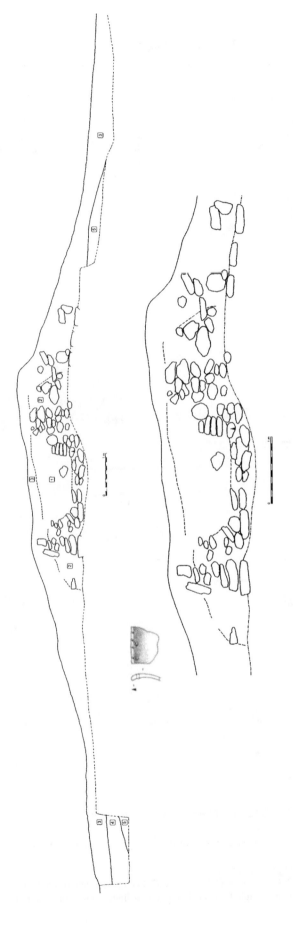

Plate 5. Cross-section and analysis of the rampart at Kale (with close-up of the central part, including pottery shard discovered in the profile wall, at ▲).

Description of layers:
1 - thin horizontal layers where light yellow clay interchanges with dark sandy loam, containing small pebbles;
2 - yellow clay and burned lime with small pebbles used to pack the stones in the front and the back wall;
3 - topsoil, sandy loam containing small pebbles and stones, humuous, rich in charcoal, brown to brown black in colour;
4 - calcareous sandy loam loaded with lime pebbles and occasional pottery shards, dark brown grey, lighter than layer 3;
5 - virgin soil, clayey layer, compact, medium brown in colour.

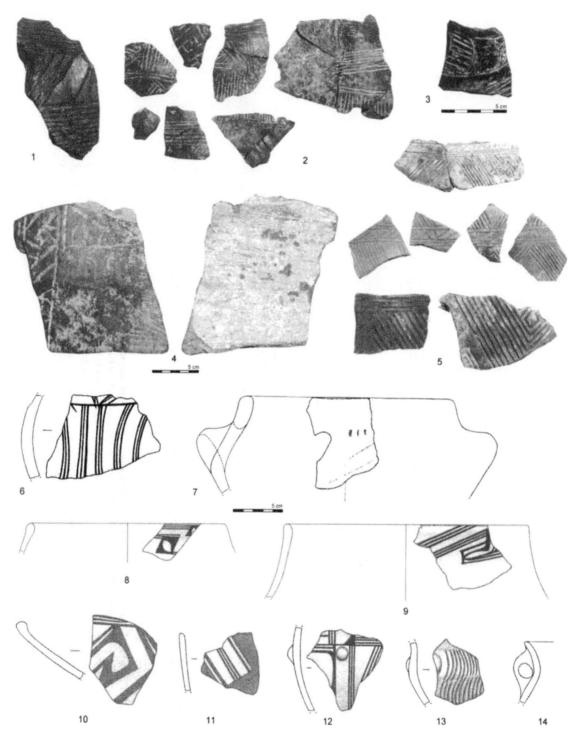

Plate 6. Pottery of Ezero, 1st to 3rd settlement.

1st settlement (Early Copper Age): 1, 2, 5 - not to scale; 3 - incrusted with yellow pigment; 4 - internal surface brushed and lime plastered.

2nd settlement (Late Copper Age): 6 - graphite painted shard.

3rd settlement (Late Copper Age): 7 - Trench B (Ø 25 cm); 8 (Ø 36 cm) & 9 (Ø 44 cm) - graphite painted, Trench A; 10-12 - graphite painted, Trench A; 13 - Trench A; 14 - graphite painted with multiple horizontal and oblique lines below, not rendered, Trench B.

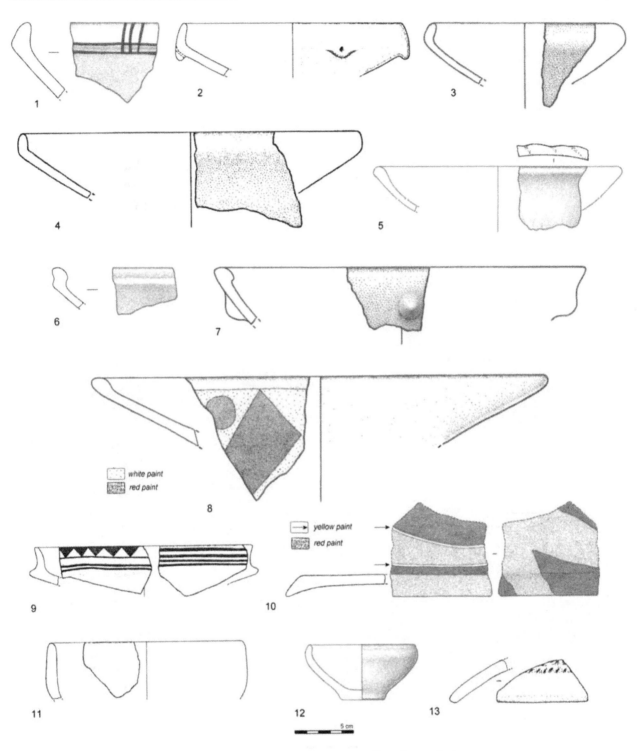

Plate 7. Pottery of Ezero, 3rd settlement (Late Copper Age).

1 (Ø 28 cm) - graphite painted, Trench B; 2 (Ø 16 cm) - Trench B; 3 (Ø 14 cm) - Trench A; 4 (Ø 28 cm) - Trench A; 5 (Ø 20.5 cm) - Trench A; 6 (Ø ~36 cm) - Trench B; 7 (Ø 28 cm) - Trench A; 8 (Ø 38 cm) - Trench A; 9 (Ø 18 cm) - Trench A; 10 (Ø 23 cm) - Trench B; 11 (Ø 16 cm) - Trench A; 12 (Ø 9.2 cm) - Trench A; 13 (Ø 16 cm) - Trench A.

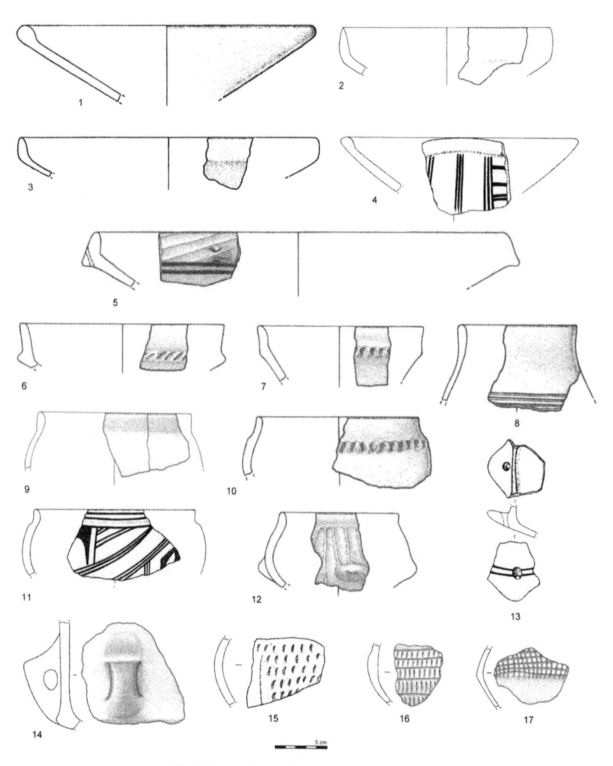

Plate 8. Pottery of Ezero, 4th settlement (Late Copper Age).

1 (Ø 26 cm) - Trench A; 2 (Ø 18 cm) - Trench A; 3 (Ø 26 cm) - Trench A; 4 (Ø 24 cm) - Trench C; 5 (Ø 40 cm) - Trench B; 6 (Ø 18 cm) - Trench A; 7 (Ø 14.5 cm) - Trench A; 8 (Ø 10 cm, arch type) - Trench A; 9 (Ø 13.5 cm) - Trench A; 10 (Ø 16 cm) - Trench A; 11 (Ø 14 cm) - Trench A; 12 (Ø 10.5 cm) - Trench A; 13-17 - Trench A.

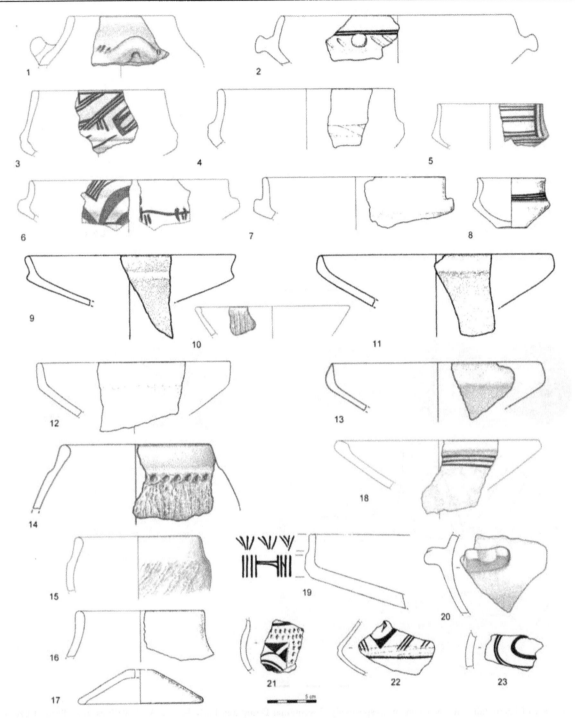

Plate 9. Pottery of Ezero, 5th settlement (etc.).

Uncertain date (4th or 5th settlement phase) - both Late Copper Age: 1 (Ø 10 cm) - Trench A; 2 (Ø ~24 cm) - graphite painted, Trench B; 3 (Ø 14 cm) - graphite painted, Trench A.

5th settlement (Late Copper Age): 4 (Ø 17 cm) - Trench B; 5 (Ø 10 cm) - graphite painted, Trench A; 6 (Ø ~18 cm) - graphite painted, internally and externally, Trench A; 7 (Ø 17 cm) - Trench A; 8 (Ø 6.8 cm) - graphite painted, Trench A; 9 (Ø 20 cm) - Trench A; 10 (Ø 16 cm) - Trench B; 11 (Ø 22 cm) - Trench A; 12 (Ø 18 cm) - Trench A; 13 (Ø 20 cm) - Trench A; 14 (Ø 14 cm) - Trench A; 15 (Ø 11 cm) - Trench B; 16 (Ø 12 cm, arch type) - Trench A; 17 (Ø 12 cm) - lid, Trench A; 18 (Ø 19 cm) - graphite painted, Trench A; 19 (Ø ~34 cm) - graphite painted, Trench B; 20-23 - Trench A; 21-23 - graphite painted.

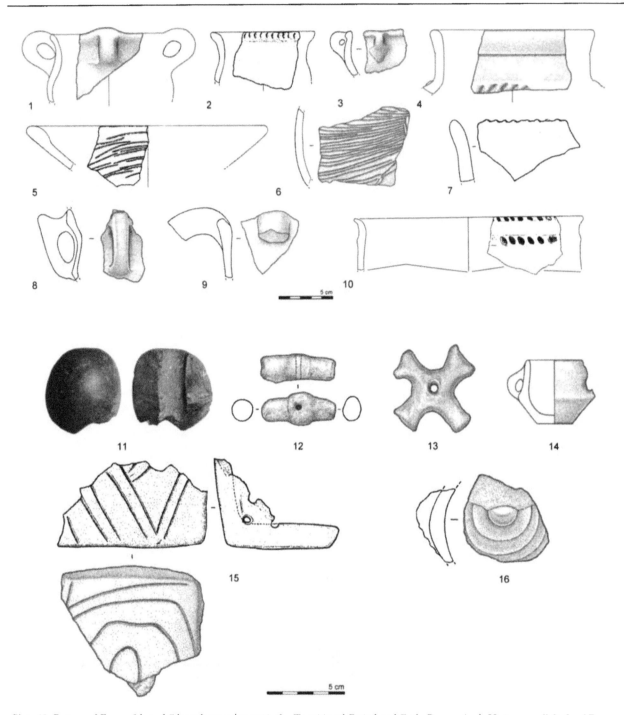

Plate 10. Pottery of Ezero, 6th and 7th settlement (respectively, Transitional Period and Early Bronze Age). Various small finds of Ezero and Kale.

Pottery of the Transitional Period: 1 (Ø 10 cm); 2 (Ø 10 cm); 3; 4 (Ø 13 cm); 5 (Ø ~22 cm, brushed then smoothed); 6; 7 (Ø ~33 cm) - Trench C; 8; 9 - Trench B.

Pottery of the Early Bronze Age: 10 - Trench A.

Various small finds: 11 - ground stone mace-head, Kale; 12 - clay model of double axe, Trench B/Ezero; 13 - cross-shaped spindle whorl, Kale; 14 - miniature vessel, Trench A/Ezero, 5th settlement phase; 15 - clay model of an up-draught kiln, Trench A/Ezero, 4th settlement phase; 16 - fragment of ceramic vessel of so-called breasted form decorated with two pairs of protrusions in the area of the shoulders, characteristic of Late Copper Age sites in NW Bulgaria (area of the KSB Culture), Trench B/Ezero.

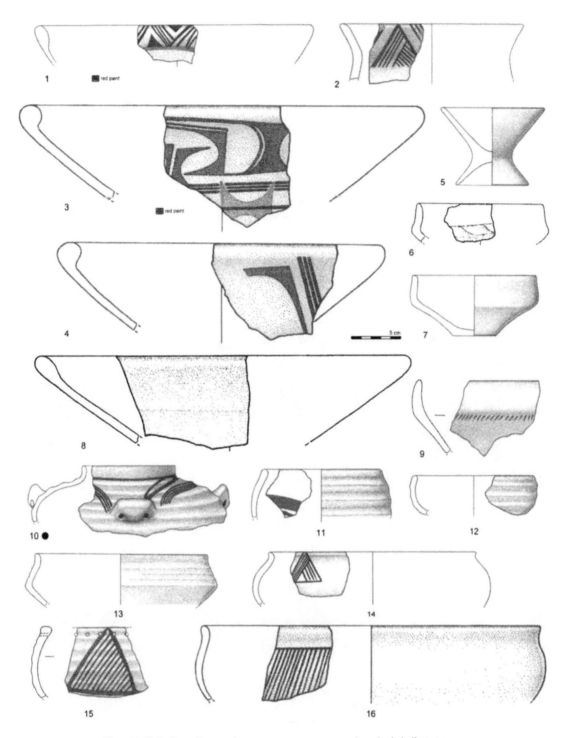

Plate 11. Kale, Late Copper Age pottery. ● – presence of crushed shells in temper.

1 - Ø 30 cm, graphite and red painted; 2 - Ø 18 cm (arch type), graphite painted; 3 - Ø 38 cm, graphite and red painted; 4 - Ø 30 cm, graphite painted; 5 - Ø 9.7, h=7.2 cm (arch type); 6 - Ø 12 cm (discovered in the trench across the rampart, top soil); 7 - Ø 12 cm, traces of red paint on the interior at the rim, found at floor level of house remains; 8 - Ø 38 cm; 9 - Ø 26 cm; 10 - Ø 7.5 cm, graphite painted; 11 - Ø 10 cm, graphite paint in the interior; 12 - Ø 12 cm, arch type; 13 - Ø 15 cm, arch type; 14 - Ø 18 cm, graphite painted; 15 - Ø 21 cm, graphite painted; 16 - Ø 31 cm, graphite painted.

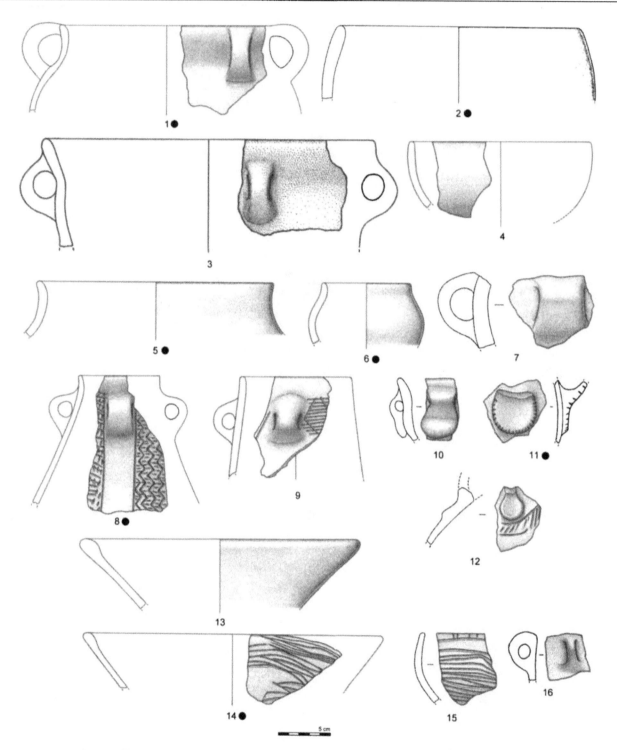

Plate 12. Kale, Transitional Period pottery. ● – presence of crushed shells in temper.

1 - Ø 18 cm; 2 - Ø 23 cm, arch type; 3 - Ø 30 cm; 4 - 16 cm, arch type; 5 - Ø 21 cm, arch type; 6 - Ø 7 cm; 7 - strap handle; 8 - 8 cm, white incrustation; 9 - Ø 10 cm; 10-12 - Scheiben/disk handles; 13 - Ø 24 cm; 14 - Ø 26 cm; 15 - fragment of bowl, brushed and white-incrusted; 16 - ear handle at the rim.

12 & 16 found in the Trench across the rampart, in topsoil.

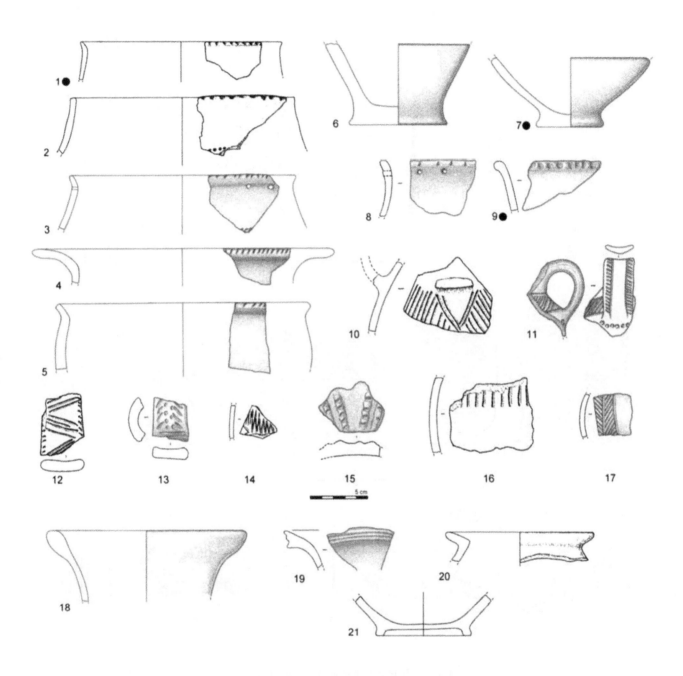

Plate 13. Kale, Early Bronze Age (EBA), and Late Antiquity pottery. ● – presence of crushed shells in the temper.

Early Bronze Age: 1 - Ø 17 cm, found in Trench across the rampart; 2 - Ø 18 cm; 3 - Ø 18 cm; 4 - Ø 24 cm, found in Trench across the rampart; 5 - Ø 20 cm, found in Trench across the rampart; 6 - Ø base 8 cm; 7 - Ø base 6 cm; 8 - Ø 14 cm, found in Trench across the rampart (at location marked with ▲ on Plate 5); 9 - found in Trench across the rampart; 10-12 - ear handles; 13 - ear handle found in Trench across the rampart; 14-17 - wall fragments, all except 15 found in Trench across the rampart.

Late Antiquity: 18-21.

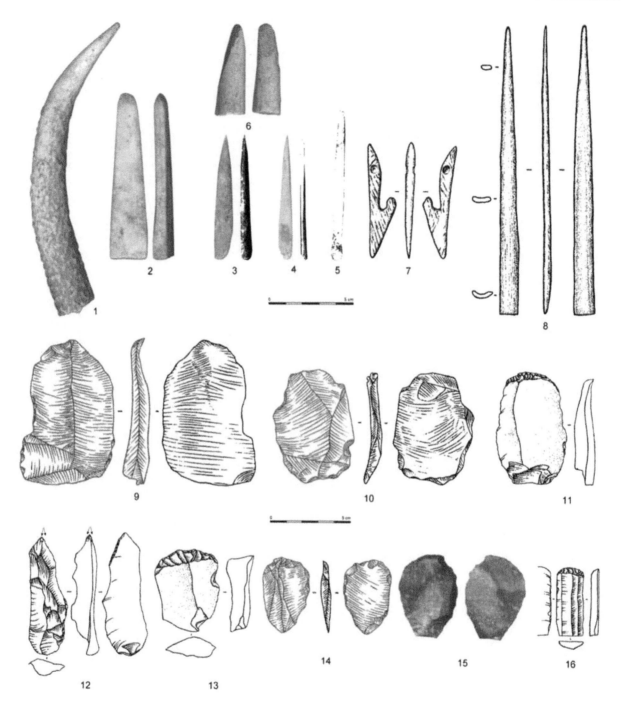

Plate 14. Bone and antler artefacts. And flints.

Locations: 1 & 5 - Kale; 2, 3 & 6 - Ezero, Trench B; 4 - Ezero, Trench A, 2nd settlement horizon; 7 - Ezero, Trench A/B?; 8 - Kale.
  Material & function: 1 - doe deer antler tine with rounded distal point and polished end = perforator(?); 2 - bevel-edged tool made on a long bone splinter = chisel, note the incised notches on the edge, l: 9.2 cm; 3 - pointed tool on long bone splinter = awl, l: 7 cm; 4 - pointed tool on long bone splinter = awl; 5 - bone pin with rounded head and flattened distal end, broken, l: 8.3 cm (EBA); 6 - distal end of shaped antler tine = wedge; 7 - unfinished net-knitting tool (harpoon point?), l: 6.3 cm; 8 - pointed artefact (pin?) made on long bone splinter, l: 13.4 cm.
  Flake and blade tools of flint: Flakes with retouch and traces of utilisation (9-10), end-scrapers (11; 13-16), and burin on retouched crested blade (12). 9, 10, 14, and 15 - Kale; 11, 12, and 13 - Ezero, Trench B; 16 - Ezero, Trench A.

Acta Archaeologica vol. 78:2, 2007, pp 79-86

Copyright 2007
ACTA ARCHAEOLOGICA
ISSN 0065-001X

THE FUNCTION OF PERFORATED SHOE-LAST AXES

Niels V. Skak-Nielsen

1. GEOGRAPHICAL DISTRIBUTION

The Linear Pottery Culture (LBK) arose c. 5500 cal BC on the middle Danube in present-day Hungary, and expanded over the following 150 years across the loess area: northward into Austria, Slowakia, the Czech Republic and Poland, westward through Germany into the Rhineland, Belgium and the Netherlands. Thousands of shoe-last axes have been found in this area, with outliers to the north and south. The distribution drops off as one leaves the loess area's fertile soil, formed during the last Ice Age when soil was blown from the north into Central Europe.

After the end of the LBK about 4900 cal BC, shoe-last axes continued to be made and used among the succeeding cultures: Stickband, Roessen, Lenguel, Gatersleben etc. According to Lutz Klassen (2004, p. 63), production ended in about 4000 cal BC. The shoe-last axe was clearly important to these cultures, and its characteristic design saw little modification over a millennium and a half. It must have served central purposes. One change did occur shortly after 5000 cal BC, when the axe was given a shaft hole near the butt.

2. SOURCE MATERIAL

This investigation is based on shoe-last axes with shaft holes found north of the loess area around the western shores of the Baltic Sea, i.e. the area of the Ertebølle Culture (EBK) of the Late Mesolithic. Following Klassen (2004, p. 26), the study encompasses northwestern Germany, from the mouth of the Oder southwest to the Elbe, then along that river to its mouth, and Schleswig/Holstein, Denmark and Scania. This selection has been made for practical reasons: Klassen (2004) offers an investigation of collections from this area where he has found 92 shoe-last axes, all

well enough preserved to be allocated to one of 15 types. Eleven further pieces whose type could not be determined were excluded from his study.

Klassen investigated the likely point of origin for each of his 15 types within the loess area. Most belong to central Germany: Lower Saxony, the middle Elbe and Saale, although similar axes have been found elsewhere. All 92 axes are post-LBK products: Klassen dates about 2/3 of them to after 4300 cal BC. Merkels (2000, p. 234) came to a similar conclusion: shoe-last axes found in the area of the Late Mesolithic Ertebølle Culture (EBK) are generally late.

Klassen's work surveys other imported artefact types found in the area in question. Thirteen pointed-butt axes are relevant to the present study, see below.

Only about a tenth of the shoe-last axes from before 4300 cal BC found in the EBK area have been found in Denmark or Scania, which are indeed the areas furthest removed from the loess. On the other hand, almost half of the later axes have been found there. This suggests (cf. Skak-Nielsen 2004) that most of the shoe-last axes found in Denmark and Scania were brought there by farmers from the loess area arriving about 4000–3950 cal BC; not, as has long been assumed, having been imported during the Ertebølle Period.

3. SHOE-LAST AXE RAW MATERIALS

Both shoe-last axes and pointed-butt axes were made of amphibolite, a very hard but not brittle kind of rock that could be shaped by sawing, grinding and drilling. The use of this material must be seen in the light of the loess soil's lack of flint and stone. Flint, the preferred material for tools during the Stone Age, is rare also in many areas adjoining the loess. Some flint was imported, but it was mainly made into sickles for harvesting, with a row of small flint blades set into a wooden frame with a handle, and for small objects such as arrowheads. In the eastern reaches of the loess, obsidian imported from the Balkans filled the same needs.

Despite much painstaking searching, the sources of the amphibolite are as yet unknown. They may have been in the mountains of central Middle Europe, possibly farther south or east. As amphibolite implements are found over such a large area, it seems likely that there were a number of sources. Klassen (2004, p. 54) states that raw material and pre-forms for shoe-last axes have been found far from any possible source, which suggests that their production was not centralised. This helps explain the axes' typological variation.

Amphibolite sources were clearly scarce. Long transportation and the labour involved in fashioning implements of such a hard rock mean that acquiring a shoe-last axe called for a lot of resources. In some areas, no amphibolite was available during certain periods, leading to the use of local surrogates such as hornblende slate and basalt. This issue has been discussed e.g. by Bakels (1987), who offers an investigation of shoe-last axes of the period 5400–4900 cal BC found along the Rhine and in the Netherlands/Belgium.

4. THE DESIGN OF THE AXES

Fig. 1 is the likeness of a well-preserved shoe-last axe. This particular specimen dates from about 4500 cal BC and is so similar to other varieties found in the EBK area that their uses must largely have been the same. As noted above, few of them are older: most date from the late 5th millennium. Among the older examples is an axe found in Holstein that retains part of the shaft, radiocarbon dated to c. 4800 cal BC (Klassen 2004, p. 40).

One difference does however bear mentioning. With 13 of Klassen's 15 variants, the length of an axe's edge never exceeds 4 cm. Two variants are set apart in this respect: types Bokel (fig. 2; 7 of 92 pieces) and Neversdorf (fig. 3; 9 of 92 pieces) have edges measuring 5–6 cm. Fig. 4. is a likeness of a late, type Böken axe. Within the EBK area, Böken axes are most com-

monly found in Denmark and Scania (15 of 19 axes), where it is also the most common type of all.

Let us discuss the uses for which axes of these 15 types were made in the loess area. The typical length of an axe is 12–20 cm, the width 6–8 cm and the thickness, usually equalling the length of the edge, 3–4 cm for most types. As shown in the figures, the edge is generally slightly curved. The length/width proportions of the implement resemble those of an adze, but the edge is in fact orientated parallel to the shaft, and it is thus an axe. How the earlier LBK axes without shaft holes were fastened to their shafts is not quite certain. There has thus been some terminological confusion: some writers in English have called these implements axes, others adzes – particularly the early non-perforated ones. The German term has always been *Schuhleistenkeile*, "shoe-last wedges", which carries no assumption about the axes' original orientation relative to the shaft, but is most likely erroneous when it comes to their function.

The implements have a polished surface, flat on the side facing away from the shaft, and commonly slightly domed on the opposite side, reminding one of a shoe-last. The shape is unusual, tapering downward. In fig. 1 it can be seen that the point is a few mm above the polished lower face. This trait is typical although often obliterated on worn specimens. Another characteristic trait is the axes' asymmetric shape (cf. Klassen 2004, p. 24). This is seen with the earlier non-perforated LBK axes as well.

Many shoe-last axes show signs of repair and intensive use. The edge has commonly been sharpened, and new shaft holes have often been drilled to replace the original when an axe has broken across the hole. Both kinds of repair produce shorter axes.

Starting from these characteristics, we shall in the following explore the possible uses for which these axes were made. The basic assumption is that traits constant among a group of implements over the course of 1000 years cannot have been the result of random chance. All traits found in all 15 axe types must have had a functional significance.

One unusual trait is seen only on some types. The axes in figs 1 and 3 have had part of the left-hand side of the butt knapped off. This is common among earlier shoe-last axes examined by Klassen. The reason must be that the axes' asymmetric shape caused

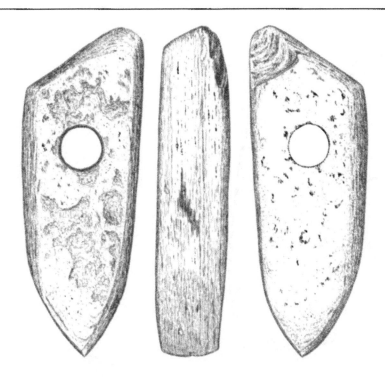

Fig. 1. Shoe-last axe with shaft hole found on Zealand in Denmark. According to Klassen (2004), type Assentorp, c. 4700–4400 BC. Left, the axe seen from the (upper) shaft face. Middle, seen from the side. Right, seen from the lower face. Length c. 19 cm. Edge c. 3.5 cm. Drawing by E. Koch (Fischer & Kristiansen 2002, p. 374).

balancing problems when they were held loosely in the shaft with the edge downward. If the shaft hole is placed on an axe's centre line the point will not be orientated exactly downward, which is awkward whatever the task at hand. By knapping off part of the butt one can shift the centre of gravity closer to the centre line. Another solution to the problem is to place the shaft hole off-centre, and the two methods may be combined. Testing this explanation would take a detailed investigation of a large sample of axes with and without an oblique butt.

The fact that the asymmetry of the form of the axe was retained for such a long time despite these balancing problems suggests that it had functional importance.

5. INTERPRETATIONS OF THE AXES' FUNCTIONAL PURPOSE

A. Ard shares. According to Buttler (1937), many early archaeologists believed that the axes were used as ard shares. This interpretation was accepted by Glob

(1951) and Brentjes (1956). Hennig (1961) and others argued against the idea after practical trials. The discussion spanned decades.

The ard is currently believed to have reached Central Europe after 4000 cal BC, but no exact date is available. In Denmark, ard furrows have been found under dolmens and passage graves, but never under the somewhat earlier long barrows with wooden structures that are dated before 3500 cal BC and the appearance of the dolmen. Although the ard may have been introduced to Central Europe earlier than to Denmark, there are chronological reasons to discount this as a purpose for the shoe-last axes. The end of the production of amphibolite shoe-last axes around 4000 cal BC (according to Klassen) may actually have something to do with an introduction of the ard around that date.

B. Weapons. The shoe-last axe was demonstrably used as a weapon. Its pointed shape made it well suited for that purpose. In southern Germany (Talheim) and northern Austria (Schletz bei Asparn), macabre finds have been made where the remains of entire

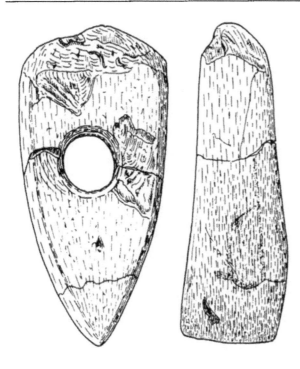

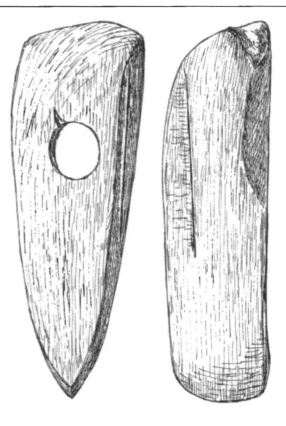

Fig. 2. Shoe-last axe with shaft hole found in Mecklenburg, Germany. According to Klassen (2004), type Bokel, c. 4700–4400 BC. Left, the axe seen from the (upper) shaft face. Right, seen from the side. Length c. 15 cm. Edge c. 5 cm. (Klassen 2004, p. 33).

Fig 3. Shoe-last axe with shaft hole found on Lolland in Denmark. According to Klassen (2004), type Neversdorf, c. 4300–4000 BC. Left, the axe seen from the (upper) shaft face. Right, seen from the side. Length c. 21 cm. Edge c. 6 cm. (Klassen 2004, p. 34).

murdered village populations show that shoe-last axes were among the weapons used by raiders (Wahl & König 1987; Teschler-Nicola et al. 1999).

This cannot however be the primary purpose for which the implement was designed. Previously mentioned characteristics such as asymmetry, one flat face and one domed face cannot be explained under this interpretation. Indeed, almost every kind of axe ever made has at times been used as a weapon, but this says nothing of their intended uses.

The era of the shoe-last axes was far from peaceful (Carman & Harding 1999; Christensen 2004), and so it seems fitting that an implement designed for peaceful work could also be used efficiently as a weapon. Such considerations may have influenced the axes' design, e.g. by making them heavier than would otherwise have been useful.

C. Woodworking tools. An interpretation as a woodworking tool was clearly one of the first suggested by German archaeologists (or laypeople): cf. the term used, "shoe-last wedge". In recent decades most ar-

chaeologists have seen this as the implements' main purpose (e.g. Hennig 1961; Nieszery 1995). Characteristically, experimental trials performed with the axes (e.g. Mamoun 1990; Lüning 2005) have been designed to test their suitability for woodworking, not for other tasks such as agriculture (see below). Some scholars (e.g. Bakels 1987) have voiced doubts as to the axes' uses, and Klassen (2004, p. 258) avoids the issue as he feels that it has not been comprehensively investigated in recent years.

To build log houses you need axes. Recent German finds of very large and deep LBK wells also have a bearing on the issue. One at Kückhoven in the Rhineland has been dendro-dated to 5303 BC (Bahn 1991). This well was lined with planks made out of large oak trees, and such structures bear witness to a high standard of woodworking. Wet conditions in the wells have preserved wooden objects such as a rake, a hoe (that does not however seem very apt for weed-

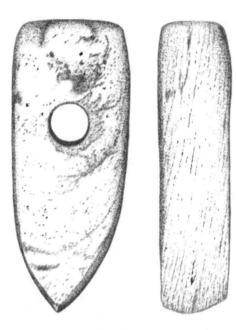

Fig 4. Shoe-last axe with shaft hole found on Zealand in Denmark. According to Klassen (2004), type Böken, c. 4300–4000 BC. Left, the axe seen from the (upper) shaft face. Right, seen from the side. Length c. 15 cm. Edge currently c. 3.2 cm. Klassen 2004, p. 30). Within the EBK area, Böken axes are most commonly found in Denmark and Scania (15 of 19 axes), where it is also the most common type of all.

ing) and what seems to have been a spade (Lüning 2005). Shoe-last axes may have been used to shape wood roughly when making such objects, but for the felling of trees and the making of well-planking you need a wider-bladed type of axe or adze.

As most shoe-last axes studied by Klassen have an edge measuring only 3–4 cm, they are not well suited for woodworking, as shown by experimental tests (Köcheler 1991). But the LBK and succeeding cultures had wide-bladed axes too (Ge. *Flachbeile, Flachhacke*) filling that need (Böhm & Pleyr 1990, p. 260). Such axes were used alongside non-perforated shoe-last axes in the LBK (Bakels 1987, p. 77), and the two implements must have served different purposes. To use a *Flachbeil* for weeding in gardens, which its shape does not rule out, it would have to be hafted as an adze.

The shaft hole drilled through shoe-last axes for a millennium shows that they cannot have been intended as wedges to split logs or planks. Such a wedge often becomes stuck in the wood, and you must hit its butt with a mallet to split the wood and free the

wedge. The risk of breaking a wedge is greatly increased if a shaft hole is drilled near the butt. Most shoe-last axes are also too small and light to be used for such purposes. But they appear to be useful for removing branches from trees, e.g. when collecting leaf fodder, or for making preforms for smaller wooden objects such as bowls or axe shafts.

When shoe-last axes occur in graves (Bakels 1987) they are generally (perhaps always) found in male graves. Some scholars (e.g. Nieszery 1995) have taken this as an indication that the axes were used for woodworking. Ethnographic parallels suggest that at least the heavier steps in woodworking would have been a male activity, while agriculture (before the introduction of the ard) and pottery belonged to the female sphere.

There are, however, other activities perceived as male ones that may explain the axes' placement in male graves, primarily their use as weapons. Furthermore, nothing excludes male participation in agriculture of the time, e.g. making furrows for sowing.

D. Garden-scale agricultural implements. Some scholars have suggested that shoe-last axes would have been used as implements in the LBK's garden-scale agriculture. Thus Buttler (1937, p. 38) believed that the axes were used to make furrows in the soil where grain could be sown. These ideas have largely been discounted since, partly because of the discovery of LBK wells in whose construction shoe-last axes were believed to have been used.

New research into loess-area agriculture during the LBK and its successor cultures has recently been published. British archaeobotanist Amy Bogaard (2004) has looked at the issue, covering almost the entire area from 5000 BC onward. Before that period, there is not enough material to allow use of her methods. She concludes that the entire loess area saw at least a millennium of labour-intensive agriculture with livestock manure on a garden scale.

Bogaard found that grain was sown in the autumn, but it cannot be determined whether this was done in holes made with a digging stick or in furrows. In other areas the digging stick was used at the start of the Neolithic. Sowing in rows, which is seen by many as by far the most likely method, is an easy way to save time and labour and may already have been taken into use before the neolithisation of Hungary and the genesis of the LBK.

Sowing grain (and probably also beans) in rows during the autumn entails four steps in principle.

- Weed the field.
- Make a furrow to sow in.
- Cover over the seed grain with soil.
- As the grain sprouts during the autumn, weed between the rows. Repeat during the spring and summer until the harvest.

This is a labour-intensive process where a shoe-last axe would be very useful. The farmer draws up a furrow by moving backward, pushing the point of the shoe-last axe into the earth. After sowing, some earth is put back over the seed in the furrow with the side of the axe. The sides of the axe can also be used for weeding the surface prior to sowing, and later on to weed along and between the rows of sprouting crops.

The axes' above-mentioned characteristics are explained by their intended use as garden-patch implements. The reason that the point of the axe is a few mm above the polished bottom face is that it prevents the implement from getting stuck in the earth when used to draw up a furrow. The shoe-last shape caused earth to be thrown up to either side as the farmer moved backwards making the furrow. The asymmetric shape of the axe may have been convenient for weeding along the rows. The user would not have to rotate the shaft in their hand or move from one side of the row to the other, when, after having weeded one side of the row, they wished to weed the other.

The posited advantage may seem small from a user's perspective. But neither can making the axes asymmetric instead of symmetric have taken much work. The benefits of asymmetric axes may have been discovered by chance.

A problem in using a shoe-last axe for agriculture is its weight. At a length of 15 cm, an axe typically weighs 400–500 g, and hefting an implement like that in the field makes for tiring work. Most likely, Neolithic farmers worked in a stooped position with a fairly short shaft on the axe. Many early axes, however, were quite light (Nieszery 1995, pp. 247–248).

The size of the shaft hole varies. Usually the diameter is about 2 cm, but larger and heavier axes may have a shaft hole diameter exceeding 3 cm.

E. Symbol of status or office. A worker's or artisan's main tool often acquires a particular identity-shap-

ing significance. It may become a symbol of status or office. This is probably one reason that tools and weapons are among the most common furnishings in graves. They may also be used ceremonially. Such a function for the shoe-last axe would have been secondary to practical considerations and is unlikely to have influenced the axes' design.

One important exception should however be noted. A few unusually large shoe-last axes have been found, measuring nearly half a metre. It is difficult to imagine any practical use for such large axes. Analogies abound both in ethnography and Scandinavian archaeology, such as Early Neolithic wetland deposits of large unused flint axes and the unwieldy cultic axes of the Bronze Age. Giant shoe-last axes may however have acted as a deterrent to enemies in hostile situations if their wielders looked as if they might be able to use them. They may have been made for chieftains, war leaders or cult functionaries.

6. CONCLUSIONS AS TO THE AXES' USES

The design details of shoe-last axes appear primarily to have been determined by the demands of agricultural use. Many traits can only be explained in such a light. It also helps explain the abundance of the axe type in its cultural context: in daily life it was the most commonly used implement.

However, it is also clear that agriculture alone cannot account for the axes' shape. There is good evidence for them having been used as weapons, which led to the production of long, large axes that were not optimal for garden work. Axe-makers must have balanced these considerations against each other, aiming for a compromise, or making axes of different size classes where the small ones were only really useful for agriculture. When equipping a household or village with shoe-last axes, it was of course advantageous to have implements of various sizes. Extremely small axes may have been made for children taking part in garden-patch work.

A third use is woodworking, mainly in making smaller wooden objects. An axe useful for tree-felling and heavier woodworking needs a much longer edge, leading to greater dimensions and an increased weight. The axes in figs 2 and 3 have edges measuring

5 and 6 cm, indicating that the woodworking function was a rather high priority. But through the centuries, short-edged axes became more common. Beside the shoe-last axe, there was need for a wider axe such as a *Flachbeil* in heavier woodworking.

In his survey of imported objects in the EBK area, Klassen also lists axes appropriate for tree-felling. He has found a total of 13 pointed-butt amphibolite axes, all with an edge measuring 5–6 cm. About half of them have been found in Denmark or Scania. Klassen (2004, p. 63) argues convincingly that these 13 axes (compared to 92 shoe-last axes) must underestimate the actual proportion at the time of pointed-butt axes relative to shoe-last axes. Their shape is similar to that of the Scandinavian Early Neolithic's pointed-butt flint axes. It appears likely that immigrant farmers brought not only shoe-last axes but also pointed-butt amphibolite axes, and that the latter type was soon copied in flint. Shoe-last axes designed for loess soil did not work well as agricultural implements in the stony moraine of southern Scandinavia, and so the imported axes were either sacrificed in wetlands or soon became damaged. Copying them in flint would have been useless.

According to Merkel (2000, p. 231), the pointed-butt axe appeared in the loess area not long after 4500 BC. The spread of this axe type may be assumed to have taken place in lockstep with the shortening of the shoe-last axes' edges, which made them better for agriculture.

7. WHY A MULTI-PURPOSE TOOL?

Why design a tool for several conflicting purposes, allowing it to become optimal for none of them? Usually, tools are specialised and made optimal for a narrow purpose.

The answer probably has to do with raw material resources. With flint a rare imported commodity, another material had to be found, viz amphibolite. This rock was also rare but had many valuable characteristics in the context of Neolithic toolmaking (see section 2 above). Demand was high, and its rarity must have made it expensive. People controlling the amphibolite sources would have been able to barter the material quite dearly. Loess area farmers thus could not afford to make large kits of specialised tools. Instead they settled for something that could be used in many contexts, albeit not in an optimal way. Such an implement would be in constant use, and the durability of the amphibolite made it long-lived. Valuable tools deposited in graves are a prehistoric commonplace.

8. FINAL REMARKS

The above refers to conditions after the end of the LBK. Could the results be applied to the six-century lifespan of that culture as well? Were the axes used in the same way already at that time?

To my mind, it appears likely, but more research is needed. LBK amphibolite implements published by Bakels (1987), Nieszery (1995), Behrens (1973) and Lüning (2005) suggest that this era saw a greater variety of implements than the later 5th millennium BC. Some LBK shoe-last axes are furthermore so narrow that they would have worked rather poorly for weeding. For that purpose, a wooden hoe or preferably an amphibolite *Flachhacke* would have been much better. Shafted differently, these could also be used as axes (see above, section 5c). Multi-purpose tools were most likely made already during the LBK (Lüning 2005, p. 48, caption), and the issue of how they were shafted has not yet been settled.

During the LBK, amphibolite must have been more abundant, and so there was less incentive to economise on its use. Scarcity set in only later.[1]

---

1 *Translated from the Danish by Dr. Martin Rundkvist.*

REFERENCES

Bahn, P.G. 1991. The Great Wooden Well of Kückhoven. Nature, 354:269 1991.

Bakels, C.C. 1987: On the adzes of the northwestern Linearbandkeramik. Analecta Praehistorica Leidensia 20, 1987, 53-85

Behrens, H 1973: Die Jungsteinzeit im Mittelelbe-Saale Gebiet. Veröffentlichungen des Landesmuseums für Vorgeschichte. Halle. 27.

Bogaard, A. 2004: Neolithic Farming in Central Europe: An archaeobotanical study of crop husbandry practices. London: Routledge.

Böhm, K. & Pleyr, R. (1990) Geschliffene Geräte aus Felsgestein des älteren und mittleren Neolithikums aus Altbayern: Herställung, Schäftung, praktische Anwendung in: Mamoun, Fansa 1990, 257-262

Brandt, K.H. 1967: Studien über steinerne Äxte und Beile der Jüngeren Steinzeit und der Stein-Kupferzeit Nordwestdeutschlands. Münstersche Beiträge Zur Vorgeschichtsforschung Band 2. Hildesheim.

Brentjes, B 1956: Der Schuleistenkeil - Pflugschar oder Holzbearbeitungsgerät? Germania 34, 1956, 144-147.

Buttler, W. 1937: Der Donauländische und der Westische Kulturkreis der Jüngeren Steinzeit. Handbuch Der Urgeschichte Deutschlands. 2. Leipzig.

Carman, J. & Harding, A. ed. 1999: Ancient warfare: Archaeological Perspectives. Strauds 1999.

Christensen, J. 2004: Warfare in the European Neolithics. Acta Archaeologica vol. 75 Issue 2 :129-156

Fischer, A. & Kristiansen, K. (ed.) 2002.: The neolitisation of Denmark. 150 years of debate. Sheffield.

Glob, P.V. 1939: Der Einfluss Der Bandkeramischen Kultur in Dänemark. Acta Archaeologica X, 1939, 131-140

Glob, P.V. 1951: Ard og Plov i Nordens Oldtid. Jysk Arkæologisk Selskabs Skrifter 1. Århus.

Hennig, E. 1961: Untersuchungen über den Verwendungszweck urgeschichtlicher Schuleistenkeile. Alt-Thüringen 5, 1961: 189-222.

Jensen, J. 2001: Danmarks Oldtid, Bind 1: Stenalder. 13000-2000 f. Kr. København.

Klassen, Lutz 2004: Jade und Kupfer. Jutland Archaeological Society, vol. 47, Århus.

Köcheler, A. 1991/92: Jungsteinzeitlishe Siedlungen zwischen Maintal und Itzgrund. Fränkische Heimat am Obermain heft 29

Lüning, Jens 2005: Der Urwald wird mit Steinäxten gerodet, in ders. (Hrsg.), Die Bandkeramiker, erste Steinzeitbauern in Deutschland. Rahden/Westf.

Mamoun, Fansa, ed. 1990: Experimentelle Archäologie in Deutschland, Oldenburg.

Merkel, Michael, 2000: Überlegumgen zur Typologie frühneolitische Felsgesteinräte. Ein Beitrag zur Neolithisierung Norddeutschland und Südskandinavien. Offa 56 1999, 223-238

Nieszery, Norbert 1995: Linearbandkeramische Gräberfelder in Bayern. Espelkamp.

Petrequin, Pierre & Christian Jeunesse, 1995 La hache de pierre. Carrière vosgiennes et échanges de lames polis pendant le Néolithique (5400-2100 av. J.-C.) Editions Errance,Paris

Skak-Nielsen, N.V. 2003: Hvordan kom bondebruget til Sydskandinavien? + Addendum. Fornvännen 98 (2003.1&2).

Skak-Nielsen, N.V. 2004: The neolithization of Scandinavia - how did it happen? Adoranten 2004: 89-102

Teschler-Nicola, M., F. Gerold, M. Bujatti-Narbeshuber, T. Prohaska, Ch.Latkoczy, G. Stingeder & M. Watkins. 1999 Evidence of Genocide 7000 BP – Neolithic Paradigm and Geoclimatic Reality." Coll. Antropol. 23 (1999): 437-450.

Wahl, J., & H.G. König 1987: "Anthropologisch-traumatologische Untersuchung der menschlichen Skelettreste aus dem bandkeramischen Massengrab bei Talheim, Kreis Heilbronn." Fundberichte aus Baden-Württemberg 12 (1987): 65-193.

Weiner, Jürgen, 1990: Noch ein Experiment - Zur Schäftung altneolithischer Dechselklingen. Staatl. Mus. Naturkde. u. Vorgesch. (Hrsg.) in: Mamoun, Fansa (red) 1990 Experimentelle Archäologie etc. : 263-272

Whittle, Alasdair 1996: Europe in the Neolithic, Cambridge University Press.

Author's address
Gentoftegade 42, 2 tv.
DK-2820 Gentofte
Denmark
ns-n@mail.dk

Acta Archaeologica vol. 78:2, 2007, pp 87-110
All rights reserved

THE AHRENSBURGIAN GALTA 3 SITE IN SW NORWAY

DATING, TECHNOLOGY AND CULTURAL AFFINITY

INGRID FUGLESTVEDT

INTRODUCTION

Galta 3 is part of a site complex located on the north-western side of the island of Rennesøy in Rogaland, Southwest Norway (Fig. 1). This part of the island takes the shape of a peninsula facing north into the Boknafjord basin. On the Galta Peninsula, as it is called, 24 sites are known (Fig. 2). In connection with a major road construction project, sites 1, 2, 3, 5 and 48 were investigated by Mari Høgestøl in 1989-90 (Høgestøl 1995). Artifacts from the remaining sites have been discovered through surface collections, or from test pits. A shore-displacement curve of the area makes 9600 BP the upper date limit for habitation at the Galta sites (ibid, 96), and 9800 BP for Galta 3, making this the highest positioned site of the complex. In the early stages of the project, emphasis was placed on dating the site more precisely using geological expertise. At the same time, the high number of diagnostic "Ahrensburgian" points brought up a new issue in the study of the oldest Stone Age in Norway; how should these earliest sites be understood? Are they a direct "prolongation" of the Late Upper Palaeolithic settlement known from the northwestern plains of continental Europe? Could the term "Ahrensburg" provide a more relevant understanding of Galta's cultural context? Or is the connection to Late Upper Palaeolithic continental Europe of a more "indirect" character and therefore justifying the use of local terms like "Fosna?" In this article I will pursue the former approach, i.e. the Ahrensburgian.

The "Ahrensburg-connection" has been mooted by others than myself (cf. Fischer 1978, 34; Høgestøl 1995, 50; Prøsch-Danielsen & Høgestøl 1995, 124). This connection, however, is based on an examina-

tion of projectile points. The aim of this paper is to investigate parts of the technological chains represented at Galta 3. The issue in question is whether the typification of this site as being of Ahrensburgian "origin" can be attributed based on the way blades are manufactured, i.e. to the schema opératoires typical of Late Upper Palaeolithic northern Europe. At Galta 3 a number of flake axes are also present. The presence of these artifacts raises another intriguing issue when discussing the Late Upper Palaeolithic / Early Mesolithic transition in this area; should flake axes be regarded as a purely Maglemosian / Fosna element, or should this artifact type be considered part of assemblages from younger Ahrensburgian contexts? Following the discussion of blade technology at the site and before my final conclusion, an evaluation of operational chains in the manufacture of flake axes will be conducted. First, however, a background will be laid describing dating results, geological context and excavation method.

DATING, GEOLOGY AND EXCAVATION

Dating by artefacts. The oldest Stone Age phase in Norway, the Fosna phase, is defined as consisting of those "sites older than 9000 BP". The typical Fosna assemblage in West and Mid-Norway is characterised as including "flake and core adzes of flint, small tanged points, burins, microliths, macro flakes, unifacial blade cores and coarse macro blades" (Bjerck 1986, 107, 110). The Fosna phase is a blanket label which covers a period of more than 1000 years of development in material culture, and does not give a good

Acta Archaeologica

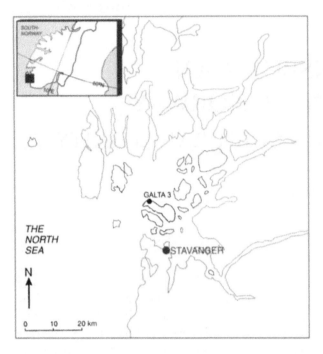

Fig. 1. Geographical position of the Galta site complex (modified after Høgestøl 1995, 23).

basis for accurate dating of the oldest settlement stage in West Norway (see Fig. 1). However, a pattern now seems to be emerging which indicates that in the period 10 000 to 9500 BP tanged points dominated in the beginning and are later succeeded, but not replaced by Zonhoven points and lanceolates. Some small elements of micro-burin technique may also occur in this period. However, microliths with microburin facets, accompanied by a high number of microburins, seem to be present at sites dated to, or younger than 9500 BP (Bang-Andersen 1990, 218f, 222; Kutschera 1999; Kutschera & Warås 2000, 69pp). On these sites tanged points are usually absent.

The tool assemblages of the Galta sites display a connection between the type of points found at the respective sites and their elevation above sea level. At Galta 3, tanged points are found in all layers, whereas Zonhoven points and lanceolates only occur in the three uppermost layers (30 cm) (ibid, 50; Prøsch-Danielsen & Høgestøl 1995, 124). Points classified as 'lanceolates' or 'simple lanceolates' are not manufactured by the microburin technique and microburins are absent from the collection.

Dating by scientific methods. Galta 3 is situated close

to Tranhaug hill which marks the highest point of the peninsula (Fig. 3a and 3b). The find area stretches from 16 to 20 m a.s.l. in a cove on the eastern slope of Tranhaug. Just below the cove, the bedrock forms a natural threshold toward the sea in the east (Prøsch-Danielsen & Høgestøl 1995, 124) (Fig. 4). The topographical position has caused the deposition of sediments from the Younger Dryas transgression. As a consequence, the Galta 3 find material is embedded in beach deposits. Only a short description of the material's relationship to its geological history will be referred to here:

The stratigraphy of Galta 3 consists of three units, 1) greyish till, 2) yellowish brown to rusty bed-beach gravel, and 3) yellowish brown sandy gravel (Fig. 5). Unit 1 was deposited before the area was deglaciated in 14 000, or perhaps as early as 16 000 -18 000 BP (Anundsen 1996, 208f). Unit 2 represents a lower beach phase during which the beach was not directly affected by swash processes. It may have developed subtidally during marine transgression and/or regression. Unit 3 represents an upper beach phase during which the beach was directly affected by swash. The unit is interpreted as having been deposited during a regression phase.

Dating of the sediments at Galta was based on the following information: Two samples from unit 3 were selected for thermo luminescence (TL) and optically stimulated luminescence (OSL) datings, combined with palaeomagnetic measurements. A shore-level displacement curve for Rennesøy was worked out wwwhich included a solid base of additional information and datings. The combined information drawn from these studies (sediment and shore-displacement curves) provides evidence that the beach sediments, including artifacts (units 2 and 3), were re-deposited during a transgression and/or regression phase taking place in the time period between ca. 11 200 and 9 800 BP.

During this Younger Dryas transgression, the maximum sea level was 28.2 m. Under these conditions Tranhaug (now 33.7 m a.s.l.) appeared as a small rock outcrop not suitable for habitation. The Galta 3 finds are situated at 16-20 m a.s.l. This leads to the conclusion that the occupation of Galta 3 must have been contemporary with, but most likely older than, 1) the transgression, or 2) the regression affecting the zone

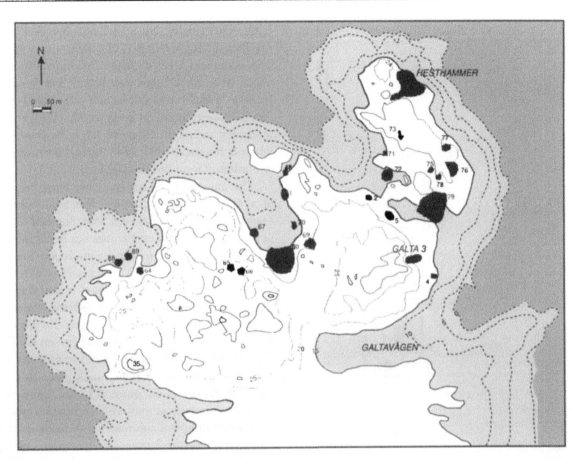

Fig. 2. Excavated and surveyed sites on the Galta peninsula. Shorelines below 15 m a.s.l. are dotted, above 15 m a.s.l. are solid lines (after Høgestøl 1995, 25).

between 16 and 20 m a.s.l. Habitation may thus have taken place prior to 11 000 BP, or in the time interval between 10 400 and 9 800 BP (for a thorough description, see Høgestøl 1995, 39-44, 47 and Prøsch-Danielsen & Høgestøl 1995, 126-129 with references).

Conclusion concerning age. A high number of the tanged points from Galta 3 fulfill the criteria to be classified as Ahrensburgian points (Fischer 1978, 34; Høgestøl 1995, 50; Prøsch-Danielsen & Høgestøl 1995, 124).[1] Furthermore, there is a group of points which can be compared with the Zonhoven points known from typologically late Ahrensburgian sites

on the Northwest European plain (Taute 1968, 183; Høgestøl & Prøsch-Danielsen 1995, 126). Overall, the entire collection of points from Galta 3 resembles those from classical Ahrensburgian sites like Stellmoor and Remouchamps (Fischer 1996, 165). Other tool categories from Galta 3 show a clear Late Upper Palaeolithic affinity (see Høgestøl 1995, 52(4)).

The Ahrensburg culture is traditionally dated to the Younger Dryas chronozone (11 000 -10 000 BP). However, nine C-14 dates from the well known type site of Stellmoor in Northern Germany, suggest occupation in the time period between 10 140 ± 105 and 9 800 ± 100 BP (Fischer & Tauber 1986, 9). According to the scientific dating of the site, the most probable habitation date of Galta 3 would have been 10 400 - 9 800 BP (Prøsch-Danielsen & Høgestøl 1995, 129). The age values of Stellmoor, however, allow us to suggest an even narrower dating of Galta 3. If we assume that the chronology between the two sites more-or-less

---

1 The tanged points at Galta 3 do not, in this way, differ from tanged points at other early sites (predating 9 500 BP) in western Norway (e.g. Bang-Andersen 1990; Gjerland 1990; Kutschera & Warås 2000). What makes Galta 3 special is the very large number of points. This means that the Ahrensburgian element can not be overlooked and has led to a renewed focus on the "Ahrensburg-Fosna-relation".

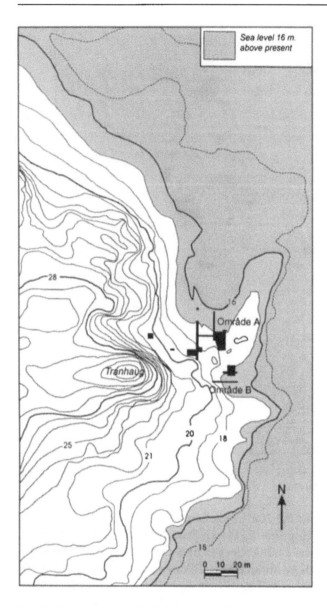

Fig. 3a. Topography at Galta 3, Rennesøy, with a shoreline 16 m a. s. l. (solid line). The excavated areas are marked in black (after Høgestøl 1995, 39).

EXCAVATION, SETTLEMENT & POST-DEPOSITIONAL FACTORS

The settlement area at Galta 3 is estimated to cover about 1000 m². Of this area 141 m² has been excavated in 5 different sections and 5 trenches (Fig. 6). Artifacts were found as deep as 90 - 110 cm within the beach sediment (Høgestøl 1995, 39; Prøsch-Danielsen & Høgestøl 1995, 124). Altogether there are 17 539 artifacts from the site (Table 1).

The material from section 1 has been the subject of a thorough refitting study. The total number of conjoined pieces is, however, low. The fact that only about 13% of the settlement area has been uncovered is probably the main reason for the lack of success in refitting.

The distribution of the refitted material indicates that most artifacts have been moved from the position where they were originally deposited. No clear activity distribution pattern seems to be preserved (Fig. 7). The disturbances would have been mainly due to the post-depositional forces which took place in connection with the regression phase at Galta. Assuming that the site represents at least two occupation phases, it is also probable that the material remains from each visit overlapped the former and that space was organised differently from one phase to the next. Material deposited during former occupation phases may well have been re-used. Disturbances at the site may thus have been the result of cultural as well as natural factors. Based on this background it is obvious that the material from Galta 3 is not well suited for intra-site analyses.

AN "AHRENSBURGIAN APPROACH" TO GALTA 3

Scope of the article. The material from Galta 3 could be immediately placed under the Fosna label, and thereby perhaps contribute to a discussion of the backward limit of this tradition (compare Bjerck 1986:107 with tab. 1). Here, I would like to start from a different point of view: We have seen that Galta 3, with regards to both dating and tool material, may have an affinity with the Late Upper Palaeolithic; not necessarily in terms of absolute dating, but in terms of being part of a palaeolithic tradition and belonging to the youngest of these, i.e. the Ahrensburg.

overlapped, the time period 10 200/ 10 000 – 9 800 BP is perhaps the most likely dating of Galta 3.

Some of the artifacts are water rolled and/or patinated, while others are pristine. This indicates that the material was deposited at different times. Therefore, there is reason to suggest that there were at least two occupation phases at the site, taking place in the time period between 10 200/ 10 000 and 9 800 (ibid, 126).

Fig. 3b. Photograph of the excavated area at Galta 3 facing westwards, with the Tranhaug hill in the background (photo: Museum of Archaeology, Stavanger).

The scope of this article is to demonstrate that not only tools, but also the technological processes that took place, make Galta 3 a typical Ahrensburgian site. In this connection tanged points will not be taken into consideration. The proposed continental Late Upper Palaeolithic affinity will here be demonstrated primarily through blade technology. A description of a selected number of refitted series from "felt 1" (see Fig. 6) will form the basis for the following discussion, in which non-fitted material will also be brought in to deepen the understanding of the material: Flake axes have not traditionally been part of the Ahrensburg assemblage. The character and presence of 19 flake axes at Galta 3 will be given a separate description. Finally, I will discuss the results in relation to the concept of a Fosna-tradition in Norway.

A definition of Ahrensburg. In his article on finds from Northern Friesland in Germany, Sönke Hartz describes the blade material of the assemblages from Ahrenshöft as being characterised by a conspicuous coalescence between remnants of the execution of an acute angle technique, a thorough reduction of the core, marginal on the platform and frequent preparation of the core edge. These features point to a soft hammer, direct percussion technique (Hartz 1987, 21; see also Madsen 1992, 120). The sites at Ahrenshöft belong to the Havelte phase of the Hamburgian culture/period, i.e. the end of the Bølling chronozone 13 000 - 12 000 BP.

In the same connection, Hartz goes on to study material from the Late Upper Palaeolithic classic sites in order to make an assessment of the technology of each phase. In his study, including sites like Teltwisch 2, Eggstedt and Stellmoor, he finds that the technology of the Ahrensburgian assemblages shows more diversity. For instance, very big blades, the so called

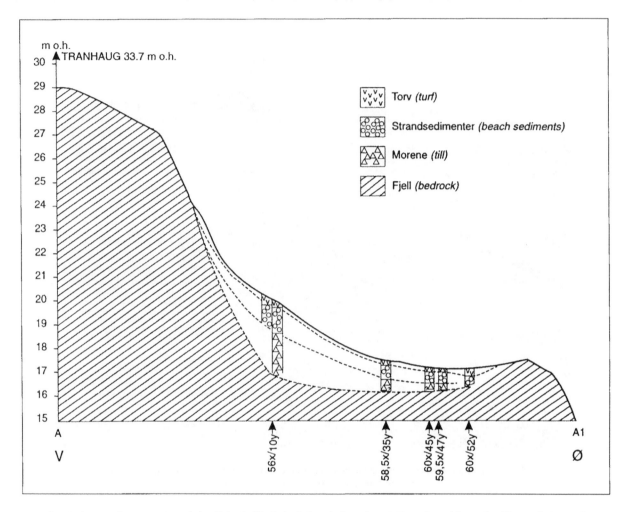

Fig. 4. A vertical cross-section, A-A1, Galta 3. (ill.: Lisbeth Prøsch-Danielsen & Bjørn Ingvaldsen, after Høgestøl 1995, 53).

Riesenklingen might have been manufactured using a hard technique, and do not always show traces of core preparation on the dorsal side. However, in "normal blades", i.e. Schmalklingen/Klingen, the technology is similar to the Hamburgian way of manufacture. According to this study, characteristic artefacts and features in Ahrensburgian assemblages are: Unifacial cores with one platform, platform rejuvenation Tablets, blades struck with an acute angle of percussion (> 70°), non-parallel scars on blade dorsal surfaces, lips, small platform remnants on blades as well as traces on blades and cores / core fragments of a thorough platform edge preparation (Hartz 1987, 26, 27 abb. 9).

This assessment of the blade technique is in accordance with other appraisals of the Ahrensburgian blade technology (e.g. Fischer 1982, 92f; 1988, 17, 20;

Madsen 1996, 72; Schild 1984, 203f; Zagorska 1996, 268f). However, the cited studies point to a higher frequency of unifacial cores with two opposed platforms, and not just one platform, as in Hartz' study.

QUESTIONS ON THE REDUCTION SEQUENCES AT GALTA 3, SECTION 1

The efforts devoted to the refitting of the Galta 3-collection corresponded to a work period of 3-4 months. Early in the work process the collection turned out to be not very promising in terms of accomplishing complete sequences and a high refitting percentage. Altogether there are 84 refitted series, each consisting of only 2 - 8 pieces. The percentage of refitted pieces is estimated to constitute

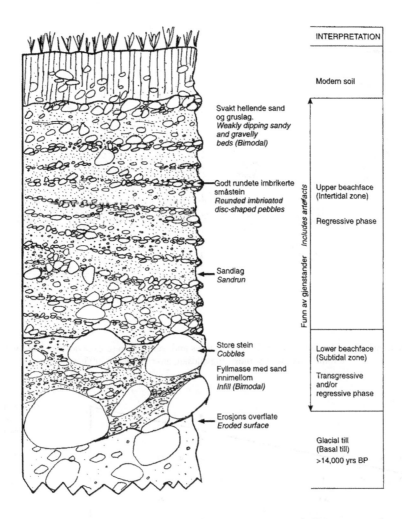

Fig. 5. Stratigraphic outline and interpretation of Galta 3 (after Høgestøl 1995, 43).

2-3 per cent of the total collection from Galta 3. The poor success in refitting is probably due to a number of different factors. The site is far from totally excavated (see Fig. 6) and as described earlier, has been strongly exposed to post-depositional movements, probably causing original activity areas – containing sets of "total" reduction sequences – to move away from their original spot (see Fig. 7). Thus, it is very likely that the "missing parts" of several reduction sequences remain in the unexcavated area of the site. Furthermore, the site has, in all probability, been visited more than once and reuse of material, trampling and clearing of soil surfaces may have erased the original arrangement of activity areas. Finally, it is possible that shortcomings in the author's

refitting abilities may also be a factor explaining the low refitting percentage.[2]

Despite this background, I cannot see any reasons why the existing results should not be representative of the work chains that actually took place at Galta 3. In the study of refitted series, my questions can be formulated as the following. To which degree: (1) is the Ahrensburgian technology defined above, materially present in the Galta 3 reduction sequences; (2) do the reduction sequences show a technical competence comparable to what is documented in continental Eu-

2 It should be mentioned though, that colleagues who are experienced in the field of refitting tried to help me out, but likewise judged the collection to be not very promising.

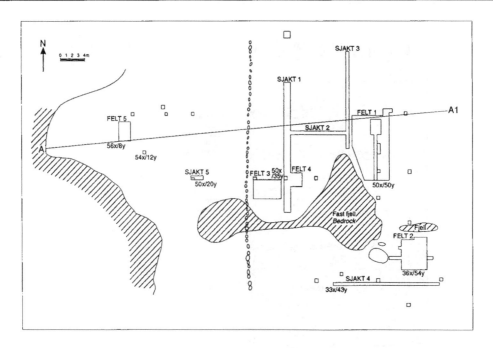

Fig. 6. Excavated sections, trenches and test-pits at Galta 3. The sections and trenches were excavated in m , with mechanical layers of 10 cm (ill.: Evy Berg & Bjørn Ingvaldsen, after Høgestøl 1995, 41).

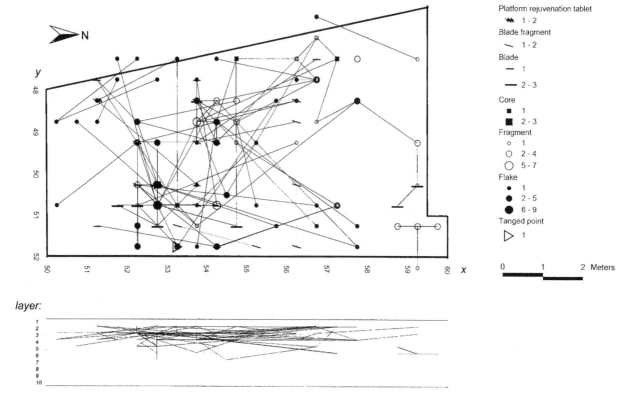

Fig. 7. Chart of refitted pieces at Galta 3, section 1 (all refits by the author, ill.: Stine Melvold).

ropean contexts; and (3) does the quality of the raw material impose limitations on the accomplishment of the operation.

With only a few exceptions (quartz, quartzite, rhyolite), the Galta 3 assemblage consists entirely of flint of varying quality. Three basic categories of flint raw material will be used in the description; a high quality senon-like flint, a coarse Danien-like flint and an intermediary type. The Senon-like category can be characterized as smooth, cryptocrystalline and usually without inclusions of coarser material. Grey, black and a brownish colour are common. The danien-like category could be described as having the type of coarseness associated with concrete cement, often consisting of smaller inclusions of better quality which give the material an irregular character throughout the core. The intermediary category is frequently opaque and grey or brown in colour. It may have a "plastic" appearance, sometimes with smaller inclusions of a coarser material.

A selection from the refitted series will be described and interpreted in detail. This presentation aims at interpreting the intentions of the responsible flint knapper, i.e. the chaîne opératoire (e.g. Edmonds 1990, 57; Eriksen 2000) of each series. An evaluation of the technical competence displayed in each series was carried out during a work-shop in March 1997 at the Museum of Archaeology in Stavanger. The work-shop included Anders Fischer, Morten Kutschera and the author. Since the statistical basis is low for both the number of pieces in each series and the total number of series, only the basic categories competent or incompetent, although used with some variation, could be applied.

REDUCTION SEQUENCES

Series 1. 2 flakes, 2 fragments, 1 blade, 2 blade fragments (Fig. 8). Flint quality: Danien. Purpose of manufacture: Blade production. Core: Unifacial, one platform. Technical competence: Competent knapper

The nodule was "opened" by the removal of two flakes which were struck from opposite directions. A blade front surface was provided represented by the one refitted blade which is positioned behind the two "opening" removals. The two refitted blade fragments bear evidence that a few (2-4?) were produced. Thus, the knapper succeeded in manufacturing a blade core and came close to the process of blade production. The viscosity of the raw material, however, placed strict limitations on how much of the core could be utilized. The primary opening of the nodule was probably carried out by the use of a hard hammer, whereas the manufacture of the blades was executed by direct percussion with a soft hammer.

Series 2. 1 platform rejuvenation tablet, 1 flake, 1 fragment, 1 blade, 1 core (Fig. 9). Flint quality: Danien. Purpose of manufacture: Blade production. Core: Unifacial, one platform. Technical competence: Competent knapper

The platform rejuvenation tablet attests to a previous generation of blade production and the two platform edges show evidence of being well prepared. Features of the flakes indicate the use of soft hammer percussion technique. From the second reduction sequence, only the last blade is present. After this removal the core was abandoned. An outcrop on the core made the cleavage surface uneven, and production of a good blade was impossible. Production of a blade could not have terminated in anything but a hinge. Even a highly skilled knapper working with this low quality flint could hardly have succeeded in evening out the curve on the core. The unsuccessful removal probably represents the last defiant attempt at producing a blade.

Series 3. 2 flakes, 1 core (Fig. 10). Flint quality: Danien. Purpose of manufacture: Probably blade production. Core: Unifacial, possibly one platform. Technical competence: Competent knapper.

The first "outer" removal contains scars indicating a well trimmed platform edge. The platform remnant of this blade-like flake has a lip: evidence of direct soft hammer percussion technique. The intention of this removal was not necessarily to produce a blade, but to even out the cleavage surface after the previous termination had resulted in a hinge from the opposite direction, "documented" by the negative scar. A retry to even out the surface, documented by the "next" underlying flake seems to represent a last endeavor. However, a few negatives present on the outer refitted flake, and on the core cleavage front, show that the manufacture of some quite successful pieces had taken place prior to and eventually after the documented knapping sequence. Negative scars along the platform edge indicate a later shift to a hard hammer as a knapping instrument. The intention was probably to make the outward curve on the cleavage surface sufficiently convex to be able to remove it; the intended result seems once again to have been to make a straight front on the core. Removal of the outcrop was, however, not carried out. The knapper probably evaluated the platform surface as being too small and concluded that the operation would cause the core to fracture into unintended pieces. The knapper had a good knowledge of the possibilities and limitations of the raw material.

Series 4. 3 flakes, 2 platform rejuvenation tablets (Fig. 11). Flint quality: Danien

Purpose of manufacture: Blade production. Core: Unifacial. Technical competence: Probably a competent knapper.

The two outer cortical flakes were probably removed in order to prepare a first generation platform, represented by the "oldest" platform rejuvenation Tablet. Another generation of reduction is evidenced on the next generation platform rejuvenation Tablet. The two platform edges bear traces of being well-trimmed and the soft hammer technique seems to have been competently carried out. There is not sufficient evidence to evaluate the knapper's skill. The chaîne opératoire seems to indicate systematic planning, however, one could question how well this plan was carried out in practice. The knapper could be characterized as a person who knew the "theory" but needed to catch up on the practical side.

Series 5. 4 blades (Fig. 12). Flint quality: Intermediary, "Senon-like Danien"

Purpose of manufacture: Blade production. Technical competence: Highly competent knapper.

Every blade in the series is thoroughly trimmed. The quite good quality of the raw material made the intention of manufacturing a series of very good blades possible to realise. Lips are present on the platform remnant of three of the blades, and partly present on one. The series represents a soft hammer punch technique and the angle of percussion can be estimated to 70 degrees. The missing blades to follow this sequence, would have, in all probability been longer, thus filling the requirements of being classified as "real" blades. Blade production using this technique could not have been conducted in a more competent way.

Series 6. 2 blade fragments (Fig. 13). Flint quality: Intermediary, "Senon-like Danien", but not as good as in series 5. Purpose of manufacture: Blade production

Technical competence: Competent knapper

Blade production was carried out by an experienced knapper. The intention was probably to place the blow as marginally as possible on the platform, in order to produce thin blades. The last blade in the sequence missed the platform remnant, indicating that the blow was a bit too marginal, i.e. slightly misjudged (see also series 13).

Series 7. 2 blades (Fig. 14). Flint quality: Intermediary, "soft Danien". Purpose of manufacture: Blade production. Technical competence: Competent knapper

The refitted pieces are an example of blade production with a soft hammer. The angle of percussion can be estimated to 80 degrees.

Series 8. 1 tanged point, 1 blade, 1 core (Fig. 15). Flint quality: Intermediary, contains bryozoes but is close to Senon quality. Purpose of manufacture: Blade/tanged point production. Core: Unifacial, two opposite platforms. Technical competence: Highly competent knapper.

The series is a nice example of blade production by way of two opposed platform cores. Both platforms are well trimmed all along the edge, i.e. there are traces of a conscious use of the two opposite platforms interchangeably. The second removal, i.e. the unworked blade is thin, concave and has a small platform remnant. The well-trimmed platform edges, along with the features of the blade, give typical evidence of a soft hammer direct percussion technique. There have probably been several previous generations of platforms constituting blade fronts: the core might have been twice as long. The soft hammer technique as evidenced in these refitted pieces, is well suited to the manufacture of tanged points because the blades produced naturally run into a feather. Tanged point production is concretely confirmed by a refitted specimen: the first removed blade of the sequence. The projectile measures 2 cm. The tip of the point is manufactured on the bulbar end of the blade.

Series 9. 3 flakes, 3 fragments, 1 blade (Fig. 16a & 16b). Flint quality: intermediary, "soft Danien". Purpose of manufacture: Decortication, probably blade production. Technical competence: Competent knapper

The presence of platform remnants (Fig. 16a) on the three oldest cortical flakes reveals the use of a hard hammer during the process of decortication. The non-cortical straight flake, which was refitted perpendicular to this sequence (Fig. 16b), has a distal end representing remnants of a well-trimmed platform edge. This indicates the start of real blade production on a unifacial core, and not

least, the change to a soft hammer. Thus, the refitted series probably represents a fragment of a blade core's outer shell.

Series 10. 3 fragments, 4 flakes (Fig. 17). Flint quality: Intermediary, "soft Danien". Purpose of manufacture: Production of macroflakes / flake axes. Technical competence: Probably a competent knapper

The series represents the decortication of a fairly big nodule. Even if not directly documented by refits, blade production does not seem to have been the intention, but was rather the production of macroflakes for the further manufacture of flake axes. Ventral and dorsal sides on the flakes show that macroflakes similar to those represented in the series had been present. Distinct platform remnants containing punch scars and cone formation represent typical evidence of a hard hammer technique. The small inner flake to the right has a faint lip (not visible on the photograph) on the platform remnant, indicating the use of soft hammer technique. There is a possibility that this flake was removed in connection with surface flaking of a flake axe originating from this part of the nodule.

Series 11. 3 side edge flakes (Fig. 18). Flint quality: Intermediary, containing bryozoes. Purpose of manufacture: Side edge preparation of flake axe. Technical competence: Probably competent.

The series gives an insight into a limited part of the operation sequence of the preparation of a flake axe.

Series 12. 2 blade fragments (Fig. 19). Flint quality: Intermediary, "soft Danien"

Purpose of manufacture: Blade production. Technical competence: Competent knapper.

This small series provides a glimpse of a successful sequence of blade production. The youngest blade has a lip, however, which only covers parts of the platform remnant. Probably the same striking instrument was used to produce both blades, i.e. a soft hammer.

Series 13. 2 blades (1 blade, 1 proximal fragment and 1 distal fragment of the same blade) (Fig. 20). Flint quality: Intermediary, "soft Danien". Purpose of manufacture: Blade production

Technical competence: Competent knapper. The first and oldest blade of the sequence has a bulbar scar indicating it was removed either by a hard antler or a soft stone. Whenever the intention is to produce thin blades, one has to place the blow as marginally as possible on the platform. When working with viscous material, it often ends up in a "collapse" of the platform, as evidenced by the oldest blade in this sequence (see also Series 6). The second blade (the two fragments) has an uneven platform remnant, partly consisting of a lip, indicating the use of a soft hammer.

Series 14. 4 flakes, 1 core (Fig. 21). Flint quality: Danien. Purpose of manufacture: Uncertain. Technical competence: Possibly an incompetent knapper

The possibility of being able to manufacture good blades from this kind of raw material is almost zero. Therefore, it is hard to decide whether the reduction is due to the very bad raw material, or to incompetent technical skills. The removal of the outermost flake marks a good start. Bad trimming of the platform edge, however, could indicate shortcomings in the knapper's competence.

Series 15. 3 fragments, 1 core (Fig. 22). Flint quality: Danien. Purpose of manufacture: Uncertain. Technical competence: Competent knapper.

Due to a very irregular consistence, this series consists of an extremely low quality raw material. At first glance it seems almost unbelievable that anyone even tried to work it. At least 4 flakes were removed until the core was given up. Negative scars of flakes show that

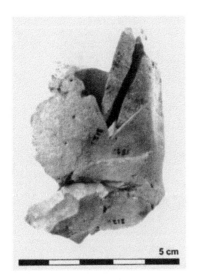

Fig. 8. Series 1 (all photographs by Museum of Archaeology, Stavanger, see text for explanation).

Fig. 9. Series 2.

Fig. 10. Series 3.

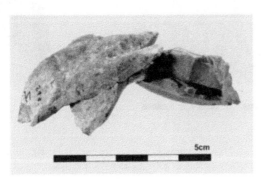

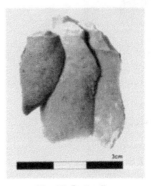

Fig. 11. Series 4.

Fig. 12. Series 5.

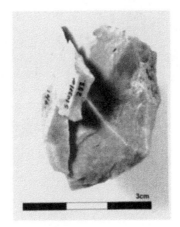

Fig. 14. Series 7.

Fig. 15. Series 8.

Fig. 13. Series 6.

Fig. 16. Series 9.

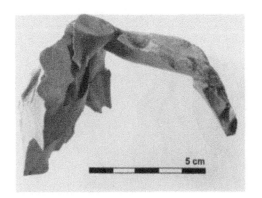

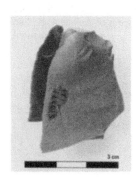

Fig. 17. Series 10.   Fig. 18. Series 11.   Fig. 19. Series 12.

Fig. 20. Series 13.   Fig. 21. Series 14.

Fig. 22. Series 15.

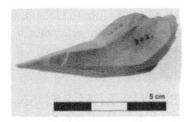

Fig. 23. Series 16.

Fig. 24. Series 17.

Fig. 25. Series 18.

they have been struck from parts of the core containing a more even type of flint. The outermost refitted flake is representative of this. The documented sequence gives evidence of an advanced technique; the outward curving cleavage surface was successfully straightened out by removal of the next flake of the sequence. After this removal, the core parts containing a better flint quality were minimal, which probably lead to the abandonment of the operation.

Series 16. 2 flakes (Fig. 23). Flint quality: Intermediary Purpose of manufacture: Side edge removals, flake axe production. Technical competence: Competent knapper.

The series shows two removals of what most probably represents the working of an edge of a flake axe. The two flakes may have been struck by different instruments; the first one of the sequence with a soft hammer, the next with either a hard antler or a soft stone.

Series 17. 3 blades (Fig. 24). Flint quality: Danien, containing bryozoes

Purpose of manufacture: Blade production Technical competence: Competent knapper.

The blades show well-trimmed edges and contain lips on parts of the platform remnants. The extremely coarse material imposed strict limits on the manufacturing process, revealed by the existence of hinges on both ventral and dorsal sides. Two hinged scars on the

ventral side are evidence of two unsuccessful attempts in evening out the cleavage surface. The series gives an example of raw material limitations met by an experienced knapper. It is obvious that it otherwise would have represented a successful blade production sequence.

Series 18. 1 blade, 1 blade fragment (Fig. 25). Flint quality: Senon. Purpose of manufacture: Blade production. Technical competence: Competent knapper.

The series represents one of the few concrete examples of blade production with a dual opposed platform core. Again a soft hammer technique was used, probably with a unifacial core. The small size of the blades shows to what extent flint of senon quality have been utilized for blade production.

DISCUSSION

Raw material usage. As will be commented on further below, the refitted series are dominated by coarse raw material. Refits of high quality flint are fewer and the pieces comprising series of high quality flint are generally smaller. From the examination of the refitted series, a general impression of raw material utilization can be summed up in the following way.

(1) Blade production with coarse flint ('intermediary' and Danien quality): The viscosity of the coarse raw material imposed a limit on how much of each block could be utilized. It is easy to produce uneven surfaces and they are hard to correct, even for competent knappers. Most series appear to have been created by competent individuals, who had knowledge of the possibilities and limitations of the raw material. The shape and distribution of the cortex of the cores, in relation to the size when they were abandoned, indicate that the number of blades produced from each block can be estimated to only 2-4. A general lack of blades indicates that most specimens were chosen for further manufacture, i.e. tool production. Blade production is accompanied with a frequent rejuvenation of the platform, sometimes probably one rejuvenation per blade. Cores in the coarse flint category, however, must be classified as unifacial: only one platform seems to be commonly represented. Features of the proximal end of blades (small platform remnant, weak bulb, lip) indicate that the blades were manufactured with a soft hammer direct percussion technique. In some series a direct hard hammer (soft stone or hard antler) may have been used. Impact blows from an acute angle are sometimes clearly documented.

(2) Blade production with high quality flint (Senon-

like quality): Manufacture by competent individuals is documented. Use of terms like "highly competent" is limited to refitted series of high quality flint. The few refitted series of senon-like flint indicate the use of unifacial cores with two opposed platforms. Features of proximal blade ends demonstrate the use of a soft hammer direct percussion technique. The refitted cores and blades are small, thus indicating a high utilization of the material.

A striking aspect of the refitted series from Galta 3 section 1 is the extent to which coarse flint is over-represented in contrast to high quality flint. An examination of the entire section 1 material also demonstrates how the total quantity of debris is dominated by coarse flint raw material. Debris of high quality flint comprises a clear minority and pieces are generally smaller than in the coarse material category. To this picture can be added that there is a conspicuous contrast between high flint quality on formal tools and the overall impression of coarse debris.

An obvious interpretation would be that the difference in flint quality gives an over-representation of coarse material in the archaeological record. This interpretation can be emphasized by relating more aspects of refitted and non-fitted material: The refitted series show signs several times, of work operations being abandoned due to limitations in the intermediary, but primarily in the low quality Danien-like flint category. The documented reduction sequences are mostly carried out by skilled knappers, and the early abandonment of cores cannot be ascribed to technical incompetence. The production of blades of coarse raw material thus produces a high quantity of debris, such as cores/core fragments, platform rejuvenation Tablets, blades and flakes from rejuvenation of the cleavage surface, in addition to general, unidentified debris and amorphous cores. The few refitted series of senon-like flint indicate a maximum reduction of nodules, due to the technical possibilities for intensive utilisation of this material. The presence of a few "normal sized" blades (7-8cm, compare Tromnau 1975) of senon-like flint, demonstrates the original presence of larger senon nodules at the site. At the same time, the few present cores of high quality flint are totally exhausted.

The use of different flint types might reflect a situation where flint from local and distant sources is used simultaneously. The coarse flint is probably picked up from beach deposits close to Galta 3, whereas the high quality material mostly originates from the European continent.

AHRENSBURG VERSUS FOSNA

The examination and discussion of the material demonstrates that the blade technology used at Galta 3 can, in all instances, be characterized as typical Ahrensburgian. This is obvious from the presence of unifacial cores (one or two platforms) and a large quantity of platform rejuvenation debris, strong evidence of frequent use of the soft hammer direct percussion technique (including some variation). The overall picture corresponds to Hartz' definition of the typical Ahrensburgian assemblage (see paragraph "A definition of Ahrensburg").

How does the Galta 3 material correspond to the definition of the Fosna assemblage? "Sites older than 9000 BP" are described as consisting of unifacial cores with one or two platforms, blades and coarse blades (Bjerck 1986, 107; Mikkelsen 1975, 26). Here, one is obviously referring to exactly the same type of blade production as described for the Galta 3 material. However, aspects related to the soft hammer technique are not recognized as being present: neither is the consequence, i.e. a close connection to continental European assemblages of the same age.

In the literature describing material of the Fosna phase, there is in my opinion a more or less implicit notion of coarseness in describing the blade technology as well as the assemblages in general (Bjerck 1986, 107, 113; Indrelid 1978, 151). This seems to be understood as an exclusively Norwegian, or rather West Norwegian phenomenon. The coarseness ascribed to the material older than 9000 BP could rather be understood, as explained in this study, as a consequence of the use of local coarse flint and the technical processes leading to an over-representation of coarse raw material in the archaeological record. When Bjerck describes macro blades of the Fosna phase as 'coarse', he is referring to the non-parallel ventral ridges of the blades (Bjerck 1986:113). When Hartz is describing Ahrensburgian blades as 'coarse facetted' ('grob facettiert', see Hartz 1987: Abb.9, s.27) he is in all probability referring to an identical phenomenon.

The idea of coarseness in the Fosna assemblages

could be placed in a wider context when looking at how the Middle Mesolithic blade technology has been taken into consideration. The appearance of "regular", i.e. blades with parallel dorsal scars, appearing in the Norwegian Middle Mesolithic period, was obviously understood as a refinement of a "bold" industry in the earlier period. Thus, blades dated to the Middle Mesolithic are described as "extremely even" (Bjerck 1986, 107). However, the present study of the Galta 3 material illustrates that blade technology of the oldest phase should rather be seen as a mere aspect of the Ahrensburgian tradition of manufacture. Soft hammer direct percussion technique requires high competence and skill and should not be attributed to a coarse "level" associated to an implicit notion of evolution in Mesolithic flint technique. It is clear that "coarseness" as a relevant concept in describing the oldest Stone Age material in West Norway, should be attributed entirely to the use of local beach flint. As a consequence of this specific raw material situation, people left behind immense quantities of coarse debris.

Previous works have pointed out an Ahrensburgian connection with the Galta 3 material on the basis of the nature of the tanged points and Zonhoven points (Fischer 1978, 34; 1996, 165; Høgestøl 1995, 50; Prøsch-Danielsen & Høgestøl 1995, 124). I have so far confirmed this same connection on the basis of blade technology. The chaînes opératoires of Galta 3 point to a set of schema opératoires that do not in any way differ from the ones characteristic of the Ahrensburg group. However, before reaching a conclusion concerning the cultural affinity of this site, the presence of flake axes needs to be examined.

FLAKE AXES
Systems of manufacture and raw material. The Galta 3 tool collection contains 19 axes of which the majority are classified as flake axes: 2 specimens could on a formal basis be described as core axes (see below).

At first glance the axes from Galta may give a deceptively simple impression (Fig. 26). However, a closer examination reveals that most specimens are produced according to a conscious system of manufacture (Fig. 27) (Fischer, unpublished). The most common system adhered to is what is known as the "Ertebølle system", where side edge flaking takes place prior to surface flaking of the axe. This operation can be carried out symmetrically as well as asymmetrically. In the Galta 3 collection both methods are represented. Furthermore two specimens could be described as being close to the "Barmose system" of manufacture, where surface flaking takes place prior to side edge flaking. One of the axes cannot be classified according to a certain system, whereas on five specimens, the original system of manufacture seems to have been erased as a consequence of intensive re-sharpening. The convex side edges of some axes are also probably due to repeated re-sharpening. The impression that the Galta 3 axes are produced according to mental schemes is strengthened by the fact that 9 out of 19 specimens have worked necks (see tab. 2).

Three axes made according to the Ertebølle system seem to have been carried out by untrained technicians. It could be interpreted as if the operation system was known "in theory" – i.e. a person having knowledge but not know-how (cf. Pelegrin 1990) – and therefore was still lacking a certain level of practical competence. This may especially be the case with specimen d, made of senon-like flint (see Fig. 27 d and tab. 3), since poor execution of the "ideal" shape cannot be explained by low quality raw material.

The choice of raw material for flake axes is worth some comments. Respectively, specimens 9, 6 and 4 are made of intermediary, senon-like and danien-like material (tab. 3). The majority of intermediary material may somehow reflect this type of flint as a preferred material for flake axe production in this cultural historical situation. What I have defined as "intermediary" also characterises the total number of 10 axes from the Ahrensburgian site Skiftesvik loc. 142 in Hordaland (Warås 2001, 101 and pers. comm.).

Debris from flake axe production. Series 10 represents the only clear evidence of the use of a hard hammer technique, and the intention must have been to produce quite thick big flakes. The flakes from series 10 resemble a large number of the flakes in the Galta material. They represent the 'macro flakes' typical of Fosna sites in general (e.g. Indrelid 1978, 151). This artifact category is often the most noticeable element in surface collections of Early Mesolithic sites in western Norway. Series 10 and other macro flakes must be seen as related to the production of flake axes. There is no other tool category that could explain the presence of macro flakes (i.e. 'skiver'). Indeed, no direct evidence exists, such as refits between flake axe and macro flakes exists from Galta 3. A refitted connection of these elements is, however, present from the Early Mesolithic site Stunner in Akershus, Southeast-Norway (Fuglestvedt 1999, Fig. 4 c). Series 16 relates to a further stage of the flake axe production, i.e. the shaping of the side edges. The flakes produced by this operation exhibit a typical wing-formed shape. These are well known in South-Scandinavia from the archaeological record as well as from experimental archaeology (Johansson 1990, 24; Petersen 1993, 133).

DISCUSSION

Dating of flake axes. The Galta 3 flake axes are mainly produced by a system of manufacture comparable to the much younger Ertebølle axes. A relevant question could be whether this represents a chronological phenomenon, involving the Ertebølle system of manufacture being used in the Ahrensburgian period and then later being superseded by the Barmose system of manufacture in the Early Magelmose phase (see Fischer 1996, s. 160f, Fig. 2). In my opinion, the two systems of manufacture are not, in this context, bound to a time scale. If we consider a 'tool-maker's perspective' the two systems of manufacture represent different "routes" to a defined end: this end being a sense of how a flake axe should and could look. The Barmose and Ertebølle systems could in this way be translated to different schema opératoires of Late Upper Palaeolithic / Early Mesolithic flake axe production.

Traditionally the flake axe is not known as an Ahrensburgian element. The presence of flake axes in collections from Ahrensburgian sites in Denmark and North Germany are explained as later disturbances, due to a tradition on the North European plain in which flake axes are exclusively known as Mesolithic (Early Maglemose and Ertebølle). At Galta 3, flake axes occur in combination with a tool assemblage and technology defined as Ahrensburgian, a fact that cannot be overlooked. Also the dating of the site covers the Ahrensburgian era (see Introduction). It is also worthwhile mentioning that a flake axe was found on the border between sediment unit 1 and 2, a position that does not suggest an age close to the younger limit of the period of habitation (9 800 BP).

Lately, the Hensbacka phase of the West Swedish Stone Age has been divided into an older and a younger phase, the first one dated to 10 500/ 10 000 - 9 700 BP (Kindgren 1995, 179). The older limit of this phase could of course be discussed (see Warås 2001, 68 pp), but what is interesting in this connection is that early Preboreal assemblages in West Sweden contain flake axes, along with artifact elements typical of the Galta 3 collection. Furthermore, flake and core axes are common elements in East-Ahrensburgian contexts in Lithuania (Zhilin 1996, s. 277). Returning to West Norway it should be worth noting that the formerly mentioned site, Skiftesvik loc. 142, has produced flake axes and core axes, the latter of the so-called Lerberg type (Larsson 1997). These elements occur in context with tanged points closely reminiscent of the so called Hintersee-type (Taute 1968, s. 12, abb. 1). The Skiftesvik site is probably younger than the Galta 3 site, according to the shore line displacement curve estimated to 9700 – 9500 BP (Warås 2001, 81). Skiftesvik and Galta are, however, only representatives of what appears to be a common trait in the first half of the Preboreal chronozone in North Europe, i.e. the co-existence of flake axes, core axes and tanged points (Ibid.).

Based on the background of evidence from Galta 3 and contemporaneous sites, it can be stated that flake and core axes should be understood as an Ahrensburgian element. It is interesting to note that at the high mountain site complex of Myrvatnet in South West Norway, no flake axes have been found (Bang-Andersen 1990). When taking into account published works, neither are flake axes represented in Ahrensburg (inland) contexts on the European continent (e.g. Fischer 1982; Hartz 1987; Rust 1943; Taute 1968; Tromnau 1975). It is thus tempting to interpret the flake axe as a coastal phenomenon within this group. However, this picture changes when actually examining the assemblages.[3] In the collections from Bonderup, Stellmoor and Teltwisch-Mitte, flake axes are physically present, but explained away as later elements, i.e. Barmosian or Ertebølleian (e.g. Tromnau 1975: 54).

---

3 In October 1998 the author, accompanied by students Morten Kutschera and Tor Arne Warås from the University of Bergen, made a study trip, in order to examine various assemblages at the Nationalmuseet in Copenhagen, and at the Landesmuseum in Schleswig.

Fig. 26. A selection of flake axes from Galta 3 (see text and Table 3 for description).

A collection of stray finds from Stellmoor Hügel contains 24 flake axes (see also Warås 2001, 73p and Fig. 22). The dating of these surface finds is of course problematic. At Teltwisch-Mitte, however, a flake axe and a core axe – and two side edge flakes – were found to have proveniences within the major find concentration areas. In other words, these artifacts indicate production sequences connected to the manufacture or maintenance of axes and they are situated within the main activity area of the site (see Tromnau 1975, Abb. 23). If these elements are regarded "Mesolithic", in the sense of Maglemosian or later, they stand alone as later disturbances at the site. This leads to the following question: How likely would it be, that younger Ahrensburgian sites were visited in later periods just for one purpose; the manufacture of flake axes?

If we tentatively conclude that flake axes are likely to appear at inland sites in South Scandinavia – as they do at coastal sites on the Scandinavian Peninsula – and simultaneously regard flake axes as a young element

within the Ahrensburg group, it gives credence to the idea that this artifact is connected to wood work. According to both local and generalized pollen curves worked out for the part of Rogaland (Paus 1988, Fig. 10; 1989, Fig. 9) where the Galta 3 site is situated, 10 000 BP marks the transition from 'open birch vegetation' to 'birch forest'. The absence of flake axes from Preboreal highland sites lends credibility to this hypothesis. If we regard the flake axe as a young element, it also gives sense to this artifact's absence at clearly older Ahrensburg sites on the continent, like Sølbjerg 1 (Petersen & Johansen 1996) and Alt Duvenstedt (Clausen 1996), along with its presumed presence at sites like Bonderup, Teltwich-Mitte and Stellmoor.

AHRENSBURG VERSUS FOSNA ONCE AGAIN

Since the detection of the 'Fosna culture' in Norway, flake axes have been considered a typical part of

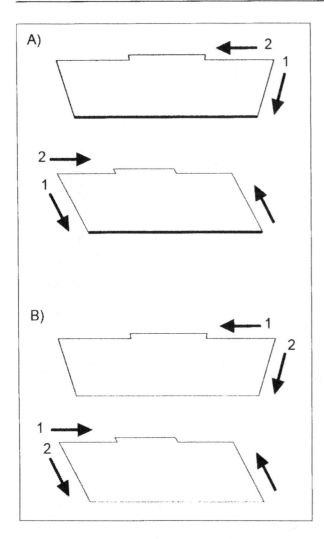

Fig. 27. Flake axe production: System of manufacture: a) Ertebølle system, b) Barmose system (Fischer unpublished, ill.: Stine Melvold).

these assemblages. However, as demonstrated here, the presence of flake axes does not make a Fosna definition of Galta 3 compelling.

Similar to the large amount of debris stemming from blade production with low quality flint, the manufacture of flake axes has produced high quantities of debris, both regarding number and the size of pieces, leading to descriptions of the Fosna phase as a period involving an "extensive use of flint" (Indrelid 1978, 151). The occurrence of this technology may have contributed to giving the sites a coarse appearance as well. In the literature 'macroflakes' as part of the Fosna definition (Bjerck 1986, 107) do not seem to be recognized

as related to flake axe production. Traditionally, the characteristic wing-shaped side edge removals (flakes) are not recognized at all. The presence of these elements as a more or less local phenomenon related to the Fosna concept, should rather, until more evidence is provided, be understood as a tool technology typical of certain geographical, or rather vegetational contexts within the Ahrensburg group's area.

Preliminary conclusion. It has here been stated that the differences in the Galta 3 material and probably other early sites, as compared to the classical or typical sites in North-Germany, are due to an over-representation of high quantities of coarse rest products. This is partly a consequence of 1) the use of local raw material in blade production and 2) the production of flake axes. Because of better technological possibilities for utilisation, the senon-like flint is under represented at the site. However, the fewer examples of high quality flint usage, reveals the skilled competence of the knappers and the Ahrensburgian affinity appears even clearer than in refitted series of coarser material. Coarseness in West-Norwegian material should not be understood as related to a lower, marginal or coarse technological practice.

In this article, the point of departure was the recognition that the site Galta 3 yields a tool assemblage (especially points) and a dating associated to the Ahrensburg group of the North European plain (Høgestøl 1995; Høgestøl et al. 1995; Prøsch-Danielsen & Høgestøl 1995). By examining a selection of refitted material from Galta 3, I have demonstrated that there exists a clear Late Upper Palaeolithic connection in blade technology as well. Lately, this notion of a coastal or non-continental version of the Ahrensburgian group, is more or less implicitly expressed in recent literature on the earliest settlement of Scandinavia (see Cullberg 1996, s. 188; Fischer 1996, s. 165; Høgestøl et al. 1995, s. 44; Kindgren 1996, s. 202; Nordqvist 1995, 188; Schmitt 1995, s. 168; see also Fuglestvedt 1999; 2001). In other words, the Ahrensburg group is extended both in space, as well as in time, since new datings make it "intrude" on the first part of the Mesolithic (>9 700 -9 500?).

Having stated that there is practically no divergence between Ahrensburgian finds in West Norway or East Norway / West Sweden, there is no reason why the Stellmoor find – or any other site in North

Germany or Denmark – should serve as a "standard" by which assemblages in the former area should be interpreted. There is, in principle, no reason why the Stellmoor find could not be described as a typical Early Fosna collection. For in Norwegian terms, this is in fact what it is (see also discussions in Warås 2001). When I prefer to use the term 'Ahrensburg' it is because it does not give the rather local associations as does 'Fosna', but rather non-regional and non-national connotations.

WHAT EXACTLY IS THE AHRENSBURGIAN GROUP?

In this article I have used the term Ahrensburg to refer to a group of things, meaning a combination of tools and artifacts resulting from a certain technology. In conclusion, I would like to suggest that the Ahrensburgian "culture" is not only something which included a combination of objects, but a number of human beings who understood themselves as a group.

There are several ways of manufacturing flint tools, but every Stone Age tradition has certain schema opératoires, or inherited skills, for accomplishing the desired results. In the daily exercising of technical practice, human beings were perpetuating and performing this tradition, which included raw material knowledge, a special motor ability, a sense of esthetics and technical experience. The regular repetition of technical methods that appear in an assemblage are, deep down, the lost fingerprints of what was once a living tradition (Madsen 1992, 94). Achieving technical ability is part of a general cultural learning process. The importance of studying technical competence, is thus a way of illustrating past people's cultural affinity. For if technology is viewed as "a mediated understanding of how to proceed under certain circumstances" (see Edmonds 1990, 56, with references), then the normative aspects, i.e. the aspects of technology as a social practice, emerges. Thus "competence" becomes part of an embodied knowledge that connects the people of a certain site to a wider human and geographical sphere.

Part of the approach in this article has been to study technical competence. Not explicitly expressed, it was important to reveal a certain technical competence in order to link Galta 3 to the classical Ahrensburgian

sites. However, my interpretations are not solely built on the recognition of a similar technical practice in Northern Europe.

As archaeologists we do not understand the past without assumptions. Underlying the "Ahrensburgian approach" is a prejudice – in the hermeneutic sense of the word (i.e. pre-judgement, see Gilje & Grimen 1995, 148) – which views the Late Palaeolithic and Early Mesolithic as a period when human groups where highly mobile and moved over distances hard for modern people to imagine. Sites in East Norway (Fuglestvedt 1999; Skar & Coulson 1987), West Norway (e.g. Fuglestvedt 2001; Høgestøl 1995; Høgestøl et al. 1995; Nærøy 1994; 1995; 2000; Kutschera & Warås 2000; Warås 2001), as well as inland (Bang-Andersen 1990; 2003a; 2003b) all indicate short occupations, lasting perhaps only a few days. This mobility may have involved movements all the way to Finnmark in Northern Norway (see Woodman 1993; Fuglestvedt 2005a; 2005b; Grydeland 2005).

By using the example of Galta 3, the continental European origin of this group is confirmed by a common technological practice. Recent research reveals more examples of a Late Upper Palaeolithic / Early Mesolithic connection between the continental and non-continental parts of North Europe (Fischer 1996; Fuglestvedt 1999; 2001; Kutschera 1999; Warås 2001).

It is important to stress that giving the group at Galta 3 a "continental origin" is not meant to indicate a permanent immigration to West Norway took place. Rather we should view Northern Europe as a total habitation area, meaning that people were frequently returning to continental Europe. In the beginning the Northern European plain was most likely the main habitation area (Welinder 1981).

In my opinion, the Fosna concept does not provide an adequate understanding of what the earliest site material in Norway really is. It gives too much local, or rather national connotations (see Fuglestvedt 1999). In opposition to this, the 'Ahrensburg culture' – in spite of its origin in a local place –connotes and connects large areas of the North-European plain in the Late Upper Palaeolithic period. The concept of an Ahrensburg group thus provides a better understanding of the assemblages discussed in this paper. The "detection" of this formerly Late Upper Palaeolithic group (now also including the first part of the Mesolithic) in the northern parts of Scandinavia, gives an extension of our understanding of the "Ahrensburgian" way of life. Erasing modern national borders gives a better picture of the situation, as in the Late Palaeolithic and Early Mesolithic of North-Europe, these kinds of borders did not exist. This Late Upper Palaeolithic / Early Mesolithic group of people embodied the same schema opératoires wherever their journeys were made. Consequently they performed similar chaînes operatoires in continental Europe as they did on the Scandinavian Peninsula.

Acknowledgements. Mari Høgestøl kindly let me use the Galta 3 assemblage for study in connection with my doctoral work. The refitting of parts of the Galta 3-assemblage was carried out by the author during two periods in 1993 and 1996/97. This work was partly financed by the Museum of Archaeology, Stavanger and the Norwegian Research Council. The evaluation of the Galta 3 work chains was carried out in a work shop in March 1997 at the Museum of Archaeology, in which Anders Fischer, Morten Kutschera and the author participated. At the same institution a work shop studying a number of West Norwegian sites was arranged by Morten Kutschera, Tor Arne Warås, Arne Johan Warås and myself in September 1998. Lasse Jaksland, Axel Degn Johansson, Bo Knarrström, Stephan Larsson and Bengt Norqvist, attended the work-shop. Thanks to every single one of you! In connection with our research travel to the National Museum in Copenhagen and the Landesmuseum in Schleswig in October 1999, we were well taken care of by Peter Vang Petersen and Klaus Bokelman. Thanks to both of you! In addition to the persons mentioned, I would like to thank Sheila Coulson, Berit Valentin Eriksen, Lykke Johansen and Birgitte Skar for their inspiring work in this field of study.

REFERENCES

Anundsen, K., 1996: The Physical Conditions for Earliest Settlement during the Last Deglaciation in Norway. In Larsson, L. (ed.): The Earliest Settlement of Scandinavia and its neighbouring areas. Acta Archaeologica Lundensia. Series in 8°, No. 24. Stockholm: Almquist & Wiksell, 207-217.

Bang-Andersen, S., 1990: The Myrvatn Group, a Preboreal Find-Complex in Southwest-Norway. In Vermeersch, P.M. & Van Peer, P. (eds.): Contributions to the Mesolithic in Europe. Leuven: Leuven University Press, 215-226.

- 2003a: Encircling the Living Space of Early Postglacial reindeer hunters in the interior of southern Norway. In Larsson, L. et al. (eds.): Mesolithic on the Move. Oxford: Oxbow Books, 193-204.

- 2003b: Southwest Norway at the Pleistocene/Holocene Transition: Landscape Development, Colonization, Site Types, Settlement Patterns. Norwegian Archaeological Review, Vol. 36, No. 1, 5 – 25.

Bjerck, H. B., 1986: The Fosna-Nøstvet Problem. A Consideration of Archaeological Units and Chronozones in the South Norwegian Mesolithic Period. Norwegian Archaeological Review, Vol. 19, No. 2. Oslo: Norwegian University Press, 103-121.

Clausen, I. 1996: Alt Duvenstedt LA 121, Schleswig-Holstein – Occurrence of the Ahrensburgian Culture in soils of the Allerød Interstadial. A Prelimnary Report. In: Larsson, L. (ed.): The Earliest Settlement of Scandinavia and its relationship with neighboring areas. Acta Archaeologica Lundensia. Series in 8°, No. 24. Stockholm: Almquist & Wiksell International, 99-110.

Cullberg, C., 1996: West-Sweden: On the Earliest Settlements. In Larsson, L. (ed.): The Earliest Settlement of Scandinavia and its relationship with neighbouring areas. Acta Archaeologica Lundensia. Series in 8°, No. 24. Stockholm: Almquist & Wiksell International, 177-189.

Edmonds, M., 1990: Description, understanding and the chaîne opératoire. Technology in the humanities. Archaeological Review from Cambridge Volume 9:1. Summer 1990. Cambridge: Department of Archaeology, 55-70.

Eriksen, B. Valentin 2000: Chaîne opératoire – den operative proces og kunsten at tænke som en flinthugger. I: Eriksen, B. Valentin (red.): Flintstudier. En håndbog i systematiske analyser af flintinventarer. Århus: Aarhus universitetsforlag, 75-100.

Fischer, A., 1978: På sporet af overgangen mellem palæoliticum og mesoliticum i Sydskandinavien. Hikuin 4. Moesgård: Forlaget hikuin, 27-50.

- 1982: Bonderup-bopladsen: Det manglende led mellem dansk palæolitikum og mesolitikum? Antikvariske studier 5. Fortidsminder og Bygningsbevaring. Fredningsstyrelsen. København, 87-103.

- 1988: A Late Palaeolithic Flint Workshop at Egtved, East Jutland - a glimpse of the Federmesser Culture in Denmark. Journal of Danish Archaeology vol. 7 1988. Odense: Odense University Press, 7-23.

- 1996: At the Border of Human Habitat. The Late Palaeolithic and Early Mesolithic in Scandinavia. In Larsson, L. (ed.): The Earliest Settlement of Scandinavia and its relationship with neighbouring areas. Acta Archaeologica Lundensia. Series in 8°, No. 24. Stockholm: Almquist & Wiksell International, 157-176.

- Unpublished: Åmose-klassifikationskoden. Et edb-orienteret beskrivelsessystem for genstande fra dansk senpalæolitikum, mesolitikum og tidligneolitikum. Fredningsstyrelsen. København.

Fischer, A., & Tauber H., 1986: New C-14 Datings of Late Palaeolithic Cultures from Northwestern Europe. Journal of Danish Archaeology vol. 5 1986. Odense: Odense University Press, 7-13.

Fuglestvedt, I., 1999: The Early Mesolithic site Stunner, Southeast-Norway. A discussion of Late Upper Palaeolithic/Early Mesolithic chronology and cultural relations in Scandinavia. To be published in: The Mesolithic of Central Scandinavia. Universitetets Oldsaksamlings Skrifter. Oslo.

- 2005a [2001]: Pionerbosetningens fenomenologi. Sørvest-Norge og Nord-Europa 10 200 / 10 000 – 9 500 BP. AmS-NETT 6 (www.ark. museum.no) Museum of Archaeology, Stavanger.

- 2005b: Contact and communication in Northern Europe 10 200 – 9 000/ 8 500 BP – a phenomenological approach to the connection between technology, skill and landscape. In: Knutsson, H (ed.): Pioneer settlements and colonization processes in the Barents region. Vuollerim Papers on Hunter-gatherer Archaeology Volume 1. Vuollerim, 79-96.

Grydeland, S.E. 2005: The pioneers of Finnmark – from the earliest coastal settlements to the encounter with the inland people of Northern Finland. In: Knutsson, H (ed.): Pioneer settlements and colonization processes in the Barents region. Vuollerim Papers on Hunter-gatherer Archaeology Volume 1. Vuollerim, 43-77.

Gilje, N., & Grimen, H., 1993: Samfunnsvitenskapens forutsetninger. Innføring i samfunnsvitenskapens vitenskapsfilosofi. Oslo: Universitetsforlaget.

Gjerland, B., 1990: Arkeologiske undersøkingar på Haugsneset og Ognøy i Tysvær og Bokn kommunar, Rogaland. AmS-Rapport 5. Stavanger: Arkeologisk museum i Stavanger.

Hartz, S., 1987: Neue spätpaleolitiche Fundplätze bei Ahrenshöft, Kreis Nordfriesland. Offa Band 44 - 1987. Neumünster: Karl Wachholtz Verlag, 5-52.

Høgestøl, M., 1995: Arkeologiske undersøkelser i Rennesøy kommune, Rogaland, Sørvest-Norge. AmS-Varia 23. Stavanger: Arkeologisk museum i Stavanger.

Høgestøl, M., Berg, E., & Prøsch-Danielsen, L., 1995: Strandbundne Ahrensburg- og Fosnalokaliteter på Galta-halvøya, Rennesøy kommune, Sørvest-Norge. Arkeologiske Skrifter No. 8 - 1995. Bergen: Arkeologisk institutt, Universitetet i Bergen, 44-64.

Indrelid, S., 1978: Mesolithic economy and settlement patterns in Norway. In Mellars, P. (ed.): The Early Postglacial Settlement of Northern Europe. London: Duckworth, 147-176.

Johansson, A.D., 1990: Barmosegruppen. Præboreale bopladsfund i Sydsjælland. Århus: Aarhus Universitetsforlag.

Kutschera, M. & Warås, T.A. 2000: Steinalderlokaliteten på "Breiviksklubben" på Bratt-Helgaland i Karmøy kommune. I Løken, T. (red.): Åsgard – Natur- og kulturhistoriske undersøkelser langs en gassrør-trasé i Karmøy og Tysvær, Rogaland. Ams-Rapport 14. Arkeologisk museum i Stavanger, 61-96.

Kindgren, H., 1995: Hensbacka-Hogen-Hornborgasjön: Early Mesolithic coastal and inland settlements in western Sweden. In Fischer, A. (ed.): Man & Sea in the Mesolithic. Coastal settlement above and below present sea level. Oxbow Monograph 53. Oxford: Oxbow Books, 171-184.

-1996: Reindeer or seals? Some Late Palaeolithic sites in central Bohuslän. In Larsson, L. (ed.): The Earliest Settlement of Scandinavia and its neighbouring areas. Acta Archaeologica Lundensia. Series in 8°, No. 24. Stockholm: Almquist & Wiksell, 191-205.

Larsson, S. 1997: Lerbergsyxan. Regional innovation och utveckling under tidigmesolitikum. Unpublished C-thesis. Göteborgs Universitet.

Madsen, B., 1992: Hamburgkulturens flintteknologi i Jels. In Holm, J. & Rieck, F.: Istidsjægere ved Jelssøerne. Hamburgkulturen i Danmark. Haderslev: Skrifter fra Museumsrådet for Sønderjyllands amt, 91-131.

- 1996: Late Palaeolithic Cultures of South Scandinavia - Tools, Tradition and Technology. In Larsson, L. (ed.): The Earliest Settlement of Scandinavia and its relationship with neighbouring areas. Acta Archaeologica Lundensia. Series in 8 , No. 24. Stockholm: Almquist & Wiksell International, 61-73.

Mikkelsen, E., 1975: Mesolithic in South-eastern Norway. Norwegian Archaeological Review, Vol. 8, No. 1. Oslo: Scandinavian University Press, 19-35.

Nordqvist, B., 1995: The Mesolithic settlements of the West Coast of Sweden - with special emphasis on chronology and topography of coastal settlements. In Fischer, A. (ed.): Man & Sea in the Mesolithic. Coastal settlements above and below present sea level. Oxbow Monograph 53. Oxford: Oxbow Books, 185-196.

Nærøy, A.J., 1994: Troll-prosjektet. Arkeologiske undersøkelser på Kollsnes, Øygarden k., Hordaland, 1989-1992. Arkeologiske rapporter 19. Arkeologisk institutt, Universitetet i Bergen.

- 1995: Early Mesolithic Site Structure in western Norway – a case study. Universitetets Oldsaksamling. Årbok 1993 / 1994. Oslo, 59-77.

- 2000: Stone Age Living Spaces in Western Norway. BAR International Series 857. Oxford.

Paus, A. 1988: Late Weichselian vegetation, climate and floral migration at Sandvikvatn, North Rogaland, southwestern Norway. Boreas Vol. 17,113-139.

- 1989: Late Weichselian vegetation, climate and floral migration at Eigebakken, South Rogaland, southwestern Norway. Review of Palaebotany and Palynology 61, 177-203.

Pelegrin, J. 1990: Prehistoric Lithic Technology: Some aspects of research. Technology in the humanities. Archaeological Review from Cambridge Volume 9:1. Summer 1990. Cambridge: Department of Archaeology, 116-125.

Petersen, P. Vang, 1993: Flint fra Danmarks oldtid. København: Høst & Søn / Nationalmuseet.

Petersen, P. Vang & Johansen, L. 1996: Tracking Late Glacial reindeer hunters in eastern Denmark. In: Larsson, L. (ed.): The Earliest Settlement of Scandinavia and its relationship with neighboring areas. Acta Archaeologica Lundensia. Series in 8°, No. 24. Stockholm: Almquist & Wiksell International, 75-88.

Prøsch-Danielsen, L., & Høgestøl, M., 1995: A coastal Ahrensburgian site found at Galta, Southwest-Norway. In Fischer, A. (ed.): Man & Sea in the Mesolithic. Coastal settlement above and below present sea level. Oxbow Monograph 53. Oxford: Oxbow Books, 123-130.

Rust, A., 1943: Die Alt- und Mittelsteinzeitlichen Funde von Stellmoor. Neumünster: Karl Wachholtz Verlag.

Schild, R., 1984: Terminal Paleolithic of the North European Plain: A Review of Lost Chances, Potential and Hopes. In Wendorf, F. & Close, A.E. (eds.): Advances in World Archaeology. Volume 3. London: Academic Press, 193-274.

Schmitt, L., 1995: The West Swedish Hensbacka: a maritime adaptation and a seasonal expression of the North-Central European Ahrensburgian? In Fischer, A. (ed.): Man & Sea in the Mesolithic. Coastal settlement above and below present sea level. Oxbow Monograph 53. Oxford: Oxbow Books, 161-170.

Skar, B., & Coulson, S., 1987: The Early Mesolithic Site Rørmyr II. A re-examination of one of the Høgnipen sites, SE-Norway. Acta Archaeologica Vol. 56 - 1985. København: Munksgaard, 167-183.

Taute, W., 1968: Die Stielspitzen-Gruppen im nördlichen Mittel-Europa. Ein Beitrag zur Kenntnis der späten Altsteinzeit. Fundamenta. Reihe A. Band 5. Köln/Graz: Böhlau Verlag.

Tromnau, G., 1975: Neue Ausgrabungen im Ahrensburger Tunneltal. Ein Beitrag zur Erforschung des Jungpaläolithikums im Nordwesteuropäischen Flachland. Neumünster: Karl Wachholtz Verlag.

Warås, T.A. 2001: Vestlandet i tidleg preboreal tid. Fosna, Ahrensburg eller vestnorsk tidlegneolitikum? Unpublished thesis, Arkeologisk institutt, Universietetet i Bergen.

Welinder, S., 1981: Den kontinentaleuropeiska bakgrunden till Norges äldsta stenålder. Universitetets Oldsaksamling. Årbok 1980/1981. Oslo, 21-34.

Woodman, P., 1993: The Komsa Culture. A Re-examination of its Position in the Stone Age of Finnmark. Acta Archaeologica, Vol. 63 - 1992. København: Munksgaard, 57-76.

Zagorska, I., 1996: Late Palaeolithic Finds in the Daugava River Valley. In Larsson, L. (ed.): The Earliest Settlement of Scandinavia and its relationship with neighbouring areas. Acta Archaeologica Lundensia. Series in 8°, No. 24. Stockholm: Almquist & Wiksell International, 263-272.

Zhilin, M.G., 1996: The Western Part of Russia in the Late Palaeolithic - Early Mesolithic. In Larsson, L. (ed.): The Earliest Settlement of Scandinavia and its relationship with neighbouring areas. Acta Archaeologica Lundensia. Series in 8°, No. 24. Stockholm: Almquist & Wiksell International, 273-284.

Author's address
IAKH/#Archaeology, Oslo University
P.O. Box 1008 Blindern
N-0315 Oslo
Norway
ingrid.fuglestvedt@iakh.uio

ARTEFACT / TOOL TYPE	NUMBER
Flake axes	19
Tanged points	82
Single edged points	89
Fragments of tanged or single edged points	17
Lanceolates	7
Simple lanceolates	35
Zonhoven points	21
Fragments of unidetified points	26
Fragments of possible points	23
Probable and possible burin spalls	17
Knives and scrapers (blades)	17
Retouched blade and blade fragments	21
Retouched flakes	45
Retouched fragments	2
Blades, flakes and fragments with working edge edges	52
Unifacial cores with one platform	36
Unifacial cores with two opposed platforms	9
Multifacial and amorphous cores	38
Core fragments, platformrejuvenation blades/flakes/tablets	193
Blades and blade fragments	682
Flakes	13 624
Fragments	1 827
Total	17 539

Table. 1. List of artifacts from Galta 3 (modified after Høgestøl 1995, 50).

FIND NUMBER	FLINT QUALITY	SYSTEM OF MANUFACTURE	WORKED NECK
a	intermediary	Ertebølle, symmetric	X
b	intermediary	Ertebølle, symmetric	X
c	intermediary	Ertebølle, symmetric	X
d	senon-like	Ertebølle, symmetric, incompetent	X
e	intermediary	Ertebølle, symmertic, incompetent	
f	danien-like	Ertebølle, symmetric, incompetent	X
g	danien-like	Ertebølle, asymmetric	
h	intermediary	Ertebølle, asymmetric	X
i	senon-like	Ertebølle, asymmetric	X
j	danien-like	Ertebølle, asymmetric	
k	intermediary	close to Barmose, symmetric	
l	senon-like	probably Barmose, asymmetric	X
m	senon-like	no special system	X
n	danien-like	? system erased, intensive resharpened	
o	intermediary	? system erased, intensive resharpened	
p	intermediary	? system erased, intensive resharpened	
q	senon-like	? system erased, intensive resharpened	
r	intermediary	transformed into "core axe" by resharpening	
s	senon-like	transformed into "core axe" by resharpening	

Table. 2. List of flake axes from Galta 3, with information about flint quality, system of manufacture and presence of worked neck.

Acta Archaeologica vol. 78:2, 2007, pp 111-142
All rights reserved

Copyright 2007
ACTA ARCHAEOLOGICA
ISSN 0065-001X

THE NORTHERN PERIPHERY OF THE TRB
GRAVES AND RITUAL DEPOSITS IN NORWAY

EINAR ØSTMO

THE FUNNEL BEAKER CULTURE & THE BEGINNINGS OF FARMING

The presence in Norway of archaeological finds attributable to the Funnel Beaker Culture (TRB) was the subject of a much-quoted work by Erik Hinsch published in 1955 (Hinsch 1955). In later years, the Norwegian TRB has been discussed in general surveys by Egil Mikkelsen and the present author (Mikkelsen 1984; Østmo 1990; Glørstad 2005; Østmo and Skogstrand 2006; also see the summary by Boaz 1998, 43ff). The interpretation of these finds as indicative of Early Neolithic (EN) agriculture in the Oslo Fiord region of SE Norway has not really been questioned since the controversy between the geologist Andreas M. Hansen and the young A. W. Brøgger a hundred years ago, Brøgger maintaining that the finds of point-butted, thin-butted and thick-butted flint axes concentrated in farming districts to such a degree that they must have been left by an established farming population (Brøgger 1906, esp. 139ff). Hansen, who rather like Christopher Prescott in recent years, was sceptical of a Norwegian Neolithic, however also admitted an exception concerning "the southeast region, where the few graves with stone implements might be accompanied by other genuine northern stone age finds", as he put it (present author's translation from Hansen 1904, 99 and 146); again like Prescott, who while mischievously asking "Was there really a Neolithic in Norway?" nevertheless restricts his doubts to the part of Norway outside the Oslo fiord region immediately affected by TRB influences (Prescott 1996, 77, 83 and 85). Even more recently, Håkon Glørstad has put forward arguments in favour of a more widespread occurrence of TRB in Norway as far west as Rogaland, including both material culture, parts of Neolithic economy and certain elements of ritual and

symbolic behaviour, i.e. the possibly sacrificial deposition of locally produced stone axes of TRB or "sub-TRB" (the present author's expression) types (Glørstad 2005; similarly Hallgren 2005).

These contributions are part of the long and ongoing debate concerning the nature and extent of the Norwegian TRB and EN farming (e. g. Bjerck 1988 with comments). This remains an important issue in Norwegian archaeology, the more so as new and illuminating as well as intriguing discoveries have been made in recent years, providing new fuel for the discussions. So, there may still be room for considering the more precise nature of the historical events indicated by the TRB in Norway. In this paper, two general themes will be considered. One concerns the dynamic nature of the TRB, which spanned some one thousand years according to recent chronology (3850-2800 BC, summarized in Koch 1998, 180ff), and the other regards the marginal character of the Scandinavian TRB, which certainly in Norway reached its northern limit. Special attention will be given to finds which may be interpreted as ritual deposits - either votive offerings or graves, and especially the megalithic graves of Southeast Norway, which may fairly be considered as monuments to the floruit of the Norwegian TRB.

Regarding the chronological framework for studying the Norwegian TRB, a somewhat simplified chronology will be adopted here, compared to some of the more ambitious chronologies which have been developed in South Scandinavia (Becker 1948; 1955b), however with many revisions in later years (e.g. Madsen og Petersen 1984; Nielsen 1985). Karl-Göran Sjögren in a recent work distinguishes between an early period, called "Formative" and embracing the years 5000-4700 BP (uncal.), followed by a middle or "Climax" period during the years 4700-4400 BP and a late "Degenerative" period in 4400-4200. The middle period was when the megalithic graves were built (Sjögren 2003, 14f). This chronology is reminiscent of the ceramic chronology proposed by Anna Lagergren-Olsson concerning settlement site finds in Scania, with an early period of small imprints (4000-3500 calBC), a middle period of belly lines (3500-3100 calBC) and a late period of tooth stamps (3100-2800 calBC) (Lagergren-Olsson 2003, 197ff). A similar three-partite chronology also seems adaptable to Norwegian conditions, in that the Norwegian material allows the identification of an early period before building of megalithic graves commenced, and with pottery decorated with small imprints just as in Scania and elsewhere in South Scandinavia, followed by a period when the TRB influence reached a peak and indeed included erection of megalithic monuments, and a late period when the TRB influence was much weaker and of a different, regional character. The Scanian pottery styles however do not adapt all that well to Norwegian conditions, and indeed it would seem from Lagergren-Olsson's own material that a period which might be called that of the cord stamp (tvärsnodd in Lagergren-Olsson's Swedish) may be identified, embracing the earlier part of her middle period, that of the belly lines, cf. Lagergren-Olsson 2003, 200, fig. 20), perhaps the years 3500-3300 calBC. As cord stamp-decorated pottery certainly is of significance to the understanding of the formation of the Norwegian TRB, it would appear reasonable to take this aspect of the chronology into account here. Concerning the early, "Formative" period, it would seem to embrace all the various periods, phases or styles claimed in the pre-megalithic TRB in South Scandinavia. The late, "Degenerative" period would embrace MN A II-V, which in their strict South Scandinavian sense seem to be of little relevance north of Scania (Lagergren-Olsson 2003, 204). However, rather than adopting Sjögren's somewhat charged period names, we shall follow Lagergren-Olsson's suggestion and use the more neutral terms Early, Middle and Late TRB to denote the three periods which have been described, with the qualification that the Middle period may be sub-divided in an Early Middle and a Late Middle period.

The Norwegian finds which may be attributed to the TRB are few enough for each one to be of paramount interest. In particular, this applies to settlement sites, ritual contexts including graves and indeed all finds of TRB pottery. There was a time not all that many years ago, when the only piece of undisputed TRB pottery in Norway was a potsherd of a late EN Virum-style vessel however without specified provenance which was part of a 19th century private collection acquired by the University Museum in Christiania (Oslo) in 1890 (Hinsch 1955, 71f). This situation is changing slowly, although TRB pottery is still scarce, as we shall see.

A summary of the source material available to the student of the Norwegian TRB may begin with the observation that settlement finds dominated by pottery decorated in TRB style remain few (Østmo and Skogstrand in prep.). Recently, however, several coastal sites with early Neolithic, arguably TRB pottery have been excavated at Svinesund on the Swedish-Norwegian border (Berget 2, Tørhaug 2002; Vestgård 3, K. B. Johansen 2004 and Vestgård 6, Jaksland and Tørhaug 2004). Otherwise there is one site at Lundvoll in Tune, Østfold which was discovered accidentally in 1983 and which has produced some Middle TRB pottery and a small collection of flint waste (No. C36796 a-f (1) in the museum register; Østmo 1988a, 154f). It remains quite uncertain, however, whether this was a settlement or a grave or for that matter none of the two. In the autumn of 2003, another site, possibly a settlement, with similar middle TRB pottery was discovered at Børsebakke in Rygge, Østfold. Yet another with quite similar pottery, at Bede in Sarpsborg, Østfold, came to light in 2007. Outside Østfold, two similar finds have come to light quite recently at Vøyenenga in Bærum just west of Oslo (Østmo and Skogstrand 2006) and in 2007 at Dønski in the same region. Otherwise, a few potsherds arguably belonging to the TRB have been claimed in hunter-gatherer (or perhaps rather fishing) settlement finds from both mountain and coastal sites all around the South Norwegian coast as far as north of Bergen (Fig. 1). However, the typical TRB funnel beaker profile and the characteristic Middle TRB belly lines still have been found only at the Narestø II settlement site in Arendal, Aust-Agder (C23892 ll, Nummedal og Bjørn 1930; cf. Hinsch 1955, 93f and 103; also Mikkelsen 1984, 106f

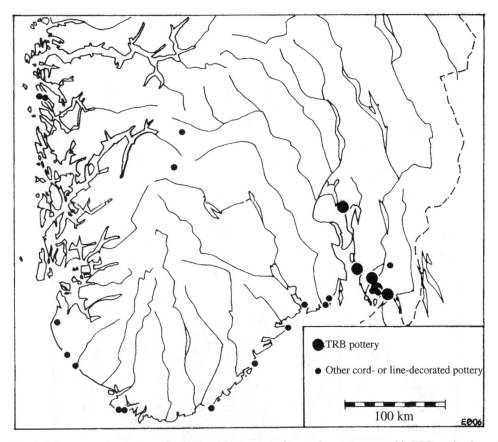

Fig. 1. Map of South Norwegian settlement sites with EN and MN pottery. Sites with certain or possible TRB potsherds are highlighted.

and Fig 10) and a recently excavated site at Skjoldnes in Farsund, Vest-Agder (personal communication from Stine Melvold). Elsewhere, the discussion has concerned small vessel fragments with impressed cord ornaments. Svein Indrelid and Asle Bruen Olsen have attributed such potsherds to the TRB in settlement site finds such as Nordmannslågen 526 (B12239) on the Hardangervidda mountain plateau and likewise the large Ramsvikneset (B11511; also B11256, 11369 and 11416) and Kotedalen (B14500-14505) coastal settlement sites just north of Bergen (Indrelid and Moe 1983; Olsen 1992). All these sites have indeed produced radiocarbon datings that would seem to fit reasonably well with the TRB. A similar situation exists elsewhere, too, for instance at well-known settlement sites like Holeheia in Klepp and Slettabø in Hå, both Rogaland (Skjølsvold 1977; 1980). However, when no other TRB material has been found, caution would seem to be in order. Cord impression ornaments cannot be claimed to be an unambiguous TRB cultural

element either, taking into account their presence in considerable quantity on what appears to be local pottery from a still mostly unpublished settlement site excavated in the 1970s by Perry Rolfsen at Hæstad in Lillesand, Aust-Agder (C38602; cf. Skjølsvold 1977, 236f; 1980, 51, note 1 and Mikkelsen 1984, 120, note 19 and illustrations of some of the pottery in Resi 2000, 20f, figs. 5 and 6). This site has been dated to c. 4500-4000 BP (Hufthammer 1997, 43), that is, approximately 3300-2500 BC in calendar years, and could represent an adaptation to the south Norwegian coast of the TRB or the early stages of a local development from such influences.

Rather than proving the presence of a clear-cut TRB of South Scandinavian type in a South Norwegian neolithic or "sub-neolithic" hunter-gatherer environment, such finds may serve to illustrate the comparative autonomy of the coastal hunters and fishermen of South Norway during the EN and MN - at least in archaeological terms, but arguably his-

Acta Archaeologica

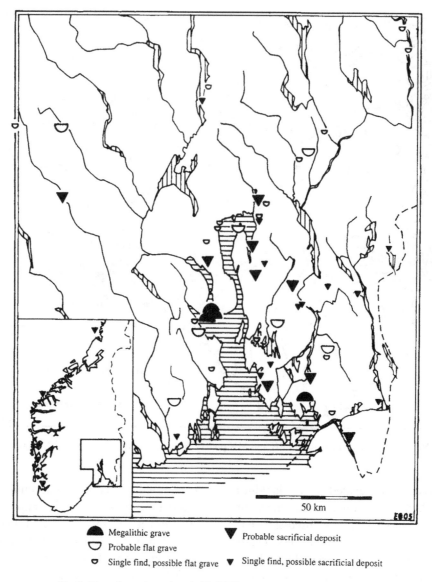

Fig. 2. Map of certain and probable TRB graves and hoards in Norway.

torically as well. It seems ever clearer that the more fully equipped TRB in the Oslo fiord region existed side by side with a local hunting and fishing culture present along most of the coast from North Bohuslän in West Sweden to Western Norway far north of Bergen (Fig. 1). No up-to-date comprehensive assessment has yet been published of this rapidly growing group of finds, but publications of individual sites are numerous, as are the views expressed about dating and interpretation of the material (2). Whether the whole or parts of these finds should be considered simply as

a South Norwegian local group of the TRB, or rather as a local stone age culture more or less strongly influenced by the South-Scandinavian TRB may be a purely academic point, but it may well prove fruitful to accord the TRB larger scope than has hitherto mostly been the case in the formation of this, in so many basic characteristics different cultural entity, at least in its early stages (cf. Olsen 1992; Glørstad 2005; Hallgren 2005). Those stages are characterized by pottery decorated with lines, pits and cord impressions (especially at Hæstad) and by transversal points (again especially at Hæstad and now also Berget 2 and other Svinesund sites) as well as tanged points and slate points, with calibrated radiocarbon ages embracing most of the 4th millennium BC. Pottery decorated with the on these sites ubiquitous cord-stamp ("whipped cord"), so common as to serve as a denominator of the whole group of finds or even culture, may according to some datings not belong to its earliest stages (mostly unpublished, but see Østmo 1993), but rather derive from TRB influences (the "Virum" style) during the Early Middle TRB.

When one is looking for more easily recognizable TRB finds to represent both the geographical distribution and the changing fortunes of the culture in Norway, one is left with single finds, mainly of stone axes, which are typical of the TRB and at the same time numerous enough to establish some feeling of statistical representativity. The main axe categories in question are the point-butted and thin- and thick-butted axes of flint and other stone and the polygonal and so-called double-edged types of battle-axes. Hinsch recognized a total of 384 such pieces in Norway (Hinsch 1955) and this number probably still gives a fair idea about the size of the material even if it certainly is too low.

In broad terms, the axe types may be dated to all of the previously outlines periods, and in consequence allow the identification of three main stages of the TRB in Norway. The earliest stage is represented by point-butted axes of flint and other stone and type I of polygonal battle-axes which are associated with the so-called "Oxie" or "A" phase of the South Scandinavian EN TRB (cf. Østmo 1998a). These types total 12 items in Norway, and these admittedly quite few finds have mostly been found east of the Oslo fiord, in the counties Østfold and the southern part of Akershus (the district of Follo) (a map may be found in Østmo 1986, 192).

The middle period comprises the main bulk of the Norwegian TRB finds, representing the remainder of the EN and the MNA I-II. These finds are the subject of maps prepared by Mikkelsen for his 1984 survey of the SE Norwegian TRB (Mikkelsen 1984, Figs. 5 and 7). As the finds defining this phase include some material associated with the early Svaleklint/Volling group in Denmark, there may be a degree of overlap with the Early TRB. Even so it remains quite clear that the TRB during this period still was

present foremost in the Oslo fiord region, however much more wide-spread than before and in greater strength. This has been substantiated by recent investigation of the finds kept in the archaeological museums in Stavanger, Bergen and Trondheim, which has shown that quite significant numbers of finds have been made both in Rogaland in SW Norway and to a lesser degree further up the west Norwegian coast, and, as has recently been demonstrated, in Trøndelag, middle Norway (Østmo 1999; 2000). It is the districts with a comparatively clement climate, combined with lightly tilled soils created by a combination of late glacial moraines and the conditions prevailing during the post-glacial land upheaval which have received the most dense concentrations of finds, certainly due to a preference for such soils for farming. Evidence for cerealia as well as pasture are present in pollen diagrams from Østfold and Vestfold from as early as the transition from the sub-atlantic to the sub-boreal climatic periods c. 4000 BC (Danielsen 1970; see also Østmo 1988a and 1998a).

The extent of the influence of the Late TRB in South Norway emerges from the distribution of finds of thick-butted flint axes and late types of double-edged battle axes. The distribution of such finds famously was interpreted by Hinsch (1955, esp. the maps figs. 11 and 13, but see also Østmo 1999; 2000) as signs of a "de-neolithization", as they seemed more numerous outside the regions presumably most suited to farming and instead concentrated in coastal environments better suited for hunting and fishing. Later, this interpretation has been confirmed by closer scrutiny of the archaeological record, including rigorous distributional studies and consideration of settlement types and inventories, which were not available to Hinsch (Østmo 1988a; 1988b). When agriculture was reintroduced in the MN B approximately 2800 BC, it seems to have been connected with the Corded Ware or Battle-Axe Culture (3).

TRB FINDS OF A RITUAL CHARACTER
While palynological findings and observation of single find distributions may be accepted as sufficient proof that farming was practiced in the Oslo fiord region from the EN onwards, and also that it was connected with the technological and aesthetic culture

Fig. 3. Anders Lorange. From a photo by an unknown photograper.

archaeologically associated with the TRB term, the nature of the TRB influence emerges in considerably more vivid colours when one considers such finds as may be interpreted in terms of the ritual practices of the TRB.

First we shall consider the evidence for hoards or sacrificial deposits, and earthen or flat graves, and finally megalithic graves. The identification of certain archaeological finds as votive offerings or sacrificial deposits or the like, or perhaps rather as hidden treasure, trade deposits or some such thing, goes back at least to Worsaae 1866, and has received renewed attention in recent years (Ø. K. Johansen 1993; Karsten 1994). The notion of TRB earthen or flat graves goes back to Friis Johansen 1917, and has also been put up for renewed consideration in recent years, last by Ebbesen 1994 and Jensen 2001. In Norway, Mikkelsen some years ago made an attempt to arrive at a reasonable idea about the relative number of earthen graves and votive offerings based on generalized considerations of the TRB axes recovered as single finds. Referring to Danish research (Mathiassen 1939; Thorvild-

sen 1941; Becker 1955; Brøndsted 1957 and Skaarup 1973), he maintained that unpolished blanks for thin-butted axes most likely had been deposited in hoards, while finished axes could come from graves or votive offerings, and fragments probably came from settlement sites. On this basis he concluded that almost one hundred or approximately 2/3 of the single finds of thin-butted axes probably had been deposited in ritual deposits such as graves or offerings, while the remaining 1/3 had been discarded on settlement sites (Mikkelsen 1984, 104f).

These numbers may look reasonable enough, and a map of whole, finished axes may give the truest representation of TRB ritual depositions. It might even be possible to identify ritually deposited pieces even more specifically among the whole axes, as Lars Sundström has done by demonstrating that long axes (at least 285 mm) form a separate group from the bulk of whole, undamaged thin-butted axes, most convincingly in the case of singly found axes from Södermanland and Närke, Sweden (Sundström 2003, 148, fig. 12). This hypothetical route will not be pursued further here, however, as focus will be on the deposition localities as constructions. Recently, a rather brief, literature-based survey of likely Stone Age graves in Norway has been published by Bergljot Solberg (2006). Reference to this work will be included where appropriate.

Point-butted and thin-butted axes are identified according to Nielsen 1977, while point-butted and thin-butted greenstone axes are as in Ebbesen 1994a, and polygonal axes according to Ebbesen 1998. Double-edged axes have been classified according to Ebbesen 1975. These are the main categories of artefacts in the finds under consideration here (4). Finally, in the absence of specific references, information about find circumstances are taken from the museum register.

HOARDS

Votive or sacrificial offerings during the Scandinavian Neolithic have been put up for recent scrutiny by Per Karsten (1994) and Christopher Tilley (1996). Karsten is primarily concerned with the Scanian finds. He defines hoards as consisting of "two or more objects deposited closely together at the same time" and which do not come from graves (p. 19, see also

Fig. 4. The Skjeltorp dolmen still standing as a ruin in 1913. Toward north-east. Photo: Museum of Cultural History, University of Oslo.

p. 186). Single objects, which have always posed a problem to students of sacrificial deposits and hoards, are included when they have been found in similar conditions as the multi-object finds, that is, in wetlands or associated with large stones or by excavation (l. c.). He concludes that during EN A-B (that is, Early TRB), most offering places were used only once, while permanent places used on repeated occasions were established during the subsequent EN C-MN II, or Middle (to Early Late) TRB. Only in a very limited degree were these however still used during the ensuing MN III-V, or Late TRB, when Karsten suggests that religious interest instead turned to settlements and megalithic monuments (summarized from op. cit., 193f).

We shall consider briefly the Norwegian finds in the light of Karsten's results. In most cases, this will be a matter of noticing finds from bogs or other wetland situations, and finds made by large stones or the like. It should be noted, though, than in some instances it may be difficult to sort hoards or sacrificial deposits from possible graves, and some finds may be more or less open to both interpretations.

Collected finds (Middle TRB)

C15440-41. Fagerholt, Idd, Halden, Østfold. Two thin-butted greenstone axes. The axes were "found together under a small, steep mountain" (Nicolaysen 1868, 72 (5)), a situation which perhaps may be considered as equivalent to proximity to large stones. C15440 is a thin-butted stone axe of Ebbesen's type IIA, 187 mm

long. C15441 is of type II C, 145 mm long. The two axes leave a quite uniform impression, and can be dated to Middle TRB. Cf. Pedersen 2003, 105.

C28624 a-b. Iseveien under Hafslund, Skjeberg, Sarpsborg, Østfold. a) The edge part of a thin-butted flint axe. All sides are carefully polished. Present length 104 mm, edge width 83 mm. Most likely of Nielsen's type III or possibly IV, considering both the dimensions, the shape of the sides and the degree of polish. b) Thin-butted flint axe. It most probably has been both re-sharpened and reworked at the butt end. Even so, it seems to have been of Nielsen's type III. Present length 121 mm. Both axes were found in July, 1952 under a stone measuring c.one by one metre, by one half metre in thickness. The stone had just been visible from above. The axes lay close together. The place lies in the flat moraine area on the Østfold Ra moraine, c. 900 m East of Hafslund bridge, c. 70 m North of Iseveien road. The find may be dated to the early part of Middle TRB. Cf. Pedersen 2003, 105.

C1097-98. Ek, Onsøy, Østfold. Two unpolished, thin-butted flint axes of Nielsen's type VI, 278 and 244 mm long. They were found apparently in 1841 when a mound on the Ek farm was dug into by the farmer. The axes were found standing on the end, close by a large pit filled with charcoal, it seems from a letter from the vicar to the Christiania (Oslo) museum (Østmo 1973; cf. Hinsch 1955, 24; Ebbesen 2002, 118; Pedersen 2003, 105). The find is datable to Middle TRB. It is the arrangement of the axes which makes an interpretation as a sacrifice more tempting than a grave in this case, although the latter certainly also is a possibility.

C22479. Østre Bøler, Spydeberg, Østfold. a) Thin-butted greenstone axe. According to the museum register it is polished at the edge, otherwise pecked. Length 168 mm. Its whereabouts is presently unknown. b) Stone axe, certainly of the thin-butted variety, however with a fairly well developed butt end. Length 113 mm. Although perhaps reworked, the axe should be classified as of Ebbesen's type II C, datable to Middle to Late TRB. Both axes have a brown patina. They were found in the same place, but at different times in 1919 and 1920, in a small plain between two

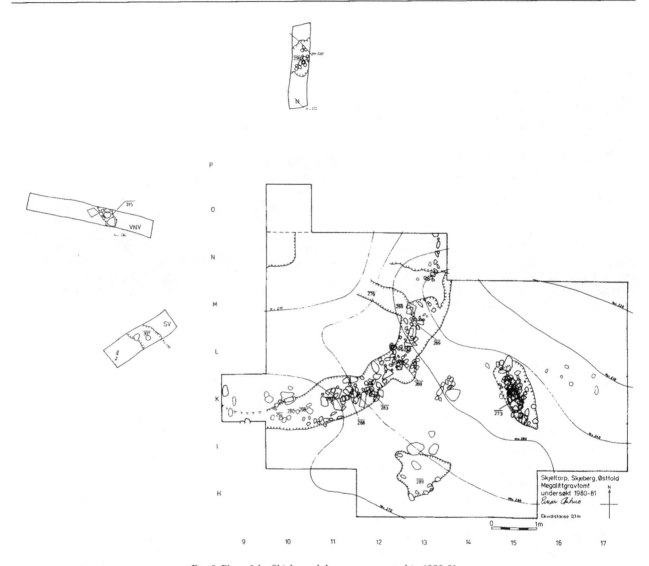

Fig. 5. Plan of the Skjeltorp dolmen as excavated in 1980-81.

rock outcrops, according to Hinsch (1955, 161) in a gravel pit. The source of this information is unclear. The larger axe was found last, c. 20 cm into the ground. Cf. Pedersen 2003, 105. Possibly, this may also be interpreted as a grave.

C27620 a-d. Østre Disen, Ø. Aker, Oslo. 3 thin-butted flint axes found together with a flint nodule at the bottom of a former bog surrounded by traces of fire about 1.5 m across (Hougen 1946). a) is 399 mm long, of Nielsen's type III, whether A or B is less certain, perhaps due to the large dimensions. b) is 388 mm long, of Nielsen's type IIIB. c) is a fragment of a similar axe, with the butt end missing. Its present length is 297 mm. Probably this, too, was of Nielsen's type IIIB. d) is a flint nodule, 303 mm long. The find may be dated to EN C or Middle TRB. Ebbesen classifies both the whole axes as of type IV, but the narrow sides appear too bulging for that (Ebbesen 2002, 118).

C10908-09. Ås landbrukshøyskole, Ås, Akershus. 2 thin-butted greenstone axes found in a bog. C10908 is of type II C and is 147

mm long (cf. Ebbesen 1984, 123). Ebbesen dates this type to MN Ia-MN III, possibly both earlier and later, that is, Middle to Late TRB. C10909 belongs to type II A and is 213 mm long. This, Ebbesen dates to EN C-MN Ia, that is, Middle TRB. Found together, these axes in consequence ought to be dated to Middle TRB.

C27309 a-b. "Trollhaugen" u. Framheim, Oppegård, Akershus. Two thin-butted stone axes found 20-25 cm apart by a small cliff. a) is a thin-butted stone axe of type II A, 223 mm long, but it is possible that the butt end is knocked off. b) also is an axe of type II A, 202 mm long, quite withered. Datable to EN C-MN A Ia, or Middle TRB.

C12207-08 and C12218. England, Røyken, Buskerud. 3 thin-butted axes of flint, which were acquired together, and have some of the characteristic brown bog patina suggesting that they may have been found together, and are accepted as a likely collected bog find by Hinsch (1955, 25). All appear to have been re-sharpened. C12207 probably belongs to Nielsen's type VI, and is 160 mm long. It would seem datable to Middle TRB. C12208 seems most close to Nielsen's type IIIb, but is only 142 mm long, and its sides are not entirely parallel. C12218 is also short, only 134 mm. It is of type V. If this is indeed a closed find, it would seem to be datable to Middle TRB, but this remains quite uncertain also in view of the somewhat disparate types of axe.

C20511 a-b. Julplassen u. Landsverk, Rollag, Buskerud. Thin-butted flint axe and a flint blade found at a depth of 1 m in a bog. a) is a thin-butted axe of a late type with unpolished narrow sides, probably of type VI or VII, but with a reworked edge. It should be dated to EN C-MN I/II (Nielsen 1977), or Middle TRB, perhaps late. b) is a quite large flint blade with partly retouched edges. Even if it does not display the edge polish characteristic of blades used as sickles (cf. Jensen 1994, 79ff), it is still tempting to suggest that it might have been intended as a sickle or reaping knife.

Single pieces

In addition to these finds, another dozen cases of thin-butted flint axes or other TRB axes found in bogs or in other contexts such as rock screes or crevices (cf. Ø. K. Johansen 1993, 91ff) indicative of special care may be mentioned (cf. Hinsch 1955, 162). It is these:

- *Early TRB*. C10020. Anstensrød, Spydeberg, Østfold. Point-butted flint axe of type 3. Only 104 mm long. Early TRB. According to Hinsch (1955, 162) found in a bog, the source of this information however is not clear.

C24215. Årbu, Aremark, Østfold. Point-butted flint axe of type 2. Quite short, and probably re-sharpened. Found in the upper layer of a bog. 111 mm long. Early TRB.

- *Middle TRB*. C19587. Skoro, Ski Akershus. Thin-butted flint axe of type IIIA, 291 mm long. Allegedly found in a narrow crevice between a rock outcrop and a large stone "which had fallen down" (Hinsch 1955, 26). Middle TRB.

C8463. Andersrød, Råde, Østfold. Thin-butted flint axe of type II. 378 mm long, found in a former bog. Dating: Early Middle TRB. Cf. Pedersen 2003, 101.

C10011. Stensrød, Trøgstad, Østfold. Thin-butted flint axe of type IIIA, 228 mm long, found in a bog. Perhaps re-sharpened. Middle TRB. Pedersen 2003, 104.

C11344. Svae, Skiptvet, Østfold. Thin-butted flint axe of type V, 185 mm long, found in a bog. Middle TRB.

C34164. Taraldrud, Rødenes, Marker, Østfold. Thin-butted flint axe of type VI, 265 mm long. Found in soil dug up from a brook (cf. also Pedersen 2003, 104). Middle TRB.

C12030. Lambertseter, Oslo. Thin-butted stone axe of type II, probably a), found in a bog, datable to Middle TRB (TN C-MN Ia, Ebbesen 1984, 122). 185 mm long.

C12043. Tukun, Rømskog, Østfold. Edge fragment of a large, thin-butted flint axe with polished, bulging narrow sides. The edge is 76 mm broad, and the axe probably was of type III. Middle TRB. According to Hinsch (1955, 162; repeated by Pedersen 2003, 101) found in a bog, but the source of this information is unclear.

C19207. Stadum, Gran, Oppland. Thin-butted flint axe of type IIIA, 186 mm long. Found in a bog. Middle TRB.

C34779. Skåra, Tjølling, Vestfold. Thin-butted flint axe found in a former, now dried-out bog. Type IIIB, 370 mm long. EN C, or Middle TRB. Ill. Mikkelsen (ed.) 1982, Fig. 5.

C36517. "Bråtan", Roe (registered as Raadegård), Råde k. Østfold. Thin-butted flint axe of type III, whether A or B is uncertain because of the large dimensions, the axe is 397 mm long, the edge width amounts to 93 mm. Found c. 25 cm below the surface. Ac-

cording to the report from the finder, the axe probably stood vertically in the ground, which may be interpreted as a special arrangement indicative of a sacrifice (Ø. K. Johansen 2002, 117ff; Pedersen 2003, 101 mentions two axes). Middle TRB.

S8070a. Thin-butted flint axe from Krogevoll, Fiskå, Strand, Rogaland (illustrated J. Petersen 1955, 20, Fig. 3). Length 194 mm. Ebbesen (2002, 118) classifies the axe as type III/VI, but the narrow sides are so straight that it would rather seem to belong to type IV. Found together with a scraper (b, illustrated J. Petersen 1955, 21, Fig. 4) and 5 flint flakes (c), beside a large boulder by a small brook. Probably Middle TRB.

B3221. Edge fragment, most likely of a thin-butted greenstone axe. Probably of type IIA. Found in a bog at Giskeødegård, Giske, Borgund, Møre og Romsdal.

B9977. a) Possibly thin-butted greenstone axe with concave narrow sides. The surface is pecked, only the edge and the butt end are polished. 181 mm long. Type IIA. b) is a pebble with pecking marks. Both pieces were found together at a depth of 2 metres on a bed of natural pebbles on the bottom of a bog at Øvre Dalland, Tysnes, Hordaland.

Several other axe finds are claimed as likely offerings by Pedersen (2003, 101ff), including C9144 from Rikesem, Hobøl, C11945 from Dal, Hobøl, Østfold, C11187 from Prestebakke, Idd, Halden, C15188 from Torper, Hærland, C19060 from Igsi, Hobøl, C19702 from Mørholt, Aremark, C20059 from Hovin, Spydeberg, C21044 from Os, Asak, Berg, Halden, C25927 from Huser, Asmaløy, Hvaler, Østfold and C31092 from Stensrød, Råde, Østfold. In none of these instances is the information about the find circumstances sufficiently detailed to bear this out. Even so, it may seem reasonable that most, if not all whole and undamaged axes which have been found, were deposited intentionally in the ground rather than accidentally lost, but such speculation falls outside of the scope of the present work. A stone axe from Brekke canal, Berg, Halden, Østfold is also mentioned by Pedersen (2003, 104), but can hardly be called thin-butted due to the unusual proportions which rather indicate that it should be viewed as some sort of thick-butted axe.

- *Late TRB*. T17452. Garstad, Vikna, Nord-Trøndelag. Double-edged battle-axe of Ebbesen's type C 2 (Ebbesen 1975, 182). Found at a depth of c. 1 m in a bog (Møllenhus 1954, 132; Østmo 2000, 87).

While most of these finds may qualify as probable votive offerings in Karsten's sense, we may note that none is indicative of permanent offering places for repeated use, even if many of the finds most probably can be dated to EN C-MN II or Middle TRB. It seems, therefore, that the establishment of permanent offering places did not reach the northern periphery of the TRB in SE Norway. Also worth pointing out is the lack of offerings from MN III-V, Late TRB, in SE Norway, just like Karsten found concerning Scania. As mentioned above, in particular the double-edged battle axes of these periods spread outside the agricultural centres of south Norway along the coast, indeed as far north as Vikna, Nord-Trøndelag, where the axe just mentioned was found in a former bog which may be indicative of a late ritual deposit. One should not press the interpretation of such a single find too far, but the possibility that customs such as that of depositing axes in ponds and bogs may live on in the periphery of a cultural region long after it has vanished in the more central parts, may be noted in this instance.

It is certainly significant that, except for the last mentioned find, only what may be called working axes have been found in the hoards, i.e. no polygonal or double-edged axes.

FLAT GRAVES

Hinsch included a thorough consideration of possible TRB graves in his 1955 survey, based on a comparison with such graves identified in Denmark, primarily by Thorvildsen 1941. Since then, more graves have been investigated in Denmark (and south Sweden), and the entire material has been subjected to renewed investigation (Ebbesen 1994a), so in this sense there exists now a much better basis for evaluating the Norwegian finds, too. Also, there are now more Norwegian finds to consider (cf. also Solberg 2006).

Ebbesen identified 86 "simple Early-neolithic graves" in Denmark. They were arranged in seven different types, on the basis of constructional elements also mostly recognized by Thorvildsen (1941) and Brøndsted (1938; 1957). They are a) Simple pit graves without stones, where the dead have been buried in wooden coffins, hides or without such cover. They are dated to the entire EN. b) Graves with surrounding stones. These are simple structures surrounded by a row of stones, and are datable to Ebbesen's phases EN 2-3. c) Graves with paved floor, that is, the floor is covered with stones, a layer of chips or a pavement. These are dated to EN 2-3. d) Graves with floor paving and surrounding stones, dated to EN in general, but particularly EN 3. e) Graves with sides lined with stones, dated to EN 2. f) Graves with stone fill, apparently precursors of the MN Jutish stone packing graves. g) Graves with large postholes at the ends, the so-called "Konens Høj"

type, dated to EN 3. h) Wooden chambers, dated to EN 3. All grave types are present in North Jutland, and some of them only there. Most of the graves were found under a level surface, but some were also found in round barrows and types g) and h) only in long mounds (Ebbesen 1994a).

We may take the characteristics of these types as a convenient starting point for identifying graves among the Norwegian finds too. In practice, it will be graves of the simpler a) type, as none of the more elaborate types seems to be represented in our material. Keeping in mind that finds from bogs or other wetland contexts probably should be interpreted as sacrifices, we shall consider finds made in sand or gravel as possible graves, in particular when they have been made at a certain depth in the ground. In a few cases, the more or less probable presence of a mound may be taken to indicate graves, too.

In principle, one ought to be prepared to find other types of graves in Norway than in Denmark. There seems however to be little reason to develop this idea further, at least concerning graves with artefacts of South Scandinavian TRB types. Some kind of identifiable physical or contextual arrangement certainly would have to be present if this were to be of relevance, and this does not seem to be the case in any of the instances under consideration here.

The Norwegian finds sufficiently elucidated to be considered as likely (distinctly as opposed to certain) graves along these lines are these (see also Hinsch 1955, 19ff):

- *Middle TRB.* C20538. Langenes u. Haraldstad, Rakkestad, Østfold. Thin-butted flint axe and retouched flint flake flint found about one half ell (0.31375 m) apart about one ell below the surface. a) is a reworked, thin-butted flint axe with only partly polished narrow sides, present length 121 mm. It should be considered as belonging to Nielsen's type V or VI. The retouched flake b) was identified as an Early Neolithic halberd by Hinsch (1955, 19), but this seems rather too grand for the quite unassuming piece (cf. Ebbesen 1994b). Datable to Middle TRB. See also Pedersen 2003, 98.

C3826, C7045. Nordby, Våler, Østfold. C3826 is a polygonal battle-axe of Ebbesen's type V. The edge has been knocked off, and the present length of the piece amounts to 150 mm. C7045 is a thin-butted greenstone axe of Ebbesen's type II C, 123 mm long. Viewed as a closed find, the dating must be Middle TRB, even rather early. According to a note in the archives of the University Museum of Cultural History (certainly the source of the reference by Hinsch 1955, 19), the axes were found together in a gravel pit in 1865. Pedersen (2003, 98) accepts this find as a possible grave.

C22694. Flaskebekk, Nesodden, Akershus. Polygonal battle-axe with the edge missing. The axe is of Ebbesen's type I or II, the preserved part is 139 mm long; the thickness at the shaft hole 50 mm. The axe was found about 1/2 m deep in the ground. "There were some small, brown rocks there which looked like sheddings, but [such matter] is not present in the bedrock there", the museum inventory states. Hinsch (1955, 22; cf. also Solberg 2006, 85) entirely plausibly suggested that these pieces might actually have been pottery.

C20524. Rydningen u. Ertesprang, Eggedal, Buskerud. Fragment of thin-butted flint axe, now 120 mm long, probably of Nielsen's type IIIB, found at a depth of 1 m by levelling a small mound. Middle TRB.

C20536 a-c. Kiste, Botne, Vestfold. One thin-butted flint axe, one reworked similar axe and one thin-butted greenstone axe found fairly close together between some middle-sized rocks in a low mound of earth, sand and rocks which was c. 3-4 m across and c. 1/2 m tall. a: small thin-butted flint axe with reworked edge, probably of Nielsen's type V. Its present length is only 108 mm. b) is an edge fragment, probably of a thin-butted flint axe, which has been reworked to resemble a kind of core axe. c) is a thin-butted greenstone axe of Ebbesen's type II C, 127 mm long. The find is datable to Middle to Late TRB. Cf. also Solberg 2006, 87.

C20702. Trevland, Kodal, Andebu, Vestfold. Thin-butted stone axe found in a gravel pit at a depth of c. 1/2 m below a square, c. 60 by 60 cm large stone. It resembles closely Ebbesen's type II A, except that it is unusually thin (only 29 mm). The length is 269 mm. Dating: Middle TRB.

- *Late TRB.* C20204 a-b. Ås, Ullensaker, Akershus. Thin-butted flint axe and thin-bladed, thin-butted flint axe, found next to each other deep in the soil in a heap of pebbles. This was the only Norwegian TRB non-megalithic grave accepted by C. J. Becker in his seminal work on the early TRB (Becker 1948, 199; also mentioned by Solberg 2006, 85). a) is a rather small, thin-butted flint axe which does not readily fit into any of Nielsen's type definitions. With its barely polished narrow sides it probably is quite late, comparable to type VI, but the butt end is not as blunt as type VI axes usually are, and the axe is only 134 mm long; its other dimensions are comparably slender. b) is a thin-butted flint chisel with unpolished narrow sides and a blunt butt end. 130 mm long. The most likely dating of this find in consequence would be early Late TRB.

SINGLE PIECES FROM GRAVEL PITS ETC.

Another group of thin-butted axes or polygonal battle-axes reported to have been found in gravel pits or at a depth of c. 30-60 cm, may perhaps also be considered indicative of flat graves (see also Hinsch 1955, 161f). It is these:

- *Early TRB.* C23722. Dikemark hospital, Asker, Akershus. Point-butted flint axe of Nielsens type 2, 130 mm long, found at a depth of 35-40 cm in sand. Early TRB.

- *Middle TRB.* C25406. Åsekjær, Berg (Halden), Østfold. Thin-butted stone axe of Ebbesen's type II A, 197 mm long, found in a gravel pit. Middle TRB.

C24249. Heenskleiva, Rakkestad, Østfold. Thin-butted stone axe of Ebbesen's type II A, 197 mm long, found at a depth of 30 cm in sand. Middle TRB.

C27798. Dillingøy, Moss, Østfold. Thin-butted stone axe, found at a depth of one spade-breadth "close by an item, perhaps

a handle, which crumbled away". Its butt end is knocked off, but the axe probably was of Ebbesen's type II A. Its present length is 176 mm. Middle TRB.

C7940. Loding, Ullensaker, Akershus. The edge part of a polygonal battle-axe, originally undamaged, found at a depth of at least 3 feet. Probably of a late type, perhaps type V resharpened. Middle TRB.

C29109a-b. Grimkelsrud, Fenstad, Nes, Akershus. Two thin-butted flint axes, found together at a depth of less than two meters in clay. Ebbesen identifies these axes as type III/VI (Ebbesen 2002, 118). Furthermore, he lists the find among hoards, which certainly is a possibility. Probably Middle TRB.

C29107. Nes, Hvalstad, Asker, Akershus. Rather small, 161 mm long polygonal battle-axe of Ebbesen's type V, however with an edge that is not splaying and only 38 mm wide; perhaps it has been resharpened in spite of being unfinished in that the shaft-hole is missing. Found under or beside a large stone, not very deep in the ground. Dating: Middle TRB. This, too, might as well allow an interpretation as a votive offering.

C29518. Vettre, Asker, Akershus. The butt end of a polygonal battle axe, certainly of Ebbesen's type V (or possibly III), found at a depth of 1,5 m together with charred coal, ashes and rocks. Dating: EN C/3 or Middle TRB.

C23895. Åsli, Sandstuveien, Oslo. Thin-butted flint axe of Nielsen's typ IIIB, 199 mm long, found at a depth of 1 m in clay. Middle TRB. Also mentioned by Solberg 2006, 85.

C22728. Disen, Oslo. Thin-butted stone axe found in a large gravel mound with other, lost items. The axe should probably be considered as belonging to Ebbesen's type II C, but it is only 19 mm thick. The length is 106 mm. Dating: Middle to Late TRB.

C20652. Ørakerbråten, Oslo. Fragment of a thin-butted stone axe found at a depth of one ell (=0,6275 m). It must have been quite large, and probably of Ebbesen's type II A. Presently it is only 72 mm long. Middle TRB.

C20427. Jonsrud, Grue, Hedmark. Thin-butted stone axe found at a depth of one half ell (=0,31375 m). It seems to be of Ebbesen's type II C, 106 mm long. Middle to Late TRB.

C9019. Sparby, Hof, Hedmark. Thin-butted flint axe of Nielsen's type III A, 342 mm long, found on the river shore, allegedly at a depth of 12 ells(!), which surely must be due to some sort of misunderstanding. (Early) Middle TRB.

C21401. Rekstad, Brandbu, Oppland. Thin-butted flint axe of Nielsen's type IIIA, 320 mm long, found at a depth of 15 inches in clay. (Early) Middle TRB.

C20481. Hyllestad, Uvdal, Buskerud. Thin-butted flint axe of Nielsen's type VI, 145 mm long, found approximately : ell (=0,470625 m) below the surface in sand. Middle TRB.

C20199-20201. Orrerød, Re, Vestfold. Three thin-butted axes, one of stone and two of flint, found not far apart at a depth of about one half ell (=0,31375 m). C20199: Unpolished thin-butted flint axe of Nielsen's type IV or V, 161 mm long. C20200: Thin-butted flint axe of Nielsen's type IIIB, 154 mm long. C20201: Thin-butted greenstone axe. The butt end is knocked off, butt appears to have had a hole, so the axe belongs to Ebbesen's type III. Its present length is 106 mm. If accepted as a closed find, the dating must be (late) Middle TRB.

C28062. Brekke, Slagen, Sem, Vestfold. Polygonal battle-axe, of Ebbesen's type V, but without a splaying edge, possibly due to resharpening. Found at a depth of 2 m in a gravel pit. Dating: Middle TRB (Ebbesen's Period FN 3, Ebbesen 1998, 88).

One of the finds mentioned by Hinsch, C10305-8 from Brevik, Enebakk, Akershus, sounds very much like it may have come from a modern clearance cairn and thus should be left out of the list. Another find, C20527 a-b from Østre Solberg, Botne, Vestfold, similarly seems not to have come from an original deposit. C26836 from Sauherad, Telemark has been wrongly attributed by Hinsch, most likely being Mesolithic.

These finds include working axes as well as battle-axes (polygonal and double-edged). Concerning the polygonal axes, one may note that their number in Norway is around 50 (Ebbesen 1998, 88), which is more than half the number found in Denmark (95 pieces in all, even more have been found in Sweden, Ebbesen 1998, 78).

It is striking that while many of the Norwegian axes fit nicely into the typological categories defined by Nielsen and Ebbesen, respectively, on basis of Danish finds, quite a few can only be attributed to this or that type if the rules are bent ever so slightly. This may have to do with the unusual dimensions of some of the axes, and this applies to large as well as small specimens. Some of the smaller axes may have been re-sharpened, and thus become too short to fit into the Danish statistics, but others apparently were produced with "too small" proportions initially. Perhaps more surprisingly, there are also a few axes which fall outside of Nielsen's measurements because they are too large, as in the case of some type III axes, which seemingly have too wide narrow sides to fit into the A subtype while at the same time having "too bulging" sides.

These observations indicate that Nielsen's type definitions are more dependent on historical conditions in Denmark than might have been expected, while finds in the Northern periphery of Norway apparently to some degree were selected according to local rules (cf. Glørstad 2005).

Recognising Ebbesen's grave types among these finds obviously will be difficult when they have not been investigated professionally and information therefore is scant. Aiming at a certain probability rather than complete certainty, it still seems fair to say that all of these finds may indeed have been simple graves. Stones or other construction details are rarely mentioned. If one accepts that conspicuous features most probably would have been noticed and commented upon had they been present, the conclusion is possible that most of these finds have been simple graves of the a) type. When stones are reported, in the

cases of Ås, Kiste and Vettre, we may have to do with one of the other grave types, possibly b-d or f. In Ebbesen's chronological terms, all graves most probably may be dated to EN 3, or Middle TRB. There are no TRB finds which provide reason for suspecting particular, local burial customs markedly different from those found in South Scandinavia. Concerning other more or less contemporary material whith different cultural connotations, some suggestions are offered by Solberg 2006.

This makes for a total of nine reasonably probable votive offerings and seven flat graves, which numbers may be increased to 25 and 23 possible such structures, respectively, if the supplementary list is also included. Considering the circumstances whereby these finds have been recovered and the uncertainty with which they may be identified, the numbers surely are not of the essence. What remains of interest, is the circumstance that these instances of the ritual practices of the TRB are present in SE Norway at all. Together with the megalithic graves, to which we shall turn in a moment, these 16 (alternatively 48) finds are indications that some rituals resembling those found in the TRB in South Scandinavia were also practised in a similar cultural environment in SE Norway during EN C-MN II (Middle TRB), and that consequently, the axes and other artefacts of TRB types found in the region are less likely to have come purely as exotic imports.

It will be interesting when the conditions in the TRB region in SE Norway may be compared not only with the South Scandinavian TRB, but also with contemporary conditions further afield, such as in Western Norway. A substantial number of indigenous axe types have been identified there (and also in Middle and North Norway), some of which can arguably be dated to the EN and MN in South Scandinavian terms (cf. Nærøy 1993). It seems, however, that votive finds as well as more or less likely graves only occur in MN B and the LN, when agriculture arguably was introduced (Berg 1993, 79); one detailed study finds no certain hoards or votive offerings among axes datable to EN or MN in a comparison between Hardanger and Sunnmøre (Aksdal 1996); the situation seems to be similar in the SW region of Rogaland (H. Gjessing 1920, 76ff, concerning grave finds). A few items from EN-MN II, especially early types of double-edged axes, however spread north to Trøndelag in Middle Norway, where

Fig. 6. Ornamented potsherds from the Skjeltorp dolmen. Photo: Ove Holst/Museum of Cultural History, University of Oslo

they have been recovered in circumstances which may indicate that they were deposited ritually, perhaps within the context of the local slate point-using hunting and fishing culture (Østmo 1999; 2000).

MEGALITHIC GRAVES

Arguably, five megalithic graves are known or believed to have existed in SE Norway. All have been considered separately in previous literature, but a detailed collected survey has been missing (6).

Whatever its origin (e. g. Midgley 1985; Sherratt 1990; 1997), the megalithic grave tradition reached South Scandinavia in the 4th millennium BC, producing what eventually became the most durable memorials of the Scandinavian TRB. The construction of megalithic tombs in South Scandinavia in the middle centuries of the 4th millennium BC reached truly feverish proportions. Today, no fewer than 7285 megalithic tombs have been identified in Denmark alone

(Kaul 1991, 229), but even this remarkable number is estimated to embrace only a fraction of such graves once in existence. Carefully considering the evidence, Ebbesen estimates that c. 25000 megalithic monuments were built in Denmark in the years 3700-3200 BC (Ebbesen 1985, 37ff; Jensen later quotes the even higher number of 40000, Jensen 2001, 347). Most are classified as dolmens, as only about 700 passage graves are known today (Nielsen 1981, 84). The numbers for Sweden are lower, totalling c. 70 dolmens and 375 passage graves (Bägerfeldt & Kihlstedt 1985, 3).

These numbers, and the truly monumental nature of many of the megalithic graves together with their often striking topographical situation easily explain why they have continued to occupy the minds of scholars and laymen alike. Indeed, they have become a symbol of Antiquity itself, appearing on stamps and banknotes ("Ever since they were built, they have been one of the symbols of the Danish landscape", Ebbesen states (Ebbesen 1985, 12)).

Understandably, this degree of veneration is not found in Norway. But megalithic aspirations did reach the country, if only just, to judge from the few surviving monuments to be found in the Oslo fiord region in the south-eastern part of present-day Norway (Fig. 2) (7). The megalithic graves arguably known to have existed in this region deserve to be studied as the northernmost occurrences of the megalithic tradition on the European mainland (8). Perhaps the place where the rapid spread of this very pronounced and resource intensive cultural expression came to a halt can contribute something toward a better understanding of the megalithic phenomenon in general.

The quite numerous megalithic graves in nearby West Sweden are part of the background against which the Norwegian ones certainly primarily ought to be viewed. Geography and common sense indicate that the megalithic graves known in the Oslo fiord area are part of and expressions of the same cultural tradition as that which produced the monuments which can be found along the West Swedish coast. Contacts with North Denmark perhaps might also be expected to manifest themselves in a similar way, but just as with North Jutish types of flat graves, pursuing this thought has not proved conclusive, certainly an indication that sea traffic at this time still was confined to coastal waters (Østmo 2005).

The Norwegian megalithic monuments were included in Lars Blomqvist's survey of all megalithic graves in Sweden (and Norway) (Blomqvist 1989), as well as in Karl-Göran Sjögren's recent work on megalithic graves, which otherwise had the numerous megalithic graves in Falbygden, Västergötland as its primary subject (Sjögren 2003; also Persson and Sjögren 2001). But while these works aim at general conclusions, necessarily focusing on the more numerous and varied Swedish graves, here we shall concentrate on the Norwegian ones as expressions of a marginal cultural phenomenon.

Developing traditional ideas, Blomqvist devised three types of dolmen. In summary, Ds 1 dolmen chambers are rectangular, Ds 2 chambers are square and Ds 3 chambers are polygonal (Blomqvist 1989, 319 and 323). In addition, Ds 1 and Ds 2 have no passage. Ds 3 may have a short passage (less than 2 m for the West Swedish region) or a polygonal chamber or both, but if there is a passage, the chamber may be rectangular (Blomqvist 1989, 52; Sjögren appears to consider that dolmens with polygonal chambers always have a passage, Sjögren 2003, 80) (9).

Based primarily on the plan of the chamber and the length of the passage, two types of passage grave have also been defined (Blomqvist 1989, 53ff). Taking account of radiocarbon datings as well as artefact finds and other typological considerations, the five types are arranged in a partly hypothetical chronological sequence, Ds 1 being dated to 3600-3500 BC, Ds 2 to 3500-3400 BC, Ds 3 to 3450-3350 BC and the two passage grave types to 3350-3300 BC and after 3300 BC, respectively (Blomqvist 1989, 110). This attempt to produce a strict typology and chronology, ultimately echoing ideas held by Oscar Montelius (1874), is not supported by Sjögren, who on the basis of a collected survey and critical assessment of all available radiocarbon datings of Scandinavian megalithic graves feels compelled to conclude that both dolmens and passage-graves were built during EN C-MN I-II (Sjögren 2003, 104). He does however admit that early dolmens do exist, at least in South Scandinavia, with archaeological material the like of which is not found in passage-graves, and it would seem a little misplaced to rule out the possibility that some dolmens may pre-date the building of passage-graves. But Sjögren may still be right to suggest that regional and local variations may be of at least equal significance to that of chronology to explain the existence of different types of megalithic graves. The individual monuments are these:

Skjeltorp, Skjeberg (Sarpsborg), Østfold. The megalithic grave at Skjeltorp (Blomqvist 1989 and Sjögren 2003 name it "Skjeberg" which is a considerably less precise geographical term) was discovered and identified as early as 1872 by that pre-eminent pioneer of Norwegian archaeology, Anders Lorange (Lorange 1876) (Fig. 3), while still standing as a ruin (10). Lorange was told that destruction of the grave had begun in 1855, when the large roof stone was taken away to be used as a sill or threshold before the barn of a neighbouring farm. The ruin existed until it was completely removed, apparently in 1930; however, in 1913 it had been the subject of a summary investigation by Gabriel Gustafson (fig. 4). It seems that no artefacts were found on this occasion, and Gustafson has not communicated any details from his investigation, but concludes that the monument "certainly has been a passage grave of the early kind common in Bohuslän, with a polygonal, not elongated chamber and a short passage" (Gustafson 1914, 8, translated from the Norwegian).

The dispersed megaliths proper (i. e. the large stones with which the grave chamber had been built) were re-assembled in the early 1940s and employed in a reconstruction of the Skjeltorp

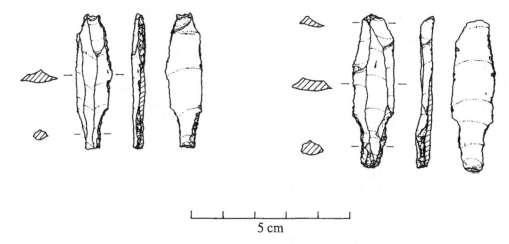

5 cm

Fig. 7. Tanged points of flint from the Skjeltorp dolmen. Drawing: Mieko Matsumoto.

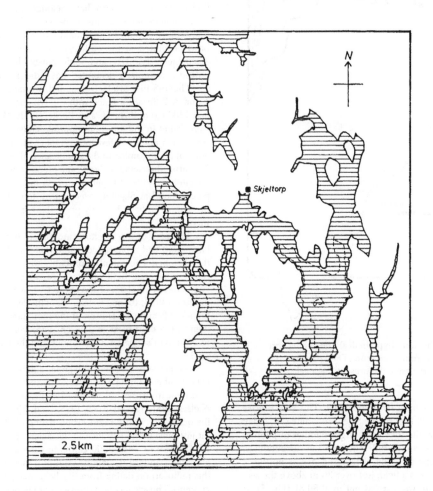

Fig. 8. Map of part of the Østfold coast with the Skjeltorp dolmen. The coast-line has been reconstructed at approximately 25 m above the present.

Acta Archaeologica

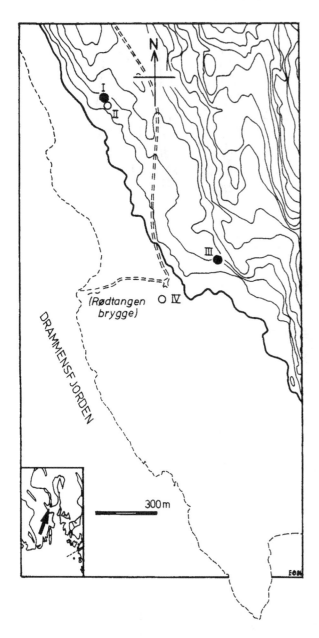

Fig. 9. Situation of the four hypothetical megalithic graves at Rødtangen, Holtenes, Hurum, Buskerud. The coast line has been drawn at 25 m above the present sea-level.

grave a little while away from its original site. This site, precise memories of which are still kept by the Skjeltorp family (11), today can also be identified by the somewhat larger number of pebbles in the soil, but otherwise is little different from the surroundings. It lies in a southern slope a couple of hundred meters northeast of the farm, in what today is a field, just over 30 m above the sea. An excavation of the site was carried out in 1980-81 (Fig. 5). It revealed that the monument had been circular with a diameter of approximately 8,6 m, and with an entrance probably in the shape

of a stone-lined passage leading into the central chamber from east-southeast. The periphery of the monument consisted of a shallow ditch which may have contained the foundations for a circle of stones. However, of the chamber itself nothing significant could be identified, as that part of the site had been all but disturbed, probably during the final removal of the monument in 1930. A number of flat, pebble-sized stones may have belonged to the dry-walling of the chamber which is mentioned by Lorange. Right outside the entrance to the passage, an oblong pit was excavated, which was filled with stones, charcoal and fragments of pots (12). A few potsherds were found in the peripheral ditch, too. Other finds were made by screening the topsoil, including most of the flint artefacts. A distribution study nevertheless suggests that even these items had been deposited in connection with the grave. A detailed study of the Skjeltorp flint material carried out by Mieko Matsumoto when drawing it for the present paper has revealed no less than nine cases of conjoinings of the flints, the largest of which consists of six pieces found in connection with the surrounding ditch and the area richest in finds immediately to the south of the entrance. Her findings will be published elsewhere.

22 of the 132 potsherds found carried impressed ornaments (Fig. 6) (13). The potsherds have belonged to several vessels, among which at least one small funnel beaker with vertical striation of the body (bowl?) could be identified (B), along with one pedestalled bowl decorated in the quite characteristic manner of the MN I Troldebjerg style (A), and some potsherds which may have belonged to a similarly decorated clay ladle (D) (14).

The 498 flint artefacts included two tanged points of types A 1 and A 2 (in accordance with the typology of Helskog, Indrelid and Mikkelsen 1976; cf. also Becker 1951; Malmer 1969), which were found in the topsoil at opposite ends of the pottery-filled pit mentioned above. A few more retouched pieces were also found, without adding much to the significance of the flint inventory (Fig. 7). Burnt flint being a significant presence in South Scandinavian megalithic graves, it is perhaps worth mentioning that eight of the pieces found at Skjeltorp were burnt, too. However, they cannot be claimed to have had any particular connection with the monument.

The plan of the Skjeltorp monument indicates that the circular mound had a passage of somewhat less than 2 m leading into the chamber. The chamber probably was roughly circular, too, or rather polygonal, built of five large stones, as both Anders Lorange's report and later observations by Sverre Marstrander (quoted in Østmo 1983, 10) make clear. All of this leads to a confirmation of the identification by Hinsch of the monument as a polygonal dolmen with a short passage (Hinsch 1955, 73), corresponding closely to Blomqvist's type Ds 3 (see above and the table Blomqvist 1989, 194).

As mentioned above, polygonal dolmens were built in significant numbers during a quite brief period around 3400 BC, at the transition from the EN to the MN (Blomqvist 1989, 110; cf. also Nielsen 1981, 77 and Koch 1998, 189f; Sjögren 2003, 104). This fits quite well with a radiocarbon dating of charcoal found in the pit just outside the entrance to the Skjeltorp dolmen, to 4560±100 BP (T-4573) or 3650-2900 calBC in calibrated ("real") years with a double standard deviation (15) (but it must be remembered that this radiocarbon dating from Skjeltorp was part of Blomqvist's argument). The artefact finds however are in perfect accordance with this dating, as the pottery style is certainly that of the MN A I. A so early dating of tanged points is unlikely by South Scandinavian standards however (for instance Rasmussen 1991, 56f; Persson 1998), but fits quite well with South Norwegian conditions (see for example Glørstad 1998). If the points are indeed contemporaneous with the building of the grave, it probably ought to be accepted as an expression of local cultural customs.

The coast on which the Skjeltorp dolmen stood can be reconstructed with a coast-line approximately 25 m above the present (Fig. 8) (16). It emerges that the coast then was heavily indented, with an undulating channel just to the south of Skjeltorp, and several larger and smaller islands and peninsulas to the west, south and east. The sea-routes led to similar places to the southeast and northwest, and to an archipelago of larger and smaller islands which extended all along the coast. Indeed, it would seem that easy access to the coastal sea routes was a main concern for the location of the Skjeltorp grave.

As regards conditions for agriculture, the soil conditions in the coastal region of Østfold are dominated by well-developed late glacial end moraines which broadly follow the direction of the coast, and which provide light, sandy soils well suited to early agriculture. In addition to this there were also low-lying plains of heavier soil which formed grassy wetlands in many places. Similar conditions obtained all along the coast of the Oslo fiord at the time, certainly south of the Drøbak straits. In general, natural conditions must have favoured a mixed subsistence economy of farming and husbandry as well as coastal hunting and fishing.

The distribution of finds of TRB axes seems to show that occupation in the two earliest stages of the Norwegian TRB, including the period when the megalithic tombs were constructed, was centred on the sandy moraine soils in the interior of the region rather than on the coast. Therefore it cannot be claimed that the Skjeltorp grave is situated in an immediate neighbourhood where traces of EN (or early MN) farming are really abundant. However, in addition to the axe finds, which are mostly stray finds with but little detailed information about find circumstances, a number of coastal settlement sites datable to the EN have been identified in the coastal districts of Østfold. Excavations and surface collections from these have produced artefacts such as points, scrapers and other smaller items which may more readily be thought of as connected with hunting and fishing, but sometimes also a few fragments of pottery and chips of polished flint axes have been found (a survey of these sites can be found in Østmo 1998a; see also Østmo 1988a, 127ff). Recently this material has bees significantly increased by the excavations of the Berget 2 (Tørhaug 2002), Vestgård 3 (K. B. Johansen 2004) and Vestgård 6 (Jaksland and Tørhaug 2004) sites. It would seem reasonable that farming eventually was introduced also in these coastal areas, and as it would probably be presumptuous to believe that all megalithic graves once built have been preserved until today, it is conceivable that the construction of megalithic monuments in the coastal region happened as the farming TRB gained foothold there, especially if we take the whole coastal region down to Gothenburg into account - pace J. G. D. Clark, who preferred to view the West Swedish megalithic graves as more likely built by a coastal hunting and fishing population (Clark 1977). One may speculate that it was precisely the confrontation with a fertile coastal culture which created the necessity for display on such a monumental scale, even if the main motive behind this custom may have been that it had become the norm within TRB societies throughout Scandinavia. A quite similar, and indeed more detailed, picture emerges from Sjögrens recent study of Bohuslän during TRB times (Sjögren 2003, 162ff). The finds from the 1980-

81 excavation at Skjeltorp are entered under the number C36732 in the museum inventory.

Holtenes (Rødtangen), Hurum, Buskerud. The Holtenes farm lies at the southern end of the Hurum peninsula between the Drammen fiord to the west and the Oslo fiord to the east, the outermost headland being known as Rødtangen. Here, about 53 km to the northwest from Skjeltorp as the crow flies, a couple of stone cists were known from early descriptions to have existed, only one of which was thought to have survived by the 1940s. Although they had never been investigated archaeologically, they were generally supposed to be of LN date (Brøgger 1938; Gjessing 1945, 428; Munch 1963, 65f). The attention accorded to these graves in later years has however established the more or less probable presence of four megalithic monuments, which have been called Holtenes I-IV from north to south (Østmo 1985, 70; 2002) (17) (Fig. 9 and 10).

- *Holtenes I.* This is the one remaining of the two "stone cists" mentioned in older literature (Fig. 10). It is situated at c. 34 m above sea level in the south-western slope beneath a cliff on which three impressive cairns of probable Bronze Age date catch the eye. The honour for its discovery must go to Miss Marriet Kiær, of Rødtangen, Hurum, in a letter to Gabriel Gustafson in 1913. Sverre Marstrander during a visit in 1943 was able to collect information establishing that 30 years earlier a large rock slab had covered the stone chamber. According to one local account, this slab was broken into pieces and used in the foundation wall of the small country house called "Birkely" which was built in 1911 (or at least during the early years of the last century) and is still standing immediately to the south of the grave monument, while others believe that it was used as a sill before the same house. Anyway, Miss Kiær's description in 1913 contains sufficient detail to assume that the stone cist at that time looked much like today, but also that the surrounding stone circle was better preserved then than it is now. A photograph of the monument taken by Jan Petersen during a visit in 1916 (Fig. 11) proves that by then, the roof stone had been removed. It also shows a large pile of stones which might perhaps be the remains of the roof slab (unless it is the remains of the stone circle).

In 1978, the monument was investigated and partly excavated by Inge Lindblom as part of a rescue campaign (Lindblom 1980) (Fig. 12). His results confirm that the grave has a chamber built of four still existing slabs, one of which has partly fallen into the chamber, as described already in 1913. The chamber is approximately square with sides of c. 1.7 m, and rises about 80 cm above the ground. Quite faint traces of the low mound once surrounding the chamber and still visible on the 1916 photograph (fig. 11) can still be seen, as can some of the stones presumably forming the periphery of the mound, the diameter of which seems to have been approximately 6 m. There is no sign of a passage, but the entrance would appear to have been from southeast, where there is an opening between two of the slabs forming the chamber walls.

Lindblom did not find any material for radiocarbon dating, nor any particularly significant artefacts. Only five flint flakes, four of which were retouched in various ways, were recovered, all from inside the chamber (C35104 a-d; Fig. 13).

The archaeological finds containing so few clues, it is perhaps understandable that Lindblom in his interpretation of the monument appears reluctant to challenge the traditional opinion that it was a stone cist (Norwegian: hellekiste) of probable LN date. He does, however, mention briefly the possibility that "Danish and Swedish dolmens could have been the models" for the Holtenes grave, but feels compelled to conclude that his investigation has brought him nowhere nearer a conclusion (Lindblom 1980, 152f).

With its almost square chamber which previously had a single slab as a roof, the surrounding, low mound and its footing of rather substantial stone slabs, interpreting Holtenes I as a dolmen seems most appropriate (Østmo 1985). Quite in line with these observations, the grave is classified as Ds 2 by Blomqvist (1989, 194). Even so, this is to some degree an afterthought, as only the excavation of the Holtenes III monument in 1984 (of which more below) paved the way for it. A similar claim probably would have met with many a raised eyebrow in 1978.

As it is, the interpretation of Holtenes I as a dolmen of the early type Ds 2, if morphologically correct, remains a hypothesis as long as datable archaeological finds are missing. But in view of the architectural characteristics mentioned, and the situation just above the EN shoreline, which probably lay approximately 30 m above the present (18) not very far from the more securely identified Holtenes III, this interpretation today stands as the more likely and is not contradicted by any observations.

- *Holtenes II.* Holtenes I, which has been described above, as mentioned is situated just north of a small country house, probably erected in 1911. Local tradition, recounted to the author by Mr. Truls Lien of Holtenes farm, maintains that at the site of this house there was previously another grave chamber similar to Holtenes I. It would seem to have disappeared without a trace, unless remains of the surrounding mound are preserved just outside the basement wall on the lower, south-western side of the house. Maybe it was removed to make way for the house prior to 1911. This hypothetical grave is entered here under the name "Holtenes II". Nothing more can be said about it, of course.

- *Holtenes III.* About 450 m to the southeast from Holtenes I, and at c. 33 m above the sea at almost exactly the same level, lies another small mound, about eight meters across and 0.5 meter high (Fig. 14). It was unknown to archaeologists until the 1970s, when it was brought to their attention by the owner of Holtenes farm, Mr. Truls Lien. In the middle of the mound, a quite substantial stone slab still can be seen rising c. 80 cm above the mound just beside a depression, almost a crater, in the mound. On the lower, more clearly defined side, the mound seems to be lined with rocks forming a footing.

Mr. Lien, who at the time was also chairman of the Hurum Historical Society, expressed an interest in investigating this monument, which has continued to intrigue him since his childhood (Dyb 1997). This investigation finally was carried out in 1984 by the present author, with financial support from the Society (Østmo 1985).

The excavation revealed that the standing slab without any doubt had formed the south-western wall of a round or polygonal stone chamber, probably with four more walls and a diameter of approximately two and a half metres (Fig. 15). A passage or even an entrance could not be identified. The chamber floor still had some of its original paving of stone tiles and otherwise consisted of fine, yellow sand.

In this floor two tanged points of flint of the types A 1 and A 3 were found, along with a possible fragment of a bit (19), one retouched flake, a small blade and a chip from a polished axe (20). The tip of a slate point was also found (Fig. 16). However, the most remarkable finds certainly were several fragments of amber ornaments, such as had never previously been found in this country (Fig. 17). At least five different pieces were identified; among them

one with transversal holes from the edges, similar to the type DO 127 and one intermediary from an amber necklace of the type DO 128 (Glob 1952, 88). It seems likely that all five pieces have belonged to this necklace.

In the crater or chamber filling we found another fragment of a slate point and some flint waste, some of which was also found in the mound filling and outside its rim on the south-eastern side, where we looked for the entrance or some pottery, alas in vain.

The amber pieces made it obvious that the grave must have belonged to the TRB (cf. Neergaard 1888; Nordman 1917, 255ff; Thorvildsen 1941, 54; Glob 1952, 23f). The other finds from the chamber floor generally are compatible with this attribution. Tanged points of type A, it will be recalled, were found also in connection with the Skjeltorp dolmen described above, and the slate points also fit into this picture (Bakka 1976; Nærøy 1993; cf. also Østmo 1980).

In absolute terms, the dating of the Holtenes III burial follows from a radiocarbon dating of a little charcoal which was found in the chamber floor, to 4660±80 BP (TUa-5828), that is, 3650-3100 calBC with a double standard deviation (21), which is almost exactly the same as at Skjeltorp, and clearly within the period of megalithic grave construction, indeed, the period of its widest distribution as indicated above.

So, the Holtenes III grave, with its chamber of large stone slabs set in the middle of a low, round mound, clearly was a megalithic grave too. No passage has been identified, but it appears likely that like the Skjeltorp grave it was a polygonal dolmen (Østmo 1985). Accordingly, it is classified as a Ds 3 dolmen by Blomqvist (Blomqvist 1989, 194). The finds from Holtenes III are entered under C36731 in the museum inventory.

- *Holtenes IV.* The fourth stone-built grave chamber at Rødtangen, Holtenes would seem to have disappeared in the early years of the 20th century, and no traces of it have been preserved; even its exact position is at present somewhat uncertain. The only source to its existence is a brief note, no more than a scrap of paper (Fig. 18) which is filed in the archives of the University Museum of Cultural Heritage in Oslo. It records the information received on January 5th., 1908, on the acquisition of a flint axe said to have been found in a grave chamber at Rødtangen "ca. 10 m n.f. Rødtangens Hotel", incidentally of which nothing more exists either. The "n.f." could mean "north of", but also possibly is short for Norw. "nedenfor", that is, below. The grave was described as "a stone cist consisting of 4 slabs which rose c. one half metre above the ground, but went far down into it. The finder said that the axe lay c. 1 2'-2' underneath some smaller tiles, which he considered to be floor tiles" (22). From the simple design at the edge of the paper it seems that the stone cist measured c. 1.5 by 1 metre. However, the measures given are described as "possibly too small". It is also mentioned that the grave was believed to be standing still and that it had not been fully excavated. In the museum catalogue it is further mentioned that the place was situated at about 20 m above the sea. Not being mentioned in the original record this piece of information does however seem secondary; one may suspect that it was taken from the maps available at the time.

So, having been recorded in 1908, this grave was known for a long time and with Holtenes I is one of the two stone graves at Rødtangen sometimes mentioned briefly in old archaeological literature. The dating of the grave would seem to rest on the correct identification and dating of the axe, the description of the grave itself being too brief to allow a decisive conclusion. The axe (Fig.

Fig. 10. The Holtenes I dolmen as restored in 1978. Photo: Inge Lindblom/Museum of Cultural History, University of Oslo

19) has been variously identified; in the museum inventory it is simply described as a thin-bladed, small flint axe (Mørck and Brøgger 1915, 42, where the information about the find circumstances also is quoted). Erik Hinsch acknowledged that it was of the thin-butted variety, but then somewhat surprisingly went on to treat it as a certain, indeed the only quite certain find of a stone cist grave attributable to influences from North Jutland during the time of the MN B Single-Grave Culture (Hinsch 1956, 33f; 175f; ill. fig. 84b p. 155; repeated by Solberg 2006, 89). However, direct influences from North Jutland across the sea to the Oslo Fiord region at this early date are not very likely from the point of view of Middle Neolithic seafaring (Østmo 2005).

The piece (C20656) in fact corresponds closely with Poul Otto Nielsen's type b1 among thin-bladed, thin-butted flint axes, i. e. the four-sided variety with polished edges with a sharp butt (Nielsen 1977, 113). As Nielsen argues quite convincingly however, the dating of such axes in no way differs from that of other thin-butted axes, which for those with polished edges covers the entire time span EN B-MN I. The datings are summarized in Nielsen 1977, 109, fig. 48. The thin-bladed axes of the late MN Single-Grave Culture on the other hand, are quite rare. Commonly, they have an oblique edge indicating their hafting as adzes, in addition to being manufactured with the seemingly less sophisticated technique favoured within the Single-Grave culture (Glob 1945, 137f). None of this fits the description of the Holtenes IV axe. In consequence, nothing about the axe can be seen to support the late dating favoured by Hinsch.

This must lead to the conclusion that the axe and therefore also the Holtenes IV grave chamber belong to the TRB, and consequently that the chamber was part of some kind of megalithic grave, certainly a dolmen. This identification is based on the identification of the flint axe, but fits reasonably well with the description of the grave chamber also. Should one venture a guess at a more precise classification, the information available is compatible with the Ds 1 characteristics as defined by Blomqvist (Blomqvist 1989, 52). The dating of the axe certainly does not contradict this classification. The main problem remaining concerns the position of the grave, which as mentioned was reported to be c. 20 m above the sea. Certainly, the area where the Rødtangen Hotel once stood lies approximately 20 m above sea level. This might seem rather too low to correspond with an EN or early MN date, but the possibility remains that the information about the level can be dismissed as a speculation on part of the museum staff receiving the information, based on a glance at the map. However, considerable uncertainty remains about precisely where the stone cist was actually discovered. The precise meaning of the expression "ca. 10 m n.f. Rødtangens Hotel" used by the allegedly somewhat reluctant, anonymous finder in 1908 cannot be reconstructed with certainty today. What the record does make certain, on the other hand, is that the axe cannot reasonably have been found in any of the two still remaining megalithic graves at Rødtangen or Holtenes (nor, for that matter, the hypothetical Holtenes II tomb). Anyway, it seems preferable to build on such facts as are available. The more likely interpretation of this monument consequently would seem to be as a dolmen, possibly of the Ds 1 type.

Fig. 11. Holtenes I, photographed in 1916. Photo: Jan Petersen/Museum of Cultural History, University of Oslo.

CONCLUSIONS. THE NORTHERN BOUNDARY OF THE MEGALITHIC TRADITION

For a certain time around the mid-fourth millennium BC, then, Holtenes was a focal point in the landscape in which the "TRB people" lived, and presumably therefore also in their minds. This was where the ancestry cult and whatever other functions that were connected with megalithic monuments were practiced. The situation of the Holtenes tombs right by the inlet to the Drammen fiord certainly is not accidental. Even so, it is not possible to connect their presence there to other archaeological vestiges of the TRB in the immediate vicinity, at least as regards the Hurum peninsula itself, where single finds of TRB axes are very few. In this respect, the situation at Holtenes is reminiscent of that at Skjeltorp and indeed the whole of West Sweden as reported by Sjögren (2003). However, in nearby Sande, just across the fiord to the south

from Holtenes, there is one of the most conspicuous of all concentrations of TRB flint axe finds known in the Oslo fiord region. This may be taken as another remainder of the significance of the sea as providing the superior means of communication during the Neolithic, rather than the divide it has all but become in later times (Malmer 2002). Indeed, from this point of view Holtenes easily emerges as particularly well-chosen, being at the same time easy to reach and difficult to avoid, since the important sea route to the fertile regions around Drammen and beyond passes by at no more than a couple of cable lengths. Prior to the development of modern communication means, this route in fact was one of the most important connections between the fertile regions in SE Norway and the western fiord country (Steen 1942, 265).

All the three megalithic graves which have been investigated archaeologically in SE Norway - Skjeltorp and Holtenes I and III - appear to have stood

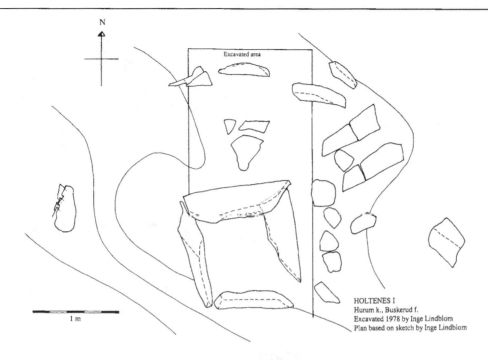

N

Excavated area

1 m

HOLTENES I
Hurum k., Buskerud f.
Excavated 1978 by Inge Lindblom
Plan based on sketch by Inge Lindblom

Fig. 12. Plan of the Holtenes I dolmen. Redrawn from Lindblom 1980. Contour interval 0,1 m.

virtually intact for more than five thousand years until destruction set in the 1850s, only 150 years ago. Today, their reduced state lends considerable uncertainty to any attempt to characterize them typologically. However, all have been shown to have been set in round, low mounds with diameters of about 6 to 8.6 m. In all cases, there are traces of a row of stones at the edge of the mounds. The chambers have been built of large, natural stones or slabs, to form square or polygonal chambers with four or five walls and roofs which in each case appears to have consisted of one large piece. Only at Skjeltorp has the presence of a passage been established with certainty.

Uncertainties notwithstanding, these descriptions fit very well with the Ds 2 and Ds 3 types of megalithic graves most common in West Sweden as described by Blomqvist. This impression is confirmed by the archaeological finds from Skjeltorp and Holtenes III as well as Holtenes IV. The pottery from Skjeltorp, the amber ornaments from Holtenes III and the flint axe from Holtenes IV prove that these monuments were used, and presumably built, within the Middle TRB at the transition from the EN to the MN. This is confirmed by the radiocarbon datings from Skjeltorp and Holtenes III to the middle of the fourth millennium BC or the time around 3400-3500 BC (Fig. 20).

The megalithic graves therefore were built during the second and most significant of the three TRB phases outlined initially.

The significance of the discovery of the Oslo fiord megaliths to our understanding of the Norwegian Neolithic perhaps is not obvious. But while the Skjeltorp grave might reasonably be thought of as the single northernmost extension of the megalithic tradition as long as it was the only one known, the discovery of the Holtenes graves changed the conditions for assessing the influence of the megalithic tradition in these northern parts.

Ideally, such assessment ought to be based on extensive knowledge about the original number of megalithic monuments and their properties in the region. Could megalithic graves not have existed elsewhere by the Oslo fiord also? In fact, this hypothesis still remains largely untested. A search might perhaps profitably be confined to the outer or southern part of the region, south of the Drøbak straits, the inner or northern part in many ways being different in terms of natural conditions and also archaeologically throughout prehistory. As the known megalithic graves were all built close by the sea-shore at the time, that level perhaps ought to be taken as a clue. This would seem to be around or slightly above the 30 m contour line,

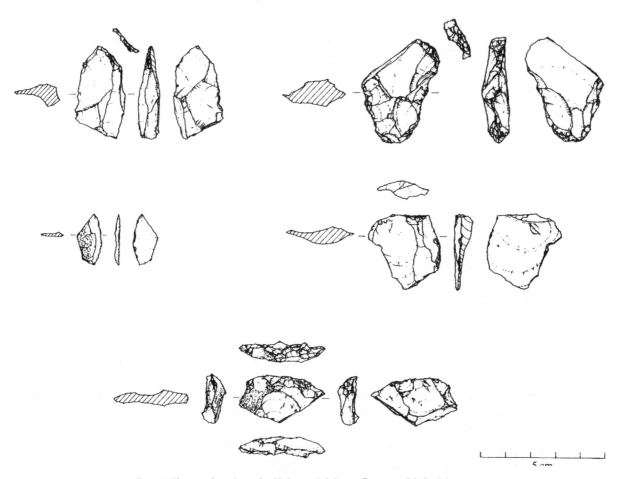

Fig. 13. Flint artefacts from the Holtenes I dolmen. Drawing: Mieko Matsumoto.

which can be read out of the available shore displacement curves for the Oslo fiord area (23). On the question of what to look for, any hopes of finding standing megalithic chambers in a good state of preservation most certainly can be laid to rest, as one must trust that they would have been discovered long ago. But if the slabs forming the chamber have been removed, the remains will look little different from the ruins of other small grave mounds. In such cases, however, excavation will certainly be needed for the nature of the monuments to be revealed.

On the Danish analogy, one could venture a guess that the number of megalithic graves in Norway once built lay in the region of 15, three times the number known. Further, when there has been so little, or indeed no knowledge about these graves, either scholarly or locally, little need will have been felt to preserve them, too. Their strong position as national symbols

in Denmark certainly, as related, is not paralleled in Norway. In theory, this could mean that their number once was substantially higher than today.

Such speculation is of but limited value, however. What remains to be explained, is the circumstance that around the time when megalithic graves were built by the thousands in South Scandinavia, a few were built also by the Oslo fiord, where the northern thrust of this cultural phenomenon subsequently came to its final halt.

The presence at Holtenes of a few megalithic tombs, rather than a single one as at Skjeltorp, representing two or possibly all three of Blomqvist's types, most probably means that the megalithic tradition existed for some time there. Hypothetically, its duration could have equalled that of the Scandinavian megalithic tradition as such, at most the time-span 3600-3200 BC. It is difficult to be more precise than

Fig. 14. The Holtenes III dolmen prior to excavation. Photo: Inge Lindblom/Museum of Cultural History, University of Oslo.

this, except to note that the radiocarbon dating from Holtenes III does fall within this period. There are, however, few definite signs of prolonged or repeated use of any the tombs, the artefact finds rather leaving the impression of singular events. Perhaps this means that it was the actual building and initial use of the graves which was of particular significance to the local TRB society; building a monument was perhaps more important than having one (this notion is developed in detail by Tilley 1996, 157ff). However, the presence in two of the graves (Skjeltorp and Holtenes III) of tanged "A" points, if found in South Scandinavia certainly would have been considered to prove later use of the chambers by the so-called Pitted-Ware Culture. As noted previously, this does not apply to Norway, tanged points having been in use since the beginning of the Neolithic or even the Late Mesolithic (Glørstad 1998 with refs.). Rather, these points demonstrate that by the time the megalithic graves were built, the TRB in this region was following local custom in terms of point technology. The slate point fragments from Holtenes III may be another indication of this local connection, as may several other cross-over finds from various places in south and middle Norway (Østmo 1999). It is worth noting that none of the graves has been found to have been used during the later, Corded-Ware or LN phases, as so often has turned out to be the case in South Scandinavia.

This impression of an unstable or short-lived tradition of applying TRB ritual standards in the Oslo fiord region is, it will be seen, a confirmation of what we found concerning votive sacrifices and flat graves, none of which can be taken to support a notion of permanent ritual places. Typologically, too, the TRB in this region leaves a poorer impression than in South Scandinavia, concerning all three categories of finds and observations.

This perhaps is just what one should expect at the very edge of a wide-spread tradition such as that of the TRB and its megalithic tombs and other signs of elaborate rituals. The TRB spread quickly across the Continent and South Scandinavia, but only briefly touched Middle Scandinavia, in fact only at Holtenes establishing a cult of some duration. Elsewhere it vanished almost as rapidly as it had appeared. Similarities in pottery styles and ornaments across South and Middle Scandinavia testify to the strength of the cultural impulses and the speed of their dissemination. It says something for the effectiveness of communications at the time that the TRB and in particular the megalithic tradition could become so wide-spread at all. But being obviously extremely demanding of both material, social and spiritual resources, it could not be expected to last, and various local developments inevitably would take over. All along its northern border, the TRB seems to have been transformed into other cultural manifestations, in which farming

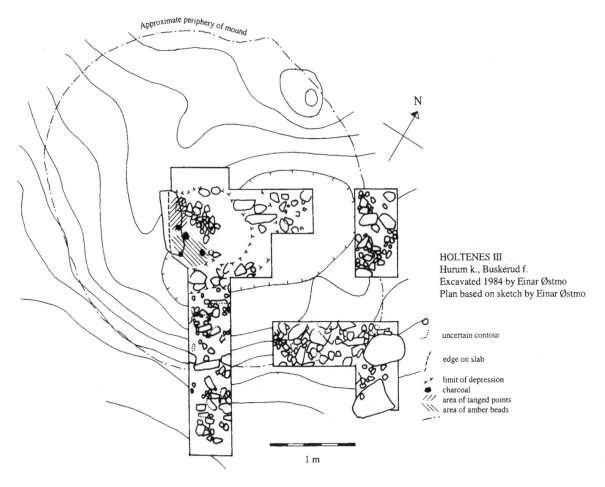

Fig. 15. Plan of the Holtenes III dolmen. Contour interval 0,1 m.

played little or no part but with strongly increased emphasis on coastal hunting and fishing, and with different aesthetic and ideological priorities from the TRB. The flint and slate points recovered from the Norwegian megalithic graves may actually indicate that the process was already under way when the graves were still in use. Hans Browall has suggested that a transformation along such lines took place in middle and southern Sweden, beginning in the north in the Mälaren valley c. 2550 bc (3300-3100 calBC), and reaching North Denmark c. 2250 bc (2900-2700 calBC). As Browall also suggests, a similar situation may have obtained in the western part of middle Scandinavia, that is, in Norway and west Sweden. This view is if anything strengthened by closer consideration of the sacrificial deposits and earthen and megalithic graves found in Norway such as carried

out here. It may however need some modification under influence from the continued investigations of the coastal hunting settlements of EN and MN, which increasingly seem to have developed prior to the megalithic tradition and simultaneously with the TRB in all its phases, as more radiocarbon datings and refined analysis of pottery styles become available from all around the South Norwegian coast (Østmo 1993; Glørstad 2004; 2005; Hallgren 2005). Instead of a succession of cultures, we may have to do with co-existing cultural expressions and practices, based on the one hand on a strong local continuity from the Mesolithic, connected with the exploitation of local hunting and fishing resources, and on the other on the combined economic, ideological and aesthetic properties of the TRB with their strongest roots in South Scandinavia. When this gave way after the megalithic

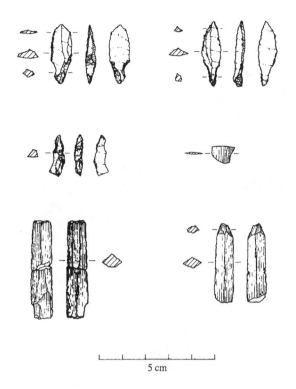

Fig. 16. Artefacts of flint and slate from the Holtenes III dolmen. Upper row: Two tanged point of flint. Middle row: Point of bit and chip of polished axe, both of flint. Lower row: Two fragments of slate points. Drawings: Mieko Matsumoto.

episode, it was to a transformation of the local culture, or rather a merger of the two strains into something new and largely independent.

The archeaological finds from the Norwegian TRB make it quite clear that the expansion of the TRB on the European mainland reached its northern limit in present-day Norway, its most extremely northern manifestations recovered approximately at the Arctic Circle (Østmo 1999). And, even if the archaeological finds attributable to the TRB in Norway in technical and aesthetic terms are comparable to those preserved in the TRB core regions in South Scandinavia, their number as well as their scope appear comparably limited, as demonstrated here concerning both megalithic graves, flat graves and sacrificial deposits. It might be expected that the TRB under these circumstances assumed some form of "borderline" character, that it was somehow affected by the extreme position in which it found itself. The TRB perhaps might be expected to "behave" differently north of the 60th parallel than in its core areas

on the North European Plain in Poland, North Germany, Denmark and Scania.

This would reasonably concern the relationship between the TRB and other cultural influences at work in the region, as well as its relationship with the surrounding natural conditions. This was pointed out by Hulthén and Welinder, who were able to show that the northern limit of the TRB in the SE Norwegian Oslo Fiord region, as well as in Mälardalen, Middle Sweden, in the main followed the same course as that of brown-soil, broadleaf forest 6000-5000 BP (Hulthén and Welinder 1981, 156ff, esp. fig. 17.1-5.).

The limit of any natural or cultural phenomenon can in itself assume many different forms. In Norway, as in similar heavily indented coastal regions elsewhere, many such borders follow exceedingly complicated courses. The coastline itself is a prime example of this - the border between land and sea in Norway is undulating, to put it mildly. As a consequence, the sea is usually never far away, and has always been of prime concern to those living here, affecting Norwegian culture to produce one of the great seafaring civilizations of the world. Similarly complicated distribution patterns will be found to characterize many other natural phenomena in the rugged Norwegian landscape, concerning everything from geology and soil conditions to climate, vegetation and historically attested fauna. The combined effect of many such conditions is a complex web or landscape of great variety and dynamism. At all times this has produced the effect that people living anywhere in the country are surrounded by quite differentiated natural conditions and a great variety of natural resources, often at short distances.

The effects of this on culture have been of concern to scholars interested in the cultural history of Norway for a long time, and arguably could be said to be the main content of A.W. Brøgger's particularly Norwegian school of archaeological thought, which he launched to considerable attention from 1925 onwards (Brøgger 1925; 1926), and which has continued to play an important part in Norwegian archaeology ever since, in addition to being of acknowledged inspiration outside Norwegian archaeology as well (e.g. Clark 1952). The ideas of this school could be said to be twofold, concerning both close connections between cultural and natural history long before some-

Fig. 16. Artefacts of flint and slate from the Holtenes III dolmen. Upper row: Two tanged point of flint. Middle row: Point of bit and chip of polished axe, both of flint. Lower row: Two fragments of slate points. Drawings: Mieko Matsumoto.

thing similar became common with the advent of "New Archaeology" around 1970, and the notion that life in Norway and indeed elsewhere under similar natural conditions always was dependent on a variety of natural resources and complex economic strategies to exploit them.

The scope for assuming a "pure", agricultural TRB in Norway in this perspective sometimes has been small, and certainly has affected the thinking of those scholars inclined to view the TRB as an exception to "normal" conditions in the Norwegian Neolithic, e.g. Christopher Prescott's reluctance to accept the existence of a "Norwegian Neolithic" quoted earlier (p. XX), indeed without doubt a late expression precisely of A.W. Brøgger's archaeological heritage. But the reality remains that the TRB in Norway, even if undoubtedly present at least by the Oslo Fiord in many significant aspects (Østmo and Skogstrand 2006), in most of the country will have been surrounded at close quarters by, and possibly challenged by natural conditions inviting other forms of subsistence than those adopted by the South Scandinavian TRB. The

hunters and fishermen inhabiting the shores, fiords and valleys of South Norway when the TRB to some degree became established here, may have continued to represent more of a presence, and perhaps more of a challenge than the case may have been in Kujawia and Denmark, and the adoption of some TRB cultural elements as far north as Trøndelag and Nordland may have been more connected with traditional forms of life than similar developments farther south.[1]

1 Acknowledgements. A word of gratitude is due to the Foundation for Danish-Norwegian Cooperation (Fondet for Dansk-Norsk Samarbeid), a generous grant from which enabled me to begin work on this paper during a pleasant week at Schæffergården in Copenhagen in February, 2000. Also, special thanks are due to Mieko Matsumoto for her enthusiastic and insightful work on the flint materials from Skjeltorp and Holtenes. At various stages during the writing of this paper, insightful and encouraging comments were offered by Håkon Glørstad and Christopher Prescott, for which I am happy to express my sincere gratitude. Any errors or other failings however remain the sole responsibility of the author.

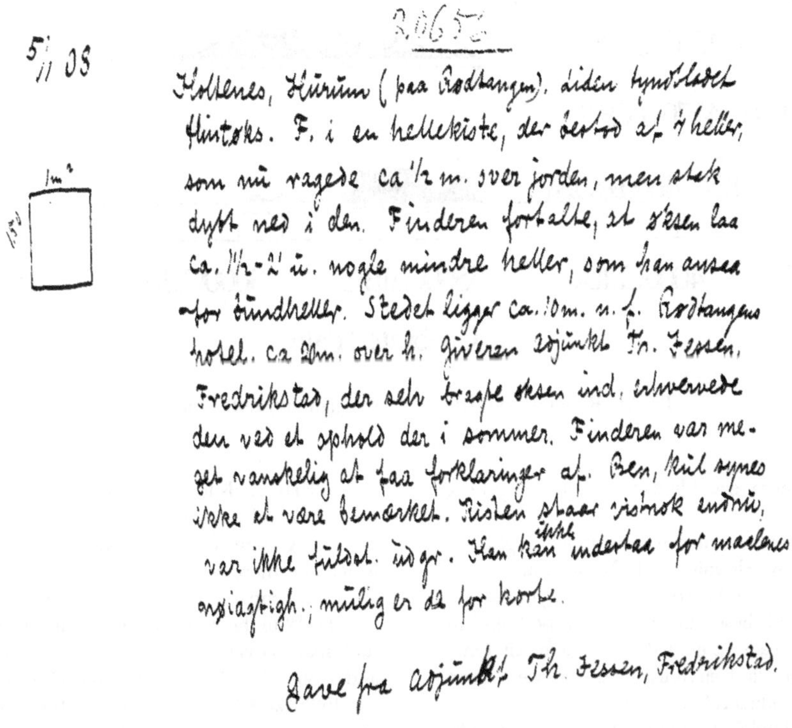

[handwritten note in Norwegian/Danish cursive]

Fig. 18. The note and outline of the Holtenes IV grave chamber preserved in the archives of the Museum of Cultural History, University of Oslo.

NOTES

(1) Museum inventory numbers in Norwegian archaeological museums take the form e. g. C20000 a, where C denotes the museum in question (C=Oslo [originally Christiania], B=Bergen, S=Stavanger, T=Trondheim and Ts=Tromsø), 20000 denotes the find or actual collection at hand, and a is a subsidiary number concerning a single item or collection of similar items. For a survey of the system, see Østmo 1998b.

(2) Some of the more prominent sites are published in Bakka (†) 1993 (Ramsvikneset): Bang-Andersen 1981 (Gjedlestadvika); Gustafson 1900 and Skjølsvold 1980 (Holeheia); Ingstad 1970 (Rognlien); Müller og Ingstad 1965 (Sluppan); Nummedal og Bjørn 1930 (Narestø, Viten); Olsen 1992 (Kotedalen); Skjølsvold 1977 (Slettabø); Østmo 1993 and Østmo, Hulthén and Isaksson 1996 (Auve, preliminary publications); Østmo 2004 (Solbakken 3, preliminary publication).

(3) Inevitably, this view is not shared by all. For other interpretations, common to which seems to be that of history as general, and uniform, progress, see e. g. Bjerck 1988, Mikkelsen 1989, Pedersen 2003.

(4) So-called bog pots of TRB types, which have played such an important part in defining the South-Scandinavian TRB (Becker 1948; Koch 1998) have not been identified in Norwegian finds. The previously mentioned finds of TRB pottery from Lundvoll in Tune, Sarpsborg, Østfold (Østmo 1988, 154f) and Børsebakke in Rygge, Østfold are not sufficiently well investigated to decide whether they are sacrificial deposits or something else. The same

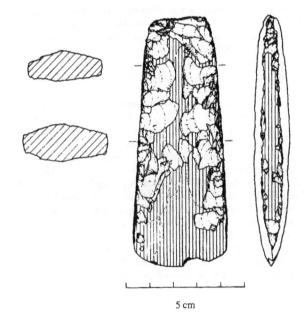

5 cm

Fig. 19. The flint axe from Holtenes IV. Drawing: Mieko Matsumoto.ig. 20. Radiocarbon datings from megalithic graves at Skjeltorp and Holtenes III. Calibration according to OxCal v. 3.10 (Bronk Ramsey 1995; 2000).

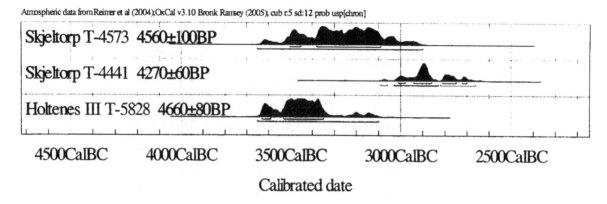

Fig. 20. Radiocarbon dates of Norwegian megalithe graves.

remark applies also to the more recent finds from Bede, Sarpsborg and from Bærum, Akershus.

(5) Information about find circumstances is usually registered in the museum inventories, which uniquely to Norway, have been published almost in their entirety in (sometimes anonymous) annual instalments. A survey of these publications can be found in Østmo 1998b, to which the reader is guided once and for all. Only when the information about find circumstances has been taken from other sources, are individual references given.

(6) Most are listed and simplified plans are shown by Blomqvist 1989; Lillehammer 1994, 61f and Solberg 2006 mention the graves in popular form; Østmo 1990 includes a brief summary of the graves and other TRB material from SE Norway.

(7) For the first Norwegians with a recorded interest in ancient monuments, the situation was different. Jens Nilssøn, bishop of Oslo from 1580 to 1600, mentions several "giant's graves" in the diaries of his visitation travels through Bohuslän, then part of the diocese of Oslo (Nilsen (ed.) 1885).

(8) In Shetland, considerably farther north than the Oslo fiord region, about two hundred megalithic tombs, or cairns are known (Wainwright 1964, 32).

(9) Particularly well-preserved examples from the Swedish west coast are Vä 5 Skee 272 (Ds 1), Vä 34 Lyse 192 (Ds 2) and Vä 79 Valla 98 (Ds 3) (all from Blomqvist 1989).

(10) Another megalithic grave was claimed by Lorange at Grålum in Tune (Sarpsborg), Østfold (Lorange 1870, 101). This was accepted with caution by Montelius (1905, 34) and Shetelig (1922, 322) as an "isolated dolmen without a passage" (Sw: "fristående dös utan gång"), neither however without actually having seen the mounument in question. During the topographical-archaeological survey in the 1960ies it was identified as an Iron Age circle of standing stones (Larsen 1985).

(11) It was a touching link with the past when our excavation at Skjeltorp in 1981 was visited by Mr. Edvard Skjeltorp, who as a young boy in 1908 had showed the way to the site to professor Gustafson.

(12) The finds from the excavation of the Skjeltorp dolmen are registered under No. C36732 a-y.

(13) A more comprehensive survey of the finds has been published elsewhere, v. Østmo 1982, 107ff.

(14) Compare for instance DO 186, Glob 1952.

(15) With the more conventional single standard deviation, the time-spans covered by the 68.2% confidence are 3500-3450 BC and 3380-3090 BC, according to OxCal, Version 3.10 (Bronk Ramsey 1995; 2000). Another radiocarbon sample cannot have been connected with the construction of the monument, to judge from the resulting age of 2520±170 BP (T-4442). This sample was taken from the peripheral ditch.

(16) The coast line for 4580 radiocarbon years bp has been reconstructed taking into consideration that the land rise has been greater along a north-easterly trajectory. The details are explained in Østmo 1988, 19ff.

(17) Less aptly named "Holmsbu 1-4" in Blomqvist 1989.

(18) Rolf Sørensen's shore-line diagram for the Ski area, which must apply to the Holtenes area also within a very small margin, places the shore line at 4500 radiocarbon years bp at c. 32 m above the present, Sørensen 1979, 243.

(19) Sometimes called a "borer" in English language Scandinavian archaeological literature.

(20) The finds from Holtenes III are entered under C36731 a-n in the museum inventory.

(21) With a single standard deviation, the periods represented are 3630-3590 BC and 3530-3350 BC after OxCal v3.10.

(22) The author's translation from Norwegian.

(23) Sørensen 1979, 243 for the Rødtangen region; cf. also Danielsen 1970, 128, Østmo 1988, 25, Sørensen 1999 and Påsse 2003 for the eastern shore in the southern part of the region (i. e. Østfold) and Henningsmoen 1979 for the western shore (i. e. Vestfold), as well as Hafsten 1956, 142 for the inner or northern part of the Oslo fiord.

BIBLIOGRAPHY

Aksdal, J. 1996: Neolitikum i Vestnoreg. Sosiale Prosessar i eit Regionalt Perspektiv. Hovudfagsoppgåve i Arkeologi. Arkeologisk Institutt Universitetet i Bergen. Vår 1996. (Unpublished Cand. philol. thesis).

Bakka, E. 1976: Comments on Typological and Chronological Problems. Stone Age Chronology in the Light of Hein 33. Norwegian Archaeological Review. Vol. 9, No. 1 1976.

- (^) 1993: Ramsvikneset - a Sub-Neolithic Dwelling Place in Western Norway. I Bergljot Solberg (ed.): Minneskrift Egil Bakka. Arkeologiske Skrifter. Historiske Museum. Universitetet i Bergen. No. 7-1993. Bergen.

Bang-Andersen, S. 1981: En fangstboplass på Eigerøy - boplassbruk og miljøtilpasning i sørvestnorsk yngre steinalder. AmS-Skrifter. 6. Stavanger.

Becker, C. J. 1948: Mosefundne Lerkar fra Yngre Stenalder. København.

- 1951: Den grubekeramiske kultur i Danmark. Aarbøger for nordisk Oldkyndighed og Historie. 1950.

- 1955: Stenalderbebyggelsen ved Store Valby i Vest-Sjælland. Aarbøger for nordisk Oldkyndighed og Historie 1954.

Berg, E. 1993; Symbolic aspects of selected groups of Neolithic axes/adzes in Western Norway. Universitetets Oldsaksamling. Årbok 1991/1992.

Bjerck, L. G. Bostwick 1988: Remodelling the Neolithic in Southern Norway: Another Attack on a Traditional Problem. With Comments by Hans Göransson, Helge I. Høeg, Kristina Jennbert, Peter Rowley-Conwey and Einar Østmo and a reply from Lisa G. Bostwick Bjerck. Norwegian Archaeological Review. Vol. 21, No 1, 1988.

Bjørn, A. 1924: Stenalderstudier. Videnskabs-Selskabets Skrifter. II. Hist.-filos. klasse 1924. No. 5. Kristiania.

- 1928: Bidrag til den yngre stenalder i Øst-Norge. Universitetets Oldsaksamling. Årbok 1927.

Blomqvist, L. 1989: Megalitgravarna i Sverige. Typ, tid, rum och social miljö. Theses and Papers in Archaeology 1. Stockholm.

Boaz, J. 1998: Hunter-Gatherer Site Variability: Changing patterns of site utilization in the interior of eastern Norway, between 8000 and 2500 B.P. Universitetets Oldsaksamlings Skrifter. Ny rekke. Nr. 20. Oslo.

Bronk Ramsey, C. 1995: Radiocarbon Calibration and Analysis of Stratigraphy: The OxCal Program. Radiocarbon 37(2), 425-430.

- 2000: Comment on 'The Use of Bayesian Statistics for 14C dates of chronologically ordered samples: a critical analysis'. Radiocarbon 42(2), 199-202.

Browall, H. 1991: Om förhållandet mellan trattbägarkultur och gropkeramisk kultur. I Hans Browall, Per Persson & Karl-Göran Sjögren (ed.): Västsvenska stenåldersstudier. Gotarc. Serie C. Arkeologiska skrifter No 8. Göteborg.

Brøgger, A. W. 1906: Studier over Norges stenalder. I. Øxer uden skafthul fra yngre stenalder fundne i det sydøstlige Norge. Videnskabsselskabets skrifter. I. 1906. Nr. 2. Kristiania.

- 1925: Det norske folk i oldtiden. Instituttet for sammenlignende kulturforskning. Serie A, Forelesninger. 6 a. Oslo.

- 1926: Kulturgeschichte des norwegischen Altertums. Instituttet for sammenlignende kulturforskning. Serie A, Forelesninger. 6. Oslo.

- 1938: Elghornøksen fra Hurum-ryggen. Viking. Bind II.

Brøndsted, J. 1957: Danmarks Oldtid. I. Stenalderen. Anden reviderede udgave. København: Gyldendal.

Bägerfeldt, L. & Kihlstedt, B. 1985: Västkustens megalitgravar. En konstruktionsanalys. Uppsats i påbyggnadskurs i Arkeologi, särskilt Nordeuropeisk, vid Stockholms Universitet framlagd vårterminen 1985. Stockholm.

Clark, J.G.D. 1977: The economic context of dolmens and passage-graves in Sweden. Ancient Europe and the Mediterranean. Studies presented in the honour of Hugh Hencken. Warminster.

Danielsen, A. 1970: Pollen-Analytical Late Quarternary Studies in the Ra District of Østfold, Southeast Norway. Årbok for Universitetet i Bergen. Mat.-naturv. Serie. 1969 No 14.

Dyb, S. E. 1997: Truls fant steinaldergraven på Villa Dag. In K. Ronge (ed.): Historiske glimt fra Rødtangen. Utgitt av Rødtangen Vel og Vannverk. S. 1.

Ebbesen, K. 1975: Die jüngere Trichterbecherkultur auf den dänischen Inseln. Arkæologiske studier. Volume II. København (Akademisk Forlag).

- 1984: Tragtbægerkulturens grønstensøkser. KUML 1984, 113-153.

- 1985: Fortidsminderegistrering i Danmark. København: Fredningsstyrelsen.

- 1994a: Simple, tidligneolitiske grave. Aarbøger for nordisk Oldkyndighed og Historie. 1992.

- 1994b: Tragtbægerkulturens dolkstave. Aarbøger for nordisk Oldkyndighed og Historie. 1992.

- 1998: Frühneolithische Streitäxte. Acta Archaeologica. Vol. 69-1998, 77-112.

- 2002: Neolitiske ravperler i Västergötland. in Situ. Västsvensk Arkeologisk Tidskrift. 2002, 85-126.

Gjessing, G. 1945: Norges steinalder. Oslo.

Glob, P. V. 1945: Studier over den jyske Enkeltgravskultur. Aarbøger for nordisk Oldkyndighed og Historie. 1944.

- 1952: Danish Antiquities. II. Late Stone Age. Copenhagen.

Glørstad, H. 1998: Senmesolitikum i Østfold - et kronologisk persepktiv. In E. Østmo (Ed.): Fra Østfolds oldtid. Foredrag ved 25-årsjubileet for Universitetets arkeologiske stasjon Isegran. Universitetets Oldsaksamlings Skrifter. Ny rekke. Nr. 21. Oslo.

- 2004: Svinesundprosjektet. Bind 4. Oppsummering av Svinesundprosjektet. Varia 57. Universitetets kulturhistoriske museer. Fornminneseksjonen. Oslo.

- 2005: Tangen - En neolittisk boplass fra Kragerø kommune i Telemark. Noen betraktninger omkring boplassens kulturmiljø og Traktbegerkulturens vestgrense. Viking. Bind LXVIII-2005, 25-54.

Gustafson, G. 1900: En stenalders boplads paa Jæderen. Bergens Museums Aarbog 1899. No. I.

- 1914: Megalitiske graver i Norge. Oldtiden. Tidsskrift for norsk forhistorie. Avhandlinger tilegnet K. Rygh, 1-8. Kristiania.

Hafsten, U. 1956: Pollen-analytic investigations on the late Quarternary development in the inner Oslofjord area. Universitetet i Bergen. Årbok 1956. Naturvitenskapelig rekke. Nr. 8.

Hallgren, F. 2005: Kommentar till Marianne Skandfer: *Fra eldre til yngre steinalder? ...+. Primitive tider. 8, 113-118.

Hansen, Dr. A. M. 1904: Landnåm i Norge. En utsigt over bosætningens historie. Kristiania (W. C. Fabritius & Sønner A/S).

Helskog, K. S. Indrelid og E. Mikkelsen 1976: Morfologisk

klassifisering av slåtte steinartefakter. Universitetets Oldsaksamling. Årbok 1972-1974.

Henningsmoen, K. E. 1979: En karbon-datert strandforskyvningskurve fra søndre Vestfold. I Reidar Nydal et al. (ed.): Fortiden i søkelyset. 14C datering gjennom 25 år. Trondheim: Laboratoriet for radiologisk datering.

Hinsch, E. 1955: Traktbegerkultur-Megalitkultur. En studie av Øst-Norges eldste, neolitiske gruppe. Universitetets Oldsaksamling. Årbok 1951-1953. Oslo.

Hougen, B. 1946: Disenfunnet. Et dyssetids votivfunn fra Østre Aker. Viking. Bind X.

Hufthammer, A. K. 1997: The vertebrate faunal remains from Auve - a palaeoecological investigation. Auve. Bind II. Tekniske og naturvitenskapelige undersøkelser. Norske Oldfunn XVII. Institutt for arkeologi, kunsthistorie og numismatikk. Universitets Oldsaksamling. Oslo.

Indrelid, S. and D. Moe 1983: Februk på Hardangervidda i yngre steinalder. Viking. Bind XLVI 1982.

Ingstad, A. S. 1970: Steinalderboplassen Rognlien i Eidanger. Et bidrag til belysning av yngre steinalder i Telemark. Universitetets Oldsaksamling. Årbok 1967-1968.

Jaksland, L. and Tørhaug, V. 2004: Vestgård 6 - en tidligneolittisk fangstboplass. In H. Glørstad (ed.): Svinesundprosjektet. Bind 3. Utgravninger avsluttet i 2003. Varia 56. Universitetets kulturhistoriske museer. Fornminneseksjonen. Oslo, 65-144.

Jensen, H. J. 1994: Flint Tools and Plant Working. Hidden Traces of Stone Age Technology. A use wear study of some Danish Mesolithic and TRB implements. Aarhus (Aarhus University Press).

Jensen, J. 2001: Danmarks Oldtid. Stenalder 13.000-2.000 f.Kr. København (Gyldendal).

Johansen, K. B. 2004: Vestgård 3 - en boplass fra tidligneolitikum. In H. Glørstad (ed.): Svinesundprosjektet. Bind 3. Utgravninger avsluttet i 2003. Varia 56. Universitetets kulturhistoriske museer. Fornminneseksjonen. Oslo, 31-64.

Johansen, K. F. 1917: Jordgrave fra Dyssetid. Aarbøger for nordisk Oldkyndighed og Historie. 1917.

Johansen, Ø. K. 1993: Norske depotfunn fra bronsealderen. Universitetets Oldsaksamlings Skrifter. Ny rekke. Nr. 15. Oslo: IAKN Oldsaksamlingen.

- 2002: Rådes eldste historie. Bind 1. De første.. Råde.

Karsten, P. 1994: Att kasta yxan i sjön. En studie över rituell tradition och förändring utifrån skånska neolitiska offerfynd. Acta Archaeologica Lundensia. Series in 8o. No. 23. Stockholm.

Kaul, F. 1991: [Review of] Lars Blomquist: Megalitgravarna i Sverige. Typ, tid, rum och social miljö. Theses and Papers in Archaeology, New Series, Published by the Institute of Archaeology at the University of Stockholm, 1, Stockholm 1989. 333 pp. With English summary. Journal of Danish Archaeology. Volume 8.

Koch, E. 1998: Neolithic Bog Pots from Zealand, Møn, Lolland and Falster. Nordiske Fortidsminder. Serie B. Volume 16. København (Det Kongelige Nordiske Oldskriftselskab).

Lagergren-Olsson, A. 2003: En skånsk keramikhistoria. Pp. 172-213 in M. Svensson (ed.): I det neolitiska rummet. Malmö (Riksantikvarieämbetet).

Larsen, J. H. 1985: Fornminner i Østfold. Rapport om topografisk-arkeologisk registrering for Det økonomiske kartverket. Tune kommune. Oslo (Universitetets Oldsaksamling).

Lillehammer, A. 1994: Fra jeger til bonde - inntil 800 e. Kr. (Volume 1 in Knut Helle (ed.): Aschehougs Norges Historie). Oslo (H. Aschehoug & Co. (W. Nygaard)).

Lindblom, I. 1980: Etterundersøkelse og restaurering av en hellekiste fra yngre steinalder, Holtenes i Hurum, Buskerud. Festskrift til Sverre Marstrander på 70-årsdagen. Universitetets Oldsaksamlings Skrifter. Ny rekke Nr. 3. Oslo.

Lorange, A. 1870: Student A. Loranges Udsigt over hans antikvariske Virksomhed i 1869. Foreningen til norske Fortidsmindesmerkers Bevaring. Aarsberetning for 1869, 97-112. Kristiania.

- 1876: Sur l'age de la pierre en Norvége [sic!]. Congrès international d'anthropologie et d'archéologie préhistoriques. Compte rendu de la 7e session. Stockholm, 1874. Stockholm.

Madsen, T. og Petersen, J. E. 1984: Tidligneolitisk anlæg ved Mosegården. Regionale og kronologiske forskelle i tidligneolitikum. KUML. 1982-83.

Malmer, M. P. 1969: Gropkeramiksboplatsen Jonstorp RÄ. Antikvariskt Arkiv 36. Stockholm (Kungl. Vitterhets Historie och Antikvitets Akademien).

Mathiassen, T. 1939: Bundsø - En yngre Stenalders Boplads paa Als. Aarbøger for nordisk Oldkyndighed og Historie. 1939.

Midgley, M. S. 1985: The Origins and Function of the Earthen Long Barrows of Northern Europe. BAR, Internatinoal Series 259. Oxford.

Mikkelsen, E. (ed.) 1982: Universitetets oldsaksamlings tilvekst 1977-1980. Oslo: Universitetets oldsaksamling.

- 1984: Neolitiseringen i Øst-Norge. Universitetets oldsaksamling. Årbok 1983/1984.

- 1989: Fra jeger til bonde. Utviklingen av jordbrukssamfunn i Telemark i steinalder og bronsealder. Universitetets Oldsaksamlings Skrifter. Ny rekke. Nr. 11.

Montelius, O. 1874: Sveriges forntid. Text. I. Stenåldern. Stockholm.

- 1905: Orienten och Europa. Ett bidrag till kännedomen om den orientaliska kulturens inverkan på Europa intill midten af det sista årtusendet före Kristi födelse. Antiqvarisk Tidskrift för Sverige. Trettonde delen.

Müller, K. V. og A.-S. Ingstad 1965: Sluppan. En fangstboplass fra yngre steinalder i Telemark. Viking. Bind XXIX.

Mørck, G. og A.W. Brøgger 1915: Universitetets oldsaksamlings tilvekst for aarene 1904-1914. Oldtiden. Bind VI første Hefte.

Munch, J. S. 1963: De første menneskene i bygda. In S. L. Eier: Hurums historie. Bind I: Bygdehistorien inntil 1807. Hurum: Hurum Bygdeboknemnd.

Nergaard, C. 1888: Ravsmykkerne i Stenalderen. Aarbøger for nordisk Oldkyndighed og Historie. 1888.

Nicolaysen, N. 1868: Tillæg til *Norske Fornlevninger+. Aarsberetning fra Foreningen til Norske Fortidsmindesmerkers Bevaring. 1867. Kristiania (Carl C. Werner & Komp.'s Bogtrykkeri).

Nielsen, P.-O. 1977: Die Flintbeile der frühen Trichterbecherkultur in Dänemark. Acta Archaeologica. Vol. 48.

- 1981: Danmarkshistorien. Stenalderen. Bondestenalderen. København (Forlaget Sesam a/s).

- 1985: De første bønder. Nye fund fra den tidligste Tragtbægerkultur ved Sigersted. Aarbøger for nordisk Oldkyndighed og Historie. 1984.

Nilsen, Y. (ed.) 1885: Biskop Jens Nilssøns Visitatsbøger og reiseoptegnelser 1574-1597. Kristiania (A.W. Brøggers Bogtrykkeri).

Nordman, C.A. 1917: Studier öfver gånggriftkulturen i Danmark. Aarbøger for nordisk Oldkyndighed og Historie. 1917.

Nummedal, A. og A. Bjørn 1930: Boplassfunn fra yngre stenalder i Aust-Agder. Universitetets oldsaksamling. Årbok 1929.

Nærøy, A. J. 1993: Chronological and Technological Changes in Western Norway 6000-3800 BP. Acta Archaeologica. Vol. 63-1992.

Olsen, A. B. 1992: Kotedalen - en boplass gjennom 5000 år.

Fangstbosetning og tidlig jordbruk i vestnorsk steinalder: Nye funn og nye perspektiver. Bergen.

Østmo, Einar 1973: Om et 130 år gammelt brev fra presten Stabell samt noe om et formodet steinalders offerfunn. Nicolay Nr. 14 1973, 8-11.

- 1980: Boplasskronologi på Skagerakkysten. Festskrift til Sverre Marstrander på 70-årsdagen. Universitetets Oldsaksamlings Skrifter. Ny rekke Nr. 3. Oslo.

- 1982: Une tombe mégalithique en Norvège. Étude sur certains aspects de l'expansion vers le nord de la civilisation des gobelets en entonnoir. Acta Archaeologica. Vol. 52.

- 1983: Megalittgraven på Skjeltorp i Skjeberg. Viking. Bind XLVI-1982.

- 1985: En dysse på Holtenes i Hurum. Nytt lys over østnorsk traktbegerkultur. Viking. Bind XLVIII.

- 1986: New Observations on the Funnel Beaker Culture in Norway. Acta Archaeologica. Vol. 55.

- 1988a: Etableringen av jordbrukskultur i Østfold i steinalderen. Universitetets Oldsaksamlings Skrifter. Ny rekke. Nr. 10. Oslo.

- 1988b: Hvor mange perioder bør vi regne med i Østlandets yngre steinalder? Et bidrag til kronologidebatten. Viking. Bind LI-1988, 43-50.

- 1990: The Rise and Fall of the TRB in Southeast Norway. In D. Jankowska (ed.): Die Trichterbeckerkultur. Neue Forschungen und Hypothesen. Material des Internationalen Symposiums Dymaczewo, 20.24 September 1988. Teil I. Poznan.

- 1993: Auve i Sandefjord - sanddynen, snorstempelkeramikken og C 14-dateringene. Viking. Bind LVI-1993.

- 1997: Rødtangen, et hellig sted for fem tusen år siden. In K. Ronge (ed.): Historiske glimt fra Rødtangen. Utgitt av Rødtangen Vel og Vannverk. S. l.

- 1998a: Da jordbruket kom til Norge. Funn fra TN A-fasen i Østfold. In E. Østmo (Red.): Fra Østfolds oldtid. Foredrag ved 25-årsjubileet for Universitetets arkeologiske stasjon Isegran. Universitetets Oldsaksamlings Skrifter. Ny rekke. Nr. 21. Oslo.

- 1998b: Register over trykte tilvekster av norske oldsaker. Delvis på grunnlag av eldre arbeider av Helge Gjessing og Per Fett. Universitetets Oldsaksamling. Årbok 1997/1998. Oslo, 177-190.

- 1999: Double-edged Axes under the Northern Lights. The northernmost finds of the Funnel Beaker Culture in Norway. Acta Archaeologica. Vol. 70 1999, 107-112.

- 2000: Elleve trøndske steinøkser. Traktbegerkulturen nordafjells. Primitive tider. Arkeologisk tidsskrift. 2000, 80-101.

- 2002: Megalittgravene i Hurum - 5500 år gamle monumenter fra jordbrukets eldste tid. Det Norske Videnskaps-akademi. Årbok 1999, 376-384. Oslo.

- 2004: En fangstboplass fra yngre steinalder på Solbakken i Idd, og en uventet elgskulptur. Et notat. Viking. Norsk arkeologisk årbok. Bind LXVII-2004, 35-48.

- 2005: Over Skagerak i steinalderen. Noen refleksjoner om oppfinnelsen av havgående fartøyer i Norden. Viking. Norsk arkeologisk årbok. Bind LXVIII-2005.

Østmo, E. B. Hulthén & S. Isaksson 1996: The Middle Neolithic settlement at Auve. Laborativ Arkeologi. Journal of Nordic Archaeological Science. 9, 31-40. Comprises: E. Østmo: Auve - an introduction, 31-33.

Østmo, E. and Skogstrand, L. 2006: Nye funn av traktbegerkeramikk ved Oslofjorden. Børsebakke og Vøyenenga. Viking. Norsk arkeologisk årbok. Bind LXIX-2006.

Påsse, T. 2003: Strandlinjeförskjutning i norra Bohuslän under holocen. I P. Persson (ed.): Strandlinjer och vegetationshistoria.

Kvartärgeologiska undersökningar inom Kust till kust projektet, 1998-2002, 31-87. Coast to coast-books - no. 7. GOTARC serie C, Arkeologiska skrifter, no 48. Göteborg: Arkeologiskt Naturvetenskapliga Laboratoriet.

Pedersen, E.-A. 2003: De eldste tider. In E.-A. Pedersen, F.-A. Stylegar and P. G. Norseng: Østfolds historie. Bind 1. Øst for Folden. Sarpsborg, 10-277.

Persson, P. 1998: Gropkeramikfenomenet på västkusten. in Situ. Västsvensk Arkeologisk Tidskrift. 1998.

- and Sjögren, K.-G. 2001: Falbygdens gånggrifter. Undersökningar 1985-1998. GOTARC Ser. C, Nr. 34. Göteborg.

Petersen, J. 1955: Oldsaksamlingens tilvekst 1954. Stavanger Museum. Årbok 1954, 7-30.

Prescott, C 1996: Was there really a Neolithic in Norway? Antiquity. Volume 70 Number 267 March 1996.

Rasmussen, L. W. 1991: Kainsbakke. En kystboplads fra yngre stenalder. Djurslands Museum, Grenaa.

Reitan, G. 2005: Neolitikum i Buskerud - skikk, bruk og erverv i et langtidsperspektiv. Hovedfagsavhandling i nordisk arkeologi. IAKH, Universitetet i Oslo. Våren 2005. (Unpublished thesis).

Resi, H. G. (ed.) 2000: Universitetets kulturhistoriske museer. Oldsaksamlinges tilvekst 1995. C. 38558-C. 39146. Oslo.

Seeberg, E. S. 1993: English-Norwegian - Norwegian-English Dictionary of Archaeology. Second and revised Edition. S. l.

Sherratt, A. G. 1990: The genesis of megaliths: monumentality, ethnicity and social complexity in Neolithic north-west Europe. World Archaeology 22 (2).

- 1997: Economy and Society in Prehistoric Europe. Edinburgh: Edinburgh University Press.

Shetelig, H. 1922: Primitive Tider i Norge. Bergen (John Grieg).

Sjögren, K.-G. 2003: "Mångfaldige uhrminnes grafvar...". Megalitgravar och samhälle i Västsverige. Gotarc Series B. Gothenburg Archaeological Theses 24. Coast to Coast-book No 9. Göteborg: Göteborg universitet. Intitutionen för arkeologi.

Skjølsvold, A. 1977: Slettabøboplassen. Et bidrag til diskusjonen om forholdet mellom fangst- og bondesamfunnet i yngre steinalder og bronsealder. AmS - skrifter. 2. Stavanger.

- 1980: Boplassen på Holeheia i Klepp. AmS-Varia 7. Stavanger.

Skaarup, J. 1973: Hesselø-Sølager. Jagdstationen der südskandinavischen Trichterbecherkultur. Arkæologiske Studier. 1. København.

Solberg, B. 2006: Graver og gravformer i norsk steinalder. In H. Glørstad, B. Skar and D. Skre (ed.): Historien i forhistorien. Festskrift til Einar Østmo på 60-årsdagen. Museum of Cultural History. University of Oslo. Occasional Papers vol. 4. Oslo, 83-93.

Steen, S. 1942: Ferd og fest. Reiseliv i norsk sagatid og middelalder. Ny utgave. Oslo (H. Aschehoug & Co. (W. Nygaard)).

Sørensen, R. 1979: Late Weichselian deglaciation in the Oslofjord area, south Norway. BOREAS. Volume 8, no. 2.

- 1999: En 14C datert og dendrokronologisk kalibrert strandforskyvningskurve for søndre Østfold, Sørøst-Norge. In L. S. og G. Lillehammer (ed.): Museumslandskap. Artikkelsamling til Kerstin Griffin på 60-årsdagen. AmS-rapport 12. Bind A. Stavanger, 59-70.

Sundström, L. 2003: Det hotade kollektivet. Neolitiseringsprocessen ur ett östmellansvensk perspektiv. Coast to coast-books - no 6. Uppsala.

Thorvildsen, K. 1941: Dyssetidens Gravfund i Danmark. Aarbøger for nordisk Oldkyndighed og Historie. 1941.

Tilley, C. 1996: An Ethnography of the Neolithic. Cambridge (Cambridge University Press).

Tørhaug, V. 2002: Berget 2 - En boplass fra senmesolitikum-tidligneolitikum med traktbegerkeramikk. In H. Glørstad (ed.): Svinesundprosjektet. Bind I. Utgravninger avsluttet i 2001. Varia 54. Universitetets kulturhistoriske museer. Oldsaksamlingen. Oslo. Pp. 73-116.

Wainwright, F. T. 1964: The Northern Isles. Edinburgh (Thomas Nelson and Sons Ltd).

Worsaae, J. J. A. 1866: Om nogle Mosefund fra Broncealder. Aarbøger for nordisk Oldkyndighed og Historie. 1866.

Author's address
Kulturhistorisk Museum, Universitetet i Oslo
Postboks 6762, St. Olavs plass
N-0130 Oslo
Norge
einar.ostmo@khm.uio.no

Acta Archaeologica vol. 78:2, 2007, pp 143-162
All rights reserved

Copyright 2007
ACTA ARCHAEOLOGICA
ISSN 0065-001X

THE MESOLITHIC SETTLEMENT IN NE SAVO, FINLAND

AND THE EARLIEST SETTLEMENT IN THE EASTERN BALTIC SEA

Timo Jussila, Aivar Kriiska & Tapani Rostedt

1. INTRODUCTION

Archaeologists in Finland have been searching for Early Mesolithic sites with the help of shore displacement chronologies since the end of the 1990s. Surveys for sites have focussed on the shores of the Ancylus Lake Stage of the Baltic Sea basin (9000–7200 cal BC; calibrated dates based on Eronen 1990, 16; Miettinen 2002, 14) after Heikki Matiskainen showed their existence in Finland in 1996 and after Hans-Peter Schulz (1996) noted that several previously known sites in the Lake District of Southern Finland could be dated to the Early Mesolithic on the basis of their find material and shore displacement age. Already before this, Torsten Edgren (1992, 30-31) had observed that the Lahti Ristola site in Southern Finland (fig. 1:1) could be dated to the Early Mesolithic Stone Age. Several new sites discovered in the Lake District of Southern Finland by surveys carried out in the 1990s were found to date to the Ancylus Lake Stage (Jussila 2000b, 13).

The intensive search for shore-related Early Mesolithic Stone Age dwelling sites requires accurate shore displacement chronologies that cover the area under investigation. Such chronologies have been constructed for the great lakes of southern Finland (Saarnisto 1970, 1971; Miettinen 1996; Jussila 1999; Tikkanen & Seppä 2001). From these, it is possible to calculate and project hypothetical shore displacement chronologies based on crust tilting caused by uneven land uplift to smaller lakes and areas outside the areas of the original chronologies (Jussila 2000b). For this purpose a computer program has been written to simulate shoreline displacement. With this program it

is possible to formulate hypothetical shore displacement chronologies for watersheds and lakes for which chronologies made by quaternary geological methods are not available (Jussila 2004). The plotting of the Ancylus Lake shores in survey areas has become a routine task to the writers of this article. In the beginning of the 21st century, more general attention has been paid to shore levels of the Ancylus Lake during surveys, and new sites dating to the Early Mesolithic have been discovered yearly in Finland.

The first systematic archaeological survey of the shorelines of the ancient Ancylus Lake was carried out in 1999 in the boroughs of Imatra and Joutseno in southeastern Finland, near the Russian border. According to the shore displacement chronology constructed for the Karelian Isthmus (projected onto the survey area by Timo Jussila on the basis of Saarnisto & Grönlund 1996), this area has been at the head of a long and narrow bay of the Ancylus Lake. 16 dwelling sites formerly located on the shores of the Ancylus Lake were discovered during the survey. Small-scale excavations were carried out at three of these in the summer of 2000 by the writers of this article. The Saarenoja dwelling site in Joutseno (fig. 1:2) was considered to be one of the oldest in the area, and this was confirmed by a 14C-date on burnt bone found in the excavation and analysed in 2003. The median value of the calibrated date was 8600 cal BC[1] (Hela-728: 9310 ± 75 BP – Jussila 2000a; Jussila & Matiskai-

---

1 Here and below the calibration of ^{14}C-dates is based on atmospheric data from Reimer et al (2004); OxCal v3.10 Bronk Ramsey (2005); cub r:5 sd:12 prob usp[chron].

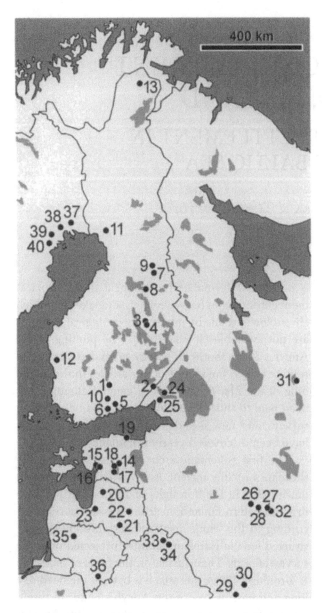

Fig. 1. Stone Age sites mentioned in text. Finland: 1. Ristola in Lahti, 2. Saarenoja in Joutseno, 3. Helvetinhaudanpuro in Juankoski, 4. Likolampi in Tuusniemi, 5. Hopeapelto in Askola, 6. Pisinmäki in Kerava, 7.Koppeloniemi in Hyrynsalmi, 8. Äkäläniemi in Kajaani, 9. Salonsaari in Suomussalmi, 10. Pukinkallio in Mäntsälä, 11. Kauvonkangas in Tervola, 12. Rävåsen in Kristiinakaupunki. 13. Sujala in Utsjoki. Estonia: 14. Kivisaare, 15. Lemmetsa I and II, 16. Pulli, 17. Sõõrikunurme, 18. Oiu I, 19. Kunda Lammasmägi. Latvia: 20. Zvejnieki II, 21. Jersika, 22. Sūlaga|s, 23. Laukskola in Salaspils. Russia: 24. Korpilahti in Antrea, and Ozero Borovskoe (Suuri Kelpojärvi in Antrea), 25. Veshevo 2 (Tarhojenranta in Heinjoki), 26. Butovo, 27. Prislon, 28. Ozerski 5, 29. Krasnoi 3 and 8, 30. Resseta 2, 31. Veretye 1, 32. Okaemovo 4. Belorussia: 33. Krumpliovo and Zamoshye, 34. Plusy. Lithuania: 35. Dreniai and Birżulis, 36 Margionys. Sweden: 37. Lillberget, 38. Alträsket, 39. Bjurselet, 40. Lundfors A-G.

nen 2003; Takala 2004, 150). During a small-scale survey on the Karelian Isthmus in 2000 and 2001, the writers of this article found ten new sites dating to the Early Mesolithic on the basis of shore displacement chronology. This survey concentrated on the shore-lines of the Ancylus Lake near the site Korpilahti in Antrea (fig. 1:24), where an ancient net dated to the Early Mesolithic had been discovered in the beginning of the 20th century (Pälsi 1920, 14; Luho 1967, 31; Carpelan 1999, table IX). The Ozero Borovskoe site (Suuri Kelpojärvi, Antrea in Finnish sources, fig. 1:24), discovered by the authors in 2000, produced a 14C-date of 8500cal BC (Hela-931: 9275 ± 120BP) on burnt bone. More sites probably dating to the Early Mesolithic were subsequently discovered in the same area in connection with research projects carried out by the Historical Museum of the City of Lahti (Takala 2004, 152, 154).

By the end of the year 2000, 18 dwelling sites in the Great Lakes District of southern Finland were presumed to predate 8000 cal BC and 23 sites were thought to be older than 7200 cal BC, assuming that these sites were originally located on the shores of the Ancylus Lake (Jussila 2000b). Sites are dated according to different shore displacement chronologies. In 2003 Jussila found a dwelling site atop an ancient Ancylus Lake cliff in Juankoski, East Central Finland. The following year, the writers of this article decided to shift the focus of their investigations concerning the Early Mesolithic from southern Karelia in SE-Finland to the northern part of Savo, Central Eastern Finland. Fieldwork began in the summer of 2004, when excavations were carried out at two Stone Age dwelling sites: Helvetinhaudanpuro in the village of Akonpohja, Juankoski and Likolampi in the village of Tuusjärvi, Tuusniemi (fig. 1:3 and 4). The first aim of these excavations was to find pieces of burnt bone that could be 14C-dated. In the summers of 2005 and 2006 investigations were continued on a larger scale at the Helvetinhaudanpuro site.

In this article we analyse the material of the Helvetinhaudanpuro and Likolampi sites from the 2004-2005 excavations, and compare it with other materials from Finland, the Karelian Isthmus, Northwestern Russia, and the Eastern Baltic area. Our aim is to interpret this material especially from the point of view of the Early Mesolithic settlements in the east-

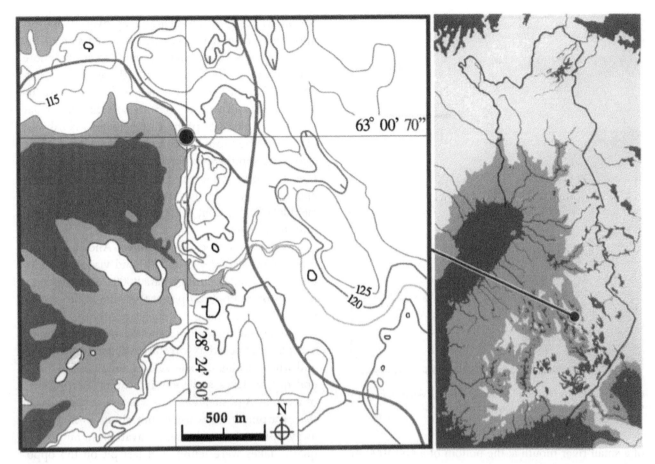

Fig. 2. Location of the site Helvetinhaudanpuro in Juankoski. Dark grey is the maximum water level of Lake Saimaa in 4800-4000 cal BC at ~99 m asl. Lighter grey is the water level of Ancylus Lake ca. 8400 cal BC at ~110 m asl.

ern Baltic Sea area. The dwelling sites in question are currently the only Mesolithic Stone Age sites in Eastern central Finland where archaeological excavations have been carried out.

2. RESEARCH HISTORY AND SITE DESCRIPTION OF THE DWELLING SITES

2.1. HELVETINHAUDANPURO IN JUANKOSKI

The Helvetinhaudanpuro site is located on top of a high and rather gently sloping fossilized 7-10 m wide ancient shore escarpment (see fig. 2). According to the shore displacement chronology of Lake Saimaa, the water level was near the top edge of the escarp-

ment (112 m asl.) about 8500 cal BC and at the foot of the escarpment (108 m asl.) about 8400 cal BC, during the Ancylus Lake Phase of the Baltic Sea basin. At this location, the highest shoreline of ancient Lake Saimaa lies some 160 m further down the gentle slope at an elevation of 99 m asl., where the water level stood c. 4800-4000 cal BC. Today, the nearest body of water is Lake Akonjärvi, a part of the present Saimaa Lake system located 1,5 km west of the site at an elevation of 82 m asl. The water has previously been at the present level in the beginning of the ancient Lake Saimaa transgression phase soon after the isolation of the Saimaa lake complex from the early Litorina Sea c. 7000 cal BC (Saarnisto 1970; 14C- dates calibrated by Jussila 1999).

The site opened towards the Ancylus Lake in the southwest and was located on the northwestern side

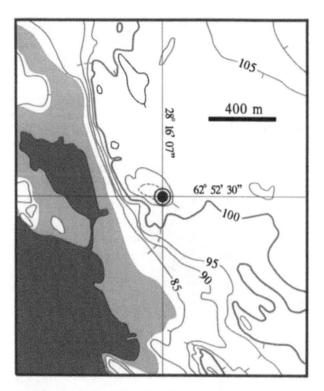

Fig. 3. Detail Map of the Early Mesolithic site of Helvetinhaudanpuro
in Juankoski.

of a small river mouth at the bottom of a 600-1000 m wide bay sheltered by an archipelago. The site lies on a c. 25 m wide terrace between the ancient shore escarpment and a gently rising slope (see fig. 3). The terrain rises in all directions except southwest and west as seen from the site. When the site was occupied, the water directly in front of it was moderately deep, but on the northwestern side the shore became shallow.

The site lies on the edge of a glacifluvial esker where the deposited sand of the esker turns into till. The soil at the site is quite loose equigranular sand; at the root of the escarpment it turns into fine sand and further downhill to silty till. Vegetation at the site is spruce-dominated mixed forest changing just above the site to pine-dominated barren moorland. To the north of the site the esker expands into a glacifluvial delta with kettleholes. 200 meters northeast of the site is a kettlehole c. 200 m in diameter with a maximum depth of some five to six meters. In this depression there has been a pond that is now almost completely paludified. From this pond, an ancient riverbed with steep banks runs directly to the southeastern edge of

the site where a small but fairly deep river discharged into the Ancylus Lake. On the opposite side of the ancient riverbed the terrain becomes somewhat more uneven and on the upper slopes there are also outcrops of bedrock. Farther towards the southeast the soil is sandy till with a stony topsoil that has so far yielded no traces of prehistoric activities. Northwest of the site the topsoil becomes stonier while the site area and its immediate surroundings are totally stone free. The fossilized erosion escarpment gradually disappears towards the northwest as the floor of the ancient lakebed in front of it gradually rises and blends into the gentle slope.

Jussila discovered the fossilized Ancylus escarpment mentioned above in 2000 and visited the location several times during years 2000-2002, digging a number of random test pits at the edge of the escarpment without noticing any traces of prehistoric activity. In the autumn of 2003, the topsoil at the location was partly exposed as a result of logging operations, and when visiting the site again Jussila observed several quartz flakes and tools indicating the presence of a Stone Age site. The site was not at the edge of the escarpment, as is usual, but about 15-20 metres away from it. Later, during excavations, a number of quartz flakes were found in a test pit on the opposite side of the riverbed. The northwestern part of the site has been partially destroyed by two 19th century charcoal-pits (see figure 3).

In the summer of 2004 a small excavation area of 15 sq. m. was opened up on the spot where the highest concentrations of quartz were observed in patches of revealed mineral soil. In the summer of 2005 the excavation area was expanded to 48 sq. m., of which 33 sq. m. was excavated that year. A small test area of 6 sq. m. was excavated at the edge of the escarpment. The finds from this second area were few and consisted of small quartz flakes. A third area of 7 sq. m. was opened up 10 meters northwest of the main area, where a small chunk of flint was found in a scarification patch. This area was excavated only to a depth of 5 cm into the mineral soil, forming a "seed" for forthcoming excavations. Fieldwork continued in 2006, revealing among other things some traces of a semi-subterranean rectangular house. The material recovered from the site in 2006 is undergoing analysis at the moment and is therefore not discussed in this

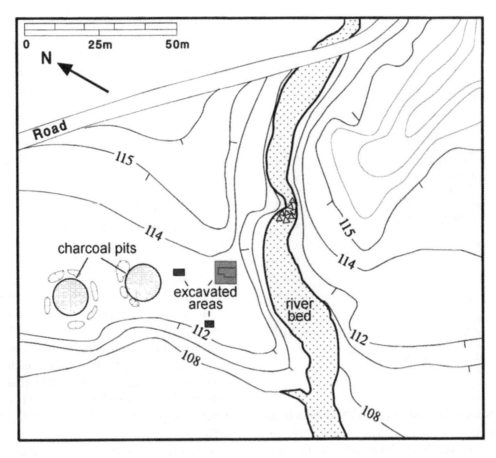

Fig. 4. Location of the site Likolampi in Tuusniemi. Dark grey is present lake. Light grey is the water level of Lake Saimaa in ca 6300 cal BC at ~84 m asl.

article. The overall size of the site is assumed to be roughly 80×25 m.

The main excavation area was characterized by a fairly thin podsol soil profile typical of the coniferous forest zone. Distinct coloured cultural layers were not discernable. Ten thousand years of podsolization processes in the loose and sandy soil had eradicated most of the visible traces of original anthropogenic dirt and sooty soil from the surface layers of the topsoil. A weakly outlined but deep pocket of dirty soil in the northeastern corner of the main excavation area also contained a concentration of small quartz flakes. The find layer was generally 30-35 cm thick and was located directly below the organic surface layer. In a limited area towards the middle of the main excavation the find layer reached a depth of 40-45 cm, and in the previously mentioned spot in the northeastern corner a depth of 70 cm.

The median date of the dated burnt fragment of elk bone from Helvetinhaudanpuro is 8400 cal BC (Hela-918: 9200±75 BP), which corresponds extremely well to the age determination given by shore displacement chronology.

2.2. LIKOLAMPI IN TUUSNIEMI

The Likolampi site is located on the southeastern rim of the level top of a gently sloping hill (fig. 4). The level area on top of the hill is about 60×40 m in size, with an elevation of 107,5 m asl. According to the shore displacement chronology of Lake Saimaa (Saarnisto 1970; 14C-dates calibrated by Jussila 1999) the water level was near the top of the hill at an elevation of 106 m at c. 8400 cal BC, when the hilltop was a small island in the inner archipelago of the Ancylus Lake, one kilometre from the mainland coast. Today, the nearest lakes, Lake Vianvesi and small Lake Likolampi (both

Fig. 5. Mesolithic site Likolampi in Tuusniemi.

parts of the Saimaa lake system), lie 300 meters from the site at an elevation of 82 m. The waters were previously at the present level about 7000 cal BC, just before the isolation of the Saimaa Lake complex from the early Litorina Sea, and again during the transgression phase of early Lake Saimaa about 6600 cal BC. The highest shoreline of the ancient Lake Saimaa in this area was 140 m from the site at an elevation of 97-98 m asl. at about 4800-4000 cal BC. The soil at the site is loose sand deposited by shore processes. Further down the hill, the soil changes to silty till.

Jouko Aroalho of the Kuopio Museum of Cultural History discovered the site in 1999 when he observed some quartz flakes in scarification patches and in a test pit. In the summer of 2004, an excavation area of 12 m2 was opened up on the southeastern side of the hilltop (fig. 5). The surface of the excavated area produced a normal thin podsol soil profile. Distinct coloured cultural layers were not observed, but some concentrations of bits of charcoal were noticed, as were also some faint spots of anthropogenic dirty soil in the deeper layers. The find layer extended to a depth of 40-45 cm as measured from the bottom of the organic surface layer. On the basis of the test pits

and surface observations, the site is assumed to be about 10×10 m in extent.

A 14C-date on a burnt elk bone from the Likolampi site did not quite fulfill expectations as it dated site to the Late Mesolithic (Hela-919: 7425±95 BP, the calibrated median being 6300 cal BC). When this site was inhabited, it was 300 meters inland from the nearest shore. The water level of ancient Lake Saimaa was about two meters higher than at present.

3. ARTEFACTS
3.1 METHODS AND TERMS
In primary lithic reduction, two different striking techniques can be distinguished in northeastern Central Finland: the platform technique and the bipolar technique. In the platform technique the core is held in one hand and supported on, e.g., the thigh when removing flakes or blades from it with a hammer. In this technique the impact point lies towards the edge of the striking platform and a platform remnant can be detected on the flake. Other characteristics of flakes or blades can be bulbs, points of percussions, or various sharp edges (e.g. Crabtree 1972, 11; Knutsson 1988a, 37).

When using the platform technique an anvil can be of good assistance. In this technique a piece of raw material or a core is placed on an anvil and flakes or blades are detached from it with blows to the platform. This technique is quite clearly platform striking, and features mentioned above can be identified in the artefacts. Especially when working with quartz, the other end of the core, flake, or blade is often crushed on the anvil. This working technique is easily identified if an artefact is crushed on the other end and yet a platform can be distinguished. Basically stones can be worked with direct or indirect blows. Direct blows are executed with a hammer. Indirect blows can be executed using a connecting piece (punch) made of, e.g., wood, antler, or bone between the core and the hammerstone. We have not observed any evidence of indirect percussion in this material.

An anvil is also used in the bipolar technique. In bipolar reduction, a chunk of raw material or core is struck directly while being rested on an anvil. As a result, tension points in the stone give way and splitting takes place through fault planes in the material. Shattered pieces that are formed with this technique often resemble segments of an orange (Crabtree 1972, 10).

As a result of bipolar striking, flakes or blades are detached from both ends of the raw material chunk. A basic mark of this technique is often that both ends of the artefact are crushed. Unlike in flakes made by the platform technique, bipolar flakes usually do not have remnants of a platform or clear bulbs of percussion. Scars of percussion do appear, and flakes made with the bipolar technique can sometimes be even thinner and narrower than those made with the platform technique (Crabtree 1972, 10-11; see also Callahan 1987, 61).

The analysed material was divided into flakes, blades, cores, and tools. The definition of flakes is slightly different from the traditional one in our classification since we include both the results of primary reduction and debris. Quartz material fragments more easily than flint, but with certain restrictions correlations with flint can be applied (see e.g. Hertell & Manninen 2002, 85, with references).

If a flake is more than two times longer than it is wide, is it classified as a blade (see, e.g., Tixier 1974, 5). Microblades are not classified as a separate group in our research, even though this has been done in some analyses. Blades are distinguished from other materials in both the bipolar and platform techniques. If a blade is complete, both distal and proximal ends can be detected. If at least one of them is missing, the artefact is classified as a blade fragment.

If at least one flake or blade has been detached from a piece of raw material, it has been classified as a core. Cores are furthermore classified as protocores or cores, depending on how much they have been prepared or worked. If more than half of the raw material cortex is left, the artefact is called a protocore. The amount and type of cortex in the material was also observed, since it can reveal something about the way raw material was obtained. Raw material could be acquired either from quartz veins in cliffs and blocks or from individual pebbles picked up in moraines or on stony shores. In vein quartz, the amount of cortex is obviously quite small when compared to other quartz materials. In separate pebbles picked up in moraines or stony shores, on the other hand, the amount of cortex seems to be much higher (see e.g. Hertell & Manninen 2002, 89; Seitsonen 2005, 25).

The basis of our tool classification is morphological: an artefact is classified as a tool only if a distinct edge made by secondary working can be observed. Definition in itself is quite subjective and is based on the expertise of the analyser in the details of quartz and flint reduction. The shape and striking technique of tools was defined with the bare eye, without a microscope. This method undoubtedly reduces the total amount of information extracted from material, but it certainly also has some advantages. Most of the research conducted around the Baltic Sea area on flint and quartz materials has been done the same way, so the comparison of different materials is easier by this method. Had we used a microscope, the proportion of tools would most certainly have increased since the use marks on quartzes would have been detected. In this research we did not do so, however. The number of tools identified in our analysis probably does not correspond to the actual number of tools used in the dwelling site, since unretouched edges could be used at least for shorter periods (see e.g. Yerkes 1990, 173; Callahan 1987, 62; Knutsson 1988b, 14, with references).

Without taking any position on the functional use of the tools we have, however, evaluated their suitability for different situations. Edges that are suitable for scraping and cutting we call scrapers, while tools called burins are better suited for gouging and grooving. On flint material we additionally distinguish one more class called microliths, with a subgroup called inserts.

Scrapers were divided into side and end scrapers based on the position of the cutting edge. When examined from above, the shape of the edge was defined as straight or convex, and when inspected from the side, the edge angle was defined as blunt or sharp. The edge was considered blunt if the angle is over 45 degrees and sharp if the angle of the edge is less than 45 degrees. Burins were observed only from above.

3.2 MATERIAL

3.2.1. *Helvetinhaudanpuro in Juankoski*

The dwelling site produced a total of 10 880 lithic artefacts in 2004-2005 (see table 1), 10 859 of which were made of quartz, 6 of flint, and 15 of other lithic materials. The find density of the artefacts was quite high, 203 pieces/sq. m. The largest group among the quartzes were flakes and blades/blade fragments,

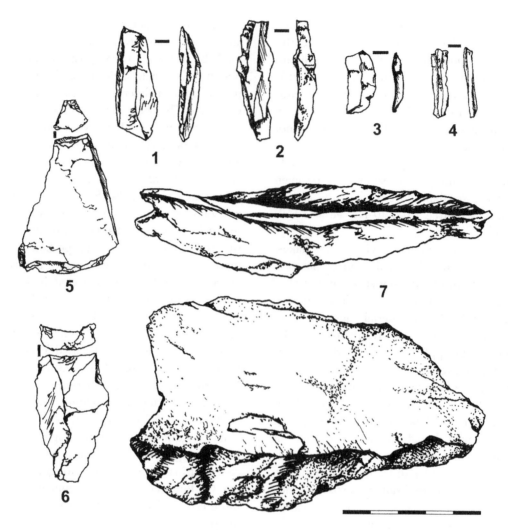

Fig. 6. Some quartz blades, blade fragments and flakes from the site of Helvetinhaudanpuro.1. Bipolar blade, 2. Platform blade modified on anvil, 3. Fragment of a bipolar blade, retouched on one side, 4. Blade made by pressure flaking, 5. Platform flake modified on anvil, 6. Platform flake, 7. Bipolar flake. (KM 35473: 180, 418, 1384, 98, 128, 64).

which amounted to 10 553 pieces (see table 2). Blades and blade fragments totalled 688 pieces (fig. 5), which is 6,5% of the total amount of quartzes. Cores and protocores numbered 173 pieces (fig. 6) or 1,6% of the total amount of quartzes.

Identified tools numbered 137, of which 133 were made of quartz (1,2% of all quartzes), 3 of flint, and one of other lithic material. 129 of the quartz tools are scrapers, 2 knives and 2 burins (fig. 8). On one scraper the other edge could also possibly have been used as a knife (KM 34661:87; KM = National Museum of Finland). Almost all quartz tools were manufactured from flakes; only one burin was made from a blade.

On the basis of to the position of the edge, 51 tools were defined as end scrapers and 42 as side scrapers. Tools with edges on both the side and end also occur; they number 31 pieces. On 9 tools, the position of the edge was not documented. Almost all edges are convex, and on two cases out of three the angle of the edge is blunt, i.e., over 45 degrees. Of the burins, one is end edged and the other side edged. The edges of both burins were created by removing several burin spalls.

Six pieces of flint were found. Of these, three are tools, two are flakes, and one is a chunk. One flake is brownish black and translucent, originating from

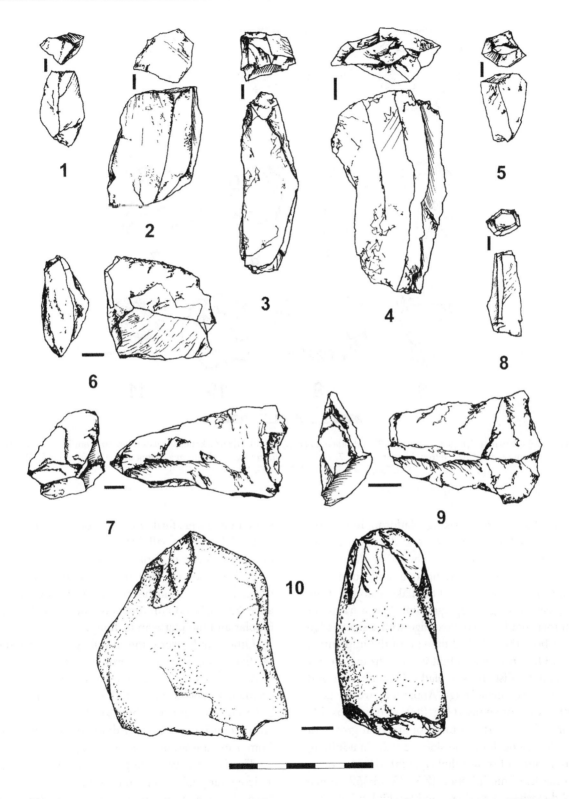

Fig. 7. Some bipolar cores (1, 3-7), platform cores (2, 8-9) and a platform-on-anvil protocore (10) made of quarz, from Helvetinhaudanpuro. (KM 35473:63, 111,348, 115, 31,469, 459,42,435, 117).

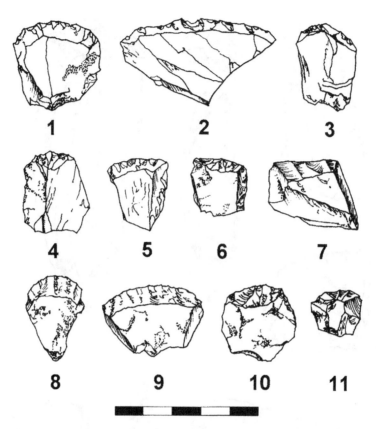

Fig. 8. Some end scrapers (4, 5, 8), side scrapers (7, 9), end-side scrapers (1, 3, 6, 10, 11) and a knife (2) made of quartz, from Helvetinhaudanpuro. Tools 1-3,9-10 from bipolar flakes, 8 from bipolar core, 6, 7, 11 from platform flakes and 4 from a fragment of a platform blade. (KM 35473: 439, 738, 1031, 630, 35, 1072, 1390, 151, 48, 420, 1185).

the edge of the core's striking platform. It features a trimmed platform remnant and three negatives of detached blades (fig. 9:4). The other flake (KM 35473:1377) is reddish grey, opaque, and quite poor in quality. The ventral side of the flake is cortex. One of the pieces is of grey opaque flint. It is a fragment of a scraper that has a convex edge with a sharp edge angle on both the side and the end of the implement (fig. 9:1). One fragment of flint is made from a nearly transparent reddish brown blade. On one side and end there is a retouched edge. Apparently we are dealing with a knife or an insert (fig. 9:3). Another possible fragment of an insert is a piece of greenish grey flint that has low retouch on one side (fig 9:2). In addition, there is a chunk of brown flint (1,2×1,0×0,8 cm), bearing no marks of modification (KM 35473:552). Since natural deposits of flint do not exist in Finland, it must have been imported here. It must therefore originate

in moraine layers further east or south of Finland. This piece of flint is so small that it was probably not carried to the site as raw material for tools.

Flakes made of other material than quartz or flint totalled 8 pieces. Furthermore, the finds included an adze (7,0×5,5×1,3 cm) that was worked with both the bipolar and the platform technique.

Other finds from the dwelling site included 5 relatively soft stones (according to the Mohs hardness scale) that we interpreted as anvil stones or their fragments. The largest of them has dimensions of 21,0×14,0×6,5 cm. On both of its wider sides there are several indentations of different sizes that derive from using the stone as an anvil (fig. 10).

The finds include one possible hammerstone. It is an irregular pebble of granite some 9×7×6 cm in size. Several indentations indicative of the bipolar technique could be detected on the sides of this artefact.

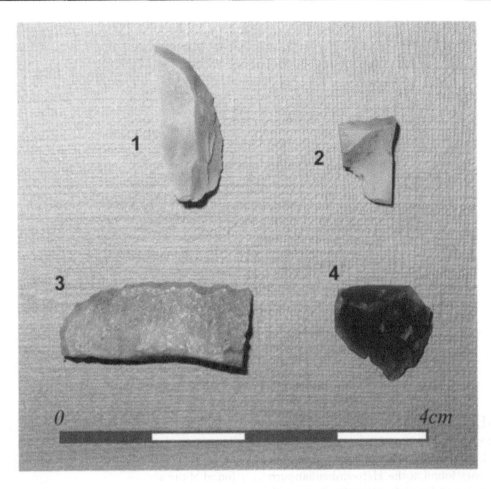

Fig. 9. Flint artefacts found from Helvetinhaudanpuro in 2004; 1. Fragment of a scraper (KM 34661: 245), 2. Fragment of a possible insert (KM 34661: 246), 3. Fragment of a knife or insert (KM 34661: 248), 4. A flake (KM 34661: 247).

The indentations are about one centimetre in diameter and their measured depth is a few millimetres. It appears that quartz could have been worked with a hard hammerstone against a softer anvil stone.

Regularities can be detected in the distribution of the artefacts. The greater part of the flakes and blades are concentrated in two areas: in the centre of the excavation area and in its northeastern sector. Even though some individual cores and tools were found inside the concentrations, most of them were not. In the southeastern section of the excavation area there are plenty of cores, indicating a cache. Weakly stained soil correlates well with the concentration areas.

3.2.2 Likolampi in Tuusniemi

This dwelling site produced 2920 lithic artefacts, of which 2916 were made of quartz and 4 of other lithic materials. The find density was relatively high, over 292 pieces/sq. m. The largest group among the quartzes were flakes and blades/blade fragments, which totalled 2853 pieces. Blades and blade fragments came to 235 pieces, which is 8,1% of the total number of quartzes. Cores and protocores numbered 61, equivalent to 2,1% of the total amount of quartzes.

Only two quartz tools, both scrapers, were identified (0,1% of all quartzes). In addition, there was one tool fragment of other lithic material, probably a part of a polished adze or axe.

The scrapers were made from flakes. One was an end scraper and other was a side scraper. On both scrapers the cutting edge was convex and the angle of the edge was blunt (over 45°).

Fig. 10. Anvil stone from Helvetinhaudanpuro (KM 34661:344).

4. BONE MATERIAL

Both sites produced only a small amount of burnt bone material. A detailed analysis was carried out only on the bones found at the Helvetinhaudanpuro site, where 12 burnt bone fragments were identified out of an overall bone material of 56 fragments. Bones of elk were the largest identified group (6 fragments), and some fragments of fish bones were also observed, including bones of pike (Esox lucius) (1), perch (Perca fluviatilis) (1), and daces (Leuciscus sp.) (2). This result agrees well with the Preboreal stadial (ca. 9600-8200 BC, calibrated dates based on Andrén et al. 1999, 369; Raukas et al. 1995, 202) and its presumed fauna.

The burnt bone fragments were heavily concentrated in the southern part of the 2004 excavation area; the distribution was quite similar to that of the quartz material. From the Likolampi site only one fragment of burnt pike bone and one elk bone were identified in the overall bone material of 90 small fragments. Looking at the bone material as a whole, the fact that beaver is totally absent is worth noting. Beaver is quite common in Early Mesolithic sites in Estonia (Lõugas 1997, 66) and in Late Mesolithic sites

in Finland (e.g., Ukkonen 1993, 256-257; 2001, fig. 2). The reason for the lack of beaver in the material may lie in the small amount of identifiable bone material found at the site.

5. ANALYSES AND COMPARISONS
5.1 QUARTZ

Taken as a whole, the quartz finds from Helvetinhaudanpuro and Likolampi include a large proportion of quartz cortex. This implies that most of the quartz has not been quarried from quartz veins but rather derives from quartz cobbles found in moraines. There are, however, also a number of pieces of quartz exhibiting features of vein quartz (angularity, jagged cortex surface etc.). When surveying the surroundings of both dwelling sites, we noted easily exploitable chunks of quartz 500 meters southeast of Helvetinhaudanpuro and 400 meters northeast of Likolampi.

The largest group in the quartz material from both dwelling sites consists of flakes. At Helvetinhaudanpuro the proportion of flakes was 97,2%, while the proportion of blades (compared to the total number of quartz flakes) is only 6,5%. In the dwelling site of

Likolampi the numbers are quite similar to Helvetinhaudanpuro; there the proportion of flakes was 97,8% and the proportion of blades 8,1%. The same phenomenon can be observed in other dwelling sites around the Baltic Sea. For example, in Finland at sites like Ristola in Lahti, Hopeanpelto in Askola, Pisinmäki in Kerava, Koppeloniemi in Hyrynsalmi and Äkäläniemi in Kajaani (fig. 1:1 and 5-8) blades have accounted for 2-3% of the whole quartz material (Schulz 1990, fig. 4). At Late Mesolithic and Early Neolithic (5800-4000 BC) sites in Estonian archipelago the percentage of blades has been 0,3-7,1% of the whole quartz material (Kriiska 2002, 38).

In the quartz material of Helvetinhaudanpuro, the reduction technique was identified in 22,6% of all finds. The bipolar technique was clearly more common than the platform technique. 15,8% of all quartzes were produced with the bipolar technique, while 6,8% were produced with the platform technique. If we consider only the quartzes whose reduction technique has been identified (2452 pieces out of 10 859), the proportion of bipolar technique is 69,9% (1715 pieces) and that of platform technique 30,1% (737 pieces)

It must be noted that the analysis of quartz fragments relies on subjective interpretation. The results depend on the quality of the material as well as on the expertise of the researcher. Looking at the finds from Helvetinhaudanpuro, we can see that the material is statistically representative enough to allow us to draw reliable conclusions.

A similar distribution of techniques can be observed in the flakes and in the tools; in both cases the proportion of identified bipolar quartzes is over 50%. The division into different reduction techniques is best seen in the blades/blade fragments, where the bipolar technique dominates with 84,8%. Of the cores, on the other hand, only 56,6% represent the bipolar technique.

In the quartz material of Likolampi in Tuusniemi the technique with which the quartz was reduced was identified in 26,2% of the whole material. In the identified material from Likolampi the bipolar technique was also clearly more popular than the platform technique. It was used on 20,9% of all quartzes. If we look at only the quartzes whose reduction technique was identified (768 pieces out of 2916), the proportion of

bipolar technique was 79,4% (609 pieces) and that of platform technique, 20,6% (159 pieces).

The same type of division in reduction technique can be observed in the flakes and in the tools; in both cases the proportion of identified bipolar quartzes at Likolampi is over 65%. Just as at Helvetinhaudanpuro, the distribution into different modification techniques is best seen in the distribution of blades/blade fragments, where the bipolar technique dominates with 88,5%. As for the cores from Likolampi, 68,9% were reduced using the bipolar technique.

It is difficult to find reference material for this kind of investigation. In Finland, a number of comparisons between differences in bipolar and platform techniques in Mesolithic times have been carried out. For example, Schulz has presented five Mesolithic dwelling sites where he came to the conclusion that the bipolar technique was dominant in cores and came to over 85% (Schulz 1990, fig. 2). Because all of the sites Schulz investigated had been at least partly in use in later periods as well, the material as a whole is not comparable with Helvetinhaudanpuro or Likolampi.

The dwelling site of Salonsaari in Suomusalmi (fig. 1:9), northeastern Finland, has been in use partly in the Mesolithic Stone Age. According to Oili Räihälä (1998, 11), the bipolar technique was represented there in 45% of all material, rising to 50% when only cores were examined. This site too has been partly in use on later times, so conclusions concerning the quartz material cannot be directly compared with our material.

The best reference for the comparison of Mesolithic stone technology is the site of Pukinkallio in Mäntsälä (fig. 1:10), Southern Finland. From its Early Mesolithic material (median age ca. 8100 BC (Hela-706: 8960 ± 65); Takala 2004, fig. 159) Mikael A. Manninen has determined that the bipolar technique was clearly dominant with a share of 74% of all identified quartzes (pers. comm. 2.2.05).

Kauvonkangas in Tervola (fig. 1:11), Northern Finland, is a dwelling site from the Neolithic Stone Age (median age ca. 3000 BC (Hela-342: 4340 ± 75; Kankaanpää 2002, 68-69), where the platform technique was almost as popular as the bipolar technique. For flakes the proportion of platform technique was 47% of the identified material as against 53% for the bipolar technique. With cores, the proportion of the bipolar technique is little higher, about 64% (Rankama 2002, 83-84, fig. 4-5). Rankama suggests that this could be explained with the change of stone technology in the middle of the modification process, as also proposed by Swedish researchers. According to her, it seems possible that the stone knappers of Kauvonkangas could have knapped quartz cores first using the platform technique and later using a bipolar method of reduction (Rankama 2002, 85; see also e.g. Callahan 1987, 60-61; Knutsson 1988b, 148-149; Olofsson 2003, 5).

The same type of modification process can explain the fact that the platform cores of Helvetinhaudanpuro and Likolampi are usually larger than those made by the bipolar technique. So far, we have identified one quartz core bearing marks of both the bipolar and the platform technique (KM 35473:302). Based on this item, the writers of this article postulate that according to this material the technique of modifying quartz has been subject to change whenever needed, even during the process itself. The bipolar technique could also be used, e.g., for crushing smaller chunks of quartz (e.g. KM 34 661:61), so the working order between the different techniques varies, depending among other things on what kind of final tools are desired (see also Hertell & Manninen 2002, 96-97).

Examples of changing techniques are found in Estonia as well. For example, the Mesolithic dwelling site Kivisaare (fig. 1:14) in Central Estonia has produced one core made of flint that was first prepared for the platform technique in order to make several blades. Later on it was also worked with the bipolar technique (Kriiska et al. 2004a, 33)

In dwelling sites dating to the Middle Neolithic Stone Age in Sweden (3400-2300 cal BC, e.g. Lundfors A-G, cf. Bjurselet; fig. 1:39-40) bipolar quartz cores were modified into scrapers in the final stage. At the end of the Stone Age and later in the Bronze Age flakes were removed from the core as long as possible, and in the final stage the core was crushed to pieces using the bipolar technique. According to researchers in Sweden, this indicates that at earlier settlements quartz technology was highly methodical but in younger settlement stages it had at least partly degenerated (Knutsson 1988a, 174-176; see also Holm 1991, 117; Broadbent 1979, 206-207).

A methodical approach to reduction was still in use in Finnish dwelling sites at least regionally in the Neolithic Stone Age. A good example of this is the Neolithic settlement at Rävåsen in Kristiinankaupunki (fig. 1:12), on the central west coast of Finland. The quartz material of several excavation areas of this site has been analysed and the bipolar technique dominates quite clearly: 59-72% of the material was reduced using the bipolar technique. Based on their study of the material and also on other analyses, Esa Hertell and Mikael A. Manninen suggest that the large proportion of bipolar technique indicates a purpose-oriented stone technology in the area. According to Hertell and Manninen, it is possible that the people at the settlement at Rävåsen sought to produce especially thin flakes that were best suited for knives and other cutting edges. For this purpose, the bipolar technique is optimal, while the platform technique is better suited for producing more robust artefacts like scrapers (Hertell & Manninen 2002, 96-97 with references and fig. 2).

On the basis of the quartz materials of Helvetinhaudanpuro and Likolampi, a trend can be observed wherein the use of the bipolar technique increases at the end of Mesolithic Stone Age as compared to its older phase. The material of Pukinkallio in Mäntsälä confirms this hypothesis, but its find collection is so small (289 pieces) that it cannot be considered completely convincing statistically. In Pukinkallio, the proportion of platform technique is 26%.

The bipolar technique is widely known around the Baltic Sea, not only in quartz but also in other lithic materials. For example, in the Mesolithic material from Kivisaare in Central Estonia more than half of the flint cores are bipolar (Kriiska et al. 2003). In the quartz material of Estonia the bipolar technique dominates throughout the whole Stone Age. For example, in the Lemmetsa I (Late Neolithic, 3200/3000-1800 cal BC; fig. 1:15) and Lemmetsa II (Middle Neolithic, 4200/4000-3200/3000 cal BC; fig 1:15) dwelling sites in southeastern Estonia only bipolar quartz flakes are present, and often flint cores represent the bipolar technique as well (Kriiska & Saluäär 2000, 13,16, 30). In Sweden the development of quartz technology is slightly different. There the bipolar technique was relatively common in the Mesolithic Stone Age, while around 4500 cal BC the platform technique started to gain more popularity and was reflected in, e.g., cores made of quartz (e.g. sites Alträsket (5000 cal BC) and Lillberget (3900 cal BC) – Halén 1994, 177-178; fig. 1:37-38; see also Lindgren 2004, 248; Knutsson 2005, 64).

5.2. FLINT

The flint material found at Helvetinhaudanpuro has not been subjected to a minerological analysis, but based on the colour, quality and reference material from Eastern and Northern Europe it is possible to draw preliminary conclusions concerning the origin of the raw material. Black translucent flint most probably derives from cretaceous layers that reach the surface in Belarus and Ukraine (for more on this flint see, e. g., Jaanits et al. 1982, 32; Zhilin 1997, 331; Koltsov & Zhilin 1999, 66; Lisitsyn 2003, 45). Nodules detached from this layer of flint do occur in the soil north of this area and can be found even in southern Lithuania. This kind of flint has been widely used by the so-called Mesolithic Post-Swiderian cultures and its use decreases the further north one goes.

In Lithuania (e.g., Dreniai, Biržulis, Margionys – Ostrauskas 2002, 94ff; Baltrūnas et al. 2006a, 43ff; Baltrūnas et al. 2006b, 23; fig.1:35-36), in Belarus (e.g., Krumpliovo, Zamoshye and Plushy – Ksenzov 2001, 20; fig. 1:33-34) and in the marshy woodlands of Zhizdra in Russia (e.g., Krasnoi 3, 8 and Resseta 2 – Sorokin 2002, 100; fig 1:29-30) this type of flint is quite common; in Estonia, on the other hand, it is known only from eleven sites (fig. 11) and in Latvia from only a few Late Palaeolithic/Early Mesolithic sites like Lauksola in Salaspils, Zvejnieki II, and Jersika (Jaanits 1989, 13; Zagorska 1999, 153-154, fig. 1:21-23). Apart from the Early Mesolithic dwelling site Pulli in Estonia (fig. 1:16), this kind of flint occurs usually only in small quantities. The Pulli site produced 1500 pieces of black flint (Jaanits 1989, 32). On the Karelian Isthmus it has so far been found only in one site, Veshevo 2 (Tarhojenranta in Heinjoki in Finnish sources – Takala 2004, 156; fig. 1:25). In Finland black flint is known from Ristola in Lahti (45 pieces; Takala 2004, 108, fig. 109), Kuurmanpohja in Joutseno (2 pieces) and Helvetinhaudanpuro in Juankoski (1 piece). Further east black flint is known from a few sites in the region of the so-called Butovo Culture in the area between the rivers Volga and Oka, e.g., Butovo 4A and Prislon (Koltshov & Zhilin 1999, 62; fig. 1:26-27).

Black flint appears to have been a very popular material in the Early Mesolithic due to its high quality. It can be found not only in areas where naturally occurring flint is completely absent (e.g., Finland) but also in areas where the local flint is poor in quality (e.g., Estonia and Latvia). It also seems apparent that black flint has been transported to areas where the local flint is of high quality (e.g., Central Russia). The flint found at Helvetinhaudanpuro extends the distribution radius of black flint to 900 kilometres from its original source (fig. 11). It may be possible, although not certain, that the grey flint found at Helvetinhaudanpuro originates from the same cretaceous layers as the black flint because differences in the colour of flint do occur even in one and the same artefact (Kriiska & Tvauri 2002, 26).

The colourful reddish brown blade made of flint apparently derives from Central Russia. Pieces made of similar flint were also found at Kuurmanpohja in Joutseno and at Veshevo 2 on the Karelian Isthmus. Other pieces of flint pointing to the east have also been found at the Kuurmanpohja site. The same kind of flint material has also been found in Estonia, e.g., at the Mesolithic sites of Pulli, Sõõrikunurme and Oiu I (Kriiska et al. 2004b, 44; fig. 1:16-18). Central Russian flint is also known from the Latvian Early Mesolithic sites Zvejnieki II, Sūļagals and Laukskola in Salaspils (Loze 1988, 16, fig. 1: 20 and 22-23).

Greenish grey flint appears sporadically in the Estonian flint material. This flint obviously derives from Silurian limestone layers deposited in the Palaeozoic period (Jürgenson 1958). It reaches the surface only in Central Estonia but can also be found in Quarternary deposits in Estonia and northern Latvia (fig. 11). Among the local materials found in Estonia, greenish grey flint is likely the most suitable for making prehistoric tools. One greenish grey flint was also found at Kuurmanpohja in Joutseno. A few exceptions notwithstanding, Mesolithic flint in Finland mainly dates to the earliest settlement of Finland c. 8800-8400 cal BC. However, it appears that the use of flint continued to some extent through the whole Mesolithic Stone Age. It is possible that some Estonian flint was imported to the southwestern Finnish coast in the late Mesolithic Stone Age (Asplund 1997, 220; definition of flint made by Kriiska).

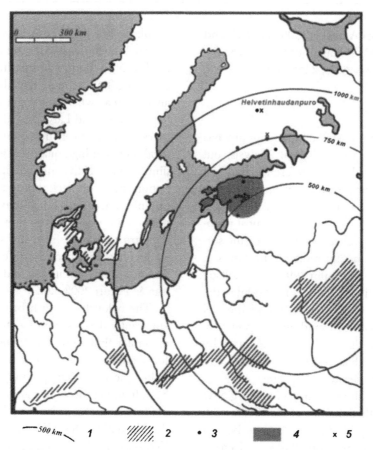

Fig. 11. 1) Distribution of artefacts made from Belorussia originating Cretaceous flint. Distance in kilometers.
2) Distribution of Cretaceous flint depositions reaching the surface. 3) Stone Age dwelling sites with Cretaceous black flint in Estonia, Latvia, Finland and Karelian Isthmus. 4) Distribution of Paleozoic flint on Quaternary deposits in Estonia and Northern Latvia (according to the investigations of A. Kriiska). 5) Early Mesolithic sites in Finland with flint resembling to Estonian flint.

6. DISCUSSION AND CONCLUSIONS

The Helvetinhaudanpuro and Likolampi dwelling sites reflect a long-term change in lithic techniques during the Mesolithic Stone Age of Finland. The Helvetinhaudanpuro site is a very important and useful source for research on the earliest settlement of Finland in the Early Mesolithic. Both dating methods, shore displacement chronology and 14C-dating of burned bone, produced the same Early Mesolithic date. The site is among the five oldest known sites in Finland and one of the two oldest in the area that was exposed by the retreat of the continental glacier after the Younger Dryas stadial (i.e. areas on the proximal side of the Salpausselkä end moraine), the other being Sujala in Utsjoki, northernmost Lapland (Rankama & Kankaanpää in press; fig. 1:13).

The location of the Helvetinhaudanpuro site indi-

cates that the ecological resources of both land and water were utilized in many ways. The site itself is not very large, although the find material from it is quite diverse. The material from the site does not reveal whether the dwelling site was settled on several occasions for longer periods or more often for short periods. Based on the finds, artefacts have been manufactured, used, and abandoned at the site and also imported.

The best comparative material for the finds from Helvetinhaudanpuro is provided by the Mesolithic sites of Eastern Finland and the Karelian Isthmus. Analogical features like the presence of flint (partly from three different original sources) and the relatively high proportion of platform technique and blades in the quartz material can be observed in the lithic materials from Ristola in Lahti and from sites at Kuurmanpohja in Joutseno.

Particularly the presence of flint in the Early Mesolithic sites of Finland makes it possible to evaluate prehistorical contact zones. The natural presence of flint in a particular area does not automatically mean that the population of Helvetinhaudanpuro would have derived from these areas. Many sites in Northern and Eastern Europe indicate the presence of extensive contact networks in the Early Mesolithic. Through the help of direct and indirect contacts even exotic raw materials could drift hundreds of kilometres without major migrations.

Apparently the colonisation of the site took place from nearby areas. From the 14C-datings of Early Mesolithic sites in Estonia, the Karelian Isthmus, and Finland it can be concluded that over twenty generations lived in the areas where quartz and poor quality flint occur in soil before the site of Helvetinhaudanpuro was occupied. Adaptation to the local lithic materials had occurred already a long time before the Helvetinhaudanpuro occupation, but nevertheless traces of ancient knapping techniques can still be observed. Some features of working methods used on good quality flint have obviously survived while working with poor quality flint and quartz.

The difference in the quartz material of Helvetinhaudanpuro can clearly be observed upon comparison with Late Mesolithic materials from Finland and earlier sites in Estonia and northeastern Russia. The writers of this article consider the relatively large proportion of blades and the platform technique to be vestiges of the ancient method of shaping good quality flint. They are characteristic of the flint technology of Early Mesolithic sites in the Baltic countries and northeastern Russia and can no longer be so clearly observed in younger Mesolithic collections from Finland.

In spite of its plentiful finds, it is difficult to find parallels for Helvetinhaudanpuro. In areas where flint occurs naturally the amount of quartz used is very small. For example, in the dwelling site of Pulli in Estonia the proportion of quartz is only 0,7% compared to the number of flint artefacts. Besides, it is necessary to bear in mind that the total number of Early Mesolithic sites in Finland is still very small and in most cases the artefact material is mixed with later human activity in the area (e.g. Ristola in Lahti). Because of this, the plentiful and unmixed material of Helvetinhaudanpuro is a good reference material for

investigating the stone technology of the earliest settlement in Finland and its adaptation to quartz.

Tools made of bone would help us to elucidate the picture of the Early Mesolithic, but unfortunately unburnt bone is preserved in Finnish soil only in special conditions and only a few individual bone tools have been found in Finnish soil. Nevertheless, the bone tools that have been discovered are quite important when forming an interpretation of the earliest settlement of Finland.

If the term "archaeological culture" is understood in an instrumental way as a similarity in artefact types, we can consider that the material of Helvetinhaudanpuro together with other Early Mesolithic sites in southern Finland and the Karelian Isthmus forms one "archaeological culture". If some kind of continuity is essential here, the "Kunda Culture" in eastern Baltic and the "Butovo Culture" between the rivers Volga and Oka in Russia provide the best parallels. The oldest bone artefacts in Finland point to the same direction: the ice pick from Kirkkonummi (Äyräpää 1950, 9) and a fragment of a double cone-shaped arrowhead from Kuurmanpohja in Joutseno. There are good parallels for this kind of arrowheads in the so-called "Post-Swiderian Cultures" like "Butovo" (e.g. Okaemovo 4 and Ozerski 5 – Koltshov & Zhilin 1999, fig. 23 and 27; fig. 1:28 and 32), "Veretye" (e.g. Veretye 1 site; Oshibkina 2000, 152, fig. 3; fig. 1:31), and "Kunda" (e.g. the Kunda Lammasmägi site – Indreko 1948, 259, fig 72, 297 ff; fig. 1:19). The material we have investigated points to cultural relations to the South as well as to the East, but the direction of stronger cultural relations seems to point to the East Baltic region. The model we propose for the earliest settlement of Finland is not new, (see, e.g., Nuñez 1987; Matiskainen 1989; and Takala 2004) but its verification still requires further research.

The artefact material of Likolampi is smaller in amount than the material from Helvetinhaudanpuro and is slightly different. Likolampi produced no flint and only a few tools of quartz. The Likolampi site is located on the same ancient shoreline of the Ancylus Lake as the Helvetinhaudanpuro site. According to the radiocarbon date, however, it is Late Mesolithic, which means that the nearest shore during occupation has been out of sight, approximately 300 metres from the site. The location of this site differs clearly from the traditional shore-bound settlement model. At Likolampi, however, tools have been manufactured and some have also been left behind at the site.

A few sites in Finland and Estonia are not located directly on the ancient shoreline (Jussila & Kriiska 2006). The number of sites of this kind is very small compared to all known dwelling sites in Finland and Estonia. At the moment, there are only limited possibilities for interpreting the function of these sites. Ethnographical and anthropological descriptions have verified that the activities of hunter-gatherers have been extensive also beyond so-called base camps. Hunting and gathering, acquiring raw materials, and activities associated with religion or entertainment can leave permanent traces so ephemeral that they

are difficult for us to recognize - as of yet.[2]

2 Acknowledgements: The fieldwork was financed by the J. E. Tuovinen Foundation of the Cultural Foundation of Savo. In addition, the town of Juankoski provided fieldworkers and other supplies. Microlith Ltd. supported the investigations with field equipment and other research supplies. The Foreign Exchange Foundation of the Estonian academy of Sciences and Arheograator Ltd. have also supported the writing of this article. The collection of Estonian reference material has been supported by research project no. 5328 of the Estonian Foundation of Sciences and the research project "Interdisciplinary archaeology: the interaction of culture and environment in the past" of the university of Tarto. We are grateful to all of the organizations mentioned above. We also wish to thank Kati Salo, MA, for the osteological analysis, Mikael A. Manninen, MA, for the information on Pukinkallio in Mäntsälä, prof. Högne Jugner, PhD, for radiocarbon dating, Kristel Külljastinen for artefact drawings, Jarmo Kankaanpää, PhD, for revising the English text, and also Jouko Aroalho, director of the Kuopio Cultural History Museum, for co-operation and most valuable background support.

8. REFERENCES

Andrén, T., Björck, J. & Johnsen, S., 1999: Correlation of Swedish glacial varves with the Greenland (GRIP) oxygen isotope record. Journal of Quaternary Science, 14/4, 361-371.

Asplund, H., 1997: Kemiön suurpitäjän esihistoria. Kemiön suurpitäjän historia I. Kemiö, 213-282.

Baltrūnas, V., Karmaza, B., Kulbickas, D., Ostrauskas, T., 2006a: Distribution of raw material for prehistoric flint artefacts in South Lithuania. Geografija 42:2, 41–47

Baltrūnas, V., Karmaza, B., Kulbickas, D., Ostrauskas, T., 2006b: Siliceous rocks as a raw material of prehistoric artefacts in Lithuania. Geologija 56, 13–26

Broadbent, N., 1979: Coastal Resources and Settlement Stability. A critical study of a Mesolithic site complex in Northern Sweden. AUN 3.

Bronk Ramsey, C., 2005: OxCal Program v3.10. http://www.rlaha.ox.ac.uk/oxcal.htm

Callahan, E., 1987: An Evaluation of the Lithic Technology in Middle Sweden during the Mesolithic and Neolithic. AUN 8.

Carpelan, C., 1999: On the Postglacial Colonisation of Eastern Fennoscandia. Huurre, M. (ed.), Dig it all – papers dedicated to Ari Siiriäinen. Helsinki, 151-171.

Crabtree, D. E., 1972: An introduction to the technology of stone tools. Occasional papers of the Idaho State University Museum, no. 28.

Edgren, T., 1992: Den förhistoriska tiden. Finlands historia I. Esbo.

Eronen M., 1990: Geologinen kehitys jääkauden lopussa ja sen jälkeen. Suomen kartasto, vihko 120-123 (Maaperä) , luku 2.3

Halén, O., 1994: Sedentariness during the Stone Age of Northern Sweden in the light of the Alträsket site, c. 5000 B. C., and the Comb Ware site Lillberget, c. 3900 B.C. Source critical problems of representativity in archaeology. Acta Archaeologica Lundensia Series in 4:o, no 20.

Hertell, E. & Manninen M. A., 2002: Rävåsens kvartsmaterial. Finskt Museum 2002, 84-100.

Herforth, A. & Albers H. J., 1999: Geologische Grundlagen des Feuersteinbergbaus in Europa. 5000 Jahre Feuersteinbergbau. 3.

Auflage. Deutschen Bergbau-Museum Bochum Nr.77, 14-20.

Holm, L., 1991: The use of Stone and hunting of reindeer. A Study of Stone Tool Manufacture and Hunting of Large Mammals in the Central Scandes c. 6000-1 BC. Archaeology and Environment 12.

Indreko, R., 1948: Die mittlere Steinzeit in Estland. Mit einer Übersicht über die Geologie des Kunda-Sees von K. Orviku. Kungl. Vitterhets Historie och Antikvitets Akademiens Handlingar, 66.

Jaanits, L., Laul, S., Lõugas, V. & Tõnisson, E., 1982: Eesti esiajalugu. Tallinn.

Jaanits, 1989 = Янитс К. Л. Кремневый инвентарь стоянок кундаской культуры. Диссертация на соискание ученой степени кандидата исторических наук. (Manuscript in the archive of the Institute of History in Estonia, Tallinn)

Jurgenson, 1958 = Юргенсон Э. О кремневых образованиях в ордовикских и силурийских карбонатных породах Эстонской ССР. - Eesti NSV Teaduste Akadeemia Geoloogia Instituudi uurimused, II, 87-93

Jussila, T., 1999: Saimaan kalliomaalausten ajoitus rannansiirtymiskronologian perusteella. In: Kivikäs, P. & Jussila, T. & Kupiainen, R.: Saimaan ja Päijänteen alueen kalliomaalausten sijainti ja syntyaika. Kalliomaalausraportteja 1, 113-133.

- 2000a: Joutsenon Kuurmanpohjan kivikautisten asuinpaikkojen koekaivaus v. 2000. Excavation reports published in: http://www.mikroliitti.fi/~microlit/kuurmanp/esipuhe.htm (2.2.2005).

- 2000b: Pioneerit Keski-Suomessa ja Savossa. Rannansiirtymisajoitusmenetelmien perusteita ja vertailua. Muinaistutkija 2, 13-28.

- 2004: Pienvesistöjen rannansiirtymisen simulointi. In: Pesonen, P. & Raike, E. (eds.), Luonnontieteelliset menetelmät ja GIS. Arkeologiapäivät 2003. Hamina, 97-104.

Jussila, T. & Kriiska, A., 2006: Pyyntikulttuurin asuinpaikkojen rantasidonnaisuus. Uusia näkökulmia Suomen ja Viron kivi- ja varhaismetallikautisten asuinpaikkojen sijoittumiseen. In: Pesonen, P. & Mökkönen, T. (eds.), Arkeologia ja kulttuuri. Uutta kivikauden tutkimuksessa. Arkeologipäivät 2005. Hamina, 36-49.

Jussila, T. & Matiskainen, H., 2003: Mesolithic Settlement During The Preboreal Period In Finland. In: Larsson, L., Lindegren, H., Knutsson, K., Loeffler, D. & Åkerlund, A. (eds.), Mesolithic on the move. Papers presented at the Sixth International Conference on the Mesolithic in Europe, Stockholm 2000. Oxford, 664-670.

Kankaanpää, J., 2002: The House Pits at Kauvonkangas, Tervola. Huts and Houses. Stone Age and Early Metal Age Buildings in Finland. Jyväskylä, 65-78.

Knutsson, K., 1988a: Making and using stone tools. The analysis of the lithic assemblages from the Middle Neolithic sites with flint in Västerbotten, northern Sweden. AUN 11.

-1988b: Patterns of tool use. Scanning electron microscopy of experimental quartz tools. AUN 10.

-2005: The Historical Construction of "Norrland". Coast to coast - arrival: results and reflections: Proceedings of the final Coast to Coast Conference, 1-5 October 2002 in Falköping, Sweden, Coast to coast 10, 45-71.

Koltsov and Zhilin, 1999 = Кольцов Л. В., Жилин М. Г., 1999: Мезолит Волго-Окского междуречья. Памятники бутовской культуры. Москва.

Kriiska, A., 2002: Lääne-Eesti saarte asustamine ja püsielanikkonna kujunemine. Keskus-tagamaa-ääreala. Uurimusi asustushierarhia ja võimukeskuste kujunemisest Eestis. Muinasaja teadus, 11, 29-60.

Kriiska, A., Allmäe, R., Lõhmus, M. and Johanson, K., 2004a: Archaelogical investigation at the settlement and burial site of Kivisaare. – Arheoloogilised välitööd Eestis 2003, 29-44.

Kriiska, A., Haak, A., Johanson, K., Lõhmus, M., Vindi, A., 2004b: Uued kiviaja asulakohad ajaloolisel Viljandimaal. – Viljandi Muuseumi aastaraamat 2003, 35- 51.

Kriiska, A., Johanson, K., Saluäär, U. & Lõugas, L., 2003: The results of research of Estonian Stone Age. – Arheoloogilised välitööd Eestis 2002, 25-41.

Kriiska, A., Saluäär, U., 2000: Lemmetsa ja Malda neoliitilised asulakohad Audru jõe alamjooksul. – Artiklite kogumik, 2. Pärnumaa ajalugu. Vihik 3. Pärnu 2000, 8-38.

Kriiska, A. & Tvauri, A., 2002: Eesti muinasaeg. Tallinn.

Ksenzov 2001 =Ксензов В. П. Культура кунда. – Гістарычна-археалагічны зборнік, 16. Мінск, 20-35.

Lindgren, C., 2004: Människor och kvarts. Stockholm Studies in Archaeology 29. Riksantikvarieämbetet Arkeologiska Undersökningar, Skrifter no 54. Coast to Coast books No. 11.

Lisitsyn, 2003 = Лисицын С. Н., 2003: Проблемы разделения смешанных комплексов финального палеолита и мезолита Двинско-Ловатского междуречья. Древности Подвинья: исторический аспект. По материалам круглого стола, посвященного памяти А. М. Микляева (6-8 октября 1999). Санкт-Петербург, 40–47.

Lõugas , L., 1997: Post-Glacial development of vertebrate fauna in Estonian water bodies. A palaeozoological study. Dissertationes Biologicae Universitatis Tartuensis, 32.

Loze 1988 = Лозе И. А. Поселения каменного века Лубанской низины. Мезолит, ранний и средний неолит. Рига.

Luho, V., 1967: Die Suomusjärvi-kultur. Suomen Muinaismuistoyhdistyksen Aikakauskirja 66.

Matiskainen, H., 1989: Studies on the Chronology, Material Culture and Subsistence Economy of the Finnish Mesolithic, 10 000-6000 b.p. Iskos 8.

- 1996: Discrepancies in Deglaciation Chronology and the Appearance of Man in Finland. The Earliest Settlement of Scandinavia and its neighbouring areas (ed. Lars Larsson). Acta Arch. Lundensia, Ser in 8, No 24, 251-262.

Miettinen, A., 1996: Pielisen jääjärven kehityshistoria. Terra 1, 14-19.

- 2002: Relative Sea-Level Changes in the Eastern Part of the Gulf of Finland during the Last 8000 Years. Ann. Acad. Sci. Fenn Geologica-Geographica 162.

Nuñez, M., 1987: A model for the early settlement of Finland. Fennoscandia archaeologica 4, 3-18.

Olofsson, A. 2003: Early Colonization of Northern Norrland: Technology, Chronology, and Culture. Pioneer Settlement in the Mesolithic of Northern Sweden. Archaeology and Environment 16, 1-96.

Oshibkina 2000 = Ошибкина С. В. Культура Веретье. Характеристика поселений. – De temporibus antiquissimis ad honorem Lembit Jaanits. Muinasaja teadus, 8, 147-180.

Ostrauskas,T. 2002. Kundos kultūros tyrinėjimų problematika. Lietuvos archeologija 23, 93-106.

Paškevičius, J., 1997: The Geology of the Baltic Republics. Vilnius.

Pälsi, S., 1920: Ein Steinzeitlicher Moorfund bei Korpilahti im Kirchspiel Antrea, Län Viborg. Suomen Muinaismuistoyhdistyksen Aikakauskirja XXVIII: 2, 1-19.

Rankama, T., 2002: Analyses of the Quartz Assemblages of Houses 34 and 35 at Kauvonkangas in Tervola. Huts and Houses. Stone Age and Early Metal Age Buildings in Finland. Jyväskylä, 79-108.

Rankama, T. & Kankaanpää, J. (in press): The earliest postglacial inland settlement of Lapland. In: P. Pavlov & A. Volokitin (eds.), Kamennyy vek Evropeiskogo Severa = Каменный век европейского Севера

Raukas, A., Saarse, L. & Veski, S., 1995: A new version of the Holocene stratigraphy in Estonia. – Proceedings of the Estonian Academy of Sciences. Geology 44:4, 201-210.

Reimer et al. 2004: Reimer P.J., Baillie M.G.L., Bard E., Bayliss A., Beck J.W., Bertrand C., Blackwell P. G., Buck C. E., Burr G., Cutler K. B., Damon P. E., Edwards R. L., Fairbanks R. G., Friedrich M., Guilderson T. P., Hughen K. A., Kromer B., McCormac F. G., Manning S., Bronk Ramsey C., Reimer R. W., Remmele S., Southon J. R., Stuiver M., Talamo S., Taylor S. W., van der Plicht J., and Weyhenmeyer C. E. Radiocarbon 46:1029-1058.

Räihälä, O., 1998: Suomussalmen Salonsaari – kivikautinen leiripaikka Kiantajärven rannalla. Kentältä poimittua 4. Kirjoitelmia arkeologian alalta. Museoviraston arkeologian osaston julkaisuja N:o 7, 5-23.

Saarnisto, M., 1970: The late Weichselian and Flandrian History of the Saimaa Lake Complex. Comm. Phys.-Math. Vol 37.

- 1971: The upper limit of the Flandrian transgression of Lake Päijänne. Comm. Phys.-Math. Vol 41, No. 2.

Saarnisto, M. & Grönlund, T., 1996: Shoreline displacement of Lake Ladoga - new data from Kilpolansaari. In: The First International Lake Ladoga Symposium : proceedings of the First International Lake Ladoga Symposium: ecological problems of Lake Ladoga, St. Petersburg, Russia, 22-26 November 1993. Hydrobiologia 322 (1-3), 205-215.

Schulz H.-P., 1990: On the Mesolithic Quartz Industry in Finland. Iskos 9, 7-23.

- 1996: Pioneerit pohjoisessa. Suomen varhaismesoliittinen asutus arkeologisen aineiston valossa. Suomen Museo 1996, 5-45.

Sorokin 2002 = Сорокин А. Н. Мезолит Жиздринского полесья. Проблема источниковедения мезолита Восточной Европы. Москва.

Takala, H., 2004: The Ristola site in Lahti and the Earliest Postglacial Settlement of South Finland. Jyväskylä.

Tikkanen, M. & Seppä, H. 2001: Post-galcial history of Lake Näsijärvi, Finland, and the origin of the Tammerkoski Rapids. Fennia 179: 1, 129-141.

Tixier, J., 1974: Glossary for the Description of Stone Tools. – Newsletter of Lithic Technology, Special Publication, No. 1.

Ukkonen, P., 1993: The post-glacial history of the Finnish mammalian fauna, ANN. ZOOL. FENNICI 30, 249-264.

-2001: Shaped by the Ice Age. Reconstructing the history of mammals in Finland during the Late Pleistocene and Early Holocene. Helsinki. Yliopistopaino, 7-41.

Yerkes, R. W., 1990: Using Microwear Analysis to Investigate Domestic Activities and Craft Specialization at the Murphy Site, a Small Hopewell Settlement in Lichting County, Ohio. The Interpretative Possibilities of Microwear Studies. Societas Archaeologica Upsaliensis 14, 167-176.

Zagorska, I., 1999: The Earliest Settlement of Latvia. Environmental and Cultural History of the Eastern Baltic Region. PACT 57. Rixensart, 131-156.

Zhilin, M. G., 1997: Flint raw material from the Upper Volga basin and its use in the Final Palaeolithic-Neolithic. In Schild, R. And Sulgostowska, Z. (eds.), Man and Flint. Proceedings of the VIIth International Flint Symposium Warszawa – Ostrowiec Świętokrzyski September 1995. Warszawa.

Äyräpää, A., 1950: Die Ältesten steinzeitlichen Funde aus Finland. Acta Archaeologica XXI, 1-43.

Authors

Aivar Kriiska, University of Tartu, Ülikooli 18, 50090 Tartu, Estonia, aivar.kriiska@ut.ee

Timo Jussila, Mikroliitti Oy, Ivisniemenkatu 2, 002280 Espoo, Finland, timo.jussila@mikroliitti.fi

Tapani Rostedt, Peltokatu 18, 20540 Turku, Finland, tapani.rostedt@gmail.com

Lithics n	Helvetinhau-danpuro	Likolampi
Quartz	10859	2916
Flint	6	0
Other	15	4

Table 1. Lithic material from Helvetinhaudanpuro and Likolampi sites.

Quartz	Helvetinhaudanpuro			Likolampi	
	n	%		n	%
Total	10859			2916	
Flakes	10553	97,2	% of total	2853	97,8
blades	686	6,5	% of flakes	235	8,2
Cores	173	1,6	% of total	61	2,1
Tools	133	1,2	% of total	2	0,1
Identified	2452	22,6	% of total	766	26,3
Bipolar flakes	975	64,7	% of identified flakes	112	23,8
Platform flakes	531	35,3	% of identified flakes	358	76,2
Bipolar blades	582	84,8	% of identified blades	27	11,5
Platform blades	105	15,3	% of identified blades	208	88,5
Bipolar cores	98	56,6	% of identified cores	19	31,1
Platform cores	75	43,4	% of identified cores	42	68,9
Bipolar tools	60	69,8	% of identified tools	1	50,0
Platform tools	26	30,2	% of identified tools	1	50,0
Unidentifed	47	35,3	% of tools	-	-

Table 2. Quartz artefacts from Helvetinhaudanpuro and Likolampi sites.

Acta Archaeologica vol. 78:2, 2007, pp 163-178

Copyright 2007
ACTA ARCHAEOLOGICA
ISSN 0065-001X

THE COMPOSITION OF MESOLITHIC FOOD

EVIDENCE FROM THE SUBMERGED SETTLEMENT ON THE ARGUS BANK, DENMARK

ANDERS FISCHER, MIKE RICHARDS, JESPER OLSEN, DAVID EARLE ROBINSON, PIA BENNIKE, LUCYNA KUBIAK-MARTENS, JAN HEINEMEIER

INTRODUCTION

What was the relative importance of hunting, gathering and fishing in Mesolithic subsistence? Clarification of this question can be attempted through the study of a variety of sources, not least food remains and ratios of stable isotopes in human bones. In addition, supplementary evidence of a more indirect nature can be derived, for instance, from settlement site location and from stable isotope measurements of associated bones of domestic dogs.

The combined effects of various taphonomic factors make it highly unrealistic to assume a straightforward relationship between the plant and animal remains preserved and the food actually consumed, even at the most well preserved Mesolithic sites. Furthermore, practical constraints on the execution of archaeological excavations normally introduce severe discrepancies between what is preserved and what is actually recovered. Traces of hunting will almost always be over-represented relative to remains arising from fishing and, not least, from the gathering of plant foods.

This is one of the reasons for the growing interest in the stable isotope approach, which is considered (with the reservations mentioned below) to have the potential to inform us concerning the average diet of specific individuals. When the analyses are undertaken on collagen extracted from the compact bones of adults, the isotope data reflect food consumption over a period of up to about twenty years prior to death (Manolagas 2000; Wild et al. 2000; Geyh 2001). In non-compact adult human bone this period falls to around 4 years, and in juveniles and infants even faster bone turnover rates can be expected (Martin et al. 1998).

However, the approach has its limitations. The most thoroughly tested and widely applied technique, mass spectrometer measurements of $\delta^{13}C$ and $\delta^{15}N$ in bone collagen, measures primarily the dietary protein component. The food's content of carbohydrates and lipids is more difficult to assess in this way - especially in case of diets rich in protein (Ambrose & Norr 1993; Schwarcz 2000; Milner et al. 2004; Hedges 2004).

The paper should be seen as a preliminary attempt to establish a broad-based, multi-disciplinary approach to the study of Mesolithic diet. It examines material collected from a submerged settlement on the Argus Bank, Denmark (Fig. 1) in three different ways: (1) by looking at the site topography, (2) by examining the preserved faunal and floral food remains and (3) by measuring stable isotopes in collagen from human and dog bones found at the site.

Like many other submerged coastal Stone Age sites, the Argus settlement has excellent conditions for the preservation of organic remains, including food residues (Fischer et al. 1987). Some of the material even survived the generally very rough method of recovery that was applied here. This site has also produced a small but unusually varied assemblage of bones from the site inhabitants themselves – children, adults and dogs. The finds from the Argus Bank represents the earliest Mesolithic assemblage yet available from Denmark offering the opportunity for isotope-based dietary studies on a number of individuals of differing age and gender.

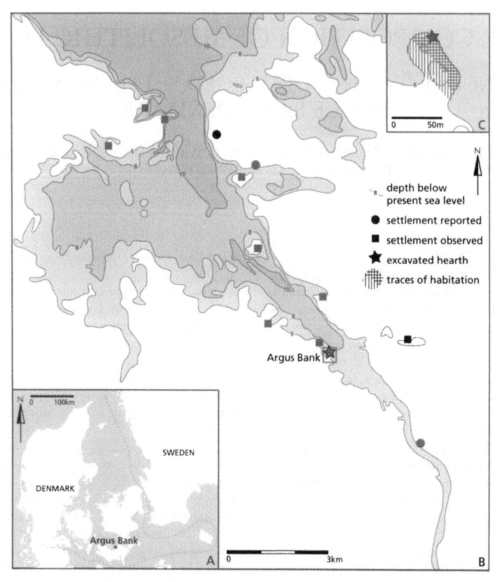

Fig. 1. The geographical and topographical setting of the submerged settlement on the Argus Bank; the site lies 2 km off the present day coast of Southern Denmark (A). Originally the site was located by the shore of a fjord - on a small peninsula (C) with a freshwater system in its hinterland (B). Map B includes other sites from the Kongemose culture recorded in the area. Round symbols indicate sites reported by the crew members involved in gravel extraction on the Argus Bank. Sites recorded during systematic archaeological underwater survey are marked with rectangular symbols. The depth contours are based on The National Survey and Cadastre's maps at a scale of scale 1:20,000.

THE SITE

The settlement is located on the Argus Bank which lies off the coast of Southern Denmark at a depth of 4 to 6 m below present sea level. It was discovered in 1956 during industrial gravel extraction (Fig. 2) (Axel 1957). Over the subsequent couple of years a considerable assemblage of flint, antler and bone was pumped up from the site (Fig. 3). In 1984-86 it was subjected to a brief archaeological surface survey and trial excavation. A section was cut through water-lain deposits containing organic refuse from the occupation. In addition, a 2½ m² area, including a hearth and a specialised flint workshop for the manufacture of arrowheads, was excavated on the periphery of the site (Fischer 1987, 1993: 89-91).

For many years, the site was claimed to be the

Fig. 2. The gravel extraction boat in action on the Argus Bank. Knud Melsen photo 1956, reproduced from Fischer 1987.

most deeply submerged Stone Age settlement in the World to have been subject to professional archaeological excavation. On a global scale, it is probably still the oldest and deepest site on the sea bed to have produced such a rich and varied selection of food remains and human bones.

Based on the typology of the flint artefacts (Fig. 4) and the bone and antler tools (Fig. 5), the settlement can be assigned to the Middle Mesolithic Kongemose culture. According to the local flint arrowhead chronology, the assemblage belongs to the middle stage of the Kongemose period (cf. Petersen 1984; Fischer 1987, 1994; Sørensen 1996). It is, therefore, significantly older than the better known settlements from the Danish sea bed that all date from the Late Mesolithic Ertebølle culture (Andersen 1985; Skaarup & Grøn 2004).

The four more or less intact flint arrowheads (Fig. 4. A-C + Fig. 8.B) relate almost certainly to hunting. Of the other 224 formally manufactured artefacts of flint, stone, bone and antler, no other item seems to have served a purpose directly connected with the procurement or preparation of food.

The five ^{14}C-dates available from the site confirm the typological date (cf. Fischer 1987; Fischer et al. 2007). Three of them are based on charcoal from one and the same hearth. When the human and animal samples are corrected for the marine reservoir effect all the resulting dates fall within an age range extending from 5970 BC to 5570 BC (68.2% confidence intervals), suggesting that the Mesolithic habitation of this site took place during a relatively brief period of time (Table 1; note that the age range could probably be narrowed down if account could be taken of the age at death of the charcoal samples).

According to the local shore displacement chronology (Christensen 1995; cf. Christensen et al. 1997; Fischer & Hansen 2005) the site has been submerged – even at low tide - ever since the Kongemose period. Consequently, the marine transgression must have put an effective stop to the accumulation of settlement debris and the digging of burials at the site. Therefore, despite the lack of stratigraphic control over the major part of the assemblage, we consider the bones of humans, dogs and terrestrial game that are the subject of this paper to be a chronologically well defined unit, dating from the Kongemose period.

TOPOGRAPHY

Marine gyttja and beach sediments beneath a hearth (Smed 1987) demonstrate that the site was originally located at the coast, directly on the seashore. A coastal location for the site is also suggested by the charred fragment of a salt-/brackish water plant from the same hearth (Table 3). The sum of field observations implies that the habitation lay adjacent to water, the surface of which stood at around 5.5 to 6 m below present sea level (Fischer 1987:41).

The topographic characteristics of the site are typical of many of the larger coastal settlements of the Middle and Late Mesolithic in Denmark. It lay well protected from larger waves on a small headland where a shallow fjord gradually turned into a submerged valley (Fig. 1). The valley served as an outlet for a number of streams and streamlets. This location gave the inhabitants easy access, by boat or on foot, to a variety of marine, freshwater and terrestrial environments rich in food.

The eastern side of the peninsula would have been an ideal location for catching fish using weirs built perpendicular to the shore (cf. Fischer 1997). The use of such wooden constructions at this time has been demonstrated at several Danish sites (Kapel 1969; Pedersen 1997; Fischer 2001, 2007). Along this sheltered shore, there was only a minimal risk of these relatively fragile structures being damaged by waves or currents.

The location of the site offered good opportunities for successful weir fishing throughout much of the year, since a variety of fish species would regularly pass close to the shore. Local brackish-water species could be trapped during their daily foraging movements along the inlet. There was also a good chance that seasonally migratory species, heading to or from the streams of the hinterland, would be caught in weirs jutting out from the shore adjacent to the site.

Modern local experience suggests that 'freshwater' species (mainly pike and perch) would have been at least as common in the catch from stationary devices set up along the seashore adjacent to the site as genuinely marine species (cf. Fischer 1987). Recent observations also suggest that the local potential for gathering of molluscs was probably insignificant relative to the returns from fishing.

HUMAN REMAINS

The Argus assemblage includes 32 human bones (Bennike 1987). One was recovered during an archaeological survey (Fig. 6) and was found in an area cov-

Fig. 3. Most of the artefacts available from the site were recovered manually from below this sieve onboard the extraction boat. Knud Melsen photo 1956.

ered with re-deposited material from gravel extraction, while the remainder were picked up by the crew of the gravel extraction boat. The colour, surface condition and general state of preservation of these bones give us no reason to doubt their association with the Mesolithic assemblage from the site comprising bone and antler artefacts and marrow-fractured bones of forest game. The most reasonable explanation for the presence of these human bones in the assemblage is that they are from graves struck accidentally by the gravel extraction boat.

On the basis of the structure, colour, shape, size and stage of development of the 32 human bones, at least four individuals can be identified:

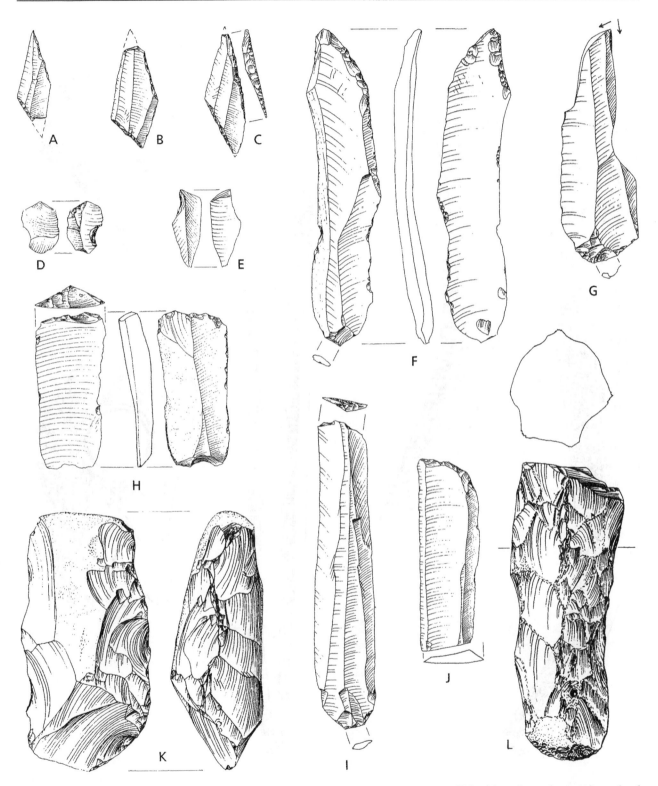

Fig. 4. Examples of flint tools from the Argus Bank. Rhombic flint arrowheads (A-C); micro burins (debris) from the production of arrowheads (D-E); drill (F); burin (G); blades with end-retouch (H-I); knife (J); core axe (K); distal end of large pick (L). One of the arrowheads (A) was found in a hearth, where it had been cracked and crazed by fire. The micro burins (D-E) were recovered near the same hearth. 3:4. Drawing E. Koch.

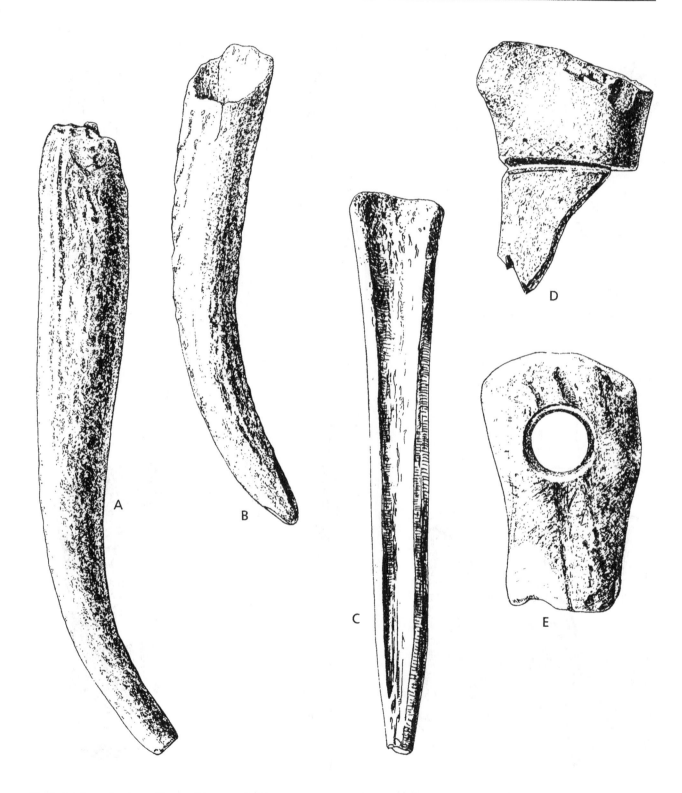

Fig. 5. Artefacts of antler and bone. Fabricators (A-B); awl or skinning knife (C); ornamented antler (part of antler axe?) (D); shaft-hole axe of red deer antler (E). 3:4. Drawing H. E. Jensen, reproduced from Fischer 1987.

- a child 2-3 years of age, represented by two bones
- a child 4-5 years of age, represented by two bones
- a female of around 20 years of age, represented by 12 bones (Fig. 7)
- an adult male whose exact age cannot be determined or estimated from the seven bone fragments available. The isotope analyses indicate that these bones derive from at least two persons (see below).

The bones do not exhibit any visible changes or abnormalities that could reflect malnutrition. Similarly, there is no evidence of pathological conditions. The only recorded lesion is a roughly rectangular, partially-healed wound (30 x15 mm) on the upper left side of the frontal bone of an adult male (Bennike 1987).

When the site was found, local newspapers wrote sensational stories about cannibalism on the Argus Bank. This was based on the observation that several of the human bones had been broken in antiquity. Since the bones in question do, to some extent, have large internal cavities, deliberate fracturing for the extraction and consumption of marrow was considered a possible explanation. None of the broken human bones does, however, display the semi-conical percussion marks on the inside of the bone wall, which characterise many mammalian bones that have been subject to marrow extraction. Such fractures can, however, be seen on many of the long-bones of large forest game animals found at the site. Our re-evaluation of the fractures suggests, therefore, that humans were not on the menu at the Argus Bank, even if the possibility cannot be entirely ruled out.

DOG BONES

In his study of the faunal evidence from the Argus site, Ulrik Møhl (1987) identified nine bone fragments from dogs. Subsequently, other scholars have reported their reservations concerning the identification of one of the bones as that of a young dog. One of the anatomical characters is very typical of dog, while others indicate roe deer (Rosenlund personal communication 2003). The stable isotope data cannot resolve this identification problem, even though they do seem to be more consistent with dog than

Fig. 6. A diver surfaces after an archaeological inspection of the Argus Bank. The shadow seen in his bag is the left humerus of a young human female. It could immediately be established that the bone did not derive for a recent drowning accident. On the contrary, its patina and state of preservation indicated that it had been imbedded in the sea floor like the many bones of Mesolithic forest game that had previously been dredged up here. Subsequently, a radiocarbon analysis proved the bone to be of Middle Mesolithic date. A. Fischer photo 1984.

roe deer. If the original identification is accepted we are dealing with an interesting example of a dog that may have spent most of its short life elsewhere than at the coast. However, due to the doubts surrounding the identification, this aspect will not be discussed in detail here.

There is no evidence of how the dog bones reached the site. They may be the remains of human food. Unlike the situation reported at some other Mesolithic settlements (e.g. Degerbøl 1943: 173; Karsten 2001: 58, 64) none of the dog bones from the Argus site shows traces of skinning or butchering. They may, therefore, just as well represent ceremonial burials like those known from the Late Mesolithic site of Skateholm in Sweden (Larsson 1989).

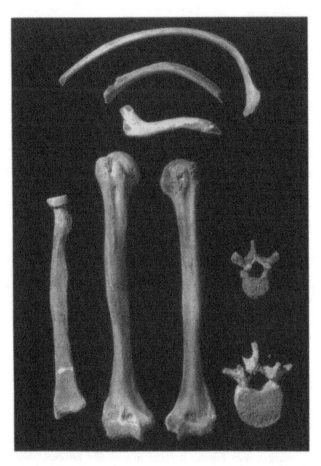

Fig. 7. Well preserved bones of an adult human female. They probably all belong to the same individual and may derive from a grave disturbed by gravel extraction. The lack of many parts of the skeleton is probably due to the nature of method by which the bones were brought to the surface. L. Larsen photo.

ANIMAL FOOD

Table 2 lists the 757 animal bones identified to species and published by Ulrik Møhl (1987). By far the largest number of faunal remains (e.g. Fig. 8) was recovered from the extraction boat, where small bones had a very limited chance of being seen and recovered. Accordingly, remains of small species, not least fish, are obviously under-represented in the total assemblage. This is illustrated by the fact that fish bones dominate the small faunal assemblage resulting from wet-sieving of sediment from the archaeological excavation of the hearth (Fig. 9). This latter assemblage comprises 101 fish bones and seven small fragments of mammal bone. Most of the former and all of the latter are too fragmentary to permit identification to species.

Due to the low recovery rate for bones of small species and a host of taphonomic factors, Table 2 is obviously a highly biased reflection of the fauna consumed on site. Therefore, it cannot form the basis for a quantified assessment of the relative dietary importance of hunting versus fishing. Even the much more carefully excavated faunal assemblage from the hearth does not permit this question to be answered. The species composition it reveals is probably also biased by taphonomic factors and certainly need not be representative of what was generally consumed at the site. Neither can we exclude the possibility that some of the non-charred bones of fish and seal were deposited by way of natural processes after the site became submerged. The relative importance of fish remains in the assemblage from the hearth, some of which clearly show the effects of fire, allows us, on the other hand, to conclude that fish may very well have played a significant role in the subsistence of the settlement inhabitants. This impression is supported by observations of very large numbers of bones and scales of fish on other well preserved Mesolithic coastal and inland sites from Denmark, where the excavation procedure has included sieving of the archaeological layers.

It should be noted that all four species of fish recorded from the site are classified as freshwater species. Except from their earliest life stages they are, however, also seen frequently in brackish waters (Muus & Nielsen 1998: 278-282; Muus 1998: 78 ff., 122ff., 156-160).

The shallow fjord around the Argus site was brackish and bones of fish caught here may, therefore, have fairly "marine" stable isotope values, even though they belong to "freshwater" species such as pike. This possibility is illustrated by a number of pike bones found at the Swedish Stone Age settlement of Västerbjers, which was originally located on the coast of the brackish Baltic Sea (Eriksson 2003b). These have $\delta^{13}C$-values ranging from −10.9 to -13.0‰ and are, accordingly, relatively marine in their isotope signature.

PLANT FOOD

Around 100 kg of sandy sediment arising from the excavation of a hearth (Fig. 9) was collected for the purpose of studying small food remains, including those of plant foods. Four 2 litre samples were processed by

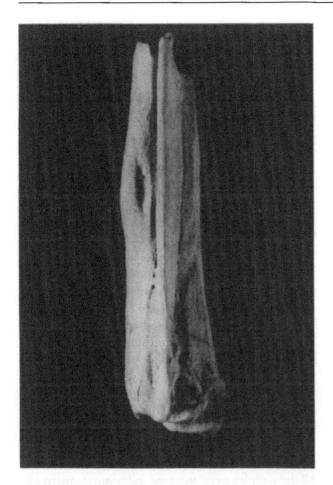 

Fig. 8. A bone of red deer (A), the end of which has been knocked off in order to gain access to the nutritious marrow. The oval depression on its left side, surrounded by a slightly swollen area, is the mark of a healed wound from a flint projectile – the frontal part of which can still be seen partly embedded in the bone (B). G. Brovad photo.

flotation and the rest of the sediment was wet-sieved using a 4 x 4mm mesh (which we now acknowledge was much too coarse). Subsequently all the botanical sample flots and residues were examined using a stereo binocular microscope (magnification x 6.3 – x 50). Small fragments of wood charcoal comprised the main component of the sample residues; other plant macrofossil remains were exceedingly rare (Table 3).

Food plant remains were restricted to charred hazelnuts (fragments of shells and an entire kernel, cf. Malmros 1987:112), and both charred and non-charred achenes (pips) of raspberry/blackberry. Further to this, the skipper of the gravel extraction boat reported that hazelnut shells were seen in great quantity when pumping sediments along the eastern fringe of the site (Fischer 1987).

The remains of fruits of raspberry or blackberry from the Argus hearth are the oldest examples of this kind of food yet available from Denmark. Within the category "seasonal fruits and nuts", only hazelnuts are known from earlier contexts.

The role of hazelnuts in the diet of European hunter-gatherers is the subject of active debate, prompted by the general abundance of nutshell remains at Mesolithic sites. Hazelnuts are often considered as a Mesolithic staple (Zvelebil 1994). It is important to emphasise, however, that evidence from recently investigated Mesolithic sites in Europe indicates that their importance may have been overestimated, especially in relation to resources such as roots and tubers (Mason et al. 2002). Although it is difficult to estimate the real significance of hazelnuts to people at the Argus

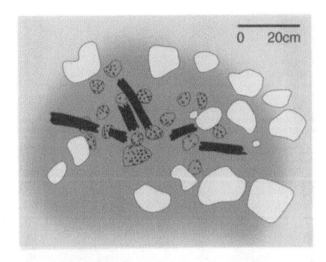

Fig. 9. A Mesolithic hearth excavated on the Argus Bank. It consisted of stones (white), charred branches (black), pieces of burnt flint (mottled) and ashes (dark grey). Among the ashes were remains of plants, fish and mammals.

site, it is assumed that they comprised a dietary component of some importance, especially in the light of their high fat and protein content and presumed extensive availability.

Other plant remains recovered from the Argus hearth were seeds and fruits of salt/brackish water plants, including eelgrass, horned pondweed and beaked tassel weed (Table 3). Only the latter was charred. The other remains could conceivably be later contaminants.

The plant macrofossil analyses of the sediment from the Argus hearth were, at the time (1988), the first of their kind on material from a submerged Mesolithic site. The results proved that seeds, fruits and other plant material could be preserved at such sites and that a sampling strategy aimed at recovering these remains, although difficult and demanding in terms of both time and resources, was justified.

Subsequently, samples have been collected and analysed from a number of submerged sites dating from later in the Mesolithic and lying either submerged off the Danish coast or within areas of reclaimed fjord (Robinson 1992; Robinson & Harild 1997, 2002; Kubiak-Martens 1999, 2002). Based on these studies we can conclude that Mesolithic people exploited various parts of a wide range of plant species, both for food and other purposes. It is sug-

gested that vegetative organs such as roots and tubers, and also green vegetables, were of particular importance in Mesolithic subsistence. The lack of remains of starch-rich root vegetables in the form of charred parenchyma (vegetative tissue) in the Argus hearth does not imply that the inhabitants of the site did not use these plant resources. This specific hearth may simply have served other purposes than for cooking roots and tubers - for instance softening tar for fixing flint tips on arrow shafts.

STABLE ISOTOPE DATA

Measurements of the stable isotopes ratios of carbon ($\delta^{13}C$) and nitrogen ($\delta^{15}N$) for human and faunal bone collagen from the Argus site are presented in Table 4. Each value listed in the table (i.e. each horizontal line) present the average of a series of measurements. The standard deviation for these series is $\pm$ 0.2‰ for $\delta^{13}C$ and $\pm$ 0.3‰ for $\delta^{15}N$. Most of the samples are of acceptable quality, since they have C:N-ratios within the range 2.9 to 3.6 (DeNiro 1985). The two samples that do not fulfil this criterion have been excluded from the following considerations.

In several cases, the same bone has been measured in both the Bradford and Aarhus laboratories. All the samples were prepared following standard extraction procedures (Longin 1971; Brown et al. 1988; Arneborg et al. 1999). The average deviation between laboratories is (0.3 $\pm$ 0.7) ‰ for $\delta^{13}C$ and (0.2 $\pm$ 0.6) ‰ for $\delta^{15}N$. Since the deviations are zero within the limits of experimental error, we have chosen to use mean values of duplicate series of measurements from the two laboratories in the following discussion and graphic presentation.

It should be noted that the isotope values for the two adult human female bones are very similar and may, therefore, be from the same individual (Fig.7). A femur and a tibia, which both represent a life age of 2-3 years, are also so similar in their isotopic signatures that they probably belong to the same person. In contrast, the $\delta^{13}C$ values for the two adult human male samples differ significantly (deviation 0.95‰, corresponding to 3.36σ), and are probably from two different individuals.

In order to interpret the human isotopic data optimally it is essential to have comparative isotopic data for the associated fauna from the same area and time period. This is necessary as geographical and chronological variations in $\delta^{13}C$ values are known to exist (e.g. Heaton 1999), and since clear variations in $\delta^{15}N$ occur through time and between different climatic regions (Heaton et al. 1986; Richards & Hedges 2003). It is, however, comforting to note that our measurements are very similar to the previously published terrestrial $\delta^{13}C$ and $\delta^{15}N$ data from other Mesolithic sites in Southern Scandinavia (e.g. Noe-Nygaard 1995; Eriksson 2003b; Eriksson & Lidén 2003; Lidén et al. 2004).

Curatorial priorities have prevented us from presenting more than one successful measurement of the stable isotopes in fish bones from the Argus site. However, we were able to measure the isotopic values for an otter – a species which, judging from the fragmentation of its bones, seems clearly associated with the human occupation of the site (Møhl 1987). As a consequence, our small sample number for aquatic animals obviously does not represent the full range of marine and freshwater species present, and possibly does not represent the full range of inter-specific variability. It is, therefore, important regarding our subsequent inferences to note that close parallels to the relatively "marine" isotope values for the Argus pike are seen in measurements for fish bones from other Danish Mesolithic coastal sites (Fischer et al. 2007). These recent measurements indicate that fully marine species from this region and of this age have $\delta^{13}C$-values of around -10.0‰.

ISOTOPIC EVIDENCE OF DIET

The stable isotope data are plotted in Figure 10. The isotope values for the six adult deer cluster in the lower left corner of the diagram, averaging $\delta^{13}C$ = -23.0‰ and $\delta^{15}N$ = 4.8‰, in good agreement with the expected values for terrestrial herbivores (e.g. Lidén et al. 2004). The pike value is located at the extreme right of the diagram with $\delta^{13}C$ = -12.3‰. This is as expected for an animal from the marine environment (Schoeninger & DeNiro 1984) and its elevated $\delta^{15}N$ value (11.2‰) is indicative of a species at a high trophic level. Note that similar pike values have been reported for the Neolithic site of Västerbjers on the Baltic Sea (Eriksson 2003b).

The two seals, an adult harp seal and an infant grey seal, display significantly lower $\delta^{13}C$ values than the pike, in spite of the fact that these are marine animals. This seems to be a peculiarity of seals in general, as seals from sites in Denmark, Sweden and Greenland often have relatively negative $\delta^{13}C$ values, compared to fish or other marine mammals (unpublished data, Aarhus AMS Laboratory; cf. Eriksson 2003b, Craig et al. 2006). Therefore, the Argus seal isotope values do not necessarily indicate an atypical local environment, but they do point to a potential complication in interpreting the marine isotope signal in humans who may have consumed significant amounts of seal.

When reconstructing diet from the above-mentioned data, account should be taken of the diet-to-consumer offset (trophic level offset). The offset values used here are 1‰ for $\delta^{13}C$ and 3.5‰ for $\delta^{15}N$ (Post 2002; Bocherens & Druckner 2003; cf. Masao & Wada 1984; Schoeninger & DeNiro 1984; Lidén 1995:17; Richards & Hedges 1999; Sponheimer et al. 2003). This phenomenon can be illustrated by a hypothetical individual whose dietary protein came only from eating herbivores, the bone collagen of which had $\delta13C$ and $\delta^{15}N$ values of -23.0‰ and 4.8‰ respectively, i.e. the average of roe and red deer from the Argus site. The bone collagen of this person would consequently have $\delta^{13}C$ and $\delta^{15}N$ values in the order of -22.0‰ and 8.3‰.

In isotope-based studies of diet it has often been assumed that human bone collagen carbon and nitrogen isotopes reflect the isotope values of the protein component of the diet, i.e. that the consumed protein is routed directly to the bone collagen (the routing model). As pointed out recently by Hedges (2004), this assumption is not necessarily valid in all cases - especially for very low protein diets, where carbon in non-essential proteins may be obtained from carbohydrates and lipids (the mixing model). In the present case the human nitrogen isotope values, which can only come from dietary protein, are very elevated compared to those of terrestrial herbivores (Fig. 10). This indicates that by far the greatest proportion of protein came from high trophic level aquatic (marine or freshwater) foods. The similarly clearly elevated values, seen in the human $\delta^{13}C$ values, can only be derived from the consumption of marine foods.

A diet dominated by carnivorous marine and

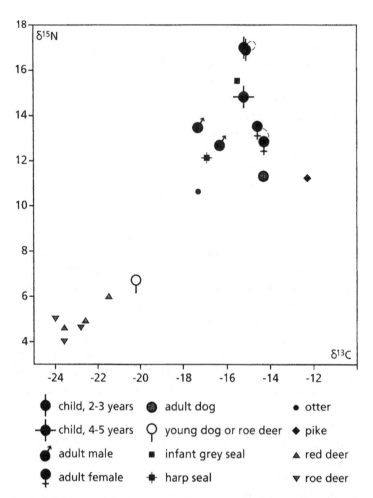

Fig. 10. δ¹³C and δ¹⁵N values for the inhabitants of the Argus site and their prey. Red deer and roe deer (in the left part of the diagram) represent terrestrial food, while pike (to the far right) represents marine food. The seals also represent the marine environment (see text). The otter appears to have subsisted on a mixture of freshwater and marine/brackish food of relatively low trophic level. The very elevated δ¹⁵N values of the humans compared to the terrestrial herbivores imply that the bulk of their dietary protein came from high trophic level aquatic animals. The elevated δ¹³C values indicate that a dominant part of this protein came from brackish or marine environments. The two samples from bones of a human female and the two samples from bones of a 2 year-old human child probably derive from the same two individuals.

freshwater animals implies food rich in protein – regardless of whether the species in question are whales, seals or fish. On this basis, it can be concluded that the diet of the Argus inhabitants was high enough in protein (even though it may also have included a substantial proportion of terrestrial plant food) that the routing model is applicable.

For the adult humans, the δ¹⁵N values lie in the range from 12.7‰ to 13.5‰, implying that their average protein intake originated from food more than one trophic level higher in the food chain than terrestrial carnivores. Such elevated nitrogen values can only result from a protein diet strongly dominated by

high trophic level aquatic animals such as pike, pikeperch and seal.

Both the humans and the dogs from the Argus site show δ¹³C values in the range -14.3‰ to -17.4‰. A comparison with the faunal data (Fig. 10) indicates that half or more of the dietary protein of these individuals was derived from marine fish or mammals. From the combined carbon and nitrogen data, the tentative conclusion can be drawn that the collagen of these individuals originated to a much greater extent from aquatic carnivores than from terrestrial plants or herbivores. An attempt to quantify this phenomenon is described in Fischer et al. 2007.

The carnivorous marine and freshwater animals implied are species such as whale, seal, cod, pike, pike-perch and perch. Bones of marine mammals are relatively rare, not just in the Argus bone assemblage but in almost all assemblages from Mesolithic sites in Denmark. This is in spite of the fact that their size and robustness should grant them a good chance of survival and recovery. It therefore seems highly likely that the dominant aquatic source of protein in the diet of the Argus inhabitants was carnivorous fish.

Henrik Tauber's studies of $\delta^{13}C$ values in human bones (Tauber 1981, 1987) gave substantial support to the impression, long held by sections of the indigenous research community, that seafood was a basic staple of the Middle and Late Mesolithic populations of coastal Denmark. With the introduction of $\delta^{15}N$ measurement of human bone collagen we now have clear evidence that aquatic food played a very dominant role in supplying dietary protein to the people inhabiting the settlement on the Argus Bank. On the basis of the isotope data, it appears that fishing was the fundamental subsistence base for the Mesolithic "hunter-gatherers" living here.

Figure 10 shows that the male and female adult humans have similar $\delta^{15}N$ values but different $\delta^{13}C$ values. The fact that the isotope ratios of the two male bones appear 'less marine' than the two female ones, may be explained in two different ways. Either these men had a greater consumption of seal and a smaller consumption of marine fish than the woman or they consumed more freshwater fish. The latter have $\delta^{15}N$ values similar to those of marine fish, but their $\delta^{13}C$ values are usually much lower than their marine counterparts (Fischer et al. 2007). Perhaps the males (and possibly also the young animal identified as either a dog or a roe deer) were away from the coast for parts of the year, during which time they subsisted largely on freshwater fish. The latter interpretation corresponds well with presently available information on inland settlement during the Kongemose culture (e.g. Larsson 1983; Fischer 2003).

The $\delta^{13}C$ values for the two children are similar to those of the female, indicating that their dietary protein also came mainly from marine sources. The 2-3 year-old Argus child has a $\delta^{15}N$ value approximately 3.5‰ higher than the adults. This could indicate that this child was breast-fed right up until the time of its death, since predominantly breast-fed children have $\delta^{15}N$ values that are elevated by approximately 3‰ – i.e. almost one trophic level - relative to their mothers (cf. Herring et al. 1998; Schurr 1998; Richards et al. 2002). The 4-5 year-old child has a $\delta^{15}N$ value around 1‰ above that of the adults. Its $\delta^{15}N$ represents not only the diet for the period immediately prior to death, but also a proportion of that consumed in its earlier years. Solid food must, therefore, have constituted the major part of this child's diet over the last year or two prior to its death.

Data for two securely identified dog bones from animals of clearly different age are given in Table 4. Their $\delta^{13}C$ values are similar to those of the humans, indicating a mainly marine diet. The $\delta^{15}N$ value is only known for the adult dog. It indicates a diet of relatively low trophic level compared to that of the humans. The marine component of the dogs' food must have come from the humans, either from sharing their food or through the consumption of kitchen refuse and/or human faeces.

CONCLUSION

The inhabitants of the Argus site had a splendid view over the fjord, inlet and forest, but what mattered most to these people were surely the excellent opportunities that the site's location provided for food procurement from these very environments. Most importantly, aquatic foods could be acquired easily, constantly and abundantly much of the year from stationary fish weirs built directly off the beach running alongside the site.

When estimating the dietary importance of each of the above-mentioned three environments, there appears to be a clear discrepancy between the information gained from the faunal remains and from the isotope analyses. Taken at face value, the food remains point to a menu dominated by large forest game, while the stable isotopes testify to a protein diet dominated by high trophic level aquatic animals. This apparent contradiction can, however, be accounted for by considering the generally very rough methods of recovery employed at the site. The remains of large forest game are over-represented and small bones, especially those of fish, are under-represented in the assemblage collected during gravel extraction. Fish bones are, however, represented – and where sieving of sediments was carried out they are numerous and clearly associated with the habitation. Moreover, the topographic characteristics of the site indicate that the potential for fishing was the determining factor in the choice of site location. Accordingly, a conclusion is favoured, based on measurements of stable isotopes, that most of the human inhabitants' dietary protein was of aquatic origin and that, to a large extent, it may have been derived from large carnivorous fish.

With humans fed on protein-rich foods, the bone collagen seems to originate almost exclusively from the protein components of diet. Since the Mesolithic flora of Northern Europe offered very little in the way of protein, it is understandable, therefore, that no traces of plant food are seen in the isotope data. Potential plant sources of starch, flavourings and vitamins were, on the other hand, plentiful in the environment around the site. It may, therefore, come as a surprise that only scattered remains of hazelnut and raspberry / blackberry and no parenchyma from starch-rich roots and tubers could be demonstrated in the ashes of the carefully excavated hearth. On the other hand, this specific hearth may not have had a function related to food preparation.

The evidence now available permits the tentative conclusion that the main sources of protein and calories at the Argus site were, in decreasing order of importance, fish, game, nuts and fruits. Fishing certainly seems to have been a more important element in the site subsistence base than hunting. Further archaeozoological and archaeobotanical studies (both based on material from new excavations), combined with additional bone chemistry analyses, are needed, however, if we are to establish the real significance of the different categories of food resources consumed by the inhabitants of the site.

Dietary habits within the Argus population do not seem to have been completely uniform. The female ate more marine fish than the males. The adult dog apparently had to be satisfied with marine food of a lower trophic level than that consumed by the humans.

An explanation for the non-uniform food habits of the Middle Mesolithic Argus population could be that the adult males (and a young dog) lived for part of the year along the rivers and lakes of the hinterland and during these periods subsisted primarily on freshwater fish. Detailed discussion of such questions will, however, be left to future studies. In so doing we would like to stress that some of the coastal sites that were abandoned immediately prior to being permanently submerged, present unique opportunities for the exploration of past subsistence and diet. Imagine what could be learned if such sites became the subject of detailed excavation and analysis.

Acknowledgements. The Danish Research Council for the Humanities provided the funding (grants no. 25-02-0555 and 25-04-0239), which made it possible for Anders Fischer to run this project. Thanks are due to museum director Lisbeth Pedersen and her staff at Kalundborg Regional Museum for administrating the project funding. Lolland-Falsters Stiftsmuseum, the National Museum of Denmark and the National Cultural Heritage Agency are acknowledged for making data from their files available and for allowing samples to be taken from bones collected under their auspices. Thanks are also due to curator Kim Aaris-Sørensen and keeper Knud Rosenlund of the Zoological Museum in Copenhagen for making bone samples available for the isotope study. Likewise, thanks to Jeppe Møhl and Niels Lynnerup of the Zoological Museum at University of Copenhagen and the Anthropological Laboratory of the Panum Institute at University of Copenhagen, respectively, for drilling stable isotope samples from bones of dogs and humans. In addition we would like to thank Gundula Müldner, Mandy Jay and Andrew Gledhill, Department of Archaeological Sciences, Bradford University, for assistance with the isotope analyses. Designer Bendt Nielsen, Ry, is acknowledged for completing the publication graphics. We are indebted to Henrik Loft Nielsen (Aarhus) for invaluable help with the manuscript.

REFERENCES

Ambrose, S. H. & Norr, L. 1993: Experimental Evidence for the Relationship of the Carbon Isotope Ratios of Whole Diet and Dietary Protein to Those of Bone Collagen and Carbonates. In J.B. Lambert & Grupe, G. (eds) Prehistoric Human Bone. Archaeology at the Molecular Level: 1-37. Berlin: Springer-Verlag.

Andersen, S.H. 1985: Tybrind Vig. A report on a submerged Ertebølle settlement on the west coast of Fyn. Journal of Danish Archaeology 4, 52–69.

Arneborg, J., Heinemeier, J., Lynnerup, N., Nielsen, H.L., Rud, N. & Sveinbjörnsdóttir, Á. E. 1999: Change of diet of the Greenland Vikings determined from stable carbon isotope analysis and ¹⁴C dating of their bones. Radiocarbon 41(2):157-168.

Axel, K. 1957: Kystkultur-bopladsen på Argusgrunden. Lolland-Falsters Historiske Samfunds Aarbog XDXCVII: 351-360.

Bennike, P. 1987: Menneskeknogler fra stenalderbopladsen på Argusgrunden (summary in English: The Mesolithic Skeletal Remains of Human Beings from the Argus Settlement). Fortidsminder og kulturhistorie, Antikvariske studier 8: 94-106.

Bocherens, H. & Drucker, D. 2003: Trophic level isotopic enrichment of carbon and nitrogen in bone collagen: a case study from recent and ancient terrestrial ecosystems. International Journal of Osteoarchaeology 13, 46-53.

Bronk Ramsey, C. 1995: Radiocarbon Calibration and Analysis of Stratigraphy: The OxCal Program. Radiocarbon 37(2): 425-430.

Bronk Ramsey, C. 2001: Development of the Radiocarbon Program OxCal. Radiocarbon 43(2A): 355-363.

Brown, T.A., Nelson, D.E. & Southon, J.R. 1988: Improved collagen extraction by modified Longin method. Radiocarbon 30: 171-177.

Christensen, C. 1995: The littorina transgressions in Denmark. In Fischer, A. (ed.) Man and Sea in the Mesolithic. Coastal settlement above and below present sea level. Oxford, Oxbow:15-22.

Christensen, C., Fischer, A. & Mathiassen, D.R. 1997: The great sea rise in the Storebælt. In Pedersen, L., Fischer, A. & Aaby, B. (eds) The Danish Storebælt since the Ice Age – man, sea and forest. Copenhagen. A/S Storebælt Fixed Link: 45-54.

Craig, O.E., Ross, R., Andersen, S., Milner, N. & Bailey, G.N. 2006: FOCUS: Sulphur isotope variation in archaeological marine fauna from Northern Europe. Journal of Archaeological Science: 1642-1646.

Degerbøl, M. 1943: Dyrelivet i Aamosen i Stenalderen, in T. Mathiassen 1943 Stenalderbopladser i Aamosen: 165-206. Nordiske Fortidsminder 3/3. Copenhagen. Kongelige Nordiske Oldskriftselskab.

DeNiro, M.J. 1985: Post-mortem preservation and alteration of in vivo bone collagen isotope ratios in relation to paleodietary reconstruction. Nature 317: 806-809.

Eriksson, G. 2003a: Norm and difference. Stone Age dietary practice in the Baltic region. Theses and Papers in Scientific Archaeology 5. Stockholm. Archaeological Research Laboratory, Stockholm University.

Eriksson, G. 2003b: Part-time farmers or hard-core sealers? Västerbjers studied by means of stable isotope analysis. Journal of Anthropological Archaeology 23: 135-162.

Eriksson, G. & Lidén, K. 2003: Skateholm revisited: new stable isotope evidence on humans and fauna, in Eriksson, G. 2003a.

Fischer, A. 1987: Stenalderbopladsen på Argusgrunden (summary in English: The Stone-Age Site on the Argus Bank). Fortidsminder og kulturhistorie, Antikvariske studier 8: 11-58.

- 1993: Stenalderbopladser på bunden af Smålandsfarvandet. En teori afprøvet ved dykkerbesigtigelse (English text: Stone Age settlements in the Småland Bight. A theory tested by diving). Hørsholm. Skov- og Naturstyrelsen.

- 1994: Dating the early trapeze horizon. Radiocarbon dates from submerged settlements in Musholm Bay and Kalø Vig, Denmark. Mesolithic Miscellanny 15(1): 1-7.

- 1997: People and the sea – settlement and fishing along the mesolithic coasts. In L. Pedersen, Fischer, A. & Aaby, B. (eds) The Danish Storebælt since the Ice Age – man, sea and forest: 63-77. Copenhagen. A/S Storebælt Fixed Link.

- 2001: Mesolitiske bopladser på den danske havbund – udfordringer for forskning og forvaltning. In O.L. Jensen, Hansen, K. Møller & Sørensen, S.A. (eds) Danmarks jægerstenalder – status og perspektiver. Beretning fra symposiet "status og perspektiver inden for dansk mesolitikum" afholdt i Vordingborg, september 1998: 59-74. Odense. Hørsholm Egns Museum.

- 2003: Trapping up the rivers, trading across the sea. In L. Larsson, Kindgren, H., Knutsson, K., Loeffler, D. & Åkerlund, A. (eds) Mesolithic on the Move. Papers presented at the Sixth International Conference on the Mesolithic in Europe, Stockholm 2000: 393-401. Oxford. Oxbow.

- 2007: Coastal fishing in Stone Age Denmark – evidence from below and above the present sea level and from the bones of human beings. In Milner, N., Craig, O.E. & Bailey, G.N. Shell middens in Atlantic Europe, 54-69. Oxford. Oxbow.

Fischer, A. & Hansen, J. S. 2005: Mennesket og havet i ældre stenalder. In C. Bunte (ed.) Arkeologi och naturvetenskap, 277-297. Lund. Gyllenstiernska Krapperupstiftelsen.

Fischer, A., Møhl, U., Bennike, P., Tauber, H., Malmros, C., Hansen, J. Schou & Smed, P. 1987: Argusgrunden – en undersøisk boplads fra jægerstenalderen (summaries in English). Copenhagen. Skov- og Naturstyrelsen.

Fischer, A., Olsen, J., Richards, M., Heinemeier, J., Sveinbjörnsdóttir, Á.E. & Bennike, P. 2007: Coast-inland mobility and diet in the Danish Mesolithic and Neolithic – evidence from stable isotope values of humans and dogs. Journal of Archaeological Science 34: 2125-2150.

Geyh, M.A. 2001: Bomb radiocarbon dating of animal tissues and hair. Radiocarbon 43(2B): 723-730.

Heaton, T.H.E. 1999: Spatial, Species, and Temporal Variation in the $^{13}C/^{12}C$ Ratios of C3 Plants: Implications for Palaeodiet Studies. Journal of Archaeological Science 26: 637-649.

Heaton, T.H.E., Vogel, J.C., von la Chevallerie, G., & Collett, G. 1986: Climatic influence on the isotopic composition of bone nitrogen. Nature 322: 822-823.

Hedges, R.E.M. 2004: Isotopes and red herrings: comments on Milner et al. Antiquity 78: 34-37.

Herring, D.A., Saunders, S.R., & Katzenberg, M.A. 1998: Investigating the weaning process in past populations. American Journal of Physical Anthropology 105: 425-439.

Kapel, H. 1969: En boplads fra tidlig-atlantisk tid ved Villingebæk. Nationalmuseets Arbejdsmark 1969: 85-94.

Karsten, P. 2001: Dansarna från Bökeberg. Om jakt, ritualer och inlandsbosättning vid jägerstenålderns slut. Riksantikvarämbetets Arkeologiska Undersökningar Skrifter 37. Lund: Riksantikvarämbetet.

Kubiak-Martens, L. 1999: The plant food component of the diet at the late Mesolithic (Ertebølle) settlement at Tybrind Vig, Denmark. Vegetation History and Archaeobotany 8: 117-127.

- 2002: New evidence for the use of root foods in pre-agrarian subsistence recovered from the late Mesolithic site at Halsskov, Denmark. Vegetation History and Archaeobotany 11: 23-31.

Larsson, L. 1983: Ageröd V. An Atlantic Bog Site in Central Scania. Acta Archaeologica Lundensia, Series in 8o. No. 12. Lund. Institute of Archaeology.

- 1989: Late Mesolithic Settlements and Cemeteries at Skateholm, Southern Sweden, in Bonsall, C. (ed.) The Mesolithic in Europe. Papers Presented at the Third International Symposium: 367-378. Edinburgh. John Donald.

Lidén, K. 1995: Prehistoric Diet Transition. Theses and Papers in Scientific Archaeology 1. Stockholm. Archaeological Research Laboratory, Stockholm University.

Lidén, K., Eriksson, G., Nordqvist, B., Götherström, A. & Bendixen, E. 2004: "The wet and the wild followed by the dry and the tame" – or did they occur at the same time? Antiquity 78: 23-33.

Longin, R. 1971: New Method of Collagen Extraction for Radiocarbon Dating. Nature 30(5291): 241-242.

Malmros, C. 1987: Trækul fra et 7.700 gammelt ildsted på Argusgrunden Fortidsminder og kulturhistorie, Antikvariske studier 8: 111-116.

Manolagas, S.C. 2000: Birth and Death of Bone Cells: Basic Regulatory Mechanisms and Implications for the Pathogenesis and Treatment of Osteoporosis. Endocrine Reviews 21(2): 115-137.

Masao, M. & Wada, E. 1984: Stepwise enrichment of 15N along

food chains: Further evidence and the relation between δ15N and animal age. Geochimica et Cosmochimica Acta 48: 1135-1140.

Mason, S.L.R., Hather, J.G. & Hillman, G.C. 2002: The archaeobotany of European hunter-gatherers: some preliminary investigations. In S.L.R. Mason et al. (eds) Hunter-Gatherers Archaeobotany. Perspectives from the northern temperate zone: 188-196. London. Institute of Archaeology UCL.

Martin, R.B., Burr, D.B. & Sharkey, N.A. 1998: Skeletal Tissue Mechanism. Berlin/Heidelberg. Springer.

Milner, N., Craig, O.E., Bailey, G.N., Pedersen, K. & Andersen, S.H. 2004: Something fishy in the Neolithic? A re-evaluation of stable isotope analysis of Mesolithic and Neolithic coastal populations. Antiquity 78: 9-23.

Muus, B.J. 1998: Europas Ferskvandsfisk. Copenhagen. Gad.

Muus, B.J. & Nielsen, J.G. 1998: Havfisk og Fiskeri i Nordvesteuropa. Copenhagen. Gad.

Møhl, U. 1987: Faunalevn fra Argusgrunden. Fortidsminder og kulturhistorie, Antikvariske studier 8 :59-93.

Noe-Nygaard, N. 1995: Ecological, sedimentary, and geochemical evolution of the late-glacial to postglacial Åmose lacustrine basin, Denmark. Fossils and Strata 37. Oslo.

Pedersen, L. 1997: They put fences in the sea. In L. Pedersen, Fischer, A. & Aaby, B. (eds) The Danish Storebælt since the Ice Age – man, sea and forest: 124-143. Copenhagen. A/S Storebælt Fixed Link.

Petersen, P. Vang 1984: Chronological and regional variation in the late Mesolithic of Eastern Denmark. Journal of Danish Archaeology 3: 7-18.

Post, D.M. 2002: Using stable isotopes to estimate trophic position: models, methods, and assumptions. Ecology 83(3), 703-718.

Richards, M.P., & Hedges, R.E.M. 1999: Stable isotope evidence for similarities in the types of marine foods used by late Mesolithic humans at sites along the Atlantic coast of Europe. Journal of Archaeological Science 26: 717-722.

Richards, M.P., Mays, S., & Fuller, B. 2002: Stable carbon and nitrogen isotope values of bone and teeth reflect weaning at the Mediaeval Wharram Percy Site, Yorkshire, U.K. American Journal of Physical Anthropology 199: 205-210.

Robinson, D.E. 1992: Bestemmelse af planterester fundet i forbindelse med en stammebåd ved Møllegabet II, Ærø. NNU Rapport (1992) nr. 6. Copenhagen. National Museum.

Robinson, D.E. & Harild, J.A. 1997: Ancient plant remains from the Halsskov site. In L. Pedersen, Fischer, A. & Aaby, B. (eds) The Danish Storebælt since the Ice Age – man, sea and forest: 196-200. Copenhagen. A/S Storebælt Fixed Link.

- 2002: Archaeobotany of an early Ertebølle (late Mesolithic) site at Halsskov, Zealand, Denmark. In S.L.R. Mason & Hather, J.G. (eds.) Hunter-Gatherers Archaeobotany. Perspectives from the northern temperate zone: 84-95. London. Institute of Archaeology, UCL.

Schoeninger, M.J. & DeNiro, M.J. 1984: Nitrogen and carbon isotopic composition of bone collagen from marine and terrestrial animals. Geochimica et Cosmochimica Acta 48: 625-639.

Schurr, M.R.1998: Using Stable Nitrogen Isotopes to Study Weaning Behaviour in Past Populations. World Archaeology 30: 327-342.

Schwarcz, H.P. 2000: Some biochemical aspects of carbon isotopic paleodiet studies, in S.H. Ambrose & Katzenberg, M.A. (eds) Biogeochemical Approaches to Paleodietary Analysis: 189-209. New York. Kluwer Academic/ Plenum Publishers.

Skaarup, J. & Grøn, O. 2004: Møllegabet II. A Submerged Mesolithic settlement in southern Denmark. Oxford. British Archaeological Reports International Series 1328.

Smed, P. 1987: Argus Grund – Feltundersøgelser 1984. Fortidsminder og kulturhistorie, Antikvariske studier 8: 125-133.

Sponheimer, M., Robinson, T., Ayliffe, L., Roeder, B., Hammer, J., Passey, B., West, A., Cerling, T., Dearing, D. & Ehleringer, J. 2003: Nitrogen Isotopes in Mammalian Herbivores: hair δ15N Values from a Controlled Feeding Study. International Journal of Osteoarchaeology 13: 80-87.

Sørensen, S.A. 1996: Kongemosekulturen i Sydskandinavien. Jægerspris. Færgegården.

Tauber, H. 1981: Kostvaner i forhistorisk tid – belyst ved C-13 målinger. In Egevang, R. et al. (eds) Det Skabende Menneske. Kulturhistoriske skitser tilegnet P.V. Glob 20. februar 1981(1): 112-126. Herning. Nationalmuseet.

- 1987: Argus-bopladsen: Alder og ernæring belyst ved kulstofanalyser (Summary in English: the Argus dwelling place: age and diet elucidated by carbon analyses). Fortidsminder og kulturhistorie, Antikvariske studier 8: 107-110.

Wild, E.M., Arlamovsky, K.A., Golser, R., Kutschera, W., Priller, A., Puchegger, S., Rom, W., Steier, P. & Vycudilik, W. 2000: 14C dating with the bomb peak: An application to forensic medicine. Nuclear Instruments and Methods in Physics Research B 172: 944-950.

Zvelebil, M. 1994: Plant use in the Mesolithic and its role in the transition to farming. Proceedings of the Prehistoric Society 60: 35-74.

Authors' adresses

Anders Fischer, Kalundborg Museum (this project) and The Danish National Heritage Agency, H.C. Andersens Boulevard 2, DK-1553 Copenhagen V; afiklb@privat.dk

Mike Richards, Department of Human Evolution, Max Planck Institute for Evolutionary Anthropology, D-04103, Leipzig, Germany; richards@eva.mpg.de

Jesper Olsen, AMS ¹⁴C Dating Laboratory, University of Aarhus (this project) and Department of Earth Sciences, University of Aarhus, Hoegh-Guldbergsgade 2, DK-8000 Aarhus C; jesper.olsen@geo.au.dk

David Earle Robinson, English Heritage, Archaeological Sciences, Fort Cumberland, Fort Cumberland Road, Eastney, Portsmouth PO4 9LD, UK; DavidEarle.Robinson@english-heritage.org.uk.

Pia Bennike, Laboratory of Biological Anthropology, Institute of Forensic Medicine, University of Copenhagen, Blegdamsvej 3, DK-2200 Copenhagen N, Denmark; bennike@antrolab.ku.dk

Lucyna Kubiak-Martens, BIAX Consult, Research and Consultancy Service for Biological Archaeology, Hogendijk 134, 1506 AL Zaandam, The Netherlands; kubiak@biax.nl

Jan Heinemeier, AMS ¹⁴C Dating Laboratory, Department of Physics and Astronomy, University of Aarhus, DK-8000 Aarhus C, Denmark; jh@phys.au.dk

Sample specifications	Lab. No.	$\delta^{13}C$ ‰ VPDB	^{14}C age		Calibrated age	
			BP	Corrected BP	BC	68.2% interval BC
Bone, left humerus of human female, 20 years	K-4354	-14.3	7080±75	6825±75	5715	5771-5639 (68.2%)
Bone, tibia of young dog or roe deer	AAR-4093	-20.0	6870±50	6811±50	5710	5733-5659 (68.2%)
Charcoal, oak (Quercus sp.), 15 fragments	K-4382	-22.7	6840±105		5840	5840-5630 (68.2%)
Charcoal, lime (Tilia sp.), 66 fragments	K-4383	-23.0	6790±105		5790	5790-5610 (65.5%) 5590-5570 (2.7%)
Charcoal, lime (Tilia sp.), 51 fragments	K-4384	-23.1	6930±105		5910	5970-5950 (4.0%) 5910-5720 (64.2%)

Table 1. ^{14}C dates from the Argus site. The correction for the marine reservoir effect is based on the assumption that 100% marine and 100% terrestrial diet implies $\delta^{13}C$ values of -10.1‰ and -21.7‰ respectively and that a 100% marine diet will result in a reservoir effect of 400 years (cf. Fischer et al. 2007). The calibration to calendar years is based on atmospheric data from Reimer et al. (2004) and produced with the aid of OxCal version 3.10 (Bronk Ramsey 1995, 2001). No attempt has been made to correct the charcoal-based dates to take account of the possibly significant age at death of these samples. eimer et al. (2004) and produced with the aid of OxCal version 3.10 (Bronk Ramsey 1995, 2001). No attempt has been made to correct the charcoal-based dates to take account of the possibly significant age at death of these samples.

Species name in English	Latin name	Number of fragments identified to species
Fish	*Pisces*	29
Pike	Esox lucius L.	9
Bream	Abramis brama (L.)	3
Perch	Perca fluviatilis L.	4
Pike-perch	Lucioperca lucioperca (L.)	13
Birds	*Aves*	7
Black stork	Ciconia nigra (L.)	1
Shelduck	Tadorna tadorna (L.)	1
Mallard	Anas platyrhynchos L.	1
Red-breasted merganser	Mergus serrator L.	1
White-tailed eagle	Haliaeetus albicilla (L.)	2
Crane	Grus grus (L.)	1
Mammals	*Mammalia*	721
Beaver	Castor fiber L.	5
Dog	Canis familiaris L.	9 (8)
Otter	Lutra lutra (L.)	4
Harp seal	Phoca groenlandicus Erxl.	1
Grey seal	Halichoerus grypus (O. Fabr.)	1
Wild boar	Sus scrofa L.	155
Roe deer	Capreolus capreolus (L.)	100 (101)
Red deer	Cervus elaphus L.	446

Table 2. Faunal remains from the Argus site, identified to species. All mammalian species derive from the gravel extraction, which took place over very much larger areas than the archaeological excavations. The material recovered in the course of gravel extraction only included the larger fish bones, whereas all the smaller examples resulted from the excavation and from sieving and flotation of sediments collected in and around the hearth.

Sample No	I	II	IV	VI	VIII	X	XI
Sample preparation	Sieve	Flot.	Flot.	Flot.	Sieve	Flot.	Sieve
Weight of processed sample (g)	23	33	17	14	1.5	80	1.0
Food plants							
Hazel (Corylus avellana)	+*		+*				+*
Blackberry/raspberry (Rubus idaeus/fruticosus)				1		1*	
Plants of salt or brackish water							
Beaked tasselweed (Ruppia maritima)						1*	
Horned pondweed (Zannichellia sp.)		1					
Eelgrass (Zostera sp.)			1				
Miscellaneous							
Charcoal	+	+	+	+	+	+	+
Seaweed (recent)						+	
Cennococcum geophilum (fungal fruit body)				1			
1 = one specimen; + = several; * = carbonised							

Table 3. Plant remains – including edible nuts and berries – recovered from the sieve and flotation residues from the Argus hearth.

Sample specifications	Stable isotope analysis					Source of the stable isotope analysis	Sample registration number
	this study				previous studies		
	$\delta^{13}C$	$\delta^{15}N$	C:N	% coll.	$\delta^{13}C$		
2-3-year-old human, right tibia	-15.2	17.0	3.3	16.8		Bradford	BCH198:32
2-3-year-old human, left femur.	-15.7	16.4	3.8	4.1*		Bradford	AND-11
	-15.1	16.9	3.3	17.7		Aarhus	AAR-8856
4-5-year-old human, left femur	-15.3	14.4	3.6	7.3*		Bradford	AND-12
	-15.1	15.1	3.3	13.9		Aarhus	AAR-8857
Adult female human, left humerus	-14.3	12.8	3.3	8.3*	-14.3	Bradford	K-4354
Adult female human, right humerus	-14.3	13.3	3.3	6.2*		Bradford	AND-13
	-14.7	13.5	3.4	13.4		Aarhus	AAR-8858
Adult male human, left humerus	-17.1	13.4	3.4	5.8*		Bradford	AND-14
	-17.4	13.5	3.4	8.3		Aarhus	AAR-8859
Adult male human, right tibia	-16.3	12.7	3.2	8.0*		Bradford	F58-54 b
Adult dog, tibia	-14.3	11.3	3.4	3.5*		Bradford	Argus dog
½ year dog, right mandibula.					-16.5		K-400
Young dog or roe deer, tibia	-20.2	6.4	3.3	13.5*	-20.0	Bradford	AAR-4093
	-20.2	6.7	3.1	12.7	-20.0	Aarhus	AAR-4093
Adult roe deer, lower end of left femur	-23.5	3.8	3.2	12.1		Bradford	AAR-8610-1
	-23.6	4.1	3.3	12.1		Aarhus	AAR-8610-1
Adult roe deer, lower end of left femur	-24.0	5.0	3.3	2.2*		Bradford	AAR-8610-2
Adult roe deer, lower end of left femur	-22.8	4.6	3.2	2.4*		Bradford	AAR-8610-3
Adult red deer, lower end of right humerus	-22.8	4.8	3.2	11.4		Bradford	AAR- 8611-1
	-22.4	4.9	3.3	11.4		Aarhus	AAR- 8611-1
Adult red deer, lower end of right humerus	-23.6	4.6	3.5	0.9*		Bradford	AAR- 8611-2
Adult red deer, lower end of right humerus	-21.5	6.0	3.3	1.4*		Bradford	AAR- 8611-3
Adult otter, humerus	-17.3	10.4	3.2	13.4		Bradford	AAR-8607
	-17.3	10.7	3.3	13.4		Aarhus	AAR-8607
New born grey seal, bulla	-17.2	14.8	3.7	0.7*		Bradford	AAR-8608
	-15.5	15.5	3.3	1.3		Aarhus	AAR-8608
Adult harp seal, os occipitale	-17.0	11.7	3.2	14.6		Bradford	AAR-8609
	-16.7	12.4	3.2	14.6		Aarhus	AAR-8609
Adult (ca. 1m-long) pike, vertebra	-13.3	11.8	3.5	5.0*		Bradford	AAR-8605
	-11.3	10.6	3.4	7.3		Aarhus	AAR-8605

Table 4. Stable isotope values for humans and faunal food sources from the Argus site. The C:N-values and the collagen % are measures of sample quality. The $\delta^{13}C$ values from previous studies were produced by the former ^{14}C-dating laboratory in Copenhagen (K-400 and K-4354) and the Science Institute in Reykjavík (AAR-4093). Collagen percentages marked with an asterisk derive from samples, which have been subjected to ultra-filtration – a method that generally results in relatively low collagen values.

Acta Archaeologica vol. 78:2, 2007, pp 181-192

Copyright 2007
ACTA ARCHAEOLOGICA
ISSN 0065-001X

HISTORICAL CONTEXT
OF THE TERM 'COMPLEXITY'
IN THE SOUTH SCANDINAVIAN MESOLITHIC

Erik Brinch Petersen & Christopher Meiklejohn

INTRODUCTION

This paper examines some of the historical elements that must be considered when using the term complexity with reference to the early Holocene hunting and gathering populations of northern Europe. Though complexity, as a concept, has had considerable currency in recent discussions of prehistoric hunting and gathering populations (e.g. Ames 1994; Price and Brown 1985; Price & Feinman 1995; Schnirelman 1992), we see three major questions concerning the present use and implications of the concept. The first of these is the question of what is actually identified as complex. The second question involves the evolutionary meaning of referring to an inferred social behaviour and its intensification as complex, especially so when seeking within the European Mesolithic for the origin of succeeding Neolithic food producing societies. The third question involves the specific fit of the archaeological evidence to the complex model, or vice versa, particularly within the Mesolithic sequence of southern Scandinavia. In this paper we will consider some historical aspects of these questions.

Three historical strands lie behind the questions raised above, two of them beginning in the 19th century. The first is the development of Upper Palaeolithic and Mesolithic archaeology in Western Europe. The second involves the anthropological study and interpretation of hunting and gathering societies. The third, and the crux of the issue, is the attempt, since the 1960's, to create a synthetic archaeological and anthropological interpretation of late prehistoric hunter-gatherers and to relate them to the origin of food production.

THE DEVELOPMENT OF PREHISTORIC ARCHAEOLOGY

The interpretation of the Upper Palaeolithic and Mesolithic periods in Europe has not always been a unitary process. Underlying the concept being discussed have been two sets of ideas, sometimes in accord and sometimes in discord. To most scholars trained in the U.K. or in North America the focus has always been on work in south-western France, and especially on the Upper Palaeolithic. Such an approach is clear in the historical survey of Glyn Daniel (1975). However, work in Scandinavia has always had a different core, concentrated for obvious reasons on the Mesolithic (see Klindt-Jensen 1975).

In France, beginning with the discovery of Aurignac in 1852, there was a gradual unveiling of a late glacial age society, centred upon the hunting of large mammals, some of them now extinct, and accelerated after 1863 by the work of Edourd Lartet and Henry Christy (1865-1875). Before the First World War the major features of Upper Palaeolithic society were in view, including the basic phases, an understanding of the density of finds in key regions, the diversity of burial ritual, and the presence of a rich artistic tradition (Breuil 1912). While the details have changed the Upper Palaeolithic that we now know was recognizable.

This cannot be said for the Mesolithic of the same region, which was still effectively invisible. Early prehistorians, including Lartet and de Mortillet, saw a complete break between the Upper Palaeolithic and the Neolithic, the ancient hiatus. The presence of a sequence gradually filling this gap was demonstrated by Vielle at Fère-en-Tardenois, beginning in 1879, and by Edourd Piette at Mas d'Azil in 1887. However, its chronological setting was in doubt until the 1920's. The Azilian had been found in cave sites and had simple geometric mobile art. The remainder of the Mesolithic was largely viewed as a phenomenon of impoverished open-air sites, lacking organic material, and represented only by small collections of lithic tools dominated by microliths. Burial was uncommon and aesthetic elements were limited in type and quantity. Compared unfavourably with the preceding Palaeolithic and the succeeding Neolithic, it was not difficult to deny a dynamic evolutionary role to such a society.

Such a denial was clearly present in models presented by major synthesizers, such as Gordon Childe (1925, 1929, 1957). In the 1950's, the marginal view of the Mesolithic (the "poor starving savages" or "strandloopers" caricature) was still present. Mortimore Wheeler (1954) could accordingly describe Star Carr in the following terms: "As squalid a huddle of marsh-ridden foodgatherers as the imagination could well encompass"!

However, such a view had seldom been evident in southern Scandinavia. The first literary mention of a Danish shellmidden, Krabbesholm, actually describes it as a votive place for a heathen population (Faber 1828). Afterwards, "the raised beach ridges", as the phenomenon initially was named, were discussed by the zoologist Japetus Steenstrup in 1848, leading in the same year to the creation of a commission (Ørsted 1848). This commission was later known by two names, first as the "Lejre Kommission" after the area in which it was working, and then as the "First Køkkenmødding Kommission". The two primary members of this commission were the zoologist Steenstrup and the archaeologist J. J. A. Worsaae. Together with the third member and geologist G. Forchhammer, they noted the combination of features appearing from the excavations, all agreeing in 1851 that these middens were of human origin (Steenstrup 1851).

Ten years later, however, Steenstrup and Worsaae debated whether these finds were closer to the "Troglodytes" or the cave dwellers of western Europe (the Upper Palaeolithic) or to the "Swiss palafittes" or lake sites (the Neolithic). Worsaae framed what we now recognize as the Mesolithic in 1859 (1861) within a

bipartite Stone Age ("Ældre" and "Yngre Stenalder"), and G. Stephens immediately brought this bipartition to the attention of the international world the following year (Stephens 1862). Steenstrup (1861), in contrast, argued for a social or functional interpretation of contemporaneous groups. However, both agreed that the finds were rich in contents. As a result of ten years work the fundamental issues of the Mesolithic-Neolithic transition had already been defined in Scandinavia by the 1860's and, even today, the same questions still haunt us. Steenstrup (1888-89) even used the Hiatus ("Et gabende svælg af tid") in his discussion against the bipartition of the Stone Age, while Georg F.L. Sarauw rejected the same in 1903 based on his then recent excavation at Mullerup in 1900. This was first published in Danish (1903), then in French in 1906 and finally in German (1911-1914), but never in English.

Further work and disagreements led to the Second Kitchenmidden Commission, during the 1890's, including excavations at the original site of Ertebølle. Though burial was still not a major part of the recognized pattern, here was a culture with large, obvious, sites, associated with a strongly developed technology and the use of a broad range of fauna. The results of the investigation were published by the Commission in 1900 (Madsen et al. 1900). In that same year Sarauw opened his excavation in the bog at Mullerup, and in the process defined the Danish Maglemose (Sarauw 1903). Finally, with the description of what was later to be known as the Kongemose, by Erik Westerby at Bloksbjerg (1927), the Danish Mesolithic was in place both as a sequence and on a scientific basis. With their well defined stone, bone and antler industries, and their art, the relegation of these cultures to the prehistoric margin was certainly never an issue in South Scandinavian archaeology.

THE ANTHROPOLOGY OF HUNTERS AND GATHERERS

If one base for a discussion of complexity lay within the development of Upper Palaeolithic and Mesolithic archaeology, the second base lay within the anthropological study of living hunter-gatherers. Such studies began in the second half of the 19th century, especially with Lewis H. Morgan (1877) and E. B. Tylor

Fig. 1. "Shellmiddens next to Ørum Å". Water colour by A. P. Madsen, 1891 (National Museum of Denmark).

Fig. 2. "Shellmidden at Fannerup". Water colour by A. P. Madsen, 1860 (National Museum of Denmark).

(1881), with influences for their evolutionary models including the development of the three-age system in Scandinavian archaeology, the publication of Charles Darwin's "Origin of Species" in 1859, and the work of Herbert Spencer. Much has been said about the interplay between Christian Jürgensen Thomsen's three age system, first developed in the displays of the National Museum in Copenhagen in 1819 (Daniel 1975, Jensen 1992) and Lewis H. Morgan's "ethnical periods" of savagery, barbarism and civilization. However, insight was still limited, as both avenues of research were not producing that kind of evidence that could be beneficent to the other.

Early studies of hunting and gathering societies include those of Franz Boas on the Eskimo of Baffin Island (1888) and on the Kwakiutl of the Northwest Coast (1897), and of W.B. Spencer and F.J. Gillen (1899) on Central Australian Aborigines. At this time Boas was redirecting North American Cultural Anthropology away from evolutionary theory and towards a dependence upon the detail of the specific field experience, in what has been termed "historical particularism". This influence continued well after 1950, providing the root for later ethnographic descriptions of those areas where Boas had worked. E. A. Kroeber and Robert B. Lowie continued this approach, though Lowie returned to evolutionary models of sequence, change and explanation. From this base came such ethnographic studies of hunters and gatherers as those by F. H. Speck and Eleanor Leacock on the Algonquians in Eastern Canada.

In Europe there was a parallel reaction to 19th century evolutionary models, based in the work of Émile Durkheim. This was to become the base of "British Social Anthropology", which was developed into the study of "structural-functionalism" by A.R. Radcliffe -Brown and others, with an insistence on synchronic studies. A key element in the thread of hunter-gatherer studies lies in Radcliffe-Brown's studies of lineage, giving rise to ideas about group structure, including the concept of the horde. However, as with the reaction in North America, a need was increasingly seen for a diachronic perspective.

For hunter-gatherer studies a further breakthrough occurred in North America when Julian Steward, under the initial influence of Kroeber and Lowie, developed an evolutionary view of small-scale societies,

seen as stemming from the interaction between culture and environment. This led to the social typologies of Elman R. Service (1962) and Marshall Sahlins (1972) with their strongly developed definitions of the hunting and gathering band.

INTERACTIVE MODELS

As already alluded to above, ethnographic comparisons and interpretations of the Stone Age Hunter-Gatherers formed an integrated part of archaeological syntheses during the 19th century (Ravn 1993). The Swedish zoologist, Sven Nilsson (Stjernquist 1983) was the first to go beyond the use of the simple analogy. His initial work (Nilsson 1834) was translated the following year into Danish and Norwegian, while his major paper, appearing between 1838 and 1843 was revised and translated twenty-five years later into German by Johanne Mestorf (Nilsson 1868a), into English by John Lubbock (Nilsson 1868b), and into French by J.H. Kramer (Nilsson 1868c). Also, in 1843, Worsaae (English translation by W. J. Thoms in 1849) made use of analogies basing his description of Stone Age axe use, albeit polished ones, on a written report from the Danish natural scientist P.W. Lund at Lagoa Santa in Brazil (Klindt-Jensen 1976).

Lartet and Christy (1865-75) also relied heavily on ethnographical description when trying to explain the results of their cave excavations in southwestern France. Lubbock (Lord Avebury) is a further example (1865), while W. Sollas (1911) seems to be one of the last workers to pursue this line of reasoning in a positive way. German contributions in this area range from the literary study of "Rulaman", the "Schwäbian Bible" (Weinland 1875; 1986), to the attempts of the more northerly working researchers to confirm the presence of "Das nordisches Mensch" in the Mesolithic (Schwantes 1925) or Late Palaeolithic (Rust 1937).

Leaving these excesses aside, archaeology after Sollas tended to forget ethnographic models and went on to pursue problems of its own such as stratigraphy, chronology, typology, and ecology. This is epitomized by Graham Clark in his masterly work on the Mesolithic Settlement of Scandinavia (1936). It must not be forgotten that another line of argumentation, favoured by other traditions in France, Central and Eastern Europe, saw migrations across Europe, a tradition that even today is still viable in some areas. However, the use of direct analogy continued in such comparisons as those by Th. Mathiassen on the Eskimo blubber lamps and whaling harpoons in the Ertebølle Culture (1935) continuing a tradition going back to the early days of archaeology and even beyond. Finally, Clark, in a way, returned to the comparisons of Sollas in his work on Stone Age Hunters (1967). One brilliant exception to this general trend should be mentioned; D. F. Thompson's (1939) study of the Wik Monkan tribe of the Cape York Peninsula in Australia, though the actual application to archaeology still awaits a convincing demonstration.

As discussed above, early archaeology of the Late Palaeolithic and Mesolithic sporadically integrated ethnographic comparisons and interpretations of hunter-gatherers. A framework for a full understanding of both past and present hunting and gathering societies only developed in the 1960's following the work of J.H. Steward. Cultural constructs then included Service's evolutionary models, a framework that saw hunters and gatherers structured into small autonomous bands, kin-centred, and organized at the level of the family (1962). They were also seen to lack those political and economic structures of agriculturalists that Service referred to as tribes and chiefdoms.

However, though an anthropological understanding of hunters and gatherers was present by 1970, the evolutionary paradigm in archaeology, especially outside of Scandinavia, was creating roadblocks. Within the evolutionary paradigm sequential stages ought to involve progress. As a result, prehistoric hunting and gathering societies were expected to be less sophisticated and developed than the farming populations of the Neolithic that replaced them. The concept of a Mesolithic society that could compete with the Neolithic, rather than simply adopt the new economic pattern, was beyond the evolutionary paradigm (see Rowley-Conwy, 1986, and Zvelebil, 1986b). This is also one of the underlying problems that bedevil the "demic diffusion" model for agricultural origins in Europe (e.g. Ammermann & Cavalli-Sforza, 1984). How then can we understand hunting and gathering societies that are neither simple nor marginal, those that have come to be referred to as complex?

Some stereotypes had been broken by "Man the Hunter" (Lee & DeVore 1968), and by other synthetic works of the same period (e.g. Damas, 1969a, 1969b). In the late 1960's and the 1970's a number of workers, including one of us (Jochim, 1976; Meiklejohn, 1974, 1979; Price, 1973; Williams, 1968, 1974; Wobst, 1974, 1976), looked independently at the question of appropriate models for the social structure of the late Pleistocene and early Holocene. Though each had different cultural and biological questions in mind, all relied on a set of sources drawn primarily from small-scale hunter-gatherer populations. Societies with structures beyond Service's band level were viewed as inappropriate or historically aberrant. As a result, groups such as the ethnohistorically recorded chiefdoms of the Northwest Coast were ignored as potential models for Mesolithic society.

Though the need for change had been clearly articulated in the "Man the Hunter" volume, the primary paradigm still viewed hunters and gatherers as organized into small and mobile bands as envisaged by Service. The full recognition of the place of larger scale groups came later, in papers such as that of T.D. Price (1981). He noted that though Service's rigid framework of social structure had heuristic value, it marginalized the study of most non-agricultural groups, and confounded the categorization of societies such as those of the Northwest Coast.

Since 1980 there has been increasing recognition that larger scale societies are central rather than marginal to an understanding of the Mesolithic. They have also played an increasingly major role in studies of the transition to food production. Obvious examples in the North Temperate Zone include the later Scandinavian Mesolithic, the Japanese Jomon and the historic Northwest Coast (Aitkens et al., 1986; Hayden 1990; Koyama & Thomas, 1981; Price, 1981; Rowley-Conwy, 1986). Another, to the south, would be the Natufian of the southern Levant (Henry, 1985).

This new understanding of hunter-gatherer size and scale has created a minor revolution in American, and some European, thought. As alluded to, it has also dominated much recent discussion of the transition to agriculture. However, in Scandinavia the perception of the richness of later hunting and gathering societies had never been compromised. Understanding of the nature of these societies had changed, but in degree rather than kind.

IDENTIFICATION AND IMPLICATION OF COMPLEXITY

The issue of complexity focuses upon the definition and use of the term. Douglas T. Price and Brown (1985) describe complexity as a natural by-product of the "regular evolutionary process". What is being stated is that there is no inherent reason for hunting and gathering societies to remain simple. They are not inherently limited by their economic mode. Such a conclusion also follows from the understanding, developed in "Man the Hunter", but still unspoken, that these societies derived their specific properties from the dynamic relationship between their ecological and social environments. Though limitations might be present for specific cases they were not universal. Price and Brown extended the argument in a simple but profound way, shifting the focus from small-scale societies, believed to be central in the prehistoric record, to large-scale societies, previously viewed as aberrant. As already alluded to, we believe that this shift raises two questions that have become confused in recent discussions.

The first of these questions refers to the identification of characteristics that are complex. The key terms appear to be intensification, elaboration, sedentism and inegalitarianism. In most discussions these are inferred behaviours rather than material objects, thereby creating problems of definition (see Rowley-Conwy, 1986; Zvelebil 1986b). Within this frame of reference there is an ever-expanding group of identified societies. In a paradoxical way, it is small-scale hunters and gatherers that have become marginal and/or aberrant.

The second question concerns the evolutionary implications to be derived from large-scale or complex groups? It is here that we part company with much of the recent literature. In brief, we feel that the evolutionary paradigm has led to the conclusion that complex groups must be central to the appearance of food producing societies during the Holocene. We believe that this is a logical non sequitur, repeating many of the errors of 19th century unilinear evolution in archaeology and of orthogenetic models in biology

and anthropology. The problematic evolutionary assumption is that development of a new trait or level must be reflective of scale. The presence of parallelisms tends to be neglected or disregarded. Within this context, what evidence exists to place the origin of food producing within societies specifically identified as complex? Consider that only one study in "Prehistoric Hunter-Gatherers" (Price & Brown, 1985) is of a group and area that plays an undisputed precursor role to the primary origin of food producing. A number of these cases are of groups noted for their paradoxical late adoption of agriculture.

The study of complexity therefore raises a further issue. What is its role in the origin of food producing? Despite the discordance just noted, much of the interest in the Mesolithic and in complex societies stems from just such a question. The very title to Marek Zvelebil's volume twenty years ago, "Hunters in Transition" (1986a), makes the point, and as he states, "(t) he principal aim of this volume has been to examine the transition to farming from the hunter-gatherer perspective". However, Richard Gould (1985), in his retrospect on the "Prehistoric Hunter-Gatherers" volume, stresses the point that our conception of the transition is implicitly coloured by the fact that it, in fact, occurred and that we are its apparent beneficiaries. This leads to the suggestion that archaeologists have tended to fall into a trap that bedevils biological explanation, that of preadaptation. This idea sees structures appearing before they are really needed, failing to recognize that those structures must have had a primary purpose within the societies in which they appear.

Clive Gamble (1986) made just this point in the "Hunters in Transition" volume when discussing the use of daisy yams in Australian aboriginal subsistence, an exploited food source using food-gathering methods. Had colonization of Australia not occurred and had daisy yams become the basis for a later indigenous food production, what would be the interpretation of the beginning of such a gathering behaviour five thousand years ago? As Gamble points out using this base, the earliest use of a resource within one cultural mode tells us nothing about its use in an altered form in a different cultural mode.

So, what is it that makes complexity in hunters and gatherers so interesting? If it is primarily a new paradigm for the understanding of the transition to farming, we feel that more attention must be paid to the dynamics of the transition for any given region. In this we feel that more attention needs to be given to the status, relative to each other, of hunter-gatherers and food producers of the late Pleistocene and early Holocene. Zvelebil (1986b) made just this point in suggesting that the European Mesolithic and the Near Eastern Neolithic do not represent evolutionary stages, but were parallel developments, both concerned with increasing environmental productivity. The same point is made far more forcibly by Ian Davidson (1989) who asks two fundamental questions in his review of the Zvelebil volume, after raising the issue of developmental parallelism. Firstly, should we consider complexity or intensification to be a natural process in Holocene hunters and gatherers? Secondly, and repeating the point made above, is there any evidence that food production has derived from specifically complex groups? Finally, ideas viewing Mesolithic society as waiting for the arrival of the Neolithic have still not disappeared.

SUMMING UP

In this paper we have briefly examined some of the historical lines of thought that have underlain both the concept and understanding of the European Mesolithic, and the use of the term "complex" to describe some of the manifestations of the Mesolithic, especially with relationship to the origins of food production. The major problem seems to be how we, as prehistorians, see and measure the idea of "complexity" in the Mesolithic when we have to deal with concepts such as intensification, elaboration, sedentism and inegalitarianism; not to speak of the significance that can be attached to these values. Indeed, and ironically, most of these concepts could far better be argued for in the Upper Palaeolithic of south western France than in the final Mesolithic of southern Scandinavia, provided that such concepts can be measured at all in the archaeological record of hunter gatherers.

It is also interesting to note that, over the years, interpretations have shifted from diachronic to synchronic studies and back again. However, when seen from today's perspective it must be said that neither is useful without the other. Finally, if we can ask a

last question, do current anthropological models enlighten our understanding of the Mesolithic, or do we lack the necessary matching information from the archaeological record? Are we again too occupied with technical information, as was the case a hundred years ago? Questions that somehow mimic the ones posed by the anthropologist Carmel Schrire two decades ago about the same problem (1984).

POSTSCRIPT

The above was written some years ago. It is presented here with minor corrections, additions and amendments. For reasons beyond our control it was not published shortly after its initial formulation as a conference paper (Brinch Petersen & Meiklejohn 1995). At this point one may wonder if a paper, like good wine, can age gracefully? Perhaps not, but despite this objection we still feel that some relevant information was dealt with in the foregoing. It has also coloured a considerable amount off our further writing and thinking, as indicated by our references to it in more recent articles by ourselves (Brinch Petersen 2001; Meiklejohn et al 1998; 2000), and by others to whom we had provided copies. We therefore feel that its publication here is justified.

Today, many use complexity, especially framed within the term intensification, to characterize the later Mesolithic just before the appearance of the Neolithic. This is especially obvious in post-processual writing about Neolithic origins (see Rowley-Conwy 2004 for a review). It looks as if this expression instead of being an analytical term, a heuristic devise, has become the ultimate goal, with all Hunter Gatherers ending up with this designation. Whether one Mesolithic group was more complex, or showed greater intensification, than another has become dependent on the variables used to define the condition! Unfortunately, the tendency of today is quite clear, namely the later a Mesolithic group is to be dated, the more intensified tends to be its characterization. But, at the beginning of the 21st century, aspects of this discussion are finally receiving a more critical examination.

To fully précis the current situation is beyond the scope of this paper. However, we note that one line of critical thinking clearly implies the same set of positions that we put forward a decade ago. In an afterword to a recent volume of essays on "evolutionary change" in hunter-gatherers, Price (2002) goes over many of the areas we raised above. The gist of his comments on complexity, from one of the fathers of the model, can be seen in two critical quotes:

"... in spite of almost 20 years of discussion, the concept of complexity among foraging groups is not well defined. There is a general consensus that complexity means bigger groups, longer stays, more elaborate technology, intensified subsistence, broader residential utilization, and the like. But does complexity also mean status differentiation?" (p. 418) and "This evidence suggests that we must define the meaning of complexity more rigorously and be very cautious in attributing status differentiation to hunter-gatherers in the past". (pp. 418-419).

It was our point above that care should be taken in attributing features to the south Scandinavian Mesolithic that were not there. The early appearance of apparent status differentiation was one of the traits we queried, suggesting that issues within the evolutionary paradigm. The same issue is, interestingly, raised in the same volume in an examination of the Japanese Jomon, a culture often compared to the Mesolithic of South Scandinavia (Habu 2002). In this analysis the absence of status differentiation in the Jomon is almost treated as paradoxical. But is it within a model that does not assume the characteristics of evolutionary change referred to above?

From this perspective the new analysis of Peter Rowley-Conwy (2004) is on line with the position we took a decade ago. He now argues that there is little if any evidence for intensification in the Late Mesolithic. Arguments for intensification are seen as primarily tied to a priori suppositions of the post-processual paradigm. Critiques of the article by Rowly-Conwy are largely supportive of his position (see especially Gronenborn 2004; Louwe Kooijmans 2004; Straus 2004). Our own view from the specific perspective of the Middle and Late Mesolithic of Øresund indeed suggested that little was to be gained by adopting the paradigm of complexity when analysing the material (Brinch Petersen 2006a; Brinch Petersen 2000b).

So, what is the Mesolithic? For many, all too many, the Mesolithic is nothing, and cannot, apparently, be understood without its opponent, and successor, the Neolithic. This, of course, is a severe shortcoming to those of us who have been searching for a behavioural meaning of the concept. But perhaps, now is the time to give up that search, as there seems to be so many Mesolithic's, that a common characteristic becomes meaningless. However, the Mesolithic is a time unit in Europe, and an adaptation to the changes produced by postglacial climate. It was populated by different groups, inland, coastal and a combination of the two, showing different seasonal poses. For various reasons different groups in different regions had different responses to the process we refer to as Neolithisation.

Given that this paper is on the Mesolithic and not on the Neolithisation of Southern Scandinavia (Fischer & Kristiansen 2002; Jennbert 1984; Klassen 2004; Koch 1998; Price 2000; Rowley-Conwy 2004) and Northern Germany (Sönke & Lübke 2004) we shall here refrain ourselves for going deeper into that discussion. However, we would like to end up with some of today's code words on this particular process, as we can only regard them as preliminary and interesting postulations, situated far away from the archaeological record. These are: a population increase being threaten by an environmental crisis, or perhaps more specific, by an oyster depletion. Local groups are becoming more sedentary in bigger houses with adjacent cemeteries resulting in more intergroup violence when defending the external border of their reduced local area. This under the leadership of a big chief or entrepeneur, an organizer of feasts, as his kind for long has been receiving exotic gifts from the South, including the necessary cultigens for the brew to feast on.

Clearly, many of these code words are Neolithic traits that are being forced backwards into the Mesolithic, thus ignoring the former warning by Gamble (1986). Another interesting caveat here concerns the earliest Neolithic around the western part of the Baltic Sea? Why are most of the above listed critical values so conspicuously absent from the archaeological record of these areas? Or to put it more bluntly, when does this local TRB-Neolithic become sedentary, with longhouses, big chiefs and a redistribution of wealth?

REFERENCES

Aitkens, C., A. Melvin, M. Kenneth & D. Sanger. 1986. Affluent Collectors at the Edges of Eurasia and North America: Some Comparisons and Observations of the Evolution of Society among North-Temperate Coastal Hunter-Gatherers. In: Akazawa, T. & C. Melvin Aitkens (eds.): Prehistoric Hunter-Gatherers of Japan, 3-26. Tokyo: University of Tokyo Press.

Ames, K.M., 1994. The Northwest Coast: Complex Hunter-Gatherers, Ecology, and Social Evolution. Annual Review of Anthropology 23, 209-29.

Ammermann, Albert J. and Cavalli-Sforza, Luigi L. 1984. The Neolithic Transition and the Genetics of Populations in Europe. Princeton: Princeton University Press.

Boas, Franz, 1888. The Central Eskimo's. Annual Report of The Bureau of American Ethnology 6, 399-669.

Boas, F. & L. Farrand 1899. Physical characteristics of the tribes of British Columbia. Report of the British Association for the Advancement of Science 1898, 628-644.

Breuil, H. 1912. Les subdivisions du Paléolithique supérieur et leur signification. Congrès International d'Anthropologie et d'Archéologie Préhistorique. Comptes Rendus de la XIVième session, Genève, 165-238.

Brinch Petersen, E. 2001. Mesolitiske Grave og Skeletter. In: Lass Jensen, O., Søren A. Sørensen & K. Møller Hansen (eds.): Danmarks Jægerstenalder - Status og Perspektiver, 43-58. Hørsholm: Hørsholm Egns Museum.

Brinch Petersen, E. (2006a). Manipulation of the Mesolithic Body. In: Piek, J. & T. Terberger (eds.): Frühe Spuren der Gewalt – Schädelverletzungen und Wundversorgung an prähistorischen Menschenresten aus interdisziplinärer Sicht. Workshop Rostock-Warnemünde 2003. Beiträge zur Ur- und Frühgeschichte Mecklenburg-Vorpommerns 41:43-50.

Brinch Petersen, E. (2006b). Cultural and Social Landscapes of Mesolithic Vedbæk. In: Kind, C.-J. (ed.): After the Ice Age. Settlements, subsistence and social development in the Mesolithic of Central Europe. International Conference, Rottenburg 8-12 september 2003. Materialhefte zur Archäologie in Baden-Württemberg 78:15-31.

Brinch Petersen, E. & C. Meiklejohn 1995. Paradigm Lost: searching for "Complexity" in the Mesolithic. Unpublished paper presented to the conference "From Jomon to Star Carr: International Conference on Holocene Hunter-Gatherers in Temperate Eurasia", Cambridge/Durham, England, September 1995.

Childe, V. G. 1925. The Dawn of European Civilisation. New York: Knopf.

Childe, V. G. 1929. The Danube in Prehistory. Oxford: The Clarendon Press.

Childe, V. G. 1957. The Dawn of European Civilization (6th edition, revised). London: Routledge & Kegan Paul LTD.

Clark, J.G.D. 1936. The Mesolithic Settlement of Northern Europe. Cambridge: Cambridge University Press.

Clark, J.G.D. 1952. Prehistoric Europe: the Economic Basis. London: Methuen.

Clark, J.G.D. 1967. The Stone Age Hunters. London: Thames and Hudson.

Clark, J.G.D. 1975. The Earlier Stone Age Settlement of Scandinavia. Cambridge, Cambridge University Press.

Damas, D. (ed.) 1969a. Contributions to Anthropology: Band Societies. Ottawa. National Museums of Canada [= National Museums of Canada Bulletin 228].

Damas, D. (ed.) 1969b. Contributions to Anthropology: Ecological Essays. Ottawa, National Museums of Canada [= National Museums of Canada Bulletin 230].

Daniel, G. 1975. A Hundred and Fifty Years of Archaeology. London: Duckworth.

Davidson, I., 1989. Is intensification a condition of the fisher-hunter-gatherer way of life? Archaeology in Oceania 24, 75-78.

Faber, F., 1828. Kort Efterretning om en zoologisk Rejse til det nordligste Jylland i sommeren 1827. Tidsskrift for Naturvidenskaberne 5, 243-256.

Fischer, A. 2002. Food for Feasting. In: Fischer, A. & K. Kristiansen (eds): The Neolithisation of Denmark. 150 years of Debate, 341-393. Sheffield: J.R. Collis Publication.

Fischer, A. & K.Kristiansen (eds) 2002. The Neolithisation of Denmark. 150 years of Debate. Sheffield: J.R. Collis Publication.

Gamble, C. 1986. The Mesolithic Sandwich: ecological approaches and the archaeological record of the early postglacial. In: Zvelebil, M. (ed.): Hunters in Transition, 33-42. Cambridge: Cambridge University Press.

Gould, R. A. 1985. Now let's invent agriculture ...: a critical review of concepts of complexity among hunter-gatherers. In: Price, T. D. & J. A. Brown (eds.): Prehistoric Hunter-Gatherers: the Emergence of Cultural Complexity, 427-434. New York: Academic Press.

Gronenborn, D., 2004. CA Comment to Rowley-Conwy 2004. Current Anthropology 45, Supplement August-October, 101.

Hartz, S. & H. Lübke 2004. Zur chronostratigraphischen Gliederung der Ertebølle-Kultur und frühesten Trichterbecherkultur in der südlichen Mecklenburger Bucht. In: Lübke,H., F. Lüth & T. Terberger (eds.): Neue Forschungen zur Steinzeit im südlichen Ostseegebiet, 119-144. 46. Jahrestagung der Hugo Obermaier-Gesellschaft. Greifswald: Landesamt für Bodendenkmalpflege Mecklenburg-Vorpommern.

Habu, J. 2002. Jomon Collectors and Foragers: regional interactions and longterm changes in settlement systems among prehistoric hunter-gatherers in Japan. In: Fitzhugh, B. & J. Habu (eds): Beyond Foraging and Collecting, 53-72. New York: KluverAcademic/Plenum Publishers.

Hayden, B. 1990. Nimrods, Piscators, Pluckers, and Planters: The Emergence of Food Production. Journal of Anthropological Archaeology 9, 31-69.

Henry, D. O. 1989. From Foraging to Agriculture: the Levant at the End of the Ice Age. Philadelphia: University of Pennsylvania Press.

Jennbert, K. 1984. Den Produktiva Gåvan. Tradition och innovation I Sydskandinavien för omkring 5 300 år sedan. Acta Archaeologica Lundensia, Series in 40, N0 16.

Jensen, J. 1992. Thomsens Museum. Historien om Nationalmuseet. København: Gyldendal.

Jochim, M. 1976. Hunter-Gatherer Subsistence and Settlement Systems: A predictive Model. New York: Academic Press.

Klassen, L. 2004. Jade und Kupfer. Untersuchungen zum Neolithisierungsprozess im westlichen Ostseeraum unter besonderer Berüksichtigung der Kulturenentwicklung Europas 5500-3500 BC. Jutland Archaeological Society. Moesgaard Museum.

Klindt-Jensen, O. 1975. A History of Scandinavia Archaeology. London: Thames and Hudson.

Klindt-Jensen, O. 1976. The influence of ethnography on early

Scandinavian archaeology. In: Megaw, J.V.S. (ed.): To Illustrate the Monuments. London: Thames & Hudson.

Koch, E. 1998. Neolithic Bog Pots from Zealand, Møn, Lolland and Falster. København: Det Kongelige Nordiske Oldskriftselskab.

Koyama, S. & D. H. Thomas (eds.) 1981. Affluent Foragers. Osaka, National Museum of Ethnology [= Senri Ethnological Studies 9].

Lartet, E. & H. Christy 1865-1875. Reliquiae Aquitanicae, London.

Lee, R. B. & I. DeVore (eds.) 1968. Man the Hunter. Chicago: Aldine.

Louwe Kooijmans, L. P., 2004. CA Comment to Rowley Conwy 2004. Current Anthropology 45, Supplement August-October, 102-103.

Lubbock, J. [Lord Avebury] 1865. Prehistoric Times. London: Williams and Norgate.

Madsen, A.P., S. Müller, C. Neergaard, C. Petersen, E. Rostrup, K. Steenstrup, & H. Winge 1900. Affaldsdynger fra Stenalderen i Danmark Undersøgte for Nationalmuseet. København: C.A. Reitzel.

Mathiassen, Th. 1935. Blubber lamps in the Ertebølle Culture? Acta Archaeologica 6, 139-152.

Meiklejohn, C. 1974. Biological concomitants of a model of band society. In: Raymond, S. & P. Schledermann (eds.): International Conference on the Prehistory and Palaeoecology of the Western North American Arctic and Subarctic, 133-141. Calgary: University of Calgary Press.

Meiklejohn, C. 1979. Ecological aspects of population size and growth in late-glacial and early postglacial North-Western Europe. In: Mellars, P. A. (ed.): The Early Postglacial Settlement of Northern Europe: an Ecological Perspective, 65-79. London: Duckworth.

Meiklejohn, C., E. Brinch Petersen & V. Alexandersen 1998. The later Mesolithic Population of Sjælland, Denmark. In: Zvelebil, M., L. Domanska & R. Dennell (eds.): Harvesting the Sea, Farming the Forest. The Emergence of Neolithic Societies in the Baltic Region, 203- 212. Sheffield Archaeological Monographs, 10.

Meiklejohn, C., E. Brinch Petersen & V. Alexandersen 2000. The Anthropology and Archaeology of Mesolithic Gender in the Western Baltic. In: Donald,M. & L. Hurcombe (eds.): Gender and Material Culture in Archaeological Perspective, 222-237. Houndmills, Basingstoke, Hampshire & London.

Morgan, L. H. 1877. Ancient Society. New York: H. Holt.

Nilsson, S. 1834. Utkast till jagtens och fiskets historia på Skandinavien. Foglarna. Lund.

Nilsson, S. 1838-1843. Skandinaviska Nordens Ur-invånare. Ett fösök i den komparativa ethnografien och ett bidrag till menniskoslägtets utvecklingshistoria. Lund.

Nilsson, S. 1868a. Das Steinalter oder die Ureinwohner des Scandinavischen Nordens. Ein Versuch in der comparativen Ethnographie und ein Beitrag zur Entwicklungsgeschichte des Menschengeschlechtes. Hamburg.

Nilsson, S. 1868b. The Primitive Inhabitants of Scandinavia. London: G. Longmans.

Nilsson, S. 1868c. Les habitants primitives de la Scandinavie: Essai d'ethnographie comparee, Matériaux pour servir à l'histoire du développement de l'homme. Paris.

Price, T. D. 1973. A proposed model for procurement systems in the Mesolithic of northwestern Europe. In: Kozlowski, S. (ed.): The Mesolithic in Europe, 455-476. Warsaw: Warsaw University Press

Price, T. D. 1981. Complexity in "non-complex" societies'. In: Van der Leeuw, S. E. (ed.): Archaeological Approaches to the Study of Complexity, 53-97. Amsterdam, Instituut voor Prae-en Protohistorie.

Price, T.D. 2000. The introduction of farming in northern Europe. In: Price, T.D. (ed.): Europe's first farmers, 260-300. Cambridge: Cambridge University Press.

Price, T. D. 2002. Afterword. Beyond Foraging and Collecting: Retrospect and Prospect. In: Fitzhugh, B. & J. Habu (eds.): Beyond Foraging and Collecting, 413- 425. New York: Kluwer Academic/ Plenum Publishers.

Price, T. D. & J. A. Brown (eds.) 1985. Hunter Gatherers: the Emergence of Cultural Complexity. New York: Academic Press.

Price, T. D. & G. M. Feinman 1995. Foundations of Social Inequality. New York: Plenum.

Ravn, M. 1993. Analogy in Danish Prehistoric Studies. Norwegian Archaeological Review 26,2: 59-90.

Rowley-Conwy, P. 1983. Sedentary Hunters: the Ertebølle example. In: Bailey, G. (ed.): Hunter-Gatherer Economy in prehistory, 111-125. Cambridge: Cambridge University Press.

Rowley-Conwy, P. 1984. The Laziness of the Short-Distance Hunter: the origins of agriculture in western Denmark. Journal of Anthropological Archaeology 3, 300-324.

Rowley-Conwy, P. 1986. Between cave painters and crop planters: aspects of the temperate European Mesolithic. In: Zvelebil, M. (ed.): Hunters in Transition, 17-32. Cambridge: Cambridge University Press.

Rowley-Conwy, P. 2004. How the west was lost. A Reconsideration of Agricultural Origins in Britain, Ireland, and Southern Scandinavia. Current Anthropology 45, Supplement August-October, 83-107.

Rust, A. 1937. Das altsteinzeitliche Rentierjägerlager Meiendorf. Neumünster: Karl Wachholtz.

Sahlins, M. 1972. Stone Age Economics. Chicago: Aldine.

Sarauw, G.F.L. 1903. En stenalderboplads i Maglemose ved Mullerup sammenholdt med beslægtede fund. Aarbøger for Nordisk Oldkyndighed og Historie, 148-315.

Sarauw, G.F.L. 1906. Sur les trouvailles faites dans le nord de l'Europe datant de la période dite de l'hiatus. Prémier Congrès Préhistorique de France. Session de Périgueux 1905, 244-248. Le Mans: Imprimerie Mounoyer.

Sarauw, G.F.L. 1911-14. Maglemose. Ein steinzeitlicher Wohnplatz im Moor bei Mullerup auf Seeland, verglichen mit verwandten Funden. Beitrag zur Beleuchtung der frühneolithischen Steinzeit im Norden. Prähistorische Zeitschrift 3, 52-104 & 6, 1-28.

Schnirelman, V.A. 1992. Complex Hunter-Gatherers: Exception or Common Phenomeneon? Dialectic Anthropology 17, 183-196.

Schrire, C. 1984. Wild Surmises on Savage Thoughts. In: Schrire, C. (ed.): Past and Present in Hunter Gatherer Studies, 1-25. Orlando, San Diego, New York, London, Toronto, Montreal, Sydney, Tokyo.

Schwantes, G. 1925. Das Beil als Scheide zwischen Paläolithikum und Neolithikum. Archiv für Anthropologie 20,13-41.

Service, E. 1962. Primitive Social Organization: an Evolutionary Perspective. New York: Random House.

Sollas, W. 1911. Ancient Hunters. London: Macmillan.

Spencer, W. B. and F.J. Gillen 1899. The Native Tribes of Central Australia. London: Macmillan.

Steenstrup, J. 1851. Mødet den 10 de januar. Oversigt over Videnskabernes Selskab's Forhandlinger 1851, 1-31.

Steenstrup, J. 1861. Bemærkninger med hensyn til Professor Worsaaes Foredrag i Videnskabernes Selskab den 25de Januar 1861 over Stenalderens Tvedeling. Oversigt over det Kongelige Danske Videnskabernes Selskabs Forhandlinger 1861, 305-376.

Steenstrup, J. 1888-89. Ved fremlæggelsen af Skriftet: "Kjøkkenmøddinger, eine gedrängte Darstellung dieser Monumente sehr alter Kulturstadien". Oversigt over det Kongelige Danske

Videnskabernes Selskabs Forhandlinger 1888, 213-252.

Stjernquist, B. 1983. Sven Nilsson som banbrytare i svensk arkeologi. In: Sven Nilsson. En Lärd i 1800-Talets Lund, 157-212. Studier utgivna av Kungl. Fysiografiska Sällskapet I Lund. Lund.

Stephens, G. 1862. On an Earlier and Later Period in the Stone Age. Gentleman's Magazine. May, 1-3.

Straus, G. 2004. CA Comment to Rowley-Conwy 2004. Current Anthropology 45, Supplement August-October, 104-105.

Thompson, D. F. 1939. 'The seasonal factor in human culture, illustrated from the life of a contemporary nomadic group. Proceedings of the Prehistoric Society 5, 209-221.

Tylor, E. B. 1881. Anthropology: an introduction to the study of man and civilization. London. Macmillan.

Weinland, F. J. 1875 [1986]. Rulaman: naturgeschichtliche Erzählung aus der Zeit des Höhlenmenschen und des Höhlenbären. Stuttgart: Deutsche Verlagsanstalt [reprint].

Westerby, E. 1927. Stenalderbopladsen ved Klampenborg: Nogle Bidrag til Studiet af den Mesolitiske Periode. København, C.A. Reitzel.

Wheeler, M. 1954. Archaeology from the Earth. Baltimore: Penguin.

Williams, B.J. 1968. The Birhor of India and some comments on band organization. In: Lee, R. B. & I. DeVore (eds.): Man the Hunter, 126-131. Chicago: Aldine.

Williams, B.J. 1974. A Model of Band Society. Memoirs of the Society for American Archaeology 29.

Wobst, H. M. 1974. Boundary conditions for Paleolithic social systems: a simulation approach. American Antiquity 39, 147-178.

Wobst, H. M. 1976. Locational relationships in Paleolithic society. Journal of Human Evolution 5, 49-58.

Worsaae, J.J.A. 1843. Danmarks Oldtid oplyst ved Oldsager og Gravhøje. København: Selskabet for Trykkefrihedens rette Brug.

Worsaae, J.J.A. 1849. The Primeval Antiquities of Denmark. London: J.H. Parker.

Worsaae, J.J.A. 1861. Om Tvedelingen af Stenalderen. Oversigt over det Kongelige Danske Videnskabernes Selskabs Forhandlinger og dets medlemmers Arbeider i året 1861, 233-294. København.

Zvelebil, M. (ed.) 1986a. Hunters in Transition. Cambridge: Cambridge University Press.

Zvelebil, M. 1986b. Mesolithic societies and the transition to farming: problems of time, scale and organization. In: Zvelebil, M. (ed.): Hunters in Transition, 167-188. Cambridge: Cambridge University Press.

Ørsted, H.C. 1848. Mødet den 7de Januar. Oversigt over det Kongelige Danske Videnskabernes Selskabs Forhandlinger 1848, 14. København.

Authors

Erik Brinch Petersen, SAXO Institute, University of Copenhage, Njalsgade 80, DK-2300 Copenhagen, Denmark,
ebp@hum.ku.dk

Christopher Meiklejohn, Dept. of Anthropology, University of Winnipeg, 515 Portage Av., Winnipeg, Canada MB R3B 2E9,
c.meiklejohn@uwinnipeg.ca

Acta Archaeologica vol. 78:2, 2007, pp 193-219
All rights reserved

NEW INFORMATION ON THE STONE AGE GRAVES AT DRAGSHOLM, DENMARK

T. Douglas Price, Stanley H. Ambrose, Pia Bennike, Jan Heinemeier, Nanna Noe-Nygaard, Erik Brinch Petersen, Peter Vang Petersen, Michael P. Richards[1]

BACKGROUND

Two graves (Fig. 1) were excavated near the castle at Dragsholm in northwest Zealand, Denmark (Fig. 2), in the early 1970s by the National Museum of Denmark (Brinch Petersen 1973, 1974). Grave I contained the skeletons of two women who at that time were suggested to be 18 years old (Burial A) and 40-50 years old (Burial B), respectively. These women had been interred with 144 animal tooth pendants, a decorated bone dagger (or spatula) and a bone point, and were covered with red ochre. The published radiocarbon date of 5160±100 bp on a human bone from burial A confirmed the Mesolithic age of the two women; stable carbon isotope ratios from the bones indicated a diet dominated by marine foods, also a Late Mesolithic hallmark.

Because of the significance of these graves and recent questions about their age and contents, we have assembled new archaeological, biological, and isotopic information on the burials and some of the grave goods. Our report is organized as follows. A description of the discovery and recovery of the graves by the original excavator, Erik Brinch Petersen, provides the find context for the materials. A subsequent section by T. Douglas Price and Peter Vang Petersen concerns some issues and questions that have arisen regarding the graves; the next section deals with questions about radiocarbon calibration and the archaeological finds in the graves and their context.

Discussion of the new investigations begins with an anthropological examination of the skeletons by Pia Bennike. The specific samples of human and animal bone and enamel that were used in this study are described in the following section, along with some information on the preservation of this material and conservation measures that were used. Next, new radiocarbon determinations are described by Price and Jan Heinemeier, along with the calibration of these dates in light of reservoir effects. The following section by Michael Richards focuses on the stable isotopes of carbon and nitrogen from the burials. A subsequent section by Price and Stanley Ambrose presents the results of carbon isotopes measured in apatite and a comparison with the collagen results. In the next section, the use of strontium isotope ratios as an indicator of resi-

dence change is discussed by Price and the results of this analysis at Dragsholm are discussed. Price and Noe-Nygaard discuss the recent archaeological and geological investigations at the site relevant to understanding the situation and date of the graves. Our conclusions provide a summary of what these new radiocarbon dates and stable isotope measurements tell us about the Dragsholm graves, as well as what the Dragsholm graves tell us about radiocarbon dating, stable isotopes, and the transition to the Neolithic in prehistory.

DISCOVERY AND EXCAVATION OF THE GRAVES (EBP)

Dragsholm is the name of the castle, formerly known as "Adelersborg", located less than one km east of the coast of northwest Zealand, in the innermost part of the Bay of Sejrø at the base of the distinctive peninsula known as Ordrup Næs. Situated on a prominent rise in the landscape, the castle overlooks a reclaimed area to the east. In conjunction with the drainage of the adjacent Lammefjord in the 19th century, a primary canal was dug at Drags Mølle (2 m asl), linking the former Lammefjord with the Dragsholm inlet, draining the Lammefjord region into the bay of Sejrø.

A small island (4.65 m asl) was originally situated on the leeward side of the mouth of this fossil inlet just to the north of the canal. In fact, fill from the excavation of the canal had been piled up along parts of the island. It was precisely here in the early spring of 1973 that a double burial was first discovered by an observant plowman, Erling Pedersen, from the seat of his tractor. Mr. Pedersen was also an amateur archaeologist and photographer. The big field to the southwest of Dragsholm Slot had provided a large portion of Mr. Pedersen's collection, more than 750 objects. In the field in the spring of 1973 he noticed several bones and a distinctive red color exposed on the surface of the ground atop a small rise at the south end of the field near the Dragsholm Canal (Fig. 3). Recognizing these bones as human, he notified the National Museum.

The National Museum initiated an investigation during the early days of March headed by Per Poulsen. After recognizing the importance of the discovery - a burial of Mesolithic age containing the well- preserved skeletons of two richly adorned females covered with red ochre, it was decided to attempt to remove the double grave en bloc Unfortunately, the attempt failed partly due to the size of the burial and partly due to the sandy and stony sedi-

---

1 Editorial note: The present contribution has the format of a technical report, even with sketchy illustrations. Nevertheless, it has been published in Acta Archaeologica due to the importance of the finds and the novel analyses, in particular C-14 dates and isotope analyses.

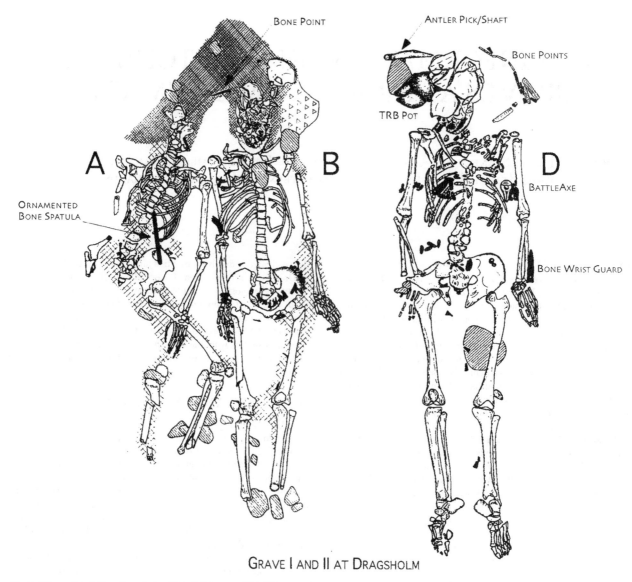

GRAVE I AND II AT DRAGSHOLM

Fig. 1. Graves I and II at Dragsholm (Brinch Petersen 1974). The second grave, less than 2 meters from the first, held the bones of a skeleton which was determined to be of a twenty-year-old male (Grave II, Burial D). This grave contained a number of artifacts including at least 60 amber beads, a stone battle axe, flint blades and projectile points, an antler pick or shaft, a bone spoon and a wrist guard, and a small ceramic beaker from the early Neolithic Funnel Beaker culture. The contents of the grave indicated a Neolithic age for this individual, confirmed by a radiocarbon date of 4840±100 bp (approximately 300 years younger than the females) and a stable carbon isotope ratio that indicated a largely terrestrial diet. The close proximity of these two burials and the very different grave goods and diets represented are remarkable. No other graves were found at this location.

ment. Poulsen was then joined by Erik Brinch Petersen and Steen W. Andersen both of the Institute of Archaeology at the University of Copenhagen, and the two interred individuals and the grave goods were recorded in situ and then removed, bone by bone and pendant by pendant.

After the harvest, a second investigation took place during August and September. Erik Brinch Petersen and Per Poulsen were now assisted by Tom Christensen, Lotte Hedeager, Leif Chr. Nielsen, and Peter Vang Petersen, students at the Institute. Some 274 m of 1 m trenches were excavated by hand across the top of the island, resulting in the discovery of the second grave situated

less than two meters from the first (Fig. 4). Again the burial was recorded in situ, followed by a lifting of the individual bones and the grave goods.

These two graves with the three buried individuals have haunted archaeologists ever since. Originally, there must have been both an Ertebølle, late Mesolithic, as well as an early Neolithic, TRB, occupation on the island, but changes in sea level and modern agriculture destroyed the cultural horizon on the top of the island. A few oyster shells were found in the fill of the second burial and a small shell midden must have been present, but whether it was of Mesolithic or Neolithic age has not been determined. The double

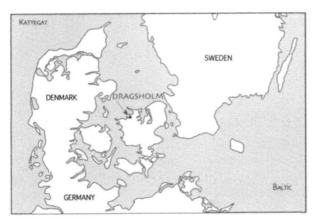

Fig. 2. The location of Dragsholm in southern Scandinavia.

burial was initially thought to be of Mesolithic age on the basis of the artifacts and the jewelry adorning the two individuals (Brinch Petersen 1973). The younger female (skeleton A) was buried with a bone dagger made from the metacarpus/metatarsus of a red deer. The dagger was ornamented on both sides with a drilled pattern in a geometrical design with a human person on one side. Behind her pelvis was a belt adorned with a string of tooth pendants, all of which, with one exception, had been made from the front teeth and the canines of red deer (Cervus elaphus), the exception being a single tooth from an Elk (Alces alces).

The older female (skeleton B) wore a similar pelvic girdle of red deer teeth. In this case, the individual teeth had been arranged in bundles, 22 in all (Brinch Petersen 1974; 1979). Placed among the red deer teeth was a single incisor from a bovid, considered to come from an auroch (Bos primigenius). Furthermore, three incisors of a wild boar (Sus scrofa ferus) were found on her right upper arm. On her chest was a pectoral consisting of seven front teeth of red deer, again all perforated. A bone pin was located next to the skull, presumably a hairpin, while a single transverse arrowhead was found above the skull. Both individuals were covered with red ochre, especially around the skulls, but also the extremities were discolored, while both torsos were largely unstained. The ornamented bone dagger and the presence of teeth from elk, aurochs, and red deer certainly suggested a Mesolithic date, although similar girdles of red deer teeth had been observed at the Neolithic cemetery of Ostorf in Mecklenburg (Bastian 1962, Schuldt 1961). Also the intensive use of red ochre pointed to a Mesolithic age for the burial.

While the first grave was oriented NW to SE with the heads towards the northwest, the second grave was laid out in a W to E direction, and with the head towards the west. Apparently, no red ochre was used, but an antler beam had been driven into the ground behind the head of the deceased. The buried individual was a male, originally identified as some twenty years of age. By the left side of his head was a ceramic pot of TRB A style (Brinch Petersen 1974, Koch 1998), while on his right side were three flint blades, four transverse arrowheads, a strike-a-light flint and a bone spatula (Fig. 1). Six additional transverse arrowheads were found between his legs. A wrist guard of bone was found along the lower part of the left arm, while a battleaxe of greenstone (Ebbesen 1998: type I) had been hammered into the ground between the upper left arm and the rib case. No less than sixty amber pendants, arranged

in six different sets, completed his adornment. One set of these pendants was found across the abdomen, one on the upper right of the stomach area, another one on the chest, one each on the upper arms, and one in the neck region.

The excavation of the two graves actually raised more questions than it resolved (Brinch Petersen 1974). On one hand the graves could be contemporaneous, making both of them Neolithic; the Neolithic designation of the second burial is obvious. Given the fact that the Dragsholm male is the oldest known Neolithic burial, the graves might provide an example of gender differences at the very beginning of the Early Neolithic period. In that case, the tooth pendant could have come from a domestic cow, and so it was unfortunately stated (Brinch Petersen 1974).

Meanwhile, the first 14C datings of the Dragsholm skeletons became available, uncalibrated, and a date around 3210±100 bc (K-2224) was accepted for the double burial; the Neolithic male was slightly younger, around 2890±100 bc (K2291). Despite the standard deviations of the two dates, H. Tauber from the Radiocarbon Lab in Copenhagen has maintained that the two burials could not be contemporaneous (Tauber 1981). However, with a calibrated date for the double burial around 4000 cal BC, it became even more difficult to favor either a Mesolithic or a Neolithic association.

Only a few years later came the discovery of the eighteen Mesolithic graves with 22 individuals from the site of Henriksholm-Bøgebakken at Vedbæk (Albrethsen & Brinch Petersen 1977). The costume of the young female in grave 8 at Bøgebakken was very similar to the two females from Dragsholm. She too was wearing a pelvic girdle, consisting of 60 red deer tooth pendants, including seven canine teeth ("Grandeln"), and a single tooth from a brown bear (Ursus arcticus). The girdle was also adorned with rows of snail shells. Exactly the same arrangement of pendants - teeth of red deer including canines, perforated shells of snails, and some teeth from wild boar and one from an elk (Alces alces) - was found in a bundle next to her head. Furthermore, an interesting pectoral was found with one of the females (individual 19C) in the triple burial at the same site, and among the elements here was an incisor from an aurochs (Bos primigenius) (Brinch Petersen 1979).

The burials at Bøgebakken were indeed Mesolithic, as shown by the 14C dates from the first three burials: Grave 3 (K-2781): 4100±75 bc; Grave 5 (K-2782): 4340±75 bc; Grave no 14 (K-2784): 3860±105 bc (all uncalibrated). It was also in this case that Tauber measured the δ13C values of the bone collagen in these individuals. Because of their high values, between -13.4‰ and -15.3‰, he suggested, that they had consumed a heavily marine diet. He then returned to the Dragsholm individuals and discovered that the two females also exhibited very marine δ13C values, -11.4‰ and -12.1‰, while the male exhibited a terrestrial value of -21.7‰. So at Dragsholm from the same locality, a dietary shift could be documented across the Mesolithic/Neolithic transition (Tauber 1981). With such high δ13C values for both the women in Grave I, they became the late Mesolithic stereotypes of coastal dwellers living from the sea, while the male epitomized an inland Neolithic life style.

The fact that not only the population from Bøgebakken, but also the two females from Dragsholm, were of Mesolithic age could now be further corroborated by the evidence that other females buried on Zealand were found with exotic tooth pendants among their sets of jewelry. Meanwhile K. Aaris-Sørensen had demonstrated (1980) that the faunal picture of Zealand during the Ertebølle period was one of depauperation with the disappearance of aurochs, elk and brown bear. We have always looked to Scania as the closest

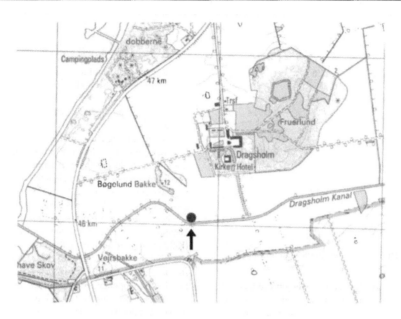

Fig. 3. The location of the Stone Age graves at Dragsholm.

place for origin for these pendants, but the same teeth could also have been procured from Jutland or even Northern Germany.

MISCELLANEOUS ISSUES (TDP AND PVP)

There are a number of minor issues relevant to the Dragsholm graves that can be addressed here in light of our study, including an unpublished radiocarbon date, a loose human bone, switched skulls, and the presence of exotic animal bones in the graves.

Two radiocarbon dates, listed above, were provided for the Dragsholm skeletons in the original publication (Brinch Petersen 1974). Tauber (1983) published these same two dates several years later with information on their calibration and carbon isotope values. This information is repeated here in Table 1. Tauber transformed the dates from radiocarbon years bp to radiocarbon years BC in the conventional way by subtracting 1,950 years. The calibration of the dates to calendar years BC was done using a table of values in Clark (1975), based on tree-ring corrections of radiocarbon dates at that time. Note also that a stable carbon isotope ratio on collagen in the bone of Burial B was measured, although a date was not reported.

There are, however, three original radiocarbon determinations listed in the records of the Radiocarbon Laboratory at the National Museum in Copenhagen and shown in Table 2. There are two important things to observe in this table. First, there is an unpublished radiocarbon date for Skeleton B of 5930±100 bp. This is 550 years older than the date for Skeleton A in the same grave and was apparently disregarded as anomalous because of the presence of conservation chemicals (Tauber 1981b: 123). Second, the date for Skeleton A of 5380±100 listed in the Museum document is 220 years older than the published date for this skeleton of 5160±100. This suggests that the original measurement was calibrated for marine reservoir effects by subtracting 220 years before the date was published. The date for the male Burial D remained unchanged. More on this later.

A Loose Human Bone. As noted above, the three burials at Dragsholm are designated as A (young female), B (older female), and D (male). Individual C is represented only by a single bone (a humerus) found on the surface near the graves at the time of the original discovery by Erling Pedersen. There was no grave associated with this find. No other parts of this skeleton were recovered and the prehistoric context of this bone is unknown.

Such loose human bones are not uncommon and are known from at least sixty different Mesolithic sites in Denmark. A number of different interpretations has been offered for this group of finds, ranging from cannibalism to burial ritual if not simply the result of disturbed or destroyed burials. Stable carbon isotopes and radiocarbon have now been measured on the humerus from Individual C. The determination (AAR-8724, 3097±44 BP, 1390-1050 B.C. at 95%) clearly indicates a Bronze Age date for this bone and means that it not relevant to the Mesolithic and Neolithic burials.

Switched Skulls. Some years ago, Christopher Meiklejohn noted that the skulls of the two Mesolithic females from Dragsholm were switched. Both skulls have the letters A and B on the inside of different segments of the cranium. Peter Vang Petersen recalls that part of one woman's skull was found after the graves had been uncovered, during the subsequent digging of exploratory trenches. Re-examination of tooth wear, bone thickness, and other characteristics of the skulls has provided a reliable assignation of skull to owner and this error has been corrected.

Exotic Animal Bones. A number of domestic animal bones were reported in the fill of the male's grave, including cow, dog, and sheep (Brinch Petersen 1974). Re-examination of the material has confirmed only the presence of domestic cow and dog. The bone pin (accession number DR 55), lying between the two women in the Mesolithic grave, has been examined by Kim Aaris-Sørensen and determined as roe deer, rather than sheep or goat.

A heavy bone chisel was found at the site during the excavation of the test pit in 1974. This bone was thought to be an elk, or perhaps aurochs, based on size and thickness. Both of these species

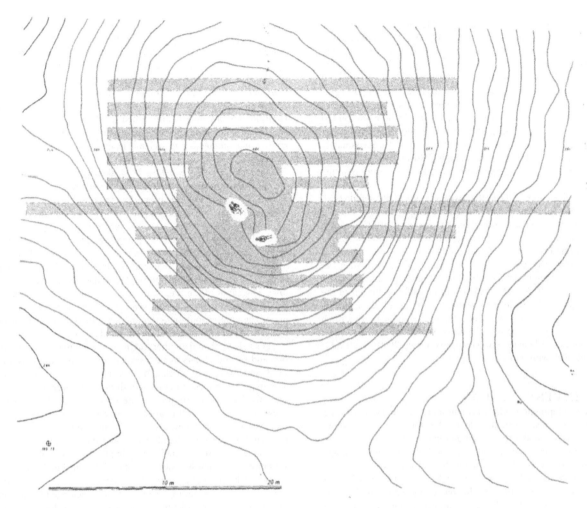

Fig. 4. The two graves and archaeological trenches at Dragsholm (Brinch Petersen 1974).

were absent from Zealand after about 6000 B.C. and their presence would be surprising. The bone is likely from a domestic cow. Stable carbon isotopes and radiocarbon have now been measured in this sample. The radiocarbon date of 4050-3770 B.C. cal (AAR-8774) confirms the Early Neolithic date for the cow and also helps to date Layer 6 at the site in which the bone artifact was found. The δ13C value for the cow is -21.5 ‰ in line with other early cows from Scandinavia (Noe-Nygaard et al. 2005).

There is an exotic species, an elk, among the animal tooth pendants in the females' grave. Another pendant was originally reported to be either a wild aurochs or domestic ox (Brinch Petersen 1973), while at the same time a third pendant, originally identified as red deer, is now classified as aurochs.

CALIBRATIONS AND QUESTIONS

Accurate dating of the Dragsholm graves is critical to resolution of a number of questions. To reiterate here, the first dates made on the Dragsholm burials were reported by Brinch Petersen in 1974 in radiocarbon years before present (bp). When initially described,

both graves were attributed to the Early Neolithic and the women's grave was called the oldest Neolithic grave in Scandinavia (Brinch Petersen 1974). Subsequent authors (e.g., Persson 1998, Larsson 1991) have emphasized the possible contemporaniety of the burials. For example, in a recent publication, Fischer (2002: 377-378) states, "the two graves at Dragsholm were constructed after the introduction of farming in the region ... The two graves may represent a man and his wives."

The original dates and calibrations are provided in Table 3, along with new calibrations. In our study, radiocarbon dates are given in calibrated years B.C. The new calibration of the original Dragsholm dates is based on recent revisions in the web-based calibration program (Calib 4.4 html version) of Stuiver et al. (1998), along with new information for marine corrections. Site-specific marine corrections are now recommended since marine waters vary substantially in the amount of incorporated old radiocarbon. The new calibrations for Dragsholm are based on recently measured marine corrections from the Kattegat just north of the site itself (Heier-Nielsen et al. 1998). The new calibration of the dates shifts the age of the female (Individual A) substantially, from ca.

4000 B.C. to ca. 3695 B.C., making the Mesolithic grave virtually identical in age to that of the male. Note that this calibration is made on the original published date. It is clear, however, from the three dates in the archives of the Radiocarbon Laboratory (Table 2) that the published date of 5380±100 had already been corrected for marine reservoir effect by approximately 220 years. How this value for the calibration was determined is unknown. This does mean, however, that any new calibration should be made on the original measurement rather than the corrected date. Calibration of the original date of 5380±100 gives a new date of approximately 4150 BC (mean of 4363 - 3980 at the highest probability of 0.991 for two sigma, Calib 4.4), approximately 500 years earlier than the male grave.

This calibration reaffirms the Mesolithic age of the female burials and casts substantial doubt on the contemporaniety of the two graves. Archaeological information also supports a different age for the graves. The original excavator, Brinch Petersen, noted that the graves had been covered by a cultural horizon, but that it had been plowed away. He also observed that the fill of the male grave contained settlement debris in the form of artifacts and oyster and blue mussel shell. No information was available on the fill of the females' grave. The male grave contained a Funnel Beaker pot, recently classified according to a new typology devised by Eva Koch (1998) as Type 1, belonging to the Early Neolithic. This type occurs in southern Scandinavia between approximately 3800 - 3500 B.C., which fits well with date for the grave.

NEW INVESTIGATIONS

Recent developments in physical anthropology, radiocarbon dating, and bone chemistry can help to resolve some of the questions that have arisen about the Dragsholm graves and to provide new information. The remainder of this report is divided into two major sections. First, a detailed re-examination of the skeletal material from Dragsholm by Pia Bennike provides new information on the characteristics, similarities and differences among the individuals. Second, isotopic studies of new samples from the graves provide a resolution of issues regarding the dating of the burials, new information on diet from carbon and nitrogen isotopes in collagen and carbon in apatite, and information on place of origin from strontium isotopes in tooth enamel. The results of our study are summarized in the conclusion.

BIOLOGICAL ANTHROPOLOGY (PB)

Renewed interest in the Dragsholm graves has given rise to several interesting anthropological questions: Is there any evidence of a familial relationship between the two Mesolithic women (A and B) in the double grave, and do they reflect a different lifestyle, including a different type of subsistence, from that of a Neolithic male skeleton (D) found in a single grave located only a few meters away? In the report below, discussion of these and other questions is organized by the topics of preservation and material, sex and age, dentition, bone mineral content, stature, asymmetry, and genetic relationships.

Preservation and Condition of Material. Although all three skeletons are incomplete, they seem to share the same degree of preservation. Several bones are more or less fragmented, while others are extremely well preserved including the jaws and most of the teeth (Fig. 5). The rather good preservation of the skeletons is reflected in the organic content of the bones which was 33 %, 28% and 34% in A, B and D respectively. It is generally known that post-mortem destruction of bone tissue mainly depends on the type of soil, its pH and humidity, and less on how long the bones have been lying in the soil. Our experience from routine measurements of organic/inorganic content in prehistoric bones (Bennike et al. 1993) shows that when the organic content is over 25%, which is the case for the Dragsholm bones, microscopic structures often remain undamaged and intact. Therefore, the bone tissue may be suitable for future microscopic studies on age-related changes or possible evidence of diseases.

In contrast to the two Mesolithic skeletons, the bones of the Neolithic male have a rather irregular surface due to taphonomic factors. This information is useful for distinguishing the stray find of the upper part of a humerus that did not belong to any of the three skeletons and must therefore belong to a fourth, designated as (C). This bone fragment has a smooth surface and its robusticity is more pronounced than that of the humeri of the two Mesolithic females, but less marked than the Neolithic male humerus. This bone has now been radiocarbon dated to the Bronze Age (see below). The caput of the fragment is fused to the shaft of the bone, which indicates that the person was more than 16-18 years old. An upper age limit cannot be determined, but there is no evidence of osteoarthritis that is sometimes seen in older people.

A single tooth and another fragment of a left mandible with the first and second molars in situ and half of an open alveolus for a third molar were found during the most recent excavations in 2003. The single tooth turned out to be a third right lower molar which may just have been erupting, as the occlusal area of the enamel shows no sign of wear, the apex of the root is not yet closed and there is no facet on the mesial area. The first and second molars in the mandible are only slightly worn, and there is no facet on the distal area of the second molar, proving that a third molar had not yet erupted. The partly visible alveolus of the third molar seems to fit well with an erupting tooth. It is therefore most probable that the separate find of a third, lower right molar belonged to the same mandible or to another young person with a similar dentition, stage of eruption and wear pattern.

The color difference between the Mesolithic and the Neolithic skeletons is striking. Following the usual pattern, the two Mesolithic skeletons (A and B) are clearly stained with red ochre, while the Neolithic skeleton (D) is not. Skeleton D is light grey in color that may partly be attributed to the remains of shells found in the grave soil. Neither of the two stray finds, the upper arm and the mandible fragment respectively, are stained with ochre. On the contrary, both appear rather gray. An attempt to find patterning in the distribution of the ochre staining on the Mesolithic bones almost failed. It seemed to be very diffuse, and both the ventral and dorsal parts of the bones of both skeletons were stained. However, the highest concentrations of ochre were found in the bones of the pelvic area and the craniums of the female skeletons. Skeleton (A) exhibits more heavily ochre-stained upper and lower vertebrae on the almost intact spine compared to those from the middle section.

The upper part of each of the three skeletons was placed in a supine position with the arms parallel to the body. One Mesolithic skeleton (B) and the Neolithic skeleton (D) lay with their legs stretched, while Mesolithic skeleton (A) lay with its legs bent at the hip with the knee joints pointing towards skeleton (B) to the left. The right side of the skeleton (A) was probably disturbed by plow-

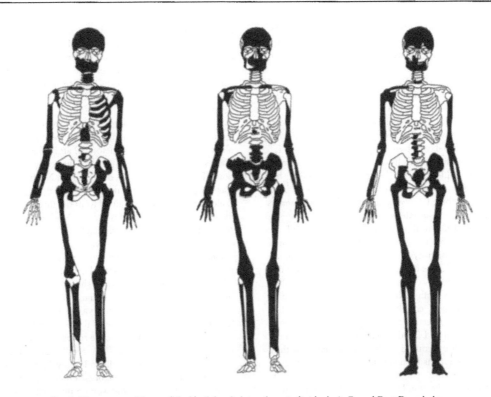

Fig. 5. The preserved bones (black) of the skeleton from individuals A, B, and D at Dragsholm.

ing, but judging from the position of the left femur, the right leg must have been lying parallel to the left.

Sex Determination. The shape and size of the bones was used for the sex determination of the skeletons, which was rather certain and concurs with the gender-related equipment found in the individual graves. The skeletons' sex was clearly reflected in the skulls and the pelvic bones as well as in several bone measurements; the femoral head measured 4.1 cm in both Mesolithic females and 4.8 cm in the Neolithic man. While we have no average values for male and female Mesolithic skeletons, the average values for Neolithic skeletons are 4.2 cm for women and 4.8 cm for men. With regard to this single measurement, the diameters of the femoral head of the two Mesolithic women were almost similar to Neolithic women. A similar pattern of sexual dimorphism as illustrated by the size of the individual femoral heads was seen in the measurements of Bone Mineral Content (BMC) (see below). Most of the variation in the size of the postcranial bones was related to such female/male differences. Unfortunately, the skulls, particularly of skeleton D, were too fragmentary for the comparison of measurements.

Age Determination. Age estimates were based on a combination of methods (excluding dental attrition) used to establish skeletal maturation (fusion of the epiphyses and dental development), structures of facies auricularis, symphysis pubica, the sternal rib-ends and the appearance of the joints with regard to any possible osteoarthritis. The study showed that individual A in the Mesolithic grave was approximately 18-20 years old when she died, while female B was over 40 years old. The considerable age difference was confirmed by almost all employed methods. The skeleton in the Neolithic grave (D) died at the age of about 30.

It is worth noting that, although dental attrition was not included in the age determination methods, the young Mesolithic woman (A) and the Neolithic man (D) exhibited very similar patterns of dental wear. However, while some of the epiphyses of the Mesolithic woman (A) had not yet fused and the third molars still had open roots, all bones of the Neolithic male skeleton had fused. In addition, some of the male's joints showed slight traces of osteoarthritis, which indicates that he must have been older than 18-20 years. This evidence was also corroborated by the results of methods based on the structures of the pelvic bones and the rib-ends. Despite the similar dental wear, it was concluded that the Neolithic man (D) was at least 10 years older than the young Mesolithic woman (A) in the double grave.

Dentition. Judging from the dental wear of skeleton A, the time of function of the third molars seems to have been 1-2 years, and their roots were not yet fully developed. These facts are in accordance with the transparency of the root (V. Alexandersen, n.d.) and the non-fusion of several epiphyses in a ca. 18-20-year-old individual.

The facial and lingual regions of the upper teeth of skeleton A exhibit polished areas. The lower frontal teeth only have polished areas on the facial sides, while calculus is seen on the lingual sides. The lower premolars and molars also have polished areas lingually. The presence of small fractures of the enamel on two teeth, frontal tooth resorption and hypercementosis in several teeth seem to confirm a pattern of severe attrition. Such severe attrition and heavy load on the teeth will also result in a reduction of the length of the roots. In such cases the apex of the root will appear rounded due to a thickening of the cement layer. This is mainly seen on the upper- and lower frontal teeth. A similar pattern has previously been noted in Eskimo dentition (Pedersen 1949). However, it cannot be determined to what degree the dentition was used as a tool, for example the chewing of hide, and whether this may have caused the polishing.

The dentition of skeleton B has some calculus and marked wear of the teeth - a flat horizontal wear of the front teeth and a helicoid wear of the molars. Together with the transparency of the roots, the age of this individual was evaluated to be ca. 40-44 years (V. Alexandersen, n.d.). Several teeth are marked with repeated linear hypoplasia of the enamel, which developed at the ages of 3, 4, 5 and 6 years. In modern children such hypoplasias usually develop during the first years of life and may be related to weaning, but prehistoric children often developed hypoplasia several years later. The causes could be attributed to seasonal crises of diet or diseases with high fevers and diarrhea or late weaning.

The dentition of skeleton B is marked by fractures of the enamel and by considerable marginal alveolar loss at the upper and lower molars. In addition hypercementoses is seen in the upper premolars, and the height of the roots is lower than average due to severe attrition. A reduced form of several teeth is related to the reduced length of the roots. Both skeleton A and B have (according to Verner Alexandersen, pers. comm.) teeth that are smaller than the average size of medieval teeth (Lunt 1969). In addition, several teeth have a reduced form and fused molar roots, but they do not have caries. The pattern of reduced roots of all second and third molars from the two dentitions is so similar that it may indicate a close genetic relationship.

The dental attrition of skeleton D is similar to the wear seen on skeleton A, which would normally suggest that the individual was about 20 years old. However, contrary to skeleton A, all skeletal epiphyses are fused, slight osteoarthritis is seen in a few joints and the auricular surfaces indicating that skeleton D was about 30 years of age. If skeleton D is about 10 years older than skeleton A, the similar dental wear may then indicate different diets. Skeleton D also has rather short frontal roots, however not to the same degree as seen in skeleton A and B, and the dentition shows no reduction in the number of roots.

Overall, the dentition of skeleton D is very different from that of both A and B. This includes both the form and size of the teeth. While the differences in size could be explained by sexual dimorphism or different environmental factors during the two periods, the various morphological differences, including the form of the crown and the fusion of the roots, may stem from a certain genetic distance between the Neolithic man on the one hand and the two Mesolithic women on the other. The two women's rather similar pattern of dentition may, as already mentioned, alternatively indicate some degree of close genetic relationship. Although Neolithic teeth often present less attrition than Mesolithic ones, the incidence of dental decay, periodontal diseases and tooth loss was higher in the former which may well be due to a new terrestrial diet (Alexandersen 1989). No caries were, however, found in the three dentitions. While one would not expect to find caries in the Mesolithic skeletons, caries has been reported in 15% of Neolithic skeletons (Bennike 1985)

Bone Mineral Content. Both the organic and the mineral content of the bones were measured with a dual photon-absorptiometry scanner. The organic bone content has already been mentioned in relation to the preservation of bone tissue. The mineral content (BMC/BMD) of the bones indicates the so-called bone mass of the two women and the man. Previous tests on archaeological bones

from various periods have shown that the measured amount of mineral in a bone (mid-diaphysis of femur) is well correlated to the area of a tranversal section of the same part of bone, with the exception of the endosteal area. This means that only few changes occur during burial when the surface of the bone is intact, even over long periods of time, in this case a period of almost 7,000 years (Bennike and Bohr 1990).

The bone mineral content (BMC) values were 4.7 g/cm for the femur of the young Mesolithic female skeleton (A), 4.3 g/cm for the older Mesolithic female skeleton (B) and 5.5 g/cm for the Neolithic male skeleton (D). In comparison, the average BMC in the same bone (femur) and site (mid-diaphysis) in Neolithic female skeletons was 4.4 g/cm (s.d. 0.55) and 5.7 g/cm (s.d. 0.49) in Neolithic male skeletons. The values obtained from the three Dragsholm skeletons fit neatly with the averages for the Neolithic, also with regard to sexual dimorphism. Unfortunately similar values for Mesolithic skeletal material are not yet available. The lower mineral content values for the two Mesolithic women as compared to the Neolithic man are probably due to sexual dimorphism. The question arises whether the Mesolithic women should not be expected to have a higher bone mineral content than the Neolithic females because of generally higher robusticity values during the Mesolithic. The femur circumferences of A and B are 79 and 84 respectively, and 88 mm in the Neolithic male; the robusticity indices (circumference middle (M8) x 100/length (M2) are 20, 21 and 21.5 respectively. However, our findings are difficult to evaluate as we have only the two Mesolithic cases. The slight difference in bone mineral content between the two Mesolithic women may also be random.

The two skeletons are those of a young woman in her late teens, and a rather older woman over the age of 40. Even though the young woman may not have reached her so-called bone peak mass, which occurs around the age of 30 in the contemporary population, her BMC is higher (4.7 g/cm) than the elder woman's BMC. The elder woman may have reached menopause, which usually occurs today in almost all populations around the age of 50-51 and initiates an age-related bone-loss (Pavelka and Fedigan 1991). However, as we have no knowledge of when menarche (onset of menses) occurred (in the modern Danish population it occurs around 12 years; during the 19th century it occurred around 16 years), nor is it known when bone peak mass was reached or the age at which menopause began during the Mesolithic, we cannot completely exclude the fact that the differences in BMC are normal variation. In our modern society we observe a decrease in bone mass from the onset of menopause, but we do not known whether this also was the case during the Mesolithic when the level of physical activity was much higher.

Stature. The stature of the skeletons was calculated from the femoral bones (Trotter and Gleser 1958). However, the method used often results in a stature estimate somewhat higher than the measured length of the skeleton in situ prior to excavation. A study of anatomical measurements of all the bones involved in the height correlated well with the length measured in situ, indicating that the calculated stature may not be reliable (Bennike, n.d.). Skeleton A in the Mesolithic grave is 153.0 cm (femur 400 mm) and skeleton B is 154.2 cm (femur 405 mm). This corresponds to the average stature of female skeletons in the Mesolithic, which is 154.0 cm. The average stature during the early Neolithic period seems to be rather similar to the Mesolithic period: 153 cm for females and 165 for males. The male skeleton (D) in the Neolithic grave was calculated to 160 cm. This is 5 cm less than the average for that period. During

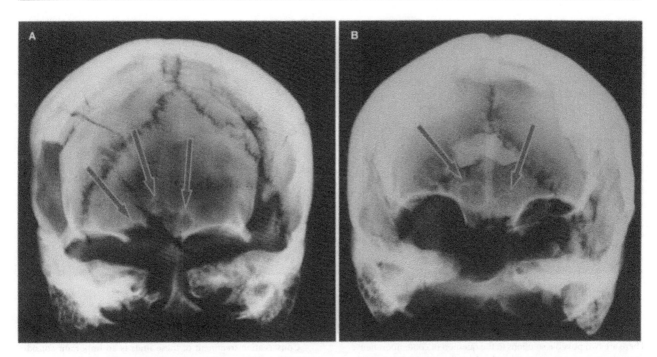

Fig. 6. X-rays of the crania of individuals A and B at Dragsholm. Arrows indicate frontal sinuses of the frontal bone.

the Neolithic the average stature increased considerably and in the late Neolithic period it had on average increased to 171 cm for men (Bennike and Alexandersen 2002).

Asymmetry. All three skeletons exhibit significant differences between the left and right humerus with regard to robusticity as seen on the traces of muscular modelling and size. The length of the preserved arm bones of the two women differed by 4-5 cm while neither the right and left arm bones were not intact on skeleton D for comparison. The difference in size between right and left side of the two Mesolithic women resemble the left/right side differences observed during the Iron Age, but the differences in the bone circumferences are larger.

Genetic Relationships. While some characteristics seem to indicate a degree of familial relationship between the two Mesolithic skeletons in the double grave, others do not. Only a DNA analysis will be able to establish whether the two women were closely related genetically. Given the quality of the skeletal material, such an analysis is unlikely to be successful.

The two female skeletons share similar form of skull and mandible, short dental roots, and characteristics of the spinal area around the sacrum, all of which seem to indicate some relationship. Skeleton A has, however, a somewhat larger skull as the circumference is c. 5% greater. In some studies the size and form of the frontal sinuses have indicated genetic relationship (Szilvássy 1986), but rather disappointingly no clear and convincing similarities were found in the pattern of the two Dragsholm skeletons, even though they were not that different. Some damage of the frontal bone of skeleton B may influence the dissimilarity (Fig. 6). However, such a difference does not mean that a genetic relationship can be excluded. This is the same situation with the presence or absence of a cranial suture of the frontal bone. Skeleton A has a frontal suture, but skeleton B does not. However, this dis-similarity in a single trait can neither exclude nor confirm genetic relationship.

Both women have an incomplete closure of the sacral spine, the so-called spina bifida occulta (Fig. 7). At least three of the lower segments were open, while the rest of the bones were too damaged to study. A survey of the pattern of sacral closure in Danish prehistoric skeletons from various periods has not yet been carried out. One is planned, so that we will have comparative parameters. It is interesting to note, however, that Ferembach (1963) found a high variation in sacral segment closure in Mesolithic skeletons from Taforalt, Marocco. She concluded that the pattern might reflect a high degree of endogamy in the population. Similarly, due to the frequent occurrence of supraacetabular grooves on the pelvic bones in the Mesolithic skeletons from Bøgebakken and Skateholm, some degree of genetic relationship between the populations has been suggested (Frayer 1988). Even though we have no material for comparison as yet, it is no less interesting that the skeleton of the Neolithic man (D) also exhibits a lack of closure in at least 2 lower sacral segments (Fig. 7). If the two women were truly genetically related, it is hard to believe that they could have been sisters because of the ca. 20-year age difference. They would more likely have been mother and daughter or mother-in-law/daughter-in-law. Only a mother/daughter relationship, however, would produce in a positive DNA analysis.

ISOTOPIC ANALYSES (TDP)

New isotopic analyses involving carbon, nitrogen, and strontium were undertaken with the materials from Dragsholm. New radiocarbon dates may either demonstrate a similar age for the burials, documenting conventionally Mesolithic and Neolithic individuals as contemporaries, or document a difference in the dates of the graves.

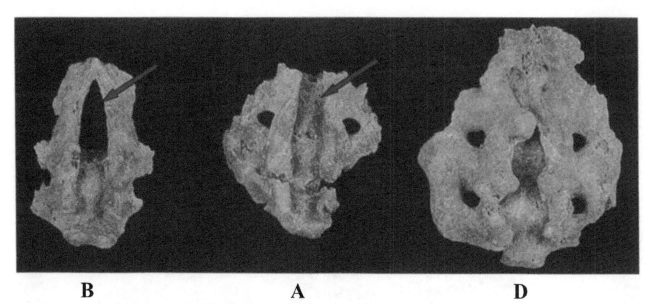

B   A   D

Fig. 7. Sacral spine of individuals A, B, and D, showing lack of closure.

There are two possible solutions to the question of contemporaneity; either the two graves were used for burial at the same time by people with very different cultural and economic backgrounds, or the two graves are of the same date, but this place continued in use as a burial ground after the beginning of the Neolithic.

Stable carbon and nitrogen isotope analysis of bone collagen and apatite can provide additional information on the diet of these individuals and help to provide a better calibration for radiocarbon dating. Dietary differences between either contemporary individuals or between the foragers of the Mesolithic and the farmers of the Neolithic will be of substantial interest. Strontium isotope analysis of tooth enamel may reveal the place of origin, indicating if any of the individuals came from another region. These analyses can provide new information on the relationship between foragers and farmers and on the nature of culture change during the transition to agriculture, one of the most momentous events in the history of our species.

This section of our study begins with a discussion of the use of preservatives in the conservation of the materials and the sampling procedures used for our analyses. Description of the collagen and apatite preparation and analysis includes the results of replicative studies in several laboratories and discussion of the differences in collagen and apatite carbon isotopes. Next, the radiocarbon dating of these samples also involved multiple analyses in two different laboratories and these results and their calibration are presented and discussed. Stable isotopes of carbon and nitrogen are considered next along with comparison of the results of carbon isotopes from both collagen and apatite.

Specimen Conservation and Sampling Protocols. Samples for the new analyses are described below. The bone and teeth were sampled largely by drilling after abrading the outer surface to remove contaminants. Specific procedures are described for the individual samples below. Human bone was sampled at the Anthropological Laboratory; human teeth were sampled at the National Museum and the Laboratory for Archaeological Chemistry; artifacts from the graves were sampled at the National Museum.

Conservation treatment of these finds is an important consideration for isotopic analyses. The finds from Dragsholm were prepared at the National Museum in the early 1970s, a period when a number of new treatments were being employed rather liberally. Primary preservatives in use included Bedacryl and Diacon. Many of the objects were treated with bedacryl during the excavation in the field. In addition some of the artifacts were dried with tertiary butyl alcohol and dipped in beeswax at 40° C (8 tooth pendants) or boiled in carnuba wax at 120° C (bone point and remaining tooth pendants). The ornamented spatula from the females' grave was repaired with Lyma-C (a nitrocellulose glue); in some of the bone artifacts from the male grave were boiled in carnuba wax and were fractures glued with Lyma-C. Specific treatments are described below along with the individual samples that were taken.

Human Femur and First Molar (DR Skeleton A NM 529/73). Grave I, younger female burial. Only known treatment was bedacryl in the field plus some glue used on cracks. Femur surface mechanically cleaned and bone powder drilled out of a series of small borings. The first molar was mechanically cleaned at the surface and powdered enamel removed by burring. Bone sample for 14C dating and light isotopes (C, N) on collagen and apatite. Enamel sample for strontium isotopes.

Human Femur (Skeleton B NM 529/73). Grave I, older female burial. Only known treatment was bedacryl in the field plus some glue used on cracks. Femur surface mechanically cleaned and bone powder drilled out. This sample released a distinct odor during drilling and the resulting powder was much finer than burials A and D. This skeleton may have been treated with an unknown substance. Bone sample for 14C dating and light isotopes (C, N) on collagen and apatite.

Human Humerus (Skeleton C NM 529/73). Isolated bone found on the surface at the time of the original discovery of the females' grave. Surface mechanically cleaned and bone powder drilled out. Bone sample for 14C dating and light isotopes (C, N) on collagen and apatite.

Human Femur and First Molar (Skeleton D NM 529/73). Grave II, male burial. Only known treatment was bedacryl in the field plus some glue used on cracks. Femur surface mechanically cleaned and bone powder drilled out. First molar was mechanically cleaned at the surface and powdered enamel removed by burring. Bone sample for 14C dating and light isotopes (C, N) on collagen and apatite. Enamel sample for strontium isotopes.

Tooth Pendant (DR 256). Animal tooth pendant mechanically abraded to remove outer surface of enamel and then enamel burred to obtain powder. Bone powder drilled from interior of root dentin. Tooth boiled in carnuba wax at 120 °C. Bone powder used for 14C dating and light isotopes (C, N) on collagen and apatite.

Ornamented Spatula (DR 147). Bone powder drilled from old crack. Spatula had been glued with Lyma C but other wise not treated. Glue was dissolved with acetone prior to drilling. Bone powder used for 14C dating and light isotopes (C, N) on collagen and apatite.

Antler Pick (DR 323). Bone powder drilled from interior of artifact. Artifact was boiled in carnuba wax at 120° C. Treated with Bedacryl in the field. Bone powder used for light isotopes (C, N) on collagen and apatite. Original sample vial exploded during transport; a second sample with more aggressive decontamination procedures was taken.

Heavy Bone Chisel (Test ditch 2, Layer 6). No known preservative. Bone powder drilled from interior of artifact. Bone powder used for 14C dating. Results from AMS determination yielded 5150 ± 65 b.p. (AAR-8774) or a range between 4050 BC – 3770 BC with a probability of 90.5%. The stable carbon isotope ratio of the sample was -21.5‰, clearly terrestrial.

Collagen and Apatite Purification and Isotopic Analysis (SHA, TDP). Several bones, teeth, and artifacts from the Dragsholm graves were selected and sampled for this project. These objects were generally well preserved, an important consideration for isotopic analysis. Table 4 shows the elemental and isotopic composition of collagen and apatite of the bones of Burials A, B and D, as determined in the Environmental Isotope Paleobiogeochemistry Laboratory at the University of Illinois. Preservation of the human bone is extremely good. Several characteristics that reflect their good condition will be discussed, after a description of the analytical methods.

Collagen purification methods are described in detail elsewhere (Ambrose 1990, 1993). Bone powder was demineralized with 0.2 M HCl (2 days), treated with 0.125 M NaOH (20 hours) to remove humic acids, solubilized at 95°C in acidified distilled water (pH3, 10 hours), filtered to remove particulate contaminants, and freeze-dried. Apatite was purified by treatment with 2% sodium hypochlorite (50% Clorox, 2 days) to remove organic matter, and 0.1 M acetic acid (0.1 ml/mg, 4 hours) to remove adsorbed carbonates (Balasse et al. 2002). Isotopic analysis of collagen (sample weight: ~400 µg) was performed by combustion and purification of CO_2 and N_2 in a Carlo-Erba elemental analyzer coupled to a Finnegan MAT 252 isotope ratio mass spectrometer. Replicate analyses of carbon and nitrogen isotopes of collagen of burials B and D are within analytical error (±0.1‰ for δ13C, and 0.2‰ for δ15N). Apatite carbonate isotopic analysis (sample weight ~700 µg) was performed by reaction with 100% phosphoric acid at 70°C in a Kiel III automated carbonate reaction device coupled to the MAT 252. Carbon and oxygen isotope ratios are simultaneously determined on the CO_2 generated by this reaction. Replicate analyses of apatite were not performed. Analytical error on this instrument is ±0.05‰ for δ13C and ±1.0‰ for δ18O (Balasse et al. 2002).

Criteria for good bone collagen preservation (Ambrose 1990,

1993; DeNiro 1985) include a yield of collagen greater than 1.8% by weight. Modern bone has ~19% to 21% collagen. Collagen was well preserved in all samples. Another criterion is the percent-by-weight of carbon and nitrogen in the extracted collagen. Modern bone collagen averages 42.7% carbon and 15.5% nitrogen. The percent of carbon in the Dragsholm bones ranges from 34.0% to 40.4%. The percent of nitrogen in the Dragsholm bones is also close to the modern average. Individual D had the lowest collagen yield, but the organic component is still relatively pure protein, as measured by its high carbon and nitrogen concentrations. An atomic carbon:nitrogen ratio (C:N) between 2.9 and 3.6 is another important criteria (Ambrose 1990; DeNiro 1985; Bocherens et al. 1996) The C:N ratio of pure collagen is 3.21 (Ambrose 1993:76). The C:N ratio in the collagen in the three human bones from Dragsholm varies from 3.18 to 3.29, which is well within this range.

The collagen carbon concentrations and C:N ratios are slightly lower, and δ13C values slightly less negative in the samples prepared in Illinois compared to those prepared in Bradford (see below). These small differences in elemental and isotopic composition are consistent with differences in purification protocols. Lipids and humic acids have low δ13C values and high C:N ratios (Ambrose 1993). They were removed by treatment with NaOH in the Illinois protocol, but not in the Bradford protocol.

The yield of carbon from apatite carbonate by percent weight provides another check for diagenetic alteration. After apatite purification, the average weight percent carbon in apatite of modern bone is ~0.9%, with a range from 0.65% to 1.3% (Ambrose 1993:80). Values of the Dragsholm burials range from 0.91 % to 1.06 %, well within the in-vivo range for bone apatite. However, as will be discussed in a later section, the isotopic composition of the apatite of burial D suggests apatite has been affected by diagenesis.

RADIOCARBON DATING AND CALIBRATION (TDP, JH)

A series of radiocarbon dates were made on materials from the Dragsholm graves. In addition to the three original skeletons, new dates were obtained from Dragsholm C, the single isolated tibia, from the mandible fragment found in 2003, and the decorated bone spatula in the grave of the females. The results of the analyses are listed in Table 5 including the lab number, sample designation, material dated, the measured age in radiocarbon years, the reservoir corrected age in radiocarbon years, the calibrated date in calendar years with probability, and the stable carbon and nitrogen isotope measurements on the bone samples, where available.

The three original skeletons were dated twice. The first set of samples dated at Aarhus came from the collagen preparation at Illinois, described above. Because of concerns about contamination from the conservation, a second set of samples from the three original skeletons were prepared using a specified procedure – hexane treatment — for the removal of preservatives. The drilled bone samples were placed in a test tube with hexane for 15 minutes at 50 °C. The test tube was then transferred to an ultrasonic bath for 15 minutes. The hexane was then decanted and replaced by acetone, which was heated and ultrasonically treated as above. This procedure was repeated with ethanol and then with a double treatment using demineralized water to remove any trace of the previous solvents. The intent is to use a series of increasingly polar

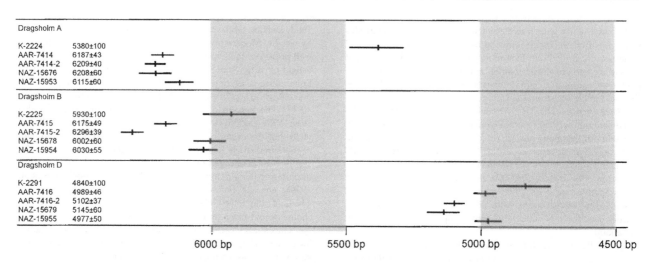

Fig. 8. Plot of multiple radiocarbon dates for the burials A, B, and D at Dragsholm.

solvents, ending with water, where each solvent is able to dissolve and remove the previous one. After decontamination the samples were subjected to normal collagen extraction procedures.

In addition to the dates obtained at the Aarhus AMS laboratory, three paired measurements were made on the human bone samples at the Rafter Laboratory, New Zealand, along with the stable isotope measurements discussed below. As can be seen in Table 6 and Fig. 8, there were differences in the dates between the two labs. For this reason, the Rafter Lab re-measured the three samples and obtained similar results to the first set of dates, with the exception of sample D. The second measurement on sample D was younger and in better agreement with the Aarhus date. As the two female individuals have clearly marine diets they both need to be corrected for the marine reservoir effect, which will change their ages by about + 400 radiocarbon years. However, even with this correction there is no overlap in dates between the female burials and the male burial.

In sum, four radiocarbon dates were obtained on bone collagen from each of the three Dragsholm skeletons. In general each set of dates show similar values but there are some anomalies (Fig. 8). The measurements on individual A show the closest values. Dates on individual B are scattered, ranging from 6030 to 6296 b.p. The Neolithic burial D also shows some variation, ranging from 4977-5145 b.p. This variation does not appear to be inter-laboratory as the values are scattered across each range. As noted, there is some difference due to preparation procedures and the removal of contaminants in the second series of dates from Aarhus. These decontaminated samples are slightly younger in date. It is also clear from the graph that the original dates from the Copenhagen laboratory are all younger than the AMS dates from Aarhus and New Zealand.

There appears to be a strong correlation between collagen preservation and the consistency of the dates between the labs. The best agreement among the dates was for Burial A which has the highest collagen concentration of 9.3%. Finally it is essential to note that the radiocarbon dates for individuals A and B should be virtually identical as these two individuals were buried in the same grave. Because of potential problems involving the marine reservoir correction for the two females with less negative stable isotope carbon isotope ratios, we also dated a bone from a ter-

restrial animal in the grave, the decorated spatula made from a red deer bone. The date on this artifact from a terrestrial animal should provide the most accurate date for the grave. This date (5983 ± 38 bp) is slightly younger than the youngest date on individual B from New Zealand (6002 ± 60 bp) and substantially younger than the youngest date from the grave, on Individual B, from Aarhus (6175 ± 49). This discrepancy suggests that the marine reservoir correction is not large enough and that marine-affected radiocarbon dates are still slightly in error. The best date for the contents of Grave I, including the two female inhabitants, comes from the bone spatula.

In the Neolithic Grave II, we also dated a terrestrial mammal in order to obtain results A similar different between marine and terrestrial samples from the same archaeological context has been noted elsewhere. For example, paired human and ungulate bone samples from Lepenski Vir in the Danube Gorges in Yugoslavia (Bonsall et al. 2000, Cook et al. 2001, 2002) showed systematic differences on the order of 540 years (uncalibrated) reflecting a freshwater reservoir effect in that region. Freshwater reservoir effects have been discussed in detail by Lanting and van der Plicht (1996), among others (e.g. Fischer and Heinemeier 2003).

A terrestrial mammal from Grave II was also dated for comparison with the results from Grave I. In Grave II we used a sample from the antler pick in the ground near the head of the male. The original sample vial exploded during air transport. The specimen was dated (AAR-7418) but not pretreated. This initial date did not match the Neolithic male (D). Because of the problem with the first date, the broken sample vial, and the known use of preservatives, a second sample was taken from the antler pick and dated. This sample (AAR-7418-2) was aggressively treated to remove preservatives. The new determination (AAR-7416-2) matches the Neolithic male in the grave very closely.

STABLE ISOTOPES: CARBON AND NITROGEN (MR)

We obtained measurements of the carbon and nitrogen stable isotopes of collagen extracted from the three Dragsholm humans as well as an ornamented spatula of red deer bone found in association with the female burials (Table 7). The two females have predominantly marine diets, reflected in the δ13C and δ15N values. These values are close to the end points that have been found in humans and mammals that consume marine foods (Schoeninger et al. 1983, Chisholm et al. 1982, Richards and Hedges 1999). Individual A has a δ13C value that is less negative than many published human and marine mammal values, which usually are at −12±1‰ (see Richards and Hedges 1999 for references). The δ13C value of -23.7‰for the red deer marks the end of the terrestrial range of diet in this area and emphasizes the importance of marine foods in the Mesolithic.

The δ15N values are elevated, as expected for a marine diet (Schoeninger et al. 1983). Schoeninger and DeNiro (1984) suggest-ed that values less than +9‰ would reflect fully terrestrial diets and values greater than +15‰ would be completely marine. Schoenin-ger et al. (1983) reported values ranging between 12.5‰ and 16.0‰ for unspecified Danish Mesolithic individuals. The high δ15N for the Mesolithic females reflects the high values of the marine food-web. These values are normal for marine diets in the temperate zone. They are not as high as has been observed for other Meso-lithic humans, which are often at 15 ± 10/00 (e.g., Richards and Mellars 1998, Richards et al. 2003, 2004), and likely indicate a diet of mainly fish and shellfish rather than marine mammals (Richards and Hedges 1999).

The male burial, individual D has δ13C and δ15N values that are consistent with a mainly terrestrial-based diet. The δ13C value is very similar to human values from the Neolithic in Denmark (Tauber 1981b) and the UK (Richards and Hedges 1999). The δ15N value is at the higher end of the scale observed for temperate Holocene Europe, and likely indicates a diet high in animal, rather than plant, protein. This value may reflect the relative importance of cattle during the Early Neolithic.

Methodology. Collagen was extracted from the human bone samples at the Department of Archaeological Sciences, University of Bradford. Approximately 200 mg of bone powder was dem-ineralised in 0.5 M HCl at 5°C for 48 hours. The supernatant was discarded the remaining solid was then gelatinised in sealed tubes, in pH3 HCl at 70°C for 48 hours. The solution was then filtered through 8 μm filters before being filtered through 30 kD ultrafil-ters. The > 30 kD fraction was then freeze-dried. The carbon and nitrogen stable isotope values were measured at Isoanalytical, Cheshire, UK. For the spatula sample the collagen was extracted at the AMS Laboratory, University of Aarhus, Denmark and the carbon and nitrogen isotopes were measured at the Stable Isotope Laboratory, University of Bradford, UK. Errors on the δ13C and δ15N values are ±0.2 ‰.

In addition to the data presented above, there are additional δ13C and δ15N values on the four samples produced at two other stable isotope laboratories (Rafter, New Zealand and the University of Illinois, Champaign-Urbana), as well as δ13C values produced in conjunction with radiocarbon dating at the AMS laboratory at Aarhus. All of these data are presented in Table 8. As can be seen there is good agreement between all of the labs, despite the differ-ent equipment and collagen extraction methods used.

Collagen vs. Apatite (SA). Krueger and Sullivan (1984) initially documented the difference in stable carbon isotope ratios between the apatite and collagen compartments of bone in the same indi-vidual. They proposed that consumer collagen carbon was derived from dietary protein and apatite from dietary energy sources. They used this model to explain systematic differences in the isotopic

composition of collagen and apatite of non-human herbivores ver-sus carnivores and omnivores, and marine versus terrestrial hu-man diets. Controlled diet experiments with rodents confirmed fundamental aspects of their model, by demonstrating that carbon isotopes in collagen preferentially reflected that of the protein por-tion of the diet, while apatite carbon reflected the isotopic compo-sition of the total diet (Ambrose and Norr 1993, Jim et al. 2004, Tieszen and Fagre 1993). The results of these experiments are not directly relevant for interpreting the isotopic composition of apatite and collagen carbon isotopes of ruminants and other animals that generate substantial amounts of 13C-depleted methane during di-gestion (Metges et al. 1990).

These experiments showed that when the protein and bulk diet have the same δ13C values, collagen is enriched by 5.0‰, and apa-tite is enriched by 9.4‰ relative to the total diet, and the apatite-collagen spacing is 4.4‰. In these experiments, the enrichment factor for apatite relative to the bulk diet was effectively constant, regardless of the isotopic composition of the dietary macronutrients (proteins, fats and carbohydrates). However, consumer collagen-diet δ13C spacing values could be systematically varied by chang-ing the δ13C value of dietary protein relative to that of the bulk diet, because more than half the carbon in collagen was derived from dietary protein. They determined that the spacing between whole diet and collagen δ13C values (Δ13Ccoll-diet) is greater when the protein component of the diet is enriched in 13C compared to the bulk diet; diet to collagen spacing is less when the protein compo-nent is less enriched compared to the bulk diet.

The results of these experiments permit more detailed recon-struction of the isotopic composition of prehistoric human diets. The bulk diet δ13C value can be reconstructed from the apatite δ13C value minus 9.4‰, and that of dietary protein can be recon-structed from the apatite-collagen difference (δ13Cap-coll). Specifi-cally, a difference of 4.4‰ occurs when the protein and bulk diet have the same δ13C value. A spacing of less than 4.4‰ indicates that dietary protein is isotopically enriched relative to whole diet. If the spacing is greater than 4.4‰, then dietary protein is isotopi-cally lighter than whole diet (Ambrose and Norr 1993, Ambrose et al. 1997, Ambrose et al. 2003, Harrison and Katzenberg 2003, Jim et al. 2004).

Marine foods, being rich in protein, will contribute dispropor-tionately to the amino acids in collagen compared to terrestrial plants. Moreover, being enriched in 13C, marine proteins will dis-proportionately increase the collagen δ13C values relative to the bulk diet, and relative to apatite δ13C. In marine contexts with no C4 plants, protein comes from mainly from 13C-enriched marine animal resources, while carbohydrates and some proteins come from 13C-depleted C3 plants and C3-feeding animals. Because the marine protein source is more enriched in the heavy carbon isotope, the diet to collagen spacing (Δ13Cdiet-coll) should be greater than 5‰, and collagen to carbonate spacing (Δ13Cap-coll) should be less than 4.4‰. Because the marine protein source is more enriched in 15N, collagen δ15N values should also be high. In a coastal environment lacking C4 plants, a positive correlation should exist between collagen δ13C and δ15N, and a negative correlation should occur between δ15N and δ13Cap-coll (Ambrose et al. 1997).

In terrestrial high latitude diets, the entire foodweb is based on 13C-depleted C3 plants, so the bulk diet and dietary protein should have very similar δ13C values. The diet-collagen spacing should be 5‰ and the apatite-collagen spacing at least 4.4‰. Stable car-bon isotope ratios were measured in the apatite of the Dragsholm samples. Values for the δ13Capatite and the spacing between apatite and collagen values (Δ13Cap-coll) are provided in Table 4. The values from the Neolithic Burial D are substantially different from the two Mesolithic females.

The δ13Cap-coll values of the Dragsholm Mesoithic and Neolithic humans are consistent with what is expected for marine versus terrestrial diets. The collagen δ13C value reflects mainly the protein 13C, plus a small amount of the non-protein 13C. For the marine diets of the Mesolithic women, the lower spacing reflects the high 13C of marine protein and thus a high collagen 13C value. The lower apatite δ13C value reflects the mix of marine foods plus C3 plants. For Burial D, both the protein and non-protein are C3, and the protein source is apparently more negative than the non-protein component (fats and carbohydrates). This pattern suggests that Neolithic people were consuming mainly terrestrial animals and plants, but the low value for protein compared to non-protein resources is unusual. This suggests diagenesis of apatite, which we shall discuss in greater detail below.

The carbon isotope ratios measured on collagen from the Dragsholm burials are -10.4 for Burial A, -11.4 for Burial B, and -19.2 for Burial D. If we use -10.0 as the end point for collagen with fully marine foods and –21.5 as the end point for fully terrestrial C3 foods, which is the equivalent of C3 and marine diet endmember 13C values of –26.5 and –15, respectively, the Mesolithic women (A and B) appear to have had an almost completely marine diet (97% for A and 88% for B). The Neolithic individual (burial D) apparently had 16% marine foods.

Apatite 13C, on the other hand, reflects the total diet 13C value plus 9.4 per mil. Using the end-member 13C values for marine and C3 terrestrial end-member diet noted above (-26.5 and –15), plus 9.4 for the diet-apatite spacing, the apatite values of –8.3 for burial A, and –9.3 for burial B would indicate diets composed of approximately 76% and 67% marine foods. Burial D has a 13C value of –12.1, and apparently consumed approximately 42% marine foods, although diagenesis may have affected this sample (see below).

The application of collagen 13C values for the calculation of diet greatly exaggerates the importance of marine foods. Because collagen is derived mainly from dietary protein, the terrestrial C3 plant dietary component has been substantially underestimated by analysis of collagen. Apatite provides a more accurate estimate of the whole diet carbon isotopic composition.

The bias of collagen toward the protein components of diet needs to be considered when evaluating the carbon isotope evidence for the transition from the Mesolithic to the Neolithic in northwest Europe. Several authors have noted the striking decrease in collagen carbon isotope ratios at the onset of the Neolithic in the British Isles, which has been interpreted as a shift to exclusive consumption of domesticated plants and animals (Hedges 2004, Richards et al. 2003, Richards and Schulting 2006, Schulting and Richards 2002, Tauber 1981a). Milner et al. (2004) have contested this evidence, but their arguments are not consistent with our knowledge of the relationship between the isotopic composition of collagen and diet (Hedges 2004). In Sweden, the collagen isotopic evidence suggests continued though significantly reduced reliance on marine protein (Lidén et al. 2004). The collagen δ13C value of –19.2‰ for Burial D indicates that marine protein was an important, though minor component of the Neolithic diet, comprising approximately 15-20% of the dietary protein.

Although apatite should accurately reflect the δ13C value of the whole diet, the Δ13Cap-coll value of 7.1‰ for burial D is higher than expected for a C3 plus marine foodweb. The high apatite δ13C value could reflect a diet with higher 13C than that indicated by collagen only when low-protein dietary resources have higher δ13C values. This would require the consumption of C4 plants. However, Denmark is far north of the distribution of C4 plants. Moreover, if the slightly elevated collagen δ13C value does reflect marine protein consumption, then the Δ13Cap-coll value for Burial D should be less than 4.4‰. Therefore it is likely that the apatite values have been shifted to somewhat higher values by postmortem isotopic exchange. The diagenetic shift is at least 2.4‰, assuming no marine foods. The sample of bone from Burial D prepared at the University of Illinois had a significantly lower collagen concentration (5.3%) than burials A (14.3%) and B (9.3%) (Table 4). Burial D bone would be more porous and thus more susceptible to apatite diagenesis than burials A and B. Apatite-based estimates of terrestrial food consumption for burials A and B are likely to be more accurate, and suggest diets with approximately 70%, rather than >90% marine input.

STRONTIUM ISOTOPE PROVENIENCE (TDP)

Another avenue of research on the Dragsholm burials involved measurement of isotopes that provide information on individual provenience or place of origin. It is now possible, however, to obtain specific clues about the migration of people in the past directly from human bone using strontium, oxygen, and other isotopes. Strontium isotopes were measured on the Dragsholm individuals.

The basic principles of the method are straightforward. Strontium isotope ratios vary with local geology, specifically with the age and composition of bedrock. Virtually all strontium in vertebrate organisms is found in the skeleton. In human bones and teeth these ratios can serve as tracers of the geology of the areas where individuals grew up and where they died, respectively. Bone undergoes continual replacement of its inorganic phase so that measurements of bone strontium reflect the last years of the life of the individual. The enamel in teeth, on the other hand, forms during infancy and childhood and undergoes very little change during life. Differences in strontium isotope ratios between bones and teeth thus reflect the residence history of the individuals under consideration. Because strontium isotope ratios vary among geological formations, strontium isotope ratios in teeth that do not match those of the local geology indicate immigrants to an area.

A number of studies have been published demonstrating the utility of strontium isotope analysis (Ezzo et al. 1997, Montgomery et al. 2000, Price et al. 1994, 2000, 2001). Each of these studies involves contexts in which migration or other residential movement has been assumed or hypothesized. Each of these areas exhibits significant variation in local geology so that differences in strontium isotope ratios between bone and tooth can be expected in situations of residential mobility. In each area, a significant number of migrants were identified and estimates made of their original homeland. For the analysis, the strontium isotope ratio in human teeth is compared to levels in archaeological fauna, which provide a measure of the local ratio. Our methods require one tooth from each individual. The analysis is destructive but only a very small amount of material is required, ca. 20 mg of the enamel from a molar. A description of analytical procedures can be found in Price et al. (2002).

In the case of the Dragsholm graves, enamel samples were taken from the first molar of one female skeleton (Burial B), the male skeleton (burial D), and a tooth pendant from red deer canine (designated as artifact Dr256) associated with the female grave. The red deer canine was used to obtain a measure of the strontium isotope ratio in the local area around the site of Dragsholm. The teeth from the older female (Burial A) were heavily worn and there was little enamel remaining. We decided not to sample this individual.

The results of the strontium isotope analysis of the three graves from Dragsholm are shown in Table 9. These results are intriguing. The strontium isotope ratio in the four red deer canine (0.710499) provides a measure of local terrestrial levels in the largely moraine landscape of northwest Zealand. The values for the two humans are close together; the Mesolithic female has a value of 0.709614 and the Neolithic male has a value of 0.709391. On first impression these results suggest that the male and female individuals were local in origin. It is important to remember that the female consumed a diet that was largely marine in origin. Unless her diet in infancy and childhood was much more terrestrial, we would expect the strontium isotope values in her enamel to be close to that of modern seawater, which is 0.7092 (Howarth and McArthur 1997). In this study, however, the Neolithic male with a diet that is largely terrestrial shows a strontium isotope ratio that is slightly closer to modern seawater than the female. Interpretation of this result is not obvious. If we assume that the red deer value is characteristic of terrestrial deposits in the region of Dragsholm, we can understand the female value as shifted from the local value as a consequence of a marine diet. The male, however, with a terrestrial diet, should resemble the red deer. The fact that he does not suggests that he may in fact be from a different area, perhaps a region where marine deposits form the primary geological substrate. The uncertainty of these results suggests that more samples of terrestrial animals and humans from this period need to be analyzed.

NEW FIELD INVESTIGATIONS

As part of the re-investigation of the Dragsholm burials, the site area was reopened in 2002 and excavations continued during the summer of 2003 and 2004. Here we describe the excavations, basic stratigraphy, and chronology of the site occupation in the context of the graves. The geological report by Nanna Noe-Nygaard focuses on the stratigraphy at the site with regard to changing sea levels in the context of the occupation on the site and the chronology of the graves. The focus in both discussions is on the nature of the Dragsholm site area at the time of shift from Atlantic to Subboreal conditions and the transition from the Mesolithic to the Neolithic, ca. 4000 B.C.

Archaeological Excavations. In the fall of 1973 Per Poulsen of the National Museum excavated a 3 x 1 m test pit (Test trench 2), approximately 40 m east of the grave site on a second, smaller rise along the Dragskanal. Several layers with cultural material were encountered in the excavations, including both Early Neolithic and late Mesolithic artifacts. These materials were taken to the National Museum.

The site was revisited 30 years later. Excavations at the site in 2002-2004 were conducted as a joint project of the University of Wisconsin-Madison and the Odsherreds Museum. The goals of these excavations were to obtain more settlement remains and to date the occupations at the site. Because of the graves and the 1973 test pit, the locality appeared promising for layers dating from the time of the transition to agriculture. A full report on the excavations will appear in another format. Here we provide a summary of the project and its findings.

In the recent excavations, a series of test pits and trenches were excavated, largely on the east side of the small island, between the Dragsholm burial site and the test pit from 1973 (Figs. 9 & 10). These excavations were largely in water-lain deposits and revealed a complex stratigraphy. The section from T11 at Dragsholm provides a good overview of the sequence of layers and the associated depositional context. T11 (Test 11) is a 2 x 1 meter unit, excavated to a depth of 2.20 m. This was the deepest section that we excavated and it exposes typical sediments in the southeast quadrant of the former small island at Dragsholm. This section is discussed both in the archaeology section as an introduction to the cultural layers and in the geology section as the sedimentary sequence at the site. The layers in this section are described in Table 10. The sedimentary history of this stratigraphic sequence is discussed in detail in a subsequent section on geology. Archaeologically layers 6, 7, and 8 are of particular interest.

Layer 6 is a heavily washed and redeposited fine sand horizon rich in flint artifacts, with some ceramics, and a few poorly preserved pieces of bone. Flint artifacts were marine patinated and rolled; ceramics were eroded and only larger pieces usually survived. Only TRB pottery is present in this layer. There is a fragment of a lugged jar, several knobs, and numerous sherds. The sherds come from medium to large Funnelbeakers and a possible clay disk. The lugged jar is probably Koch's (1998) type 2 with lugs in a ring around the base. Decoration was limited and only included stabbing and finger impressions below the rim on a few sherds. In general the ceramic assemblage would appear to belong in late ENII. Fish bone and nutshells were rare to absent. Two radiocarbon-dates on bone and charcoal from this layer suggest a date very close to 4000 B.C. the artifacts in this layer are a mix of Mesolithic and Early Neolithic that suggest these materials were eroded from higher areas of the site and redeposited here. One of the radiocarbon dates (4050-3770 B.C.) comes from a large chisel made from cow bone, reaffirming the Early Neolithic date.

Layer 7 is a complex of medium to coarse sand deposits that appear to represent a sequence of redeposition. Two radiocarbon dates from the upper and lower sections of layer 7 indicate a range from 4810-4520 B.C. to 5260-4800 B.C. This layer contains some archaeological materials. Flint was lightly rolled and patinated. Bone was concentrated in the lower part of this layer and included some fish bone. Ertebølle ceramics at the site were found in this layer. At least four medium to large vessels were represented. No small pots or lamps were recovered. Layer 7 appears to represent occupation materials from the middle Ertebølle period, given the radiocarbon dates and the presence of the pottery vessels and the absence of lamps.

Layer 8 is a deposit of gray to rust-colored fine sand with gravel and larger stones. Flint and bone were much fresher in this horizon. Bone was well preserved. Flint was sharp and unrolled. Fish bone and burned hazel nutshells recovered in these lower layers were plentiful and well preserved. The presence of small bone and flint pieces and the fresh condition of the material suggests that the artifacts in layer 8 are largely in situ, probably deposited originally in water. Two radiocarbon dates are available from Layer 8 in T11: 5320-5040 B.C. and 5480 – 5200 B.C., early Ertebølle in age. The artifact material generally fits this date and appears to be unmixed. Numerous projectile points and core axes were recovered in this layer and no pottery was present. A substantial number of bone and antler artifacts including fishhooks, bone points and awls, and three fragments of decorated antler axes were found as well.

The elevation of the site was measured from a fixed point at the Dragskanal bridge. This new elevation information indicated that the height of the small rise with the graves was less than 5m asl. Information from investigations at the Trundholm Mose, 10 km north of Dragsholm, documents a maximum transgression at the end of the Atlantic beginning of the Subboreal of +4 m asl. Clearly this area at Dragsholm would have been only a small piece of land above the water, a few tens of square meters and would have constantly been washed over by wave and storm. It is unlikely that there was any habitation at Dragsholm during this high water stand. This situation fits closely with the revised ages for the graves and the new data from the cultural horizons.

Geological Investigations. The geological context of the Dragsholm graves is discussed here on both a regional and local level. Emphasis is on changing sea levels in the area with regard to the chronology of settlement and burial. The landscape of northwest Zealand is characterized by steep end moraine ridges and eroded lowland just to the south. The ridges were formed by the Young Baltic ice stream during recessions and successive re-advances through the Storebælt strait between 18 -16,000 years ago.

The present day landscape is dominated by an end moraine arch called Vejrhøjbuerne, consisting of till and ice lake clay deposits to the northwest (brown) and a dead ice and melt water landscape to the southwest (yellow). The raised marine foreland is marked in blue. When sea level was higher in the middle Holocene, the only land passage to Odsherred, between the Sejerø Bugt and the Lammefjord, was across the narrow isthmus of land at Dragsholm. This land bridge was 2-3 km wide and consisted largely of wetlands and marsh. Much of this area is only 2 m above present day sea level and could readily be transgressed. When the adjacent Lammefjord was reclaimed in the 19th century, a primary drainage canal was dug at Drags Mølle (2 m asl), linking the former Lammefjord with the Dragsholm inlet, draining the Lammefjord region into the sea at the bay of Sejerø. Maximum sea level in the Dragsholm area during the middle Holocene was between+ 3.5 and +4 m asl (Mertz 1924). This estimate concurs with our own observations from the recent excavations at Dragsholm. The sedimentological record at the site indicates an open connection between Lammefjord and the Bay of Sejrø at +3 - +3.5 m asl. The narrow land barrier between the Dragsholm fjord and the Lammefjord was breached by the sea already during the High Atlantic transgression. The fjord became part of a strait connecting the Lammefjord with the Kattegat. Odsherred was then separated from the rest of Zealand. The formation of this connection and the estimated sea level at that time fits well with information from Trundholm Mose, 15 km to the north of Dragsholm (Kolstrup 1987, Christensen 1995).

Three major processes were involved in the changing sea levels of the mid-Holocene at Dragsholm. The local sea level is a result of the interplay between eustatic sea level, isostatic rebound after the down warping of the earth's crust from the weight of the ice cap, and the sediment input into the available accommodation space for deposition (Fig. 11). Eustatic (global) sea level rose approximately 120 m in the early and middle Holocene following the warming at the end of the Pleistocene. The rate of rise slowed substantially around 7000-6000 years ago. A rapid eustatic rise of sea level re-

Fig 9. Airphoto of the 2003 excavations at Dragsholm. The Dragskanal runs through the left of the photo. The excavation skurvogn is the large white rectangle in the upper left. The location of the two Stone Age graves at Dragsholm are marked by three individuals lying on the ground in the top center of the airphoto. Courtesy of the Royal Danish Airforce.

sults in the sea moving over the land, a transgression. When the eustatic sea level rise decreases, the isostatic rebound of the land surface may overtake the sea, resulting in a regression, where the coastline moves in a seawards direction as seen in the coastal profiles from Dragsholm, for example from Test 11 (Fig. 12).

As most of the near shore areas around the Denmark are flat and shallow, little accommodation space is available for sediment deposition. This means that even during highstands of sea level, regressions may occur as the space for infilling of sediment is limited and rapidly filled. The coastline then starts to prograde towards the sea resulting in a regression, in contrast to a transgression where the coast line moves inland. The terms transgressions and regressions thus refer to the movements of the coastline, irrespective of sea level. As the Storebælt area was flooded by the sea, beginning in the Boreal period, sedimentation changed from river, lake and bog deposits into marine silt and clays with a salt water mollusk fauna (Christensen et al. 1997). The marine transgressive surface is clearly detected in seismic profiles and sediment cores. This transgression had a major influence on adjacent areas such as northwest Zealand. A gradual degradation of low land areas and the lower reaches of the rivers took place, as ground water levels were raised by the ongoing marine inundation.

The rate of sea level rise slowed during the later Atlantic period. A combination of isostatic rebound and eustatic sea level rise resulted in a number of minor regional transgression and regression cycles called the Littorina transgressions (Iversen 1937, Berglund 1971, Christensen 1994, 1995 and 1997, Jakobsen 1981,1983). Around 6000 years ago, an interruption of the ebb and flood cur-

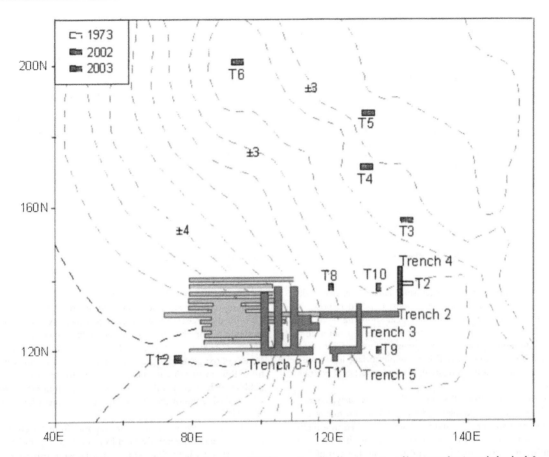

Fig. 10. Plan of the excavations at Dragsholm. The excavations from 1973 (shown in yellow) were a series of long trenches intended to look for additional burials around the first grave. T2 is the 3 x 1 m test pit that was excavated by Per Poulsen. Trench 4 is 10 m long; contour interval is 25 cm.

rent occurred, probably as a result of changes in the configuration of land and sea. That resulted in a much weaker tide with an amplitude of 0.5 m to 0.75 m, in contrast to a previously strong tidal system, with an amplitude up to 4 m, that had provided warm, salty, and well oxygenated to the inner fjords during the Atlantic time.

Around 4000 years ago, a change in the marine current system shifted the position of the tidal forces in the North Sea and cooler water foraminifera are found in the marine cores together with cold tolerant bivalves (Nordberg 1991). These changes are clearly reflected in the marine shell content of the kitchen middens. Before 6000 years ago, oysters (Ostrea edulis) were the dominant species together with other warmth and salt demanding species; after 6000 years ago low salt tolerant species such as cockles (Cerastoderma edulis) and mussels (Mytilus edulis) were predominant (Andersen 2000; Rowley-Conwy 1984). Not only did the molluscan fauna change, but also the species and distribution of fish.

The Dragsholm area is situated where highest beach lines of the Littorina transgressions occur between 3.5 m and 4.5 m asl. Based on sea level projections in this area, the small rise with the two graves was once an island in an area with a strong current and wave-dominated sea-connection between the Lammefjord and the Kattegat in Sejerø Bay. The very coarse grained sediments observed in the excavation trenches, the rather abraded state of some of the bone material, and the large amount of charcoal in many

layers are characteristics of high energy and erosion on the upper foreshore and beach environment (Fig. 12). The stray finds of a human jaw from the waterlain deposits suggest that the site has been subjected to substantial erosion by the advancing sea.

Stratigraphy and Sedimentology at Dragsholm. The general stratigraphy and sedimentology is here shown on the Dragsholm profile from Test 11 at 116 N/123E (Fig. 12). The overall trend in the multiple successions that have been measured is an upwards coarsening indicating the increasing proximity of land regression. The sequence is around 200 cm in thickness and contains three major regressive /transgressive cycles from the High Atlantic, Late Atlantic and Early Subboreal Littorina transgressions. These transgressive events seem to be more prominent in the northern part of Zealand (Iversen 1937, Jakobsen 1981, 1983, and S. Ulfeldt Hede, unpublished data from Søborg Sø). The dating of the Dragsholm transgressions is based on the bone material and charcoal from the different layers and strengthened by comparison with the well-dated contemporary sequences from the Tengslemark bog only 40 km to the north (Jessen 1937, Mortensen pers. comm. 2004). The distribution of the dates confirms the stratigraphic evidence based on the interpretation of sediment facies.

The first of three transgression cycles at Dragsholm includes the sediments deposited from 170 cm to 140 cm below surface (Fig. 12). The lowermost 30 cm from 200 cm to 170 cm can be divided

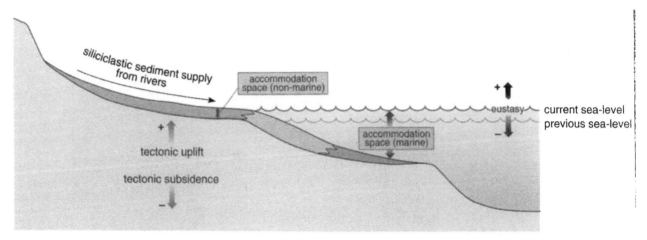

Fig. 11. Schematic illustration of the terms in near shore environment and the term accommodation space.

into two facies deposited during regression. Facies one, from 200 cm to 178 cm below surface, the lowermost exposed deposit, is a clean medium-grained cross-laminated, near shore, light-colored sand. The grain size and cross lamination indicate deposition in a near-shore, low energy, beach environment influenced by some wave activity. The sand facies at 178 cm below surface is abruptly cut by a surface of erosion (regressive), marked by a lag of cobble-sized stones.

The second facies, from 178 cm to 170 cm, is rusty, coarse-grained pebbly sand with cobbles and scattered blocks, maximum size of 20 cm in diameter. This sediment was deposited in a high-energy environment such as a wave-breaking beach zone and formed during regression in a low stand situation. On top of this facies are several rusty rotten blocks, indicating occasional exposure above Littorina sea level. The blocks originate in the adjacent moraine hill that was being eroded by the sea. The blocks have moved by sliding and tumbling, washed clean by the advancing sea, and left as a lag at the bottom of the layer.

The first transgression is, as mentioned, represented by sediments deposited between 170 cm to 140 cm (Fig. 12). The sequence starts with a drowning surface created during transgression at 170 cm below surface. The sediments consist of greenish, fine sand with clay and marine organic matter and scattered pebbles and charcoal. Throughout the facies, small bivalves (Cerastoderma edulis) and gastropods (Littorina littorea and Hydrobia spp.) occur in living position. The fine grain size and high content of glauconitic clay and organic mud indicate deposition in a low energy marine environment, either in deeper waters or in a protected area during a relative high transgression and early high stand. This green sand facies is abruptly cut by a regressive surface of erosion marked by a concentration of broken and complete shells in a gravel layer.

The second cycle occurs from 138 cm to 115 cm below surface. The shell lag is overlaid by coarse sand with large stones. The sequence becomes finer upwards into medium sand with stones (max. diameter of 20 cm). From 130 cm to 120 cm there is a gradual shift to more fine-grained, rusty sand with scattered boulders indicating deposition at lower energy, probably in deeper waters during transgression, perhaps in the upper shore zone. The boulders had a rotten, rusty surface indicating some period of subaerial exposure.

From 120 cm to 110 cm below the surface, a coarsening from medium to coarse sand occurred. The sediment now contains shell gravel and charcoal indicating an increasing proximity of land. This tendency is corroborated by the succeeding layer, from 110 cm to 95 cm, of coarse, rusty sand with plenty of charcoal and brownish streaks of oxygenated organic material. Cycle two ends with a bed, from 105 cm to 115 cm, coarsening upwards from coarse sand to pebbles with large quantities of charcoal and flint deposited in the waved-wash zone of the upper foreshore during a late high stand (Fig. 11).

The third cycle includes the deposits from 85 cm to 45 cm below surface. The pebbly sand from cycle 3 is from 85 cm to 75 cm, overlaid by light, fine to medium sand with rusty root and stem traces from in situ vegetation, probably from reeds (Phragmites comunis), indicating a water depth of less than 2 m. The fine grain size and the abrupt transition to the underlying layer indicate a drop in energy caused either by a rising water table or the closing of the passage from the Lammefjord to Sejerø bay. From 75 cm to 65 cm below surface, the sediment grain size increases to medium sand and horizontal streaks of peat occur. The sandy sequence is caped by coarse, pebbly sand with cobbles and sharp edged flint and an indistinct lamination with a sharp and erosive base. The very coarse grain size indicates deposition in a high-energy environment; the low angle, indistinct, cross-lamination suggests a beach zone. The wide areas covered by the sequence indicate rapid coastal progradation during a relative fall in sea level and erosion during regression. The regression is likely due to decreasing accommodation space caused by a combination of isostatic uplift and a low rate of sea level rise.

Similar patterns in the stratigraphic record of the transgressions can be seen at Toftevang, Tengslemark, and Smakkerup Huse. The earliest marine transgression recorded at Toftevang in the Lammefjord is radiocarbon-dated 6450 years before present (Christensen 1994), contemporaneous with the high Atlantic transgression, and correlated by pollen analysis and other radiocarbon dates with evidence from the Søborg Sø (Iversen 1937, Hede unpub. data, Mortensen unpub. data 2003, Noe-Nygaard et al. in prep.). At Toftevang, the marine succession is overlaid by terrestrial peat dated to 5870 years before present.

The Tengslemark locality today is a lake connected to the

DRAGSHOLM TEST HOLE 11   116N/123E

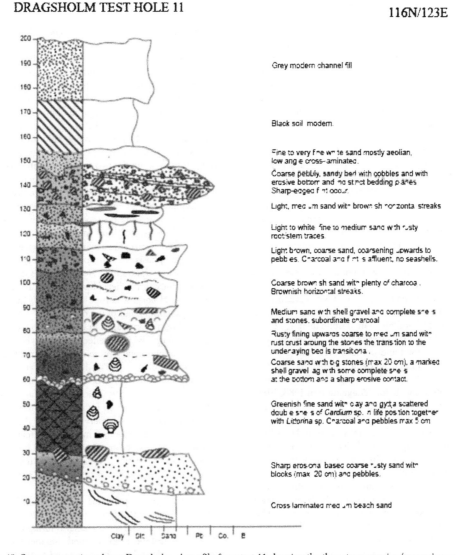

Grey modern channel fill

Black soil modern.

Fine to very fine white sand mostly aeolian,
low angle cross-laminated.

Coarse pebbly, sandy bed with cobbles and with
erosive bottom and no strict bedding planes
Sharp-edged flint occur.

Light, medium sand with brownish horizontal streaks

Light to white fine to medium sand with rusty
root/stem traces.

Light brown, coarse sand, coarsening upwards to
pebbles. Charcoal and flints affluent, no seashells.

Coarse brownish sand with plenty of charcoal.
Brownish horizontal streaks.

Medium sand with shell gravel and complete shells
and stones, subordinate charcoal

Rusty fining upwards coarse to medium sand with
rust crust around the stones the transition to the
underlaying bed is transitional.

Coarse sand with big stones (max 20 cm), a marked
shell gravel lag with some complete shells
at the bottom and a sharp erosive contact.

Greenish fine sand with clay and gytja scattered
double shells of *Cardium* sp. in life position together
with *Littorina* sp. Charcoal and pebbles max 5 cm

Sharp erosional based coarse rusty sand with
blocks (max 20 cm) and pebbles.

Cross laminated medium beach sand

Clay   Slt   Sand   Pt   Co.   B

Fig. 12. Sequence stratigraphy at Dragsholm. A profile from test 11 showing the three transgression/regression cycles.

former Klintsø fjord on the north coast of Odsherred. The pollen spectrum from Tengslemark has been compared with a diagram from Søborg Sø (Iversen 1937) in order to establish the connection with the original type site for the four Littorina transgressions (Iversen 1937). The onset of the High Atlantic transgression at Tengslemark is dated to 6210±55 14C years before present. The transgression is marked by a steep raise in the total sulphur percentage in the sediment profile. The impact of marine conditions ceased at 5775±50 years before present and normal lacustrine conditions and sedimentation returned. The onset of the Late Atlantic Littorina transgression is dated to 5295±45 years before present and the Early Subboreal transgression is dated to 5095±45 years before present. This transgression continues into and merges with the early Subboreal transgression. The two transgressions are only separated by a short-lived low stand at the end of which the elm decline occurs. The first onset of marine transgression over terrestrial

peat at Smakkerup Huse (Price and Gebauer 2005) is dated to 6140 ± 40 before present and further inland to 6100 ± 60. The onset of the late Atlantic/Early Subboreal transgression is dated at the site to 5040 ± 65 years before present.

CONCLUSIONS

A new study of the Dragsholm graves has involved more detailed investigation of the skeletal remains themselves, new isotopic analyses, and fieldwork to determine the settlement and stratigraphic context of the graves. The females' grave was originally dated to the latest Mesolithic with the possibility that calibration would place the two individuals in the Early Neolithic along with the male in the second grave. Carbon isotope analysis of the bone collagen indicated substantial differences between the two females and the male with a distinct marine diet for the two females. The burials from Dragsholm have been a contentious component of discussions of the transition from the Mesolithic to the Neolithic since their discovery.

New studies of the skeletal material itself have provided some important insights. The three skeletons and other bone fragments from Dragsholm were examined partly in order to establish whether there was any evidence of relationship between the 18 - 20-year-old and over 40-year-old Mesolithic women in the double grave, and partly to look for any evidence that may reflect different subsistence and lifestyles between the skeletons in the Mesolithic and Neolithic graves.

The two women exhibited a number of similarities with regard to the size and form of some bones and teeth, open sacral segments, short dental roots and signs of reduced dentition such as fused molar roots. They also exhibited dental differences, which are mainly attributed to cultural or environmental factors like polished areas produced by chewing hide (skeleton A) and the presence of linear enamel hypoplasia attributed to seasonal crises (skeleton B). This means that a close genetic relationship between the two women can neither be confirmed nor excluded. The more than 20-year age difference may indicate that the two women, if they were closely related, would more likely represent daughter and mother rather than sisters, although it cannot be demonstrated with certainty.

The similar patterns of dental wear in the young Mesolithic woman and the 30 year old Neolithic man, despite their age differences, may reflect the different subsistence during the two periods, different ways of preparing food and perhaps even different ways of using the teeth as a tool. It has been demonstrated that the latter produced more severe attrition in the young Mesolithic woman than is seen in the Neolithic population (Alexandersen 1988, 1989). The ochre-stained Mesolithic bones and the Neolithic grayish soil-stained bones express yet another cultural difference.

New isotopic investigations of the burials from Dragsholm were undertaken confirm the age of the skeletons and to re-measure carbon isotope values for carbon. In addition, nitrogen isotopes were measured in these materials, carbon isotopes in apatite were recorded, and strontium isotopes were measured in tooth enamel.

New radiocarbon dates were obtained on the bone collagen from the three skeletons. Two sets of samples were run using AMS dating at laboratories in Aarhus and New Zealand. These dates resulted in a correction of the original date on the two female burials. The best estimate for the age of this grave comes from the date 5983±38 bp (AAR-7417) on a red deer bone artifact in the grave. The corrected BC date lies between 4946 and 4773 BC (2 s.d., 97.7%). The dates from the human collagen of the two females, even after calibration, remain a hundred years or so too old. The date of the Neolithic male remains essentially unchanged, ca. 4989±46 (AAR-7416) on human bone collagen, corrected to between 3782 and 3637 BC (2 s.d., 99.7%). Thus the difference in age between the two graves is approximately 1000 years. They are in no way contemporary. The two females are clearly Mesolithic, while the single male belongs in the Early Neolithic period. The isolated mandible fragment found in 2003 was dated to 6310±60 BP, roughly contemporary with the two Mesolithic females from the grave.

Measurement of the carbon isotope content of bone collagen largely confirmed the original results of Tauber (1981a). A number of new measurements on the three individuals indicated a significant difference between the two females and the male. The $\delta13C$ values from the University of Illinois are A = -10.4, B = - 11.4, and D = -19.3. The new values are slightly higher (ca. 1 - 2‰ less

negative) than the original measurements. The Mesolithic females have a higher, marine-based carbon isotope ratio while the ratio for the male is largely terrestrial. The isolated mandible fragment from 2003 had a $\delta13C$ value of -11.7, which is very similar to the two Mesolithic females. The values for the Mesolithic females are close to the most positive end of the range for marine sources and suggest a diet that was composed of 90% or more of seafood. The $\delta13C$ value of D is relatively high for an exclusively terrestrial diet, and may reflect the consumption of up to 15% marine foods.

Nitrogen isotopes were also measured on bone collagen in several laboratories. Nitrogen isotope ratios from the University of Illinois were A = 13.2‰, B = 13.5‰, and D = 10.0‰. Again a distinct difference between the two females and the male is indicated. The isolated mandible from 2003 had a nitrogen isotope ratio of 14.5‰ similar to the Mesolithic females. Nitrogen isotopes should reflect the trophic level of individual. Values greater than 15‰ should reflect purely marine diets; values less than 9‰ should represent completely terrestrial food sources. The values for the Mesolithic females and the isolated mandible indicate largely marine diets, with an emphasis on fish rather than marine mammals. The nitrogen isotope ratio in the Neolithic male indicates the largely terrestrial nature of his diet. This value is at the high end observed for temperate Holocene Europe and suggests that animal protein was the major component of the diet.

Carbon isotope ratios in bone apatite should reflect sources of dietary energy, which is effectively the whole diet, while collagen reflects mainly dietary protein. Measurements of apatite produced $\delta13C$ values of A = -8.3‰, B = -9.3‰, and D = -12.1‰. Apatite carbon was not measured on the isolated mandible from 2003. The $\delta13C$ values for apatite indicate a marine component in the diet of approximately 76% in individuals A, 67% in B, and 42% in D. The relatively poorly-preserved bone of Burial D may have been affected by diagenesis and may overestimate the consumption of marine resources. From this information it is clear that the marine component of the diet is exaggerated by the protein source for the collagen. Marine foods, rich in protein, contribute disproportionately to the collagen carbon.

Strontium isotope ratios were measured in individuals B and D, along with four red deer teeth. Strontium isotopes can provide information on residential changes during an individual's lifetime. Strontium isotope ratios in tooth enamel are determined by the place of birth and can be compared to the local signature of the place of death to see if they are the same. The strontium isotope ratios in the red deer teeth (ca. 0.7105) provide the local terrestrial signal for the Dragsholm area. Seawater and marine foods should have a strontium isotope ratio of 0.7092. Both the Mesolithic female (B = 0.7096) and the Neolithic male (D= 0.7094) exhibited values below the red deer. The range from terrestrial to marine in these samples is approximately 0.0013 (0.7105 - 0.7092). The Mesolithic female strontium isotope value of 0.7096 is 0.0009/0.0013 between the two extremes. Given the high marine component of her diet documented in the carbon and nitrogen isotopes, this shift is not unexpected. In fact, the strontium isotopes might suggest that marine foods were 9/13 (ca. 70%) of the diet of the mother of individual B. This value is essentially identical to the prediction based on apatite carbon isotopes. The Neolithic male, however, did not consume as high a proportion of marine foods and his strontium isotope value even closer to seawater is surprising. This value in fact suggests that he may have been born outside of the glacial moraine that characterized much of the Danish landscape.

His place of birth was likely on marine deposits where strontium isotope values would have been 0.7092 and terrestrial foods in the diet of his mother would have shifted his enamel value slightly above the marine signal.

New archaeological excavations at the Dragsholm site have uncovered largely areas around the original burial location, collected new artifactual and human materials, and detailed the stratigraphic context of the site. These excavations opened a series of trenches along the eastern slopes of the small rise of the burial ground and in the adjacent waterlain deposits. The wide trenches on the slope of the rise did not expose any new features or burials. It appears that the graves discovered in 1973 were the only remaining intact burials at the site. At the same time it is clear from the discovery of the isolated mandible in 2003 that other graves may have been destroyed and scattered by the wave erosion of the site during the course of several transgressions.

The water lain deposits at the site indicate two major episodes of deposition. There is a lower horizon of early and middle Ertebølle materials that is largely in situ with little evidence of rolling or patination. This lower horizon contains well preserved fish bone and nut shell in great quantities along with other faunal remains. An upper horizon appears to contain late Ertebølle and Early Neolithic materials according to radiocarbon dates and the contents of the layer. This material is frequently rolled and marine patinated, bone is eroded and not well preserved. Fish bone and smaller artifacts are rare. This upper horizon appears to be secondarily deposited, presumably during a transgression or regression event at the end of the Atlantic climatic episode.

The artifactual materials recovered at the site document occupation in the late Mesolithic and Early Neolithic. Remains from the Ertebølle date from the early and middle parts of this period with little evidence of a late Ertebølle occupation. Distinctive artifacts included decorated antler axes, a greenstone trindøx, concave truncations on blades, and ceramics. In addition, there are ceramic and bone artifacts belonging the Early Neolithic in conjunction with radiocarbon dates that indicate the presence of Funnelbeaker (TRB) settlement at the site. TRB ceramics were common in the upper cultural layer at the site. Flake axes were found throughout the cultural horizons but no polished flint axes or fragments were recovered. In total, the artifactual remains and radiocarbon dates suggest a rather continuous occupation of this propitious location along the coast of the Kattegat in northwest Zealand. The fjord created here by rising sea levels during the Atlantic episode would have been a rich area for marine resources. In addition, the opening of this waterway between the Kattegat and the Lammefjord to the east may have created an exceptional situation for the capture of marine resources. The location also has strategic significance as a passage to the north into the peninsula of Odsherred.

The topographic and hydrological history of the area is revealed in the stratigraphy as Dragsholm. The sedimentary sequence documents three transgressive cycles. The dates of the three cycles were compared other northwest Zealand localities. Together they confirm that the High Atlantic transgression and the Late Atlantic/ Early Subboreal were the most pronounced and the most inland-reaching transgressions. The time of the transgressions is well dated

and established at four different localities in northwest Zealand (Table 1). The height of sea level (ca. 4 m asl) and the timing of the Late Atlantic/Early Subboreal transgression make it clear that the Dragsholm locality could not have been occupied at the end of the Atlantic period. At that time, this area would have been largely submerged just at the edge of a high-energy current connecting the Lammefjord and the Kattegat.

Taken together, the new investigations at Dragsholm provide an almost complete picture of the age and anatomical characteristics of the burials at the site, their bone chemistry and diet, the archaeological context of the graves and accompanying settlement, and the Holocene geology of the region. A great deal of new information has derived from these studies including strong evidence that the two graves are approximately 1000 years apart in age and that the two females date from the Mesolithic Ertebølle and that the male is certainly Neolithic. The stray humerus (individual C) found at the burial site comes from the Bronze Age. A new Mesolithic individual, identified from a mandible fragment, was discovered in the new excavations. Stable isotope study of the human remains replicated the earlier collagen carbon results but investigation of nitrogen and apatite carbon indicates that marine foods, primarily fish, were less important during the Mesolithic than previously believed. New flint, ceramic, bone, and antler artifacts document Mesolithic and Neolithic occupation at the site. Geological study of the sequence stratigraphy revealed a series of transgressions at Dragsholm, comparable to events elsewhere in Denmark. Sea level during these transgressions reached a maximum of +4.0 m asl and effectively prohibited human occupation at the Dragsholm site for some time at the very end of the Atlantic period. Early Neolithic materials accumulated at the site prior to this last transgression.

The Dragsholm area is rich in archaeological sites from the later Mesolithic and it is likely that new settlements and graves will be discovered in the coming years. It is our hope that the results reported here will assist in the understanding of new finds. At the same time, we believe our work has contributed to the resolution of questions regarding the age of the Dragsholm graves and the nature of the transition from the Mesolithic to the Neolithic at this place in northwest Zealand.[2]

2 *Acknowledgements*: Research excavations at Dragsholm were sponsored by the Carlsberg Foundation and the National Science Foundation of the U.S.A. with some help from the Graduate School of the University of Wisconsin-Madison. The excavation project was a collaborative effort between the Odsherred Museum, Arne Hedegaard Andersen, and the Department of Anthropology, University of Wisconsin-Madison. Special thanks to Nils Lynnerup for taking bone samples of the humans, Peter Henriksen for taking enamel samples from the humans, Jim Burton for sample preparation in Madison, Paul Fullager for sample analysis at the University of North-Carolina at Chapel Hill, Chris Meiklejohn for help with information on the Dragsholm burials, Kim Aaris-Sørensen for identification of faunal remains, Poul Otto Nielsen for permission and coordination, Verner Alexandersen for collaboration on the dentition of the burials, Peter Bøttger for permission to excavate in the fields at Dragsholm, and especially Per Paulsen for revisiting the site and helping to reestablish the previous datum. The Royal Danish Air Force kindly took care of the air photography of the site, with the help of Søren Andersen.

REFERENCES

Aaris-Sørensen, K. 1980. Depauperation of the Mammalian Fauna of the Island of Zealand during the Atlantic Period. Vidensk. Meddr. dansh. Foren. 142:131-138.

Albrethsen, S.E., & E. Brinch Petersen. 1977. Excavation of a mesolithic cemetery at Vedbæk, Denmark. Acta Archaeologica 47:1-28.

Alexandersen, V. 1988. The late Mesolithic dentition in southern Scandinavia. Rivista di Antropologia, suppl. 66:19-204.

Alexandersen, V. 1989. Description of the human dentitions from the late Mesolithic grave-fields at Skateholm, southern Sweden. In: L. Larsson (ed.), The Skateholm Project: I. Man and Environment. Stockholm, Almquist: 106-163

Ambrose SH, 1990. Preparation and characterization of bone and tooth collagen for isotopic analysis. Journal of Archaeological Science 17: 431-451.

Ambrose, S.H. 1993. Isotopic analysis of paleodiets: Methodological and interpretive considerations, in Sandford, M.K. (ed.) Investigations of Ancient Human Tissue: Chemical Analyses in Anthropology. Langhorne, Pennsylvania:Gordon and Breach Science Publishers. Pgs. 59-130.

Ambrose, S.H. & L. Norr. 1993. Experimental evidence for the relationship of the carbon isotope ratios of whole diet and dietary protein to those of bone collagen and carbonate. In Prehistoric Human Bone: Archaeology at the Molecular Level (eds) J.B. Lambert & G. Grupe. Berlin: Springer-Verlag.

Ambrose, S.H., Brian M. Butler, Douglas B. Hanson, Rosalind L. Hunter-Anderson, Harold W. Krueger. 1997. Stable isotopic analysis of human diet in the Mariana Archipelago, western Pacific. American Journal of Physical Anthropology 104: 343-361.

Ambrose, S.H., J. Buikstra, and H.W. Krueger. 2003. Gender and status differences in diet at Mound 72, Cahokia, revealed by isotopic analysis of bone. Journal of Anthropological Archaeology 22:217-228.

Andersen, S. H. 2000. 'Køkkenmøddinger' (shell middens) in Denmark: a survey. Proceedings of the Prehistoric Society 66: 361-384.

Balasse, M., Ambrose, S.H., Smith, A.B. and Price, T.D. 2002. The seasonal mobility model for prehistoric herders in the Southwestern Cape, South Africa assessed by isotopic analysis of bovid tooth enamel. Journal of Archaeological Science 29: 917-932.

Bastian, W. 1962. Das jungsteinzeitliche Flachgräberfeld von Ostorf, Kreis Schwerin. Bodendenkmalpflege in Mecklenburg. Jahrbuch 1961: 7-130.

Bennike, P. 1985. Palaeopathology of Danish Skeletons. Akademisk Forlag, Copenhagen

Bennike, P. & Bohr, H. 1990. Bone mineral content in the past and present. In. C. Christiansen and K. Overgaard (eds.) Osteoporosis: 89-91

Bennike, P., Bohr, and Toft. 1993. Determination of mineral content and organic matrix in bone samples using dual photon absorptiometry. International Journal of Anthropology 8: 111-116.

Bennike, P., and V. Alexandersen 2002. Population plasticity in Stone Age Denmark. In: A. Fischer & K. Kristiansen (eds.) The Neolithisation of Denmark. 150 years of debate. J.R. Collis Publ., Sheffield

Berglund, B. 1971: Littorina transgressions in Blekinge, South Sweeden. A preliminary survey. Föreningens i Stockholm Förhandlinger 93: 625-652.

Bocherens, H., Pacaud, G., Lazarev, P., & Mariotti, A. 1996. Stable isotope abundances (13C, 15N) in collagen and soft tissues from Pleistocene mammals from Yakutia. Implications for the paleobiology of the mammoth steppe. Palaeogeography, Palaeoclimatology, Palaeoeocology 126: 31-44.

Bonsall, C., G. Cook, R. Lennon, D. Harkness, M. Scott, L. Bartosiewicz & M. Kathleen. 2000. Stable Isotopes, Radiocarbon and the Mesolithic—Neolithic Transition in the Iron Gates. Documental Praehistorica 27, 119-132.

Brinch Petersen, E. 1973. Dobbeltgraven fra Dragsholm. Nationalmuseets Arbejdsmark 187-188.

Brinch Petersen, E. 1974. Gravene ved Dragsholm. Fra jægere til bønder for 6000 år siden. Nationalmuseets Arbejdsmark 112-120.

Brinch Petersen, E. 1979. Kvindernes smykker. Søllerødbogen: 39-56.

Chisholm, B.S., D.E. Nelson, and H.P. Schwarcz. 1982. Stable carbon ratios as a measure of marine versus terrestrial protein in ancient diets. Science 216:1131-1132.

Christensen, C., F. Fischer, & R. D. Mathiassen. 1997. Den Store Havstigning i Storebælt, pg. 45-55 In: Storebælt i 10.000 år-mennesket, havet og skoven, ed. Pedersen, L., Fischer, A. & Aaby, B. Storebælt publikationer.

Christensen, C., 1994: Lammefjorden, Undersøgelser på 4 lokaliteter i fjorden giver informationer om havniveauændringer og afkræfter formodet forekomst af tektoniske bevægelser af landjorden i atlantisk tid. Nationalmuseets naturvidenskabelige Undersøgelser 16: 1-31.

Christensen, C., 1995. The littorina transgressions in Denmark. In Man and Sea in the Mesolithic p 15-21. A. Fischer (ed.), A. Oxbow Monograph pp 440.

Clark, R.M. 1975. A calibration curve for radiocarbon dates. Antiquity 49: 251-266.

Cook, G.T., Bonsall, C., Hedges, R.E.M., McSweeney, K., Boroneanţ, V. & Pettitt, P.B. 2001. A freshwater diet-derived 14C reservoir effect at the Stone Age sites in the Iron Gates gorge. Radiocarbon 43(2A): 453-460.

Cook, G.T., Bonsall, C., Hedges, R.E.M., McSweeney, K, Booneant, V., Bartosiewicz, L. and Pettitt, P.B. 2002. Problems of dating human bones from the Iron Gates. Antiquity 76: 77-85.

DeNiro, M.J. 1985. Postmortem preservation and alteration of in vivo bone collagen isotope ratios in relation to paleodietary reconstruction. Nature 317: 806-809.

Ebbesen, K. 1988. The long dolmen at Grøfte, South-west Zealand. Journal of Danish Archaeology 7: 53-69.

Ezzo, J. A., C.M. Johnson, and T.D. Price. 1997. Analytical perspectives on prehistoric migration: a case study from East-Central Arizona. Journal of Archaeological Science 24: 447-466.

Ferembach, D. 1963. Frequency of Spina Bifida Occulta in prehistoric human skeletons. Nature 199 (4888): 100-101.

Fischer, A. 2002. Food for Feasting. In The Neolithisation of Denmark. 150 Years of Debate (eds) A. Fischer & K. Kristiansen. Sheffield: JR Collis Publications.

Fischer, Anders, and Jan Heinemeier. 2003. Freshwater reservoir effect in 14C dates of food residue on pottery. Radiocarbon 45: 449-466.

Frayer, D.W. 1988. The supra-acetabular fossa and groove: a

skeletal marker for northwest European Mesolithic populations. Human Evolution 3:163-178.

Harrison, R.G., and M.A. Katzenberg. 2003. Paleodiet studies using stable carbon isotopes from bone apatite and collagen: examples from southern Ontario and San Nicolas Island, California. Journal of Anthropological Archaeology 22: 227-244.

Hedges, R.E.M. 2004. Isotopes and red herrings: comments on Milner et al. and Lidén et al. Antiquity 78: 34-37.

Heier-Nielsen, S., J. Heinemeier, H.L. Nielsen and N. Rud. 1995. Recent reservoir ages for Danish fjords and marine waters. Radiocarbon 37-3: 875-882.

Howarth, R, J, & McArthur, J. M. (1997). Statistics for strontium isotope stratigraphy: a robust LOWESS fit to the marine Sr- isotope curve for 0 to 206 Ma, with look-up table for derivation of numeric age. Journal of Geology 105: 441-456.

Humlum, O. 1983. Dannelsen af en disloceret randmoræne ved en avancerende isrand, Höfdabrekkujölkull, Island. Dansk Geologisk Forening 1982: 11-26.

Iversen, J. 1937. Undersøgelser over Littorinatransgressioner i Danmark. Meddelelser fra Dansk Geologiske Forening, Bd. 9, 223-236.

Jim, S., S.H. Ambrose, and R.P. Evershed. 2004. Stable carbon isotopic evidence for differences in the dietary origin of bone cholesterol, collagen and apatite: implications for their use in palaeodietary reconstruction. Geochimica et Cosmochimica Acta 68: 61-72.

Koch, E. 1998. Neolithic Bog Pots from Zealand, Møn, Lolland and Falster. Copenhagen: Nordiske Fortidsminder.

Kolstrup, E. 1987. Late Atlantic and Early Subboreal vegetational development at Trundholm, Denmark. Journal of Archaeological Science 15: 5.

Krueger, H. W., & Sullivan, C.H. 1984. Models for carbon isotope fractionation between diet and bone. In Stable Isotopes in Nutrition, edited by J.R. Turnland and P.E. Johnson, pp. 205-220. American Chemical Society Symposium Series, No 258.

Lanting, J.N., and J.van der Plicht. 1996. Wat Hebben Floris V, Skelet Swifterbant S2 en Visotters Gemeen? Palaeohistoria 1998: 1-39.

Larsson, L. 1990. The Mesolithic of Southern Scandinavia. Journal of World Prehistory 4: 257-309.

Lidén, K. G. Eriksson, B. Nordqvist, A. Götherström, and E. Bendixen. 2004. "The wet and the wild followed by the dry and the tame" - or did they occur at the same time? Diet in the Mesolithic - Neolithic of southern Sweden. Antiquity 78: 23-33.

Lunt, D. A. 1969 An odontometric study of Medieval Danes. Acta Odontol. Scand. Suppl. 55,27.

Mertz, E. L. 1924: Oversigt over de sen- og Postglaciale Niveauforandringer i Danmark. Danmarks Geologiske Undersøgelser. II række, 41.

Metges, C, K. Kempe, H.L. Schmidt, 1990. Dependence of the carbon-isotope contents of breath carbon-dioxide, milk, serum and rumen fermentation products on the delta-C-13 value of food in dairy-cows. British Journal of Nutrition 63: 187-196.

Milner, N., O.E. Craig, G.N.Bailey, K. Pedersen, and S.H. Andersen. 2004. Something fishy in the Neolithic? A re-evaluation of stable isotope analysis of Mesolithic and Neolithic coastal populations. Antiquity 78: 9-22.

Montgomery, J., P. Budd & J. Evans. 2000. Reconstructing the lifetime   movements of ancient people: a Neolithic case study from southern England. European Journal of Archaeology 3: 407-422.

Noe-Nygaard, Nanna, T. Douglas Price, and Signe Ulfeldt Hede. 2005. Diet of aurochs and early cattle in southern Scandinavia: evidence from 15N and 13C stable isotopes. Journal of Archaeological Science 32: 855-871.

Nordberg, K. 1991: Oceanography in the Kattegat and Skagerak over the past 8000 years. Palaeocenography 6: 461-484.

Pavelka, M.S.M. and Fedigan, L.M. 1991. Menopause: A Comparative Life History Perspective.

Pedersen, P.O. 1949. The East Greenland Eskimo Dentition. Numerical variations and anatomy. Meddelelser om Grønland 142,3.

Persson, P. 1998. Neolitikums början. Undersökningar kring jordbrukets introduktion i Nordeuropa. Uppsala, Göteborg.

Price, T.D. 1989. The Chemistry of Prehistoric Human Bone. Cambridge: Cambridge University Press.

Price, T.D., 1995. Agricultural origins and social inequality. In T.D. Price & G.M. Feinman (eds.), Foundations of Social Inequality, pp. 129-151. New York: Plenum Press

Price, T.D. 2000. Europe's First Farmers. Cambridge: Cambridge University Press.

Price, T.D., Johnson, C. M., Ezzo, J. A., Ericson, E., and Burton, J. H. 1994. Residential Mobility in the Prehistoric Southwest United Stated: A Preliminary Study using Strontium Isotope Analysis. Journal of Arcaeological Science 21: 315-330.

Price, T.D., & A.B. Gebauer (eds.). 1995. Last Hunters — First Farmers. New Perspectives on the Transition to Agriculture in Prehistory. Santa Fe NM: School for American Research Press.

Price, T.D., & A.B. Gebauer (eds.). 2005. Smakkerup Huse. Excavations at a Late Mesolithic Coastal Site in Denmark. Aarhus: Aarhus University Press.

Price, T. Douglas, Gisela Grupe, and Peter Schröter. 1998. Migration and mobility in the Bell Beaker period in Central Europe. Antiquity 72: 405-411.

Price, T. Douglas, Linda Manzanilla, & W.H. Middleton. 2000. Residential mobility at Teotihuacan: a preliminary study using strontium isotopes. Journal of Archaeological Science 27: 903-913.

Price, T. Douglas, R.A. Bentley, Jens Lüning, Detlef Gronenborn, & Joachim Wahl. 2001. Prehistoric Human Migration in the Linearbandkeramik of Central Europe. Antiquity 75: 593-603.

Price, T.D., J.H. Burton & R.A. Bentley. 2002. The characterization of biologically available strontium isotope ratios for the study of prehistoric migration. Archaeometry 44: 117-135.

Richards, M.P., and R.E.M. Hedges. 1999. Stable isotope evidence for similarities in the types of marine foods used by Late Mesolithic humans at sites along the Atlantic coast of Europe. Journal of Archaeological Science 26:717-722.

Richards, M.P., Price, T.D. & E. Koch. 2003. Mesolithic and Neolithic subsistence in Denmark: new stable isotope data. Current Anthropology 44: 288-295.

Richards, M.P., R.J. Schulting & R.E.M. Hedges. 2003. Sharp shift in diet at onset of Neolithic. Nature 425:366.

Richards, M.P., and R.J. Schulting. 2006. Touch not the fish: the Mesolithic- Neolithic change of diet and its significance. Antiquity 80: 444–458.

Rowley-Conwy, P. 1984. The laziness of the short-distance hunter: the origins of agriculture in western Denmark. Journal of Anthropological Archaeology 3:300-324.

Schoeninger, M. J., M. J. DeNiro, and H. Tauber. 1983. 15N/14N ratios of bone collagen reflect marine and terrestrial components of prehistoric human diet. Science 220: 1381-1383.

Schoeninger, M. J., and M. J. DeNiro. 1984. Nitrogen and carbon isotopic compositionof bone collagen from marine and terrestrial animals. Geochemica and Cosmochemica Acta 48: 625-639.

Schuldt, E. 1961. Abschließende Ausgrabungen auf dem jungsteinzeitlichen Flachgräberfeld von Ostorf 1961. Jahrbuch für Bodendenkmalpflege in Mecklenburg 1961:131-178.

Schulting, R.J. & M.P. Richards. 2002. Finding the coastal Mesolithic in southwest Britain: AMS dates and stable isotope results on human remains from Caldey Island, Pembrokeshire, South Wales. Antiquity 76: 1011-1025.

Stuiver, M., Reimer, P.J., Bard, E., Beck, J.W., Burr, G.S., Hughen, K.A., Kromer, B., McCormac, F.G., v.d. Plicht, J., and Spurk, M. 1998. INTCAL98 Radiocarbon age calibration 24,000 - 0 cal BP. Radiocarbon 40:1041-1083.

Szilvássy, J. 1986. Eine neue Methode zur intraserialen Analyse von Gräberfeldern. A new method for intraserial analysis of burial sites. In: B. Herrmann (ed.) Innovative trends in prehistoric anthropology. Mitt. Der Berliner Gesellshaft für Anthropologie, Ethnologie und Urgeschichte, Berlin 7: 51-62

Tauber, H. 1973. Copenhagen radiocarbon dates X. Radiocarbon 15: 86-112.

Tauber, H. 1981a. 13C evidence for dietary habits of prehistoric man in Denmark. Nature 292: 332-333.

Tauber, H. 1981b. Kostvaner i forhistorisk tid - belyst ved C-13 målinger. In Det skabende menneske, pp. 112-126. Copenhagen: National Museum.

Tauber, H. 1983. C14 dating of human beings in relation to dietary habits. In The first international symposium on C14 and archaeology, Groningen 1981. PACT 8.

Tieszen, Larry L. and Thomas Fagre 1993. Effect of diet quality on the isotopic composition of respiratory CO_2, bone collagen, bioapatite and soft tissues. In Molecular Archaeology of Prehistoric Human Bone, edited by J. Lambert and G. Grupe, pp. 121-155. Springer, Berlin.

Trotter, M. and Gleser, G. 1958 A re-evaluation of estimation of stature based on measurements of stature taken during life and long bones after death. American Journal of Physical Anthropology 9:79-125.

Authors

Stanley H. Ambrose, Department of Anthropology, University of Illinois, Urbana, IL 61801, USA, ambrose@uiuc.edu

Pia Bennike, Laboratory of Biological Anthropology, Institute of Forensic Medicine, University of Copenhagen, 2200 Copenhagen N, Denmark, bennike@antrolab.ku.dk

Jan Heinemeier, AMS 14C Laboratory, University of Aarhus, 8000 Aarhus C, Denmark , jh@phys.au.dk

Nanna Noe-Nygaard, Geologisk Institut, University of Copenhagen, Copenhagen, Denmark, nannan@geol.ku.dk

Erik Brinch Petersen, Archaeology, Saxo Institute, University of Copenhagen, Njalsgade 80, DK-2300 Copenhagen K, Denmark, ebp@hum.ku.dk

Peter Vang Petersen, National Museum, Fredriksholms Kanal 12, 1220 Copenhagen K, Denmark, peter.vang.petersen@natmus.dk

T. Douglas Price, Laboratory for Archaeological Chemistry, 1180 Observatory Drive, University of Wisconsin-Madison, Madison WI 53706 USA, 1-608-262-2575, tdprice@wisc.edu

Michael P. Richards, Department of Human Evolution, Max Planck Institute for Evolutionary Anthropology, Leipzig, Germany, richards@eva.mpg.de

Lab #	Burial	^{14}C Years bp	Cal. ^{14}C Years BC	Years BC Cal.	δ^{13}C
K-2224	A	5160± 100	3210	4000	-11.4 $^{o}/_{oo}$
K-2225	B				-12.1 $^{o}/_{oo}$
K-2291	D	4840± 100	2890	3675	-21.7 $^{o}/_{oo}$

Table 1. Original radiocarbon data on Dragsholm Burials (Tauber 1973).

Lab Number	Skeleton	^{14}C Years bp
K-2224	A	5380± 100
K-2225	B	5930± 100
K-2291	D	4840± 100

Table 2. The three original dates from the Dragsholm skeletons in the archives of the Radiocarbon Laboratory at the National Museum Copenhagen.

Burial	^{14}C Date	δ^{13}C‰	Original Calibration	New Calibration
Mesolithic Female	5160±100 b.p.	-11.4	4000 B.C.	3650-3520 B.C.
Neolithic Male	4840±100 b.p.	-21.7	3650 B.C.	3670-3500 B.C.

Table 3. Original and New Calibration of 14C Dates from Dragsholm. Published in Brinch Petersen (1974) and Tauber (1981b).

Burial	Collagen						Apatite			
	Wt. % Collagen	Wt. %N	Wt. %C	Atomic C:N	δ^{15}N ‰	δ^{13}C ‰	Wt. % apatite	Wt. %C	δ^{13}C ‰	δ^{13}Cap-coll ‰
A	14.3	14.7	40.4	3.21	13.2	-10.4	70.8	1.06	-8.3	2.1
B	9.3	13.6	37.2	3.18	13.4	-11.3	65.7	0.99	-9.3	2.0
B*		14.4	39.3	3.17	13.6	-11.5				2.2
D	5.3	12.0	34.0	3.29	9.9	-19.3	70.2	0.91	-12.1	7.2
D*		13.1	35.9	3.19	10.1	-19.2				7.0

Table 4. Elemental and isotopic composition of bone collagen of Dragsholm human burials, determined at the University of Illinois. δ^{13}Cap-coll is the difference between apatite and collagen δ^{13}C values. Replicate analysis of collagen, indicated by *, was performed on burials B and D.

AAR#	Sample	Material	¹⁴C Age (BP)	Reservoir Corrected	Calibrated BC Range (2 s.d.)	δ¹³C	δ¹⁵N
7414	Dragsholm A	bone	6187 ± 43	5787 ± 43	4722 (94.4%) 4535	-10.52	--
7414-2	Dragsholm A	bone	6209 ± 40	5809 ± 40	4730 (86.8%) 4540	-10.82	14.03
7415	Dragsholm B	bone	6175 ± 49	5775 ± 49	4720 (96.7%) 4499	-11.47	--
7415-2	Dragsholm B	bone	6296 ± 39	5896 ± 39	4860 (94.2%) 4680	-11.67	13.74
8724	Dragsholm C	bone	3097 ± 44	2995 ± 44	1390 (95.4%) 1050	-18.84	11.30
7416	Dragsholm D	bone	4989 ± 46	4903 ± 46	3782 (99.7%) 3637	-19.17	--
7416-2	Dragsholm D	bone	5102 ± 37	5030 ± 37	3950 (95.4%) 3710	-19.47	10.40
8725	2003 Mandible	bone	6310 ± 60	5910 ± 60	4940 (95.4%) 4610	-11.72	14.45
7417	Bone Spatula	Cervus	5983 ± 38	--	4946 (97.3%) 4773	-23.47	--
7418	Antler Pick	Cervus	5799 ± 50	--	4767 (97.3%) 4552	-22.57	--
7418-2	Antler Pick	Cervus	5090 ± 65	--	3965 (97.3%) 3795	-21.46	--

Table 5. New radiocarbon dates, calibration and light isotope ratios from the Dragsholm graves. All data from the AMS Dating Laboratory, University of Aarhus.

Sample	Code	δ¹³C‰	Age BP
A	NZA-15676	-10.7	6208 ± 60
A	NZA-15953	-10.7	6115 ± 60
B	NZA-15678	-11.4	6002 ± 60
B	NZA-15954	-11.4	6030 ± 55
D	NZA-15679	-18.9	5145 ± 60
D	NZA-15955	-18.9	4977 ± 50

Table 6: AMS Radiocarbon dates from the Rafter Laboratory, New Zealand.

Sample	Description	¹³C‰	¹⁵N‰	:N	C	
A	Adult female (18 years)	-10.7	13.3	3.4	44.0	15.3
B	Adult female (40-50 years)	-11.7	13.7	3.5	43.4	14.7
D	Adult male	-19.6	10.0	3.4	43.1	15.0
AAR-7417	Ornamented spatula	-23.7	4.6	3.2	36.0	13.0

Table 7: Stable isotope and carbon:nitrogen data for the Dragsholm samples measured at Bradford. Errors on the δ¹³C and δ¹⁵N values are ± 0.2 ‰.

Sample	δ¹³C T	δ¹³C B	δ¹³C I	δ¹³C NZ-I	δ¹³C C NZ-AMS	wδ¹³C A	δ¹⁵N B	δ¹⁵N I	δ¹⁵N NZ-I	C:N B	C:N I	C:N NZ-I	%C B	%C I	%C NZ-I	%N B	%N I	%N NZ-I
A	-11.4	-10.7	-10.4	-10.4	-10.7	-10.5	13.3	13.2	12.5	3.4	3.2	3.1	44.0	40.4	33.7	15.3	14.7	12.5
B	-12.1	-11.7	-11.4	-10.9	-11.4	-11.5	13.7	13.5	14.1	3.5	3.2	3.1	43.4	38.3	33.6	14.7	14.0	12.6
D	-21.5	-19.6	-19.3	-19.1	-18.9	-19.2	10.0	10.0	11.3	3.4	3.2	3.2	43.1	35.0	39.5	15.0	12.6	14.6

Table 8. All stable isotope data produced for the three Dragsholm human samples. Codes are T=Tauber, B=Bradford, I=Illinois, NZ-I= New Zealand isotope lab, NZ-AMS=data produced during ¹⁴C dating, A=Aarhus.

Grave B	Human Tooth Enamel	First Molar	0.709614
Grave D	Human Tooth Enamel	First Molar	0.709391
Trench	Red Deer Tooth Enamel		0.710572
Trench	Red Deer Tooth Enamel		0.710465
Trench	Red Deer Tooth Enamel		0.711222
Grave B	Red Deer Tooth Enamel (Dr256)	Canine	0.710499

Table 9. Strontium isotope ratios in tooth enamel from Dragsholm graves.

Layer 1 is the plowzone, a dark brown sandy humic layer composed of the sediments removed during the excavation of the canal.

Layer 2 is the fill of the canal cut which have been redeposited along the canal. This material is a dark brown mix of humic and sandy layers also containing archaeological materials and shell. This layer may also contain (layer 3) dark decomposed sandy peat that probably represents the former ground surface following the retreat of the sea here in the middle Holocene. This area was likely a wetlands from the time of that retreat until the recent drainage of the region for agricultural purposes. Layer 3 could not be distinguished in this section. Layer 4 is drainage pipe ditch fill that was encountered in other parts of the site but was not visible here.

Layer 5, beneath Layer 2, is an aeolian fine white sand deposit with some gravel, perhaps formed during the period of marine transgression when the "dobberne" (sand dunes) to the west were developing along the coastline. This layer is sterile and continuous across the site area except above +4 m asl.

Layer 6 is a regression horizon with fine white sand, gravel, and large rolled stones, artifacts, bones, and some shell and charcoal. The cultural material in this horizon is both Early Neolithic, confirmed by several cattle teeth and bones and TRB pottery, and Ertebølle. Flint artifacts are moderately rolled and marine patinated. This mixed deposit must represent a final episode of erosion and deposition at the site as the sea was retreating from its high stand of the early Subboreal.

Layer 7 was a rich and complex sequence of gray medium sands with two major lenses of cultural material in the middle and lower parts of the layer. The cultural materials in this layer are Mesolithic, belonging largely to the middle Ertebølle. This layer likely represents a series of transgression deposits. The upper part of the layer (7a) is often leached with vertical streaks of oxidation and in some areas substantial accumulations of iron oxide. This layer contains some artifacts. A second horizon 7b is largely sterile coarse sand grading into 7a above with a few artifacts. Layer 7c is a darker, gray sand layer with substantial cultural material. Charcoal likely provides the gray color here. Shell lenses are present above 7c in some parts of the stratigraphy. Finds include ceramics and distinctive projectile points. This material is lightly rolled and probably secondarily deposited by the transgression and wave action.

Layer 8 was a layer of rust to gray colored sand and stone (variable in color across the excavation units) with lots of fish bone and hazelnut shell along with artifacts and other bone. This layer is likely largely in situ; the flint is fresh and unrolled. The cultural material in this layer is outcast material. Cultural material appears to be middle Ertebølle, confirmed by radiocarbon date on red deer bone of 6104±46 BP, 5019-5000 BC (AAR-8189).

Layer 9. Gray brown clayey sand, likely marine deposits during early transgression of the inlet here. Sterile. These lowest three layers are likely marine deposits during the early transgression of the fjord here.

Layer 10. Bedded, down-sloping coarse orange-brown sands, leached with accumulation of iron in bottom of layer. Sterile.

Layer 11. Fine, medium orange brown sand, bedded, sterile. Excavations ended in this layer at a depth of -2.2 m below ground surface, -0.73 m asl.

Table 10. Archaeological layer descriptions for T11, Dragsholm 2003.

Printed and bound by CPI Group (UK) Ltd, Croydon, CR0 4YY

09/06/2025

14686070-0005